JESUS AS THEY SAW HIM

By
J. ALEXANDER FINDLAY, M.A.

WIPF & STOCK · Eugene, Oregon

Wipf and Stock Publishers
199 W 8th Ave, Suite 3
Eugene, OR 97401

Jesus as They Saw Him
By Findlay, J. Alexander
Copyright©1920 Methodist Publishing - Epworth Press
ISBN 13: 978-1-5326-3508-3
Publication date 6/16/2017
Previously published by Epworth Press, 1920

PREFACE

In the studies which this volume contains Mr. J. A.Findlay has given the result of a great deal of honest digging into the text of the Gospels, and his delving has been done in many cases with newer and improved instruments. Synoptic criticism, for example, which he uses freely, is still, for most English theologians, a new instrument ; but those who employ it know that, in comparison with the rigid methods of interpretation (based upon a rigid theory of inspiration) which prevailed half a century since, there is almost as great a difference as there is between a Ford tractor and a primitive digging-stick. Mr. Findlay is nearer in his practical studies of the Gospels to the former than to the latter ; and in any case he digs right vigorously. The result of such toil is that once again the wilderness becomes glad and the desert blossoms as the rose—the wilderness being here understood, not of the Gospels, but of what theologians make of the Gospels, which have become overrun with briars of irrational interpretation and the thorns which grow on that un-amiable tree whose name is *Petitio Principii*.

These studies, then, are not to be taken as an exhaustive review of what has been already said by others. They are fresh investigations with the aid of new instruments. They may even be thought by some to be amateurish, but that is a first impression which will soon pass off. It is evident that the writer has brought to his theme a spiritual vision, and that those who follow his leading patiently will often find themselves enriched, not only in the knowledge of the letter, but still more in the per-ception of the things of God, which the men of the Spirit share with one another and communicate to one another.

After which brief commendation of a beloved disciple

SYNOPSIS OF PART ¹

CHAPTER I

The comparative study of the Gospels—The reason for omission in the scheme presented here of the Fourth Gospel—Discrepancies in the gospel-tradition—Their value as evidence of the trust-worthiness of the documents in which they are found—All versions of sayings *may* be true, where there are variants—If the Gospels had been concocted, they would have been made to fit—The evangelists real men, with points of view of their own—The outline portrait as built up from the three ; details to be filled in later—What the Gospels do not tell us—Their intimacy with and reverence for their Subject—Jesus like and unlike us—Unassuming friendliness, sense of leisure and ease, and readiness to listen—His openness and His reserves—Men did not know how to label Him—He would not leave them alone with their preconceived notions—How He was thrown back upon Himself—The problem of the preoccupied—Our Brother to the end—Would not be managed by His friends or countered by His foes—How He left His lovers behind and was ' classed among criminals '—The agony in the Garden—That men thought themselves better than they were the cause of His despair, but came to be the ground of His hope, for it proved that they ' knew not what they did '—The redeeming prayer on the cross—The ' dying thief '—The many and the one—The reaction and the cry of despair —Son of Man to the last extremity yet always Son of God—The water stained with blood has become the wine, the cooling cup of peace, and the power to hope. (pp. 5–22.)

CHAPTER II

Mark in the New Testament—In the tradition of the Church— His relations with Peter—Signs that his Gospel does give us Peter's version of the story—The characteristics and special merits of Mark's Gospel illustrated by words and clauses peculiar to it.

(pp. 23-38.)

CHAPTER III

Mark's portrait of Jesus—His eyes and voice and manners—His mastery of the soul—The fear which He inspired grew upon men as they knew Him better—Cases of the paralysed man, the Syrophoenician woman, the woman with the hæmorrhage, the deaf stammerer, the blind man, the Gerasene demoniac—Problem of reserve as to miracles—What Jesus thought of them—Reasons for policy of secrecy on the Galilean lakeside—Secrecy abandoned when away from this area and when ' scribes from Jerusalem present ' —The political ferment of the times and the phenomena of demon-possession—The treatment of the twelve in this Gospel—Inferences as to its genuineness from the somewhat undignified part they are made to play.   (pp. 39–57.)

CHAPTER IV

Is this Gospel disorderly ?—Rather incomplete than really lacking in order—Its main divisions—i. 14–iii. 6 ; iii. 7–vii. 23 ; vii. 24–x. 31 ; x. 32–end—Dramatic value of the Gospel illustrated—Its gaps—The riddle of the Marys and omission of Raising of Lazarus—The first sweep of success—Pharisaic jealousy and its development —Popular misunderstanding—How the two working together make public ministry in Galilee undesirable—Attempts to break the coalition of these two opposing forces—Retreat with twelve—Their wavering—The break away to Judaea—Encounter with vested interests—The union between political prejudice, professional opposition, the vested interests, disappointed ambition, to bring about the tragedy—Judas and Peter—Tragic victory through tragic defeat.   (pp. 58–98.)

CHAPTER V

The pillar-passages—Their importance as evidence of genuineness—Faith in this Gospel, illustrated by the stories of the Syrophoenician woman, the woman with the hæmorrhage, the deaf stammerer and the blind man, the father of the epileptic boy, and the paralysed man borne by four—The all-importance of intercourse with the Healer—Body and soul—' Mighty works '—The strain upon Jesus noticeable in some cases of healing, never in nature-miracles—Mark's definition of faith makes him the link between Paul and James—Inferences as to faith-healing.   (pp. 99–108.)

I

THE SYNOPTIC PORTRAIT OF JESUS

THE purpose of this book is to show the great fascination of the comparative study of the first three Gospels, the Fourth Gospel being left on one side, except for a few references, partly for reasons of space, partly also because its character is so distinctive and its importance so great that it demands separate treatment.

With the view of avoiding certain harmful misconceptions, the writer has thought it well to deal in this chapter with some features of the Lord's personality as this method has led him to see it, and in Chapter I. of Part II. with a suggestion as to His method of teaching. Each of the three Gospels is considered in what he conceives to have been the order of their publication, and it is shown how the portrait outlined in this chapter is compounded of them all. If the second part stood by itself, it might be argued that excessive attention was being paid to discrepancies between the Gospels, or—with more reason, perhaps—that more was being said about the evangelists than about their Subject. That is why he is anxious to make it clear at the outset that he does not believe that, where our authorities seem to disagree, any one of them is necessarily wrong. Of course, the same incident cannot have taken place in two different ways at the same time, and the theory that where the same story is told differently by two of our witnesses, it is because it happened twice, is dangerously easy, and therefore is not too readily to be brought into play. But when we allow for the slight changes which come into any narrative as it passes from lip to lip, even when the reporters are honest and highly educated people, we can see that minor discrepancies as to matters of actual fact, so far from

5

being a hindrance to faith, are really something like a guarantee of substantial genuineness ; for it is very much easier to arrange for precise agreement in detail when men are conspiring to concoct a story than when they are seeking independently to give a report of things which they have seen, heard, or read. If the whole conception of Jesus as outlined in the Gospels had been the invention of men who used a largely imaginative biography to propagate a cult of their own, none but very slight and accidental differences between the published accounts of the Saviour-God's sayings and doings would have been allowed to appear ; there would have been a carefully wrought consistency ; if more than one officially accepted story had been published, each would have been dove-tailed into the other. When we study the Gospels, on the other hand, we are faced with a reassuring variety—a variety which itself bears witness to the fact that both Jesus and His reporters were real men, and that there were many others who were able, when the Gospels came to be written, to contribute their memories of the Lord who had been so lately with them, the result being that, in the Third Gospel especially, the writer is almost embarrassed by the multitude of those who had something to tell.

The writer does not intend to discuss at length the question of ' sources,' but is concerned that readers should be impressed with the richness of Gospel tradition ; the fact that ' all various readings are early ' should make us not suspicious of all, but ready to take them all into consideration. When we come to discuss the sayings of Jesus, we must remember that, in the nature of the case, all four Gospels together can only give us a selection of extracts, for there were many reasons why Gospel publication would be a somewhat precarious undertaking ; in fact, it would seem that at one time there was only one copy of Mark's Gospel extant. We must not leave out of view the probability that the Master repeated some of His cardinal sayings more than once. If so, He would almost certainly improve upon the original version on the second occasion. This consideration may account for some discrepancies.

In regard to the fullness with which temperamental

peculiarities and prepossessions of the evangelists themselves are to be treated, I want to say quite clearly at the outset that even if, as we shall see reason to believe, Luke was something of a social revolutionist, while Matthew, or the compiler of the Gospel which goes by his name, was more exclusively concerned with moral issues as they bear upon problems of the individual life, I do not regard such bias—if bias it really was—as any disqualification for their task. Jesus was individualist and socialist in one, and, though the writers of the Gospels approach Him from diverse points of view, the portrait to which they all contribute forms a coherent whole ; only it is the picture of One so much greater than all that they or we can see in Him or say about Him, that all that is true in the convictions of earnest men—and there is truth in them all, opposed as they seem to be, apart from Him—finds its final expression in His words and life who is the truth. The gospel is more adequately conveyed to us because it comes to us written in four Gospels by men, who may have used, but did not copy, one another's books ; who all saw Him differently, because they saw Him through different eyes ; who saw, it may be, what they most desired to see, yet who saw truly, for all that they saw was there already. The marvel is that with all the difference of approach and colouring the picture painted by, it may be, more than four different hands, emerges in the end substantially one, with clear outlines—the portrait of One recognizably a Man, yet always something more than a mere man.

That this is true of the Fourth Gospel as well as of the others is my own conviction, but I shall make no attempt to prove this within the limits of this volume. What I am concerned to assert, and, if I can, to prove, is that the Gospels give us not a mere bundle of impressions and points of view useful for the study of Jesus, but a well-defined and convincing portrait, all the more nearly complete because at least four real men, with tastes and opinions of their own, contributed to its execution Their honesty is as evident as the limitations of their outlook. The full and final proof of their inspiration lies in the fact that, with all their differences in theory and in statement, the Spirit of God has attuned them to the same key, harmonizing them in one deep and various music, until they become a worthy echo of His tones, whose voice was as the sound of many waters.

Can we, then, draw together some of the materials for an outline-portrait of Jesus as He is painted for us in the first three Gospels? Mark tells us, as we shall see, something of His looks and tones, but we hear little of His outward appearance, as we know little of His habits in daily life. The broad impressions were so overpowering that His friends could not trace the details of His features. They hint at the light on His face, and Peter, who was closest to Him in the Galilean days, could tell of His gestures, His sighs, His manners with little children ; but even Peter's suggestions come down to us only in certain intimate references, which imply that he knew more than he cared to tell. The earliest Gospel—that of Mark— impresses the reader with a sense of intimacy, of a face and voice so freshly in the memory of the apostolic circle that description was not needed ; but our second impression is one of an overmastering awe, as though any detailed delineation were a profanation. We never hear that Jesus was ill or weary till we come to the Fourth Gospel ; only once that He slept. But of the spirit which animated Him, of His endearing tenderness and His flashes of terrible majesty, of His anger and impatience and dismayed surprise, of His homely friendliness and His enlivening humour, we find suggestions everywhere ; and we do not wonder that those who knew Him best found Him sometimes strangely removed from them, while those who were farthest away from Him in their ignorance and sinfulness often felt wonderfully at home in His free and understanding companionship. G. S. Lee, in his beautiful book called *The Shadow Christ*, has expressed the marvel of this new evangel so well that I can only repeat his words. ' It was,' he says, ' before he had heard of Christ's evangelistic methods that John had called Him '' One the latchet of whose shoes I am not worthy to unloose.'' Looking almost out of his grave to watch himself being forgotten, John in the prisoner's cell was too essentially a preacher not to question the Son of God because He was different from himself. When his disciples returned to him with '' Do you not remember those old sermons of yours, the city trooping out to meet you, strong men crying out with a sense of their disobedience, the long lines of weeping penitents that you baptized in the river? "; when, as the shadows grew long in his cell, they told him the words of Christ, " Come unto Me, all ye that labour and are heavy laden, and I will give you rest," there came into the broken old prophet-heart the thought of the greatest sermon of his life and the mighty climax of it, " Who hath warned you to flee from the wrath to come ? His fan is in His hand. He will gather His wheat into His garner, but He will burn up the chaff with unquenchable fire." And the more he heard about Jesus, His inscrutable " Abide in Me," His eating with publicans, His divine disreputable love for every one, the more He wondered how this disastrous tenderness could belong to One in whose face he had seen, one wonderful day, the shining of God.' That is all true, and devoutly as well as wittily said ; but there is more than this in the Gospels, in the first three as in the Fourth. It is gloriously obvious, as Mr. Lee goes on to say, that it was the distinctive prerogative of Jesus to open His heart with a ' beautiful recklessness,' and keep it for ever open, for ' God may be as frank as He will ' ; but the heart so widely open that we can hide in it from our own most secret doubts and fears is a heart stern in its very tenderness, as relentless in its demand for an unreserved surrender as it is various—masterful and gentle, wooing and commanding—in its approaches to us. The gospel, as Mr. Lee says, is the law ' with the heart open first.' But it *is* the law, for Jesus makes room for our weakness ; He never gives way to it. This perfect union of firmness and gentleness we shall find best expressed in the first of our Gospels, for Mark is the book of faith, Luke of hope, Matthew of love—the last the tenderest and most terrible of the three.

Even the earliest of our Gospels hints more than once at the reserves of Jesus. ' To you,' He said, ' it is given to know the mystery of the Kingdom ; but to those who are without, all things take the form of parable.' [1] Are we justified, then, in speaking of the ' beautiful recklessness ' of Jesus ? Yes, if we remember that the ' mystery

[1] Mark iv. 11.

of the Kingdom ' was an *open* secret ; there was no real
reservation, for the use of parables was only another
invitation, a call to the venture of a painstaking faith
which clears the way to the hearer's heart in his turn.
All the truth as it is in Jesus was there already, accessible
in His words and works, in parable and miracle ; but
before men could see or even faintly understand Him as
He stood revealed and revealing before them, they must
learn to think and desire in a deeper and more passionate
way. Every parable was a deliberate provocation to
thought, to the faith that will not be shaken off until
it sees and knows all that can be seen and known in
Jesus. For He was always beyond the grasp of friends
and enemies alike ; if He gave Himself up to the one or
to the other, it was because He willed to do so. He could
neither be managed by His friends nor countered by His
foes. Pharisees would entangle Him, and He lightly
escapes ; Galilean peasants would make Him their leader,
and He is gone from them ; at last His followers try
desperately to control His course, and He leaves them
behind, and only comes back when they are ready to
follow without question. The temptation story, as told
in the First and Third Gospels, suggests our Lord's
deliberate rejection of any short cut to the empire of the
hearts of men ; He will not go the comfortable way of
the well-to-do philanthropist, seeing first to His own health
and fitness, and then setting himself to make others as
warm and well-fed as He is himself. He will not appeal
to a sensation-loving public by extravagant methods.
How startling Jesus could have been if He had chosen !
He will not compromise, or go the lower way of success.
He will appear among men as one of themselves. Yet
how well He came to know that He can never be quite
one of themselves ! Men use the philanthropist, they
stare at the sensational preacher, they understand the
man who schemes to win their souls ; but as for One who
at one moment made you feel really a better man for
having come near Him, and then, when you least expected,
turned round upon you, and gave you a look which made
you feel utterly mean, you did not quite know why—
if He will not adapt Himself a little to the give and take
of life, and yet will not leave anybody alone—what can

you make of Him ? If He had set up for a saint, they would have known where to place Him ; but He was never the professional moralist. The secret of His extra-ordinary power with disillusioned people, like the woman of Samaria or the ' dying thief,' was that He drew your interest before He struck at your conscience. John the Baptist, as Mr. Lee says, would have begun with the five husbands, and would have conditioned his fellowship on amendment. ' If Jesus had approached the woman at the well with the air of being better than she was, she would either have doubted it or hated Him for it. It was because He offered her the most perfect fellowship at first, and afterwards told her all that ever she did, that He was the Son of God. A great heart keeps its secrets, like the sky, by being open.'

So we must think of Jesus as men saw Him in the early days. Their first impression, we may be sure, was that here was a new kind of prophet, quite as ready to listen as to speak, one who made you feel that He was interested in you, that you could talk about yourself ; who was always able to take time about doing good, for He never had public engagements which forced Him to hurry over private and casual interviews. This feature of our Lord's Galilean ministry shines out in every page of Mark's Gospel. An invalid woman interrupts Him when He is on His way to a desperate case ; five minutes' delay may make all the difference, for it is a matter of life or death. But He will stop and make her tell her story, at the same time keeping up the courage of the distracted father of the sick child.[1] A blind man comes to Him [2]; the Healer is careful (see page 43) to make Himself understood, and goes out of His way to inquire what coming out of darkness into light feels like, perhaps because that was one of the things that He had never experienced in His own Person ; more probably for the simple reason that He was able to help men more when they would talk about themselves ; He could read a man's soul from his mere description of his physical sensations at a great crisis. The gravamen of His charge against the men of His generation was, we remember, that He ' never knew ' them [3]; they never gave Him the chance. The

[1] Mark v. 36.   [2] Mark viii. 22   [3] Matt. vii. 23 ; Luke xiii. 27.

of Hanan—the Annas of the Gospels), and that 'the Pharisees themselves denounced such practices'; only pleading that 'we must not magnify an exception into a rule.' 'It was only under the aristocratic régime of the Temple's last decades,' he says, 'that we hear of oppression'; but it was just then that Jesus made His onslaught upon the system. Dr. Abrahams also quotes Dr. Gould as saying that His attack reveals 'not merely an invective against an illegitimate use of the Temple, but a thorough-going antipathy to trade as such.' That may be so ; but the fact that our Lord would possibly, and even probably, pass a violent condemnation upon many of the methods characteristic of commerce in all ages rather makes us restive under the suggestion that such methods are a necessary part of the social order now than acquits these bitter enemies of Jesus then. That this traffic was a public convenience would almost certainly have been the line of defence chosen by the priests, if we could have heard what they had to say for themselves ; indeed, the words 'social order' have often been used to cover a multitude of sins, for there is no abuse that has not at one time or another found shelter there. A whip of small cords was the Lord's answer to the argument, and from His action we may make what inferences we will ; at least they cannot be very comfortable ones, least of all to modern Englishmen.

So it was to a disillusioned society that Jesus came when He entered Jerusalem for the last week of His ministry— the one week of which we have a detailed history in the Gospels. Only the Galilean pilgrims were eager and expectant, joining with hilarious riotousness in the cries which welcomed His entry. The development of the situation, so far as it concerned them, will be traced with some fullness later on (pp. 66 ff.) ; here we are rather concerned with the mind and heart of the Saviour. As for the citizens of Jerusalem, the words which Luke adds to his account of the crucifixion may be said to sum up the part they played the whole week through : 'The people stood beholding'[1] only realizing that some great crime had been committed when it was too late to do anything but grieve.[2] They had seen too much of this sort

[1] Luke xxiii. 34.　　　[2] Luke xxiii. 48.

of thing to be greatly excited. They too had settled down to make a trade of the sacred city and the veneration of the Gentiles, to exploit the world which, under the Maccabees, they had hoped to conquer; and so they could not comprehend the Cross; they came to it as 'to a spectacle,'[1] the latest sensation. Yet the Lord will make His last appeal—for an appeal His death was—to His people as well as to the world. So He enters the city— that there may be no excuse for misunderstanding—upon an ass, symbol of a peaceful Messiahship. That Jesus Himself had small hope that His appeal would succeed is shown alike by His weeping over the city,[2] and by the cursing of the fig-tree—an explanation of the meaning of this strange incident is attempted later (Part ii. chap ii.). But He throws His whole soul into this last effort to save His people from the doom which He foresaw, accepting every challenge, and expounding His purposes in the thrust and parry of His daily encounters with the utmost directness and force. All the popular ideals are attacked—the revolt against Roman exactions, the conception of the Messiah as another David,[3] while both the theory[4] and the practice[5] of the priestly aristocracy are exposed in the most public and provocative manner. Not revolutionary enough for His Galilean well-wishers, too revolutionary for His Sadducean foes, with His popular influence undermined by the suspicion of zealots in the patriotic camp and by the jealousy of His Pharisaic rivals, Jesus was never busier and never more alone. While His enemies are forgetting their differences in resistance to a danger which threatened them all alike, His friends are disunited and out of touch with Him, some of them, like Peter, distracted with doubt and fear and struggling with half-suppressed resentment (pp. 91 ff.); others, like James and John, still nursing wild dreams of honours in the Kingdom[6]; others again, it may be, like Judas, plotting and arming for a decisive blow within a few hours (pp. 79 ff.). Jesus rallies them for a last evening together, and seeks to shame them out of these unnerving moods, which so unfitted them for the crisis now upon them, by an act of unparalleled condescension. For their sakes He holds back His own

[1] Luke xxiii. 48.   [3] Mark xii. 17, 37, &c.   [5] Mark xi. 17.
   Luke xix. 41.   [4] Mark xii. 27, &c.   [6] Mark x. 35 ff.

sorrows till He can hold them back no longer, and then He bids them leave Him[1] (see Part ii., chaps. vi. &c., for an exposition of this passage). But at the supper-table it is only here and there that we can discern any premonition of the agony so soon to sweep over the Saviour's soul. When the 'traitor' has gone, He can altogether shut the door upon what the next hour might bring, and give Himself wholly to the task of comforting His weaker friends. But all too soon the crisis comes. The evil which has been drawing in upon mind and heart, fastening upon His sensitive and pitiful imagination for so long, comes a step nearer, and He must leave His friends for a while. They are young, and have not gone far into the deeper waters of sin and sorrow ; they must wait, and can be dealt with a little later, when the redemption of a nation and a world given over to the power of darkness, and going down swiftly to despair, has been won.

When they will not leave Him, assuring Him that they are ready to defend Him against all comers, He allows three of them to follow Him into the garden, but forbids them to come too near. They will be safer if they can manage to keep awake an hour longer—above all, if they will prepare themselves for what is coming in prayer. But He will not have them see more of His sorrow than their weak hearts can bear. It was characteristic of Jesus that He shrank from calling upon His friends to suffer with Him. He would make them partners in His joy,[2] but would spare them the sight of His pain ; on the mountain of Transfiguration He had not forbidden them to come too close. Much less can we venture far behind the curtain which the Lord dropped behind Him when He went into the dark ; we can only try to gather up the meaning of the hints that He has given us. We faintly realize that He called Himself ' Son of Man ' because He felt Himself from the beginning one with us, because in His own Person He ever ' took upon Him our weaknesses and carried our diseases.'[3] His perfect sinlessness left the avenues of approach on both sides—Godward and manward—wide open, for it is sin that bars our way to God and man alike. Once here, He could not but throw

---

[1] Luke xxii. 35 ff.   [2] Mark ii. 19; John xvi. 22, &c.
[3] Matt. viii. 17.

in His lot with us, to sink or to swim. That is how He could be made to be sin for us,[1] 'who knew no sin'; it was no calculated condescension, but a necessity of His nature, that He should feel in every fibre of His being that our sins were His, our despair His. When we add to this identification with us His terrible penetration, already suggested, we can see that He not only felt with us, but felt for us; though our sorrows were His, His can never be ours, for we are under the merciful shadow of moral ignorance, and He was not. About the doom of the lost we only know what we have been told, and, again in consideration for our frailty, He has left us with a warning, terrible in its very vagueness, expressed in dark images which certainly do not justify any easy optimism, but still do not shut the gates of mercy on the unbelief of man. But they are most terrible, because we feel instinctively that they only faintly reflect the thoughts which haunted the Saviour's mind as He went down to grapple with the last mysteries of human lawlessness. In the garden He was wrestling with His own knowledge of the issues of sin. It was not that Mercy in the Son was pleading with Justice in the Father—that suggests an utterly false antithesis—but that His hope was battling with His fear. He could save men, the demon-haunted, the most desperately depraved sinner, when the barriers set up by pride and prejudice were broken; but what of the men, in some senses the better men, whose hearts had never seemed so fast closed to His appeal as now? Would anything ever move them, when He had failed? They had seen Him, and many of them, He knew, had known Him for something of what He was—and yet they would not let Him save them! And now sheer self-deception was leading them, more irrevocably as the minutes of the last hour fled by, to a deed which might well doom them to the hell which, in His darker hours, He had seen. Being what they were, having done what they were seeking to do with Him, how could they escape the fire of Gehenna? He had warned them[2], sought to surprise them in a storm of anger and pity into reality; but His words had only hardened their hearts against Him. It was not a question merely

[1] 2 Cor. v. 21.   [2] Matt. xxiii. 33.

B

of the particular deeds of the few specially guilty men, nor of the self-inflicted doom of one nation, sealed by the transactions of that day, though these were ingredients in His cup of agony. These men and these deeds were representative, for men are for ever crucifying Him whom they partly know to be the Christ of God ; they will grasp at security or power, and risk their souls. He will risk His soul with them, not regarding either His divine power or the peace which was His birthright as ' a thing to be grasped at,' if perchance He may save some of them. For all the while He felt strangely near akin to the men who had come to be His murderers ; if their sins were to become His, if His name, the first in the Book of Life, were to be blotted out, it should be so.

But in prayer, as always, He sees farther still, for ' an angel from heaven ' strengthens Him.[1] He had thought of His death already as a supreme appeal to men ; from the side of God, for He was God ; as an act of representative atonement from the side of man, for He was man. His death, He had seen, would be a pledge to His Father that His other children would not for ever be estranged from Him, for was He not one with them ? And if He could die with them and for them, could they not live with Him and for Him ? But since then He had become ever more aware that there was opening under His eyes a gulf which, it might be, could never be bridged. Was it possible that, even if He were lifted up from the earth, He would draw not all men, but only *some* men, to Him ? That He would become a ' ransom for *many*,' He knew. His eleven faithful men, the many whom He had saved and was saving, were evidence of that ; but what of the others, the Pharisees, the priests, the Iscariots of every age ? Did they really know what they were doing ? He would pray for them. Surely His prayers, always heard,[2] would avail ! If they knew not what they did, there was hope, for ' truth is great, and shall prevail.' In this hope, attained in prayer, Jesus rose to face His foes. So overmastering was the glory of the victory written upon His face that they sank before Him.[3] We may well believe that this peace, so hardly won, was with Him through the trials before Caiaphas and Pilate ; He is

[1] Luke xxii. 43.   [2] John xi. 42.   [3] John xviii. 6.

waiting for the great moment of redemptive prayer. Once upon the cross, when they have done their worst, He utters His commentary upon the whole history of human sin and sorrow : ' Father, forgive them, for they know not what they do." [1] We must rest in this prayer and hope of Jesus, for the Lord's hopes must come true, we know not how. That He may offer His whole Being in the great prayer, He has already refused the drug, [2] as before He had handed to His disciples the cup of good-fellowship and peace, [3] which He would not just then taste Himself.

But all is not finished yet, for Jesus never forgets the one, though His heart be strained to breaking with the sorrow of a world. He has provided for His mother, [4] prayed for friends [5] and foes [6] alike. Is not His work done ? Has not He conquered without despair ? No ; there is yet one man whom He can carry from the gates of death to Paradise, and He will not give way to His longing for rest, after His heart-shaking struggle, until He has rescued him. So He waits, gathering up, we may be sure, all His powers of mind and heart to this last mighty work. Whether Dismas—for that was the dying robber's traditional name—had heard of Jesus before, we do not know ; but we may well believe that he had. Perhaps the jailer who led him out of his cell had entertained him that morning with an account of the arrest and the uncanny power of this Man who had thrown them all to the ground with a look. Perhaps he had heard Pilate's tribute in the court, or noticed the title upon the cross, ' This is the King of the Jews. It may be that old words of Scripture had come back to his mind : ' He was despised and rejected of men. . . . He was numbered with outlaws.' Was He really a King ? At any rate, by all accounts, He was a more unfortunate man than himself. If, as he heard, He had given Himself up without a blow, there must be some reason for this strange behaviour. It was not weakness, for had He not shown what He could do ? He must try to think this out if he could, though the drug which he had taken, but Jesus refused, was creeping over his brain. We can

---

[1] Luke xxiii. 34.   [3] Mark xiv. 25, &c.   [5] Luke xxii. 32.
[2] Mark xv. 23.   [4] John xix. 26.   [6] Luke xxiii. 34.

reconstruct the biography of this man without difficulty. Possibly he had listened as a boy to some patriotic orator in his native town in Galilee, his young blood had been stirred, and he had joined a band of revolutionists, only to come into conflict with the Roman legions—an unequal struggle which could only end in one way. The band was dispersed, and the survivors, with no shelter from the Government on sea or land, took in desperation to the roads, and had been living by their wits. He had sunk very low, led on by his older companion ; and now they had been caught red-handed, and were together condemned to the cross. How he despised these people to whom he had given his life, and who would not even let him die quietly ! Anyhow, a man ought to tell the truth before he dies, and he would stop that blackguardly companion of his. He was always like that ; he might at least have the decency to hold his tongue now (' Dost thou not even fear God ? '). So he speaks, atoning for the whole sordid history of his short life by one most brave confession. Perhaps, if Jesus is indeed a King, He will remember the man who spoke up for Him when He was dying. With one short sentence the Lord lifts this lost sheep out of his despair to Paradise. The cries of the crowd are forgotten, and he drops into blissful unconsciousness. When they come to give the robbers the happy dispatch, he does not feel the blow.

But, though He saved others, the Saviour could not save Himself. Once the tension is relaxed, there comes a terrible reaction. The effort, following so closely upon the redemptive agony, was too much even for Him. There is nothing more to be done now, for He is left alone with the appalling present fact. He cannot help either Peter or Judas, or comfort His mother now. Things must take their course until this hour is over. To be unable to relieve the sorrow of those who loved Him—for how well He knew how much they could suffer in how short a time !—to see men before Him who were shouting themselves to despair ! He could not rest in the thought of a world redeemed, coming back to sanity in the far future. What of these men now ? How could they be saved from the hell which He alone of living men had seen ? Suddenly the fears which He had conquered in the garden swoop down upon Him again, and He cries out like a lost child. It is only for a moment, for He rallies once again, and passes peacefully away. He ' bows His head ' upon the cross as He could never do before.[1] At last He will let them quench His thirst, for ' It is finished.' The ' Father ' has come back, and the sun shines ; but Jesus meets the dawning of hope, never to be eclipsed again, with a broken heart, for after His passing ' one of the soldiers with a spear pierced His side, and forthwith there came out blood and water.'[2]; His heart had burst, and discharged ' its sanguineous contents in the form of red clots of blood and watery serum ' (Professor J. Y. Simpson).[3] We must hide from our fears—for the world and for ourselves little indeed compared with His, but terrible enough to us—in His riven side. He knew and saw the worst, and yet could hope, passing through deeper waters of despair than we can ever fathom to peace. We must take shelter in His hope, and rest in His availing prayer. He had once said, ' Whoever shall give one of these little ones a cooling cup, only because he is a disciple, shall not lose his reward.'[4] I think of one of the golden deeds of an older world. ' And David longed, and said, Oh that one could give me drink of the water of the well of Bethlehem, which is beside the gate ! '[5] The three mighty men overheard his muttered words, and brought him the water at the risk of their lives, breaking through the ranks of the Philistines twice to gratify their lord's momentary fancy. What they did for their captain we, said Jesus, must be ready to do for any one of these little ones, His brethren, for He has broken through to make the power to hope in such a world as this available for us. There would have been no water in the well beside the gate of Bethlehem, no satisfying music in the angel's song of ' Peace on earth ' for a world heart-sick of war and grown hard and bitter, if Jesus had not broken through to bring us His cooling cup of hope ; and as we look into the sacramental cup of peace and joy in His finished work, we see that it is stained with His blood who brought it

---

[1] Luke ix. 58 ; John xix. 30.   [2] John xix. 34.
[3] Since this was written, a medical friend of mine has suggested to me that the ' blood and water ' showed that Jesus had been suffering for some time from ' pleurisy with effusion,' contracted through exposure
[4] Matt. x 42   [5] 2 Sam. xxiii. 14 ff.

to us.   The water of our dreams has become wine indeed, and we must take it kneeling in childlike wonder.   For ' one of the soldiers with a spear pierced His side, and forthwith there came out blood and water ' [1]; the blood that heals the soul comes first, the water refreshing the spirit afterwards, and both are mingled in the sacred cup which, on the night of His agony, He refused Himself, [2] but gave to His friends as their inalienable sacrament of hope.   ' The blood of Jesus Christ . . . cleanses us from all sin'; for, before the wonder of His inrushing love and the rising to meet it of our love in answer, barriers that otherwise would part us from Him are burst asunder in a moment, and ' we love because He first loved us.'   Of these mysteries it is not easy to speak or write, and when we have said all that it is given us to say, ' the rest is silence.'   It is better so.

> For none of the ransomed ever knew
> How deep were the waters crossed.

We only know that He came back to us, and that He, this Jesus, is ours for evermore.

---

[1] John xix. 34.   [2] Mark xiv. 25; xv. 23.

II

THE GOSPEL ACCORDING TO MARK: GENERAL CHARACTERISTICS

References to John Mark in the New Testament are to be found in Acts xii. 12–25; xiii. 5–13; xv. 37–39; Col. iv. 10; 2 Tim. iv. 11; Philem. 24; 1 Pet. v. 13. His mother, Mary, was a lady of some position in Jerusalem. She had slaves, one of whom, Rhoda by name, answers the door to Peter.[1] Mark himself appears as 'attendant' upon Barnabas and Saul [2] on their visit to Cyprus. Dr. Chase (*Hastings' B.D.*, art. ' Mark ') argues that the word ' attendant,' as used here, means ' synagogue-attendant ' (cf. Luke iv. 20), not ' assistant-preacher.' He is ' cousin ' to Barnabas, so presumably of priestly descent, and connected with Cyprus. Perhaps, owing to his connexion with Peter (see below) and Barnabas, he would seem to have become restive under the growing ascendancy of Paul. In Acts xiii. we have ' Barnabas and Saul ' at the beginning of the chapter. ' Paul and Barnabas ' at the end. When ' those about Paul '—notice the submergence of Barnabas—leave Cyprus for Pamphylia, Mark returns to Jerusalem.[3] His behaviour on this occasion leads to a sharp contention between his two superiors at the beginning of Paul's second missionary journey, and results in the breaking up of their colleague-ship,[4] Mark going back with Barnabas to Cyprus. Later on, however, we find him reconciled to Paul, and making himself exceedingly useful in personal services during his imprisonment at Rome. He figures as Peter's ' son in he gospel ' in 1 Pet. v. 13.

To these New Testament allusions should be added a

Acts xii. 13.   [2] Acts xiii. 5.   [3] Acts xiii. 13.   [4] Acts xv. 39.

quotation from Papias, reported by Eusebius, as follows :
' And this the presbyter used to say : " Mark, having
been Peter's interpreter, wrote down all that he remembered of the sayings and doings of the Lord, accurately,
yet not in order." For he had neither heard the Lord,
nor ever been His disciple, but later, as I said, had attended
Peter, who composed his teachings to suit the needs of
the moment, but did not profess to make a regular collection of the Lord's sayings. And so Mark made no mistakes,
writing down the particulars just as he remembered them ;
only of one thing he made sure, not to leave on one side
or report falsely any of these reminiscences.' The
' presbyter ' to whom Papias owed his information was
apparently ' John the Presbyter,' who was prominent
in the Church of Asia at the end of the first century, and
was thought to have been a disciple of the Lord Himself.
It should be added that the quotation from ' John the
Presbyter ' only goes as far as the words ' in order,' the
rest almost certainly coming from Papias himself.

Clement of Alexandria (190–203), commenting upon
1 Pet. v. 13, says : ' Mark, a follower of Peter, when
Peter was preaching the gospel publicly in Rome before
certain members of the trading classes, and was bringing
forward many testimonies of ' (or ? ' to ') ' Christ, was
asked by these hearers to compose a permanent memorial
of Peter's discourses, and so came to write, from his
memory of them, the Gospel which is called the Gospel
according to Mark.' In another place (as reported by
Eusebius) he says that Mark composed his Gospel with
the sanction of Peter, but without his supervision.

These traditions should be received with a certain
reserve, but there are features in the Gospel that suggest
association with Peter. After a somewhat hurried and
colourless introduction, the narrative suddenly lights up
with his entrance. Moreover, the words ' passing along
the sea of Galilee '[1] take, so to say, the point of view of
the men in the boat, while ' Andrew the brother of Simon '
may well stand for ' Andrew my brother,' and ' Simon
and those with him '[2] for Peter's ' we.' So i. 29 might
be rendered in Peter's words, ' We came straight from
the synagogue to our house, and James and John were

<hr>

[1] Mark i. 16.   [2] Mark i. 36.

with us.' If the bulk of the story comes from Peter, it is a little difficult to understand why such sayings as 'Thou art Peter, and upon this rock I will build My Church,' [1] and such stories as that of Peter's walking on the water, should be omitted. Both these sections are peculiar to Matthew. We can only say that if Peter is the narrator he must have been in those days exceedingly modest. This Gospel is obviously a preacher's manual, covering, as it does, the range of apostolic preaching as reported in the early chapters of the Acts—from 'the baptism of John' to the Resurrection (cf. Acts i. 22)—and the word 'gospel' occurs frequently. Mark has this word eight times, Matthew four times (only once without the addition of the words 'of the Kingdom'), Luke never ! Compare especially Mark i. 1, 15, both peculiar to this Gospel in this particular. Sometimes to the homiletic mind a sermon outline is discernible in the very arrangement of the narrative. In a few places the style of the writer is as curt as that of a note-book (e.g. i. 1) ; in many others its very homeliness and informality reveal Mark or Peter as a first-rate story-teller. The dramatic arrangement of the material at the disposal of the evangelist also suggests to us that the ground has been covered again and again for the purposes of popular preaching.

For if we know little of Mark from history and tradition, we can arrive at a very clear idea of the qualities of his mind from his book. Every now and again we have incisive comments upon sayings or doings of Jesus, nearly all peculiar to Mark, and all showing a real faculty for getting to the main point in the fewest and simplest possible words. One of these comments deserves to be called a stroke of genius. In iii. 14 we read : 'And He appointed twelve' (not apostles) 'that they might be with Him '; compare v. 18, ix. 8, 'with themselves,' Mark only. Jesus came back from converse with Moses and Elijah to the prattle of Peter, James, and John; from the company of the great to the daily discipline of intimacy with men who would never understand Him till He was with them no longer in the flesh. The fact that they had been with Jesus accounts for the history of the glorious company of the apostles. We shall see later how Matthew

[1] Matt. xvi. 18 ; cf. xiv. 28-31.

evokes a subtler harmony from the same very simple
words. The Fourth Gospel tells us that the Lord Himself
touched this note at the climax of His prayer for His
disciples, ' Father, inasmuch as Thou hast given (them)
to Me, I will that where I am they also may be *with
Me*.'[1] Some scholars think that Mark was Luke's chief
authority in Acts, chapters i.–xii. If so, we can
recognize a genuine Marcan touch in Acts iv. 13 : ' They
took knowledge of them, that they had been with Jesus.'
Most of these comments will come under review presently,
when we try to classify the passages and phrases peculiar
to this Gospel. It is quite possible, of course, that they
only came to be added in the third edition of the book.
The fact that in most cases neither Matthew nor Luke
repeats them perhaps looks in this direction, a widely held
theory (see Professor W. W. Holdsworth's *Gospel Origins*,
passim), being to the effect that the First and Third evangelists saw and used a copy of an edition or draft of Mark's
Gospel earlier than ours. There can, however, be little doubt
that the writer of the Gospel as a whole was responsible
also for the comments, in whatever edition they were first
inserted.

The style of the evangelist reproduces the easy colloquial
manner of the popular preacher. In the Parable of the
Sower, as reported here, the convenient word ' and ' occurs
fourteen times, while Matthew has only six, Luke nine
' ands.' So in Mark xi. 29 : ' I will ask you one word, *and*
you answer Me, *and* I will tell you.' In iii. 14 ff., Dr.
Abbott tells us, ' there appears to be a confusion of two
documents, one dealing with the appointment of the twelve,
the other with the naming of some of them—the two
documents being combined by parenthesis.' The result
is certainly not a model of lucidity. The frequent repetition of the word ' straightway ' in some parts of the story
has often been pointed out. In the first chapter everything
after verse 14 happens at breathless speed. If the writer's
purpose is to give us a specimen day in the Galilean ministry
of Jesus, the recurrence of this hard-worked word ceases
to be merely monotonous, for it helps us to appreciate
the strain and stress of the Master's working day ; what
is lost in smoothness is more than made up in pictorial

[1] John xvii. 24.

effect. In many cases we feel that by this very defiance of the conventional grammar and style of reported speech Mark succeeds in giving us the actual idiom of Jesus. The first charge to newly ordained missionaries may be quoted as an example of this happy disorder : [1] ' And He summons the twelve, and began to send them out two by two, and was giving them authority over unclean spirits, and forbade them to take anything for the road except one staff ; not a loaf, not a wallet ' (the religious beggar's wallet, or collecting-bag), ' no brass in their purse ; but (let them be) shod with sandals, and *you* are not to put on two under-garments.' Moreover, our evangelist everywhere gives proof of his appreciation of the movement or gesture which reveals character at a crisis. The blind beggar in x. 50 ' throws away his upper garment,' leaps up and comes to Jesus. As a matter of fact, he probably put his upper garment on, as the oldest extant Syriac version—commonly known as the ' Lewis ' Syriac—tells us. ' I have watched,' says Mrs. Lewis, ' too closely the habits of Orientals not to know that they will more readily put on some outer garment—which they take off when they settle down to bask in the sun by the roadside—than divest themselves of anything when they are called into the presence of a superior.' The rich young ruler is said to have had a thunder-cloud upon his face when he left Jesus, while Peter [2] ' set to and began to weep ' when he had denied his Master. The Revised Version renders, ' When he thought thereon, he wept ' ; but the papyri give us the sense ' he set to.' Peter cries, as he does everything else, energetically. It is Mark also who tells us that Peter spoke ' with great vehemence ' —or, perhaps, ' with emphasis over and over again '— when he said, ' If I must die with Thee, I will not deny Thee.' [3]

But the vividness and love of telling detail characteristic of this Gospel can best be brought out by a cursory treatment of the more interesting words, phrases, and sections only found here.

i. 13 : ' He was with the wild beasts '—gives us the setting of the Temptation scene.

[1] Mark vi. 7 ff.   [2] Mark xiv. 72.   [3] Mark xiv. 31.

i. 20 : ' With the hired servants '—at once provides us with information as to the social status of Zebedee's family, and saves his sons' conduct from any appearance of callousness.

i. 26 : The demon ' tore ' its victim. Mark is always explicit upon the subject of demon-possession, and makes the driving out of these ' unclean spirits ' the outstanding feature—as it was to the Galileans—of the earlier ministry of Jesus.

i. 33 : ' And the whole city was gathered at the door.' This makes us think at once of the embarrassment of the disciples when they got up in the morning—Jesus gone, and a clamorous crowd to be appeased somehow.

i. 36 : ' And Simon and those with him (Peter's " we ") tracked Him down.' They knew His favourite retreat, and felt sure of finding Him, and bringing Him back. They did find Him, but did not bring Him back !

i. 43 : ' And speaking in stern tones (?), straightway He cast him out '—on this verse see below chap. iii.

i. 45 : The leper's disobedience and its result. Matthew omits altogether (see below), while Luke [1] simply states that the story went round, without saying how it leaked out.

ii. 2 : ' So that there was no room even near the door '—a very vivid touch.

ii. 3 : The ' paralytic ' is ' borne by four . . . they unroofed the roof where He was, and digging away, they let down the bed.' . . . Luke [2] has ' going up on to the roof they let him down through the tiles with the stretcher into the midst in front of Jesus.' Luke is evidently thinking of a Roman villa ; Mark—more correctly—of the old-fashioned workman's cottage. In the Roman house there was a hole called the ' impluvium ' in the centre of the tiled roof, but it is not likely that Peter's house would be more than a cottage built of mud. Dr. Abbott makes the interesting suggestion that there was a trap-door in the roof of some old Galilean cottages. A little chamber was often built in with the roof, and was connected with the rest of the house by means of a ladder which could be let down through the trap-door in the roof, while access to roof and roof-chamber could also be obtained by a mud or stone staircase at the back of the house, so that the lodger, such as Jesus sometimes was, could let himself in and out without disturbing the family— an excellent substitute for the modern latchkey ! This explains how it came about that Jesus was able to slip away unnoticed before the household was stirring (i. 35) ; if the trap-door had not been

[1] Luke v. 15.   [2] Luke v 19.

used for some time, it would have to be raised from outside by means
of a crowbar or some such instrument. This explains Mark's
curious phraseology, and avoids the very practical difficulty that
if part of the roof were really taken off there would have been a
heavy shower of mud and plaster on the heads of the people below !
F · the ' prophet's chamber ' see 2 Kings iv. 10, and for the trap-
do r in the sky, through which, it was thought, the rain came down,
Gen. vii. 11, viii. 2 ; 2 Kings vii. 19 ; Mal. iii. 10.

ii. 18 : ' And the disciples of John and the Pharisees were fasting.'
It was one of the Jewish fast-days.

ii. 23 : ' And the disciples began to make a way, plucking the
ears of corn.' Matthew and Luke avoid this suggestion, which
would perhaps imply a real trespass—making a path through
standing corn.

iii. 17 : ' And He surnamed them Boanerges, that is " Sons of
Thunder " or " Heavenly Twins." ' Dr. R. Harris has accumulated
a vast quantity of evidence from almost all times and conditions
to show that twins are called ' Sons of Thunder.' One MSS.
has, ' He called them in common ' (or ' familiarly ') ' Sons of
Thunder '—all the twelve ! I suppose because they ' hunted in
couples.'

iii. 20 : ' So that they could not even have a meal.' This brings
out the hurry and stress of the Galilean life of Jesus.

iv. 26–29 : The only complete parable—with the doubtful
exception of xiii. 34—peculiar to this Gospel. It will be considered later.

iv. 38 : ' On the cushion.' The word translated ' cushion ' is
somewhat puzzling ; it means ' a thing on which to lay the head.'
Theophylact says that it was ' all of wood,' but there is no
known parallel to the use of this word as meaning a wooden head-
rest in a boat. On the other hand, it might mean a wooden
cabin or shelter. Probably the language of the storm scene in
the Book of Jonah was in the mind of the evangelist. ' Jonah
had gone down into the innermost parts ' (R.V., literally ' covered
parts ') ' of the ship to sleep.' [1] There are other signs that the
contrast between Jonah and Jesus is working in the narrator's mind
here. Both slept in the storm ; but Jonah brought bad luck to the
boat, and the storm only ceased when he was waked and thrown
out, whereas ' with Christ in the vessel I smile at the storm ' ; the
danger is past when Jesus wakes and takes command. Matt. viii.
20 : ' The Son of Man has not where to lay His head,' and John

[1] Jonah i. 5.

xix. 30, ' He laid His head (down) '—at last—' and gave up His spirit,' should also be compared.

iv. 38, 39: The rather petulant tone of the disciples' cry (' Carest Thou not ? '), and the Lord's homely manner of address to the waves—as we should say, not to winds and waves, but to tiresome children, ' Hold your tongues '—are both omitted by Matthew and Luke. The second of these points is specially illuminating, as tending to show that Jesus talked to the forces of Nature—as indeed He did to the demons—in a half-scolding way (see below, p. 49). The same tone of easy and unembarrassed authority is noticeable in Mark xi. 23 and parallels ; but there it is said to be possible for us !

In **v. 13** the number of the swine is said to have been ' about two thousand,' and in verse 16 the apparently trivial addition ' and about the swine ' touches what was really the sore point with these Gerasenes. They would not have minded Jesus curing mad people, but ' what about our pigs ' ? Jesus stands here for the rights of man's soul against a vested interest.

v. 26 is very hard upon doctors. We shall see that Luke, a doctor himself, softens these rough expressions down.

v. 41: ' Talitha cum '—' Get up, darling.' The beautiful Aramaic words give an endearing touch to the story, and bring us very near to the heart of Jesus.

v. 42: ' And began to walk about '—at once, as a little girl of twelve years old would, when she began to feel better ! The whole story is a masterpiece of realistic narrative, and illustrates almost all Mark's special excellences. Other points will be noted later.

vi. 4: ' And amongst His relatives.' Omitted by both Matthew and Luke, perhaps out of regard for the family of Jesus ; compare iii. 21, also omitted by the later Synoptists, and iii. 31, ' calling Him,' softened by Matthew to ' seeking to talk with Him,' by Luke to ' wishing to see Thee.'

vi. 5: ' And He could not do,' altered by Matthew (xiii. 58) to ' He did not do.' Like many modern Christians, Matthew did not like the suggestion that there was anything that Jesus could not do (see below, p. 99).

vi. 6: For the same reason both Matthew and Luke leave out the surprise of Jesus, expressed by Mark in the words, ' And He was amazed at their unbelief.'

vi. 7: ' He *began* to send them out.' They were not sent out all at once ; a *period* of apostolic tours was begun.

vi. 13 : The disciples ' anointed with oil those who were ill.' Jesus is never said to have done this, but compare Jas. v. 14, Luke x. 34.

vi. 31 : ' They had not leisure so much as to eat.' Jesus did not care much about rest or regular meals for Himself, but went into retreat out of consideration for His disciples. Matthew and Luke both imply that He retired because He had heard of the fate of John the Baptist, and knew that Herod was cognizant of His whereabouts. Both motives may well have had a place in the motives of the Master, but Mark gives us the simplest and most human explanation.

vi. 39 : ' He bade them all lie down by parties ' (better, perhaps, ' as for a party,' with Codex Bezae) ' on the green grass, and they lay down in rows ' (literally, ' garden-beds '). Assemblies of Rabbis were often held in vineyards, where men could sit in rows or tiers. ' On the green grass ' gives us the time of year, early spring.

vi. 46 : ' Having dismissed them ' (or, better, ' bidden a regretful farewell to them '). The same word is used in Luke xiv. 33, ' Who-ever does not bid good-bye to all his possessions.' This implies a definite relinquishment of the Lord's public ministry in Galilee.

vi. 48 : ' And He would have passed by them.' It was character-istic of Jesus that He waited for an invitation before joining them ; compare Luke xxiv. 28, ' He made as though He would have gone farther.'

vi. 51, 52 : The fear and bewilderment of the disciples are graphi-cally described. Matthew especially gives us quite a different picture.[1]

vii. 19 : ' (This He said), pronouncing all kinds of food clean.' A very remarkable comment of the evangelist or some later editor. But it may just as well have come from Peter as the result of the Joppa vision.[2]

vii. 24 : ' And He *could* not escape notice.' Another thing that Jesus cannot do : Matthew again cancels.[3]

vii. 29 : ' On account of this word, Go ' (see below, pp. 46, 103).

vii. 30 : ' Lying on the couch.' Matthew [4] does not mention the prostration of the child after the departure of the ' demon.'

vii. 31-36 : A story peculiar to this Gospel, with several characteristic features, notably the sigh of Jesus, on which more hereafter (pp. 42, 106).

viii. 3 : ' And some of them come from a long way off.' These

[1] Matt. xiv. 33. [2] Acts x. 15. [3] Matt. xv. 22. [4] Matt. xv. 28.

words express the practical sympathy of Jesus with individual people in the crowds which thronged Him ; He never thought of them merely as crowds.

viii. 12 : ' With an inward sigh.' Compare the sigh of Jesus in vii. 34, also mentioned only by Mark, and see below (p. 42).

viii. 14 : ' They had taken but one loaf.' Peter would not forget that solitary loaf !

viii. 15 : ' And the leaven of Herod.' In Mark iii. 6 also the ' Herodians ' figure, and there again the other Synoptists leave them out. We shall see reason to doubt whether the Herodians existed as a distinct party at all.

viii. 17 is to be dealt with later on (p. 51).

viii. 22 ff. : Another Marcan story like that of vii. 31 ff., but with yet more vivid detail (see p. 43).

viii. 27 : ' On the road.' Luke ix. 18 says that it was while He was alone with His disciples and was praying. There is no con-tradiction here, for Jesus may often have been alone in prayer, even when He was walking with His disciples along the road.

viii. 31 : ' And He was talking over the matter freely.' The word ' began ' (verse 31) in this Gospel often marks a new stage in the life of Jesus (compare vi. 7 above).

viii. 34 : ' The crowd with His disciples.' Matthew [1] has ' to His disciples '; Luke [2] ' He said to all.'

viii. 35 : ' And the gospel.' For this distinctive Marcan word compare i. 15, where also it is found in Mark only.

ix. 3 : ' So as no laundryman on earth can bleach it.' On ix. 6 see below (p. 55).

ix. 8 : ' With themselves ' (see above).

ix. 10 : ' Discussing what rising from the dead means.' They understood ' rising from the dead ' at the last day [3] : ' after three days '—a proverbial phrase meaning ' very quickly,' or, as we say, ' in a day or two ' (compare Hos. vi. 2 ; Mark viii. 31 ; John ii. 19) —puzzled them. To avoid this ambiguity, Matthew and Luke keep to the more definite and dignified phrase ' on the third day.'

ix. 15 ; ' And straightway all the crowd seeing Him were amazed, and running up were saluting Him.' At what were they amazed ? Perhaps the Transfiguration glory had not yet quite faded from the Master's face. At any rate it is clear that something made them fall back again, for in verse 25—again Mark only—the crowd runs up a second time.   (Compare Exod. xxxiv. 30 and 2 Cor. iii. 7).

[1] Matt. xvi. 24.   [2] Luke ix. 23.   [3] John xi. 24.

Compare also x. 32, where the disciples are 'amazed' at an expression upon the face of their Leader which they had not seen before.

ix. 14: 'The scribes disputing with them.' They are making capital out of the disciples' failure.

ix. 18: 'And he gnashes his teeth, and withers up.' Another example of realistic description of the symptoms of demon-possession.

ix. 20–25a (to 'I charge thee') is all peculiar to Mark, and is to come under closer observation later (p. 103). Notice also 'and go no more unto him,' with its suggestion of the danger of relapse. In ix. 25 observe the Lord's uneasiness in the presence of an excited crowd. He makes haste to cure the patient and get away.

ix. 30: 'He did not want any one to know (it)'; compare vii. 24.

ix. 33, 34: 'On the road,' 'in the house,' 'on the road.' The importance of these details is to be emphasized later.

ix. 35: 'He sat'—the attitude of the Teacher.

ix. 36: 'He took "the child" in His arms'; compare x. 16, where 'He took them in His arms' is also Mark only. This twice-repeated word, along with 'Talitha cum,' [1] show us in an unforgettable way our Lord's habitual and instinctive 'manner' with children. There is no evidence in the text of the Gospels for the cool assumption that this model child was a little boy !

ix. 37: 'One of such little children.' Luke [2] has 'this little child.'

ix. 48–50: There is much matter peculiar to Mark in these verses.

ix. 49 especially is a standing riddle for the textual critic. There are three main readings found in three groups of MSS. The first is, 'Every one shall be salted with fire'; the second, 'Every sacrifice shall be salted with salt'; the third, 'For every one shall be salted with fire, and every sacrifice shall be salted with salt.' The third may be cast overboard at once, for it is obvious that an eminently cautious copyist has found the other two readings in two different MSS. before him, and, to be on the safe side, has put them both in. But how can we choose between the other two ? The old Latin version, known as Codex Bobbiensis, perhaps gives us the clue. It reads, 'For everything material shall be destroyed.' The Greek word evidently underlying 'material' is very much like the more familiar word 'sacrifice' ($OY\Sigma IA$, $\Theta Y\Sigma IA$), and 'shall be destroyed' is not unlike 'shall be salted.' The 'fire' has slipped down from the line above (verse 48), and the 'salt' jumped up from the line below (verse 50); hence the

[1] Mark v. 41.   [2] Luke ix. 48.

C

confusion. This reading, it should be observed, not only accounts for all the others, but explains the whole preceding passage. The reason why we should be willing, if need be, to sacrifice hand, foot, or eye, rather than the soul, is that 'everything material shall be destroyed,' while the soul remains.

x. 14: The displeasure of Jesus with His disciples is passed over in Matthew and Luke.

x. 21 : ' He looked searchingly at him, and loved ' (or ? ' caressed ') 'him.' This passage will be dealt with later (p. 41).

x. 22 : ' With a lowering face at the word.'

x. 23 : ' Looking round '—a habit characteristic of Jesus; compare iii. 5, 34 ; v. 32 ; xi. 11—all Mark only (see also below, p. 40).

x. 24 : Notice ' children,' with its reference back to verse 15 ; also that this verse, according to the best MSS., which all omit ' for them that trust in riches,' means that it is hard for anybody —not simply for specially rich people—to get into the Kingdom.

x. 28 : ' Peter began to say.' He was interrupted by our Lord's generous acknowledgement of the sacrifices of His friends before he finished what he had to say.

x. 30 : ' Houses . . . with persecutions.' This very detailed statement of the nature of the reward promised to faithful service —' houses, brothers, sisters, mothers ' (Codex Bezae reads ' mother,' and indeed we do not need more than one), ' children, and lands with persecutions . . .'—is found in this Gospel only, and seems to mean that we are to be repaid *in kind* for all that we have, for Christ's sake, to part with. It is interesting to observe, too, that ' persecutions ' are included among the rewards of service ; this exactly corresponds to the spirit of Matt. v. 11, 12 ; Luke vi. 23. The rhythm of the verse reminds us of iii. 35.

x. 32 : The most conspicuous landmark in the Gospel. Mark explains why Jesus had to ' take ' the twelve ' again '—they had begun to lag behind Him. Matthew [1] and Luke [2] both have something like this, but do not tell us why the followers of Jesus had to be brought into line once more.

x. 35 : Matthew [3] softens ' that You should do for us whatever we ask ' into the more respectful ' asking something from Him,' and tells us that it was ' the mother of the sons of Zebedee ' who came in the first instance, not James and John themselves ; while Luke omits the incident altogether.

x. 50 has been noted above.

---

[1] Matt. xx. 17.   [2] Luke xviii. 31.   [3] Matt. xx. 20.

xi. 4 : ' Outside a door in the street.' Notice the picturesque detail, which must surely have come from Peter.

xi. 10 : ' Blessed . . . of our father David ' probably reproduces the cries of the crowd. They wanted the Kingdom (Home Rule) even more than the Messiah Himself.

xi. 11 : A lifelike touch. Jesus is taking stock of the position.

In xi. 13, 14, 20 Jesus curses the fig-tree in the morning, and the twelve notice that it is withered as they go back in the evening. In Matthew [1] the effect of the curse ensues instantaneously.

xi. 13 : ' For it was not the time of figs.' This phrase betrays the bewilderment of the writer in regard to this story. I have attempted an explanation elsewhere (Part ii., chap. i). ' From afar ' is also peculiar to Mark, and suggests that the mind of the Master was dwelling upon the distant view *of the city*.

xi. 16 : ' And did not allow that any one should carry a vessel through the Temple.' Jesus sided with those who urged that the Temple should not be used as a public thoroughfare. Dr. Abrahams (*Pharisaism and the Gospels*, p. 84) cites the regulation in Cambridge against carrying trade parcels through the college precincts. The use of the aisle of St. Paul's as a public thoroughfare, until comparatively recent times, might be quoted as a parallel case.

xi. 17 : ' For all nations.' Mark here finishes the sentence taken from Isaiah,[2] and so in three words gives us the inner meaning of the vehement anger of Jesus. The cattle-market was held in the court of the Gentiles ; the guardians of the Temple were flouting the very reason for its existence.

xi. 32 : ' They feared the crowd.' Matthew [3] has ' We fear '; while Luke [4] suggests that they confessed themselves afraid of stoning at the hands of the people. It does not seem likely that the members of the Sanhedrin would own up, even in a private meeting, to fear of the common people.

xii. 27 ff. : There is much matter peculiar to this Gospel in this passage. The commendation of a scribe's insight in verse 34 is noteworthy.

xiii. 34 : A little parable not found in the same form in the other Gospels.

xiv. 5 : ' And they were speaking harshly about her.' This phrase is referred to below (p. 79).

xiv. 7 : ' And when you choose, you can do them good.' Perhaps a touch of sarcasm at the expense of people who are very generous when there do not happen to be any poor folks about.

[1] Matt. xxi. 19.　　[2] Isa. lvi. 7.　　[3] Matt. xxi. 26.　　[4] Luke xx. 6.

xiv. 30: 'Twice.' Peter would not forget this. 31: 'With great vehemence.'

xiv. 36: 'Abba.' Jesus prays in His native tongue. 'All things are possible to Thee'; compare ix. 23—also Mark only.

xiv. 37: 'Simon, sleepest thou? Couldst thou not watch one hour?' Matthew [1] has 'So, then, you could not watch one hour with Me?'; Luke [2] 'Why are you asleep?' Both Matthew and Mark say that Peter was addressed, but Matthew avoids the appearance of a special reproach to Peter.

xiv. 40: 'They did not know what answer to make'; compare ix. 6, and see below (p. 55).

xiv. 41: 'It is enough.' Evidence from the papyri tends to show that this may well mean, 'He (Judas) has the money.' The word is omitted in the oldest Syriac version, and we cannot be sure of its genuineness.

xiv. 44: 'Safely.' The oldest versions translate 'cautiously.' If the solution of the riddle of Judas suggested below (pp. 79 ff.) be accepted, this may be taken as a hint to the Temple guards that they would not find it so easy to apprehend Jesus as they expected; He was more formidable than He appeared to be. We should like to think that he was anxious that his Master should not be hurt.

xiv. 51 is more important than it looks. It has often been suggested that this young man was Mark himself; otherwise there would seem to be no point in the insertion of this trivial incident in a solemn context.

xiv. 58: 'Made with hands' and 'not made with hands.' Perhaps a distorted memory of a real saying of Jesus; compare John ii. 19 and 2 Cor. v. 1, 'Not made with hands.' If so, the latter passage gives us another Pauline reminiscence of the words of Jesus, and Mark has again given us the clue.

xiv. 65: 'And the attendants received Him with slaps'; compare Matt. v. 39. Jesus is here practising what He had preached.

In reference to the denial, it should be noticed that in Mark apparently the same girl accosts Peter twice, whereas in Matthew another girl, in Luke a man, is his assailant the second time.

xiv. 67: 'She looked searchingly at him warming himself'; compare John xviii. 18, 25. Luke [3] has another word, for reasons stated below (p. 39).

xiv. 72: 'Twice'—'when he thought thereon.' Both these features have been commented upon above.

[1] Matt. xxvi. 40.   [2] Luke xxii. 45.   [3] Luke xxii. 56.

xv. 15: 'Wishing to propitiate the crowd.' The insertion of this clause reveals true insight in the writer. The crowd was not yet actively hostile to Jesus, though they had begun to suspect Him of betraying the people's cause. They were exasperated with Him because of His non-resistance to the authorities; in their view all that had followed the triumphal entry had been a pitiful fiasco, and Bar-rabbas at least had done something more than mere talking. They revelled in the obvious embarrassment of Pilate, because they had old scores to settle with him (see Luke xiii. 1), and they knew that a riot was the one thing that Pilate must avoid at all costs, so precarious was his position with the home government. That was the very reason why they insisted upon rioting; if they could not riot in favour of Jesus, they would riot against Him, but riot they would. In other words, they loved Jesus less than they hated Pilate. They had the Governor in an impasse, and both they and he knew it; in the heat of party passion any lingering gratitude to Jesus went overboard.

xv. 23: 'Myrrhed wine,' a narcotic. Again the touch which helps us to understand.

xv. 41: 'And many other women.' Jesus had many woman friends.

xv. 43: 'Plucked up courage.' This implies secret discipleship previously (cf. John xix. 38).

xv. 44, 45: Pilate is surprised at the early passing of Jesus. This leads the way to the question: 'Why did Jesus die so soon?' and the answer, 'Because He died of a broken heart' (John xix 31 ff.).

In xvi. 5 the women see 'a young man clad in a white robe sitting on the right' in the tomb; in Matthew,[1] 'An angel of the Lord had come down,' and (apparently) moved away the stone while the women were looking on; in Luke,[2] 'Two men stood over them in dazzling garments.'

xvi. 7: 'And Peter.' Perhaps a delightful touch of reminiscent humility on Peter's part; he leaves himself out of the number of the Lord's disciples, but Jesus puts him in.

xvi. 9: 'For they were afraid.' These words are almost certainly the last words written by Mark in the Gospel as it has come down to us. The oldest and best MSS. have a blank page or pages after them, while others have an alternative conclusion. Mr. F. C. Conybeare has discovered an ancient Armenian MS. in the convent at Edschmiazin, in what was Russian Armenia, which

[1] Matt. xxviii. 2.   [2] Luke xxiv. 4.

shows the last twelve verses of this Gospel actually spaced off from the rest, and in the intervening space a line written in red, containing the words ' Ariston Eridzou '—that is, ' of Ariston the presbyter.' The only question left is whether the ' Aristion ' mentioned by Papias as a ' disciple of the Lord,' and one of his chief authorities for what he calls ' the living tradition,' is meant or not. At all events, there can be little doubt concerning the antiquity of the ending as we have it ; Paul's experience, as described in the Acts,[1] reminds us of verse 18, ' They shall take up serpents,' and it is interesting to notice that ' Aristion ' is credited with the story taken by Eusebius from Papias to the effect that Joseph Barsabas once took poison without any ill results (compare verse 18, ' And even if they drink any deadly thing,' &c.). How did the original gap come to be ? Two theories hold the field. Either Mark never finished his Gospel, being interrupted by death or persecution, or the last page of one defective copy, from which all the others without the appended verses were transcripts, had simply been worn away by constant use before it came into the copyist's hands. The latter suggestion becomes more plausible when we observe that Codex Bezae has the Gospels in the following order : Matthew, John, Luke, Mark, the apostles coming first. If the same order was observed in the parent MSS., the last page— perhaps originally containing an account of a Galilean appearance of the risen Lord—may have been lost through pure accident. Irenaeus (second century) quotes verse 9, whereas Codex Bobbiensis has the shorter alternative ending. The loss took place in the interval between the publication of the Gospel in its final form and the end of the first century. It should be observed that the recognition of an ' interpolation ' in our earliest Gospel rather strengthens the evidence for the Resurrection, for it provides us with another early witness, who has taken the trouble to fill up a gap in a Gospel of acknowledged authority with a summary of the testimonies available in his time (see Dr. Rendel Harris's *Sidelights on New Testament Research*, p. 91 ff.). It is quite likely that Matt. xxvii. 11 ff. gives us the substance of Mark's original ending, if there was one.

----

[1] Acts xxviii. 3 ff.

III

MARK'S PICTURE OF JESUS AND HIS FRIENDS

THE most valuable feature of the Second Gospel is to be found in the suggestions it provides for a picture of the Lord Himself. No description of His personal appearance is anywhere attempted in the New Testament ; but Rev. i. 12 ff. does give us an idea of the terms in which those who had been closest to Him in the days of His flesh had come in later years to think of Him. I cannot believe that all the details of the picture are merely conventional symbols of the divine majesty. The Lord as He appears there has eyes like a ' flame of fire ' and a voice deep and many-toned as the sea. Mark tells us of the strange inward glance of Jesus, and the other Gospels echo his suggestion. An unusual word, meaning to ' look into,' or, as we should say, ' searchingly at,' is used of Jesus in Mark x. 21, 27 ; Luke xx. 17 ; John i. 42 ; Luke xxii. 61. In the last two cases the whole history of our Lord's relations with Peter is contained by implication. In Mark x. 21 we have His searching glance at the ' rich young ruler ' ; in verse 27 His survey of the disciples' faces as He sought for a response to His own mood of pity and regret. The young man had come so eagerly, and gone away so disconsolately ; were they as happy as they ought to be because they were poor ? That this kind of look was native to Jesus is proved by the fact that, whereas Mark uses the same word also of the maid-servant who looked Peter up and down in the denial scene, Luke carefully substitutes for it a word meaning ' fastening her eyes upon him '—also used more than once, of Paul's intense gaze, in the Acts. Luke and John keep the word sacred to Jesus, while Matthew only has it once, in the mouth of the Lord,[1] ' examine the

[1] Matt, vi. 26.

39

wild birds.' Closely connected as it is with this 'kind
but searching glance,' we may take the Lord's habit
of looking round, passing from face to face in a
company. In Mark iii. 5 this is a look of anger;
He is searching vainly for a sign of relenting in the faces
of His enemies. In verse 34 we are shown the lingering
tenderness of Jesus. In the group round Him—not all
of one sex—there were those who could be His brothers,
His sisters, His mother. With keen delight in their
differences, He, so to say, sorts them out, glorying in His
own discoveries of the variety of human love. xi. 11 is
different, but equally suggestive. On the evening following
His triumphal entry Jesus reconnoitres the position with
a view to action on the morrow. In v. 32 He keeps looking
round ' to see her that had done this thing.' He knew
that it was a woman, and an invalid woman, by the kind
of nervous clutch at His robe, so unlike the random jostling
of the crowd. In x. 23 the same word is used of Jesus
and the twelve.

As to His voice, we have still less information. We
infer from a quotation of Isaiah in the First Gospel [1] that
it was normally low in tone; but evidently it was sometimes raised in sharp rebuke, for ' out of His mouth proceeded a sharp two-edged sword.' In Mark i. 43, Matt. ix.
30, as also in John i. 33, 38, a word is used which is translated in the A.V. of Mark and Matthew ' straitly charged,'
in John ' groaned '; literally it seems to mean ' roared,'
' growled,' or ' thundered.' In Mark xiv. 5 the same word
is applied to Mary's critics, who grumbled at her action
in harsh undertones. But here again Matthew, Luke, and
John conspire to keep the word sacred to Jesus. It is
curiously significant of the painstaking reverence with
which the writers of our Gospels treated their Subject
that, when once even so strange a word had been used of
Jesus, it should be set aside for Him. Perhaps its use in
the Septuagint version of Lam. ii. 6, of the blast of the
wrath of God, may have suggested its application to the
equally terrible indignation of Jesus. In Mark i. 43,
Matt. ix. 30, the men addressed proceed at once to disobey
Him; Jesus must have foreseen their behaviour. John xi.
33, 38, is somewhat different; at the sight of Mary's

[1] Matt. xii. 18 ff.

weeping Jesus ' groaned in spirit, and disturbed Himself.'
' In spirit ' must refer to the Lord's restraint upon His
feelings, while ' disturbed Himself ' might perhaps be
represented by our ' trembled all over.' It has been
urged that this strong emotion was caused by the
presence of death, whose seizure of his friend brought
home to Jesus the awful reality, and was another omen
of Calvary. But the twice-repeated use of a word which
everywhere else in the New Testament denotes anger
should warn us not to leave anger out of account in our
interpretation of the situation. The wrath of Jesus is
caused by the contrast between Mary's grief and the sham
tears of those Jews who had come ostensibly to condole
with the family ; actually to watch over the Lord Himself.
Grief and anger are struggling for the mastery in the soul
of Jesus, for the real omen of Calvary lay in the hatred
of His enemies. The poignancy of the scene is almost
too much for Him ; as the ' Lewis ' Syriac has it, ' The tears
of Jesus were coming.'

Mark makes it plain also that there were certain people
for whom the Lord felt an instinctive affection, while
there were others who as obviously repelled Him. He
loved at first sight the young member of the Sanhedrin[1]
who was in such a hurry for eternal life that he forgot the
dignity of his official robe, ' came running,' and kneeled
in the dust before Him.[2] On the other hand, something
in the tone or bearing of the leper in Mark i. 40–45 rouses
His anger. Codex Bezae at verse 41 reads ' being angry ' ;
other MSS., as our A.V. and R.V., ' being moved with
compassion.' Both readings cannot be right ; but Jesus
may have been angry with the man and sorry for him at
the same time. We should compare the case of Naaman,
whom, great personage as he is, Elisha will not see, but
sends his servant to bid him wash in Jordan (2 Kings v.).
Here Jesus dislikes a man, and yet goes out of His way to
touch him. Clearly one of the things that He did not like
about the leper was his use of the word ' if '—' Lord, *if*
Thou wilt,' he said, ' Thou canst make me clean.' For
at Mark ix. 23 Jesus protests on this point again. The
father of the epileptic boy said, ' But, *if* Thou canst do
anything.' The Lord answers, ' Oh that *f* Thou canst !

[1] So Luke xviii. 18.   [2] Mark   17.

All things can be to him that believes.' In one case the Lord's will, in the other His power, is questioned : in both Jesus interrupts the speaker. Impatience rather than anger is suggested by the twice-repeated inward sigh.[1] In the first case we might think that Jesus was a little wearied by the endless procession of sufferers, if it were not that a more satisfactory explanation is ready to our hand. It is clear, as we shall see more fully by-and-by, that Jesus was always anxious to get into conversation with the men and women who came to be cured. When those who came could not talk or listen to Him until they were cured, the effort needed to effect the healing would seem to have been greater ; we shall examine this possibility later on. In the second case the sigh is a deeper one—' He sighed in spirit ' ; the reiterated demand for a ' sign ' evinced a tragic failure to come anywhere near understanding Him, following as it did immediately upon the miraculous feeding of the crowd.[2] The same kind of impatience breaks out in Mark ix. 19, ' O faithless generation, how long shall I be with you ? '

More important than these occasional revealing touches is our evangelist's contribution to our knowledge of our Lord's manner of dealing with individuals who came into contact with Him. (He shows us that Jesus dealt with almost all His patients in a different way, adapting His methods in each case to His own rapid estimate of the condition of the person concerned) In nearly all cases of sane people He gives them something hard to do for themselves, and will not let them slip away, if He can help it, without the crowning blessing of salvation. This cannot come merely by power exerted from outside, apart from the effort of the soul itself. A nervous woman, who has got what she came for, is hurrying away, when she is summoned back by the mastery in the eyes and voice of Jesus, and is constrained to tell Him ' all the truth ' before the crowd. She would never forget her first and perhaps her last public speech as long as she lived. Her own power to get the words out, and, still more, the fact that the great Teacher thought it worth His while to stop and listen to her story, restored in a moment her self-respect. In verse 36 we see Jesus keeping in touch with two people at the same time ; in dealing with one, He does not forget

[1] Mark vii. 34 ; viii. 12.   [2] Cf. John vi. 30.

the other.   A blind man has to consign himself to the care of a stranger, is led right away from the familiar village, from any part of which he could find his own way without help, is cured gradually, and by the use of saliva.[1]   It may not be too fanciful to suggest that the methods used in this case were somewhat roundabout, because the man was blind, and his eyes gave his Healer no help.   Human saliva was supposed to have medicinal virtues.   Doubtless the man thought so, and would be instantly reassured when he felt that something he could understand was being done.   The same method is used, we may observe, in the case of the deaf and dumb man.[2]   But the story of the blind man's cure is specially interesting in more respects than one.   Here again Jesus takes pains to get the man (cf. v. 33) to talk about himself.   After the first touch He asks him, 'Do you see anything?'   And he answers, 'looking *up*,' ' I think I see men, walking about like trees ' (I follow the vivid reading of Codex Bezae, which drops out ' because ' and ' I see ').   Jesus is reading the man's soul through his attempt at self-expression, training his faculties and probing them at the same time.   The result is a delightfully natural impressionistic picture : men like trees, their arms and legs like branches.   But viii. 25 is still more suggestive : ' Then again He laid His hands upon his eyes, and he saw *through* ' (not ' *up*,' for now he was recalled to the Master Himself away from his tour through a new-discovered world), and was restored, and with a ' searching glance ' (our old friend again), ' was seeing into all things ' (or perhaps ' every one ') ' clearly.'   The touch of Jesus on the one hand, the effort to see Him on the other, brought the perfect vision ; we are reminded of the beautiful reading of Tatian in x. 51—which ought to be true, if it is not—' Rabboni, that I may see *Thee*.'   It is clear that it was not simply the touch of Jesus, but the intercourse of the souls of men with His, that wrought the perfect cure.   Before we leave the twin-stories in Mark vii. 32 ff., viii. 22 ff., we ought to notice another link between them.   In each case Jesus leads His patient away from the crowd ; ' Jesus,' as Mr. Bradfield once said in my hearing, ' is like a Lover, who takes you for a walk in the dark, and you are not sure at first where He will

[1] Mark viii. 22 ff.   [2] Mark vii. 33 f.

· take you, and whether you can altogether trust this most unceremonious Wooer.'

With the Gerasene demoniac the Master's methods are more startling still, but it is manifest that He is here condescending to a man of very low estate. This case differs from all other cures of the same class reported in the Gospel, in that here the Healer talks to the man himself. The answer given to the question as to his name gives the Lord His cue. The madman had watched the Roman legions thunder past his lair, and that was what, to his wild mind, his own life had become—an endless succession of tormentors trampling him down. In the expressive Syriac phrase, ' They rode upon him,' and he carried them about with him everywhere, for he was they, and they were he. The man's name for himself was quite enough to show that he was not beyond the consciousness of his own condition. To many Eastern peoples, as to the Jews, the pig was a sacred animal—that is, it was the home of a spirit, and not to be touched. If the man associated the ' legion ' of his oppressors with the herd of swine which had become a feature of his landscape, we begin to understand why the demons were sent into the swine. According to Mark [1] the demons, speaking through the mouth of their victim, asked not to be sent ' out of the country. The ' country ' was Decapolis, a district held by ten Greek cities, of which Gerasa was one. We must remember that we are rummaging in a madman's mind now, and also that we are concerned with a case of what would now be called ' multiple personality.' Perhaps the man was a Jew, taken over the border and ' dumped ' upon Greek territory —a trick which is not unknown in the East during an epidemic of plague or cholera : if any one dies in your house, get rid of the inconvenience by simply leaving him at a neighbour's when the tenant is not at home. The poor outcast shrinks from going home again—' out of the country ' would mean into Galilee, or more probably Perea —for fear that the demons were not really gone ; only quiet for once because Jesus was there. What would he do with these unclean heathen demons of his if they broke out again among the respectable folks at home ? Better stay where he is, now he has gone so far ! There is strong

[1] Mark v. 10.

evidence to show that Jesus did believe in the reality of demon possession, and we who are appointed to live in an age which often seems to be demon-ridden are not so ready as were the men of the last generation to scout the idea as mere superstition.   Whether the Lord Himself held that these particular spirits had anything to do with the pig we do not know ; nor does it greatly matter.   We are not able, on the one hand, to say outright that none of what we still call ' animal ' sins have any connexion whatsoever with certain animals.   Shakespeare, when he wrote *King Lear*, seems to have been haunted by the idea that they had something to do with the ' brute ' creation.   Nor can we be certain, on the other, that Jesus shared the beliefs of His own age upon this subject.   We do know that His concern was not to teach the man sound theories of the origin of disease, but to prove to him that his tyrants were gone for ever   Another notion common to all who believed in the real existence of demons was to the effect that the demons were more afraid of water than they were of anything else ; that is why the ' unclean spirit ' of Matt. xii. 43 ff. ' goes through waterless places,' because he dare not venture near the water.   If visible proof will help the man's haunted mind to believe that the incubus is done with, visible proof on a large scale he shall have.   There were the pigs—two thousand of them, Mark says—and here was the lake ; what better way was there than to send the demons into the pigs, and the pigs into the water ?   How much better than two thousand pigs is a man ?   Surely he had been tortured enough, and whatever is likely to help him at the moment, precisely that Jesus will do. ' Never mind about your pigs,' we can imagine Him saying to the indignant owners of those profitable beasts, and to us who find the pigs a difficulty and the whole story a mystery, ' look at the man ! '   In this case the end does certainly justify the means ; Jesus simply uses the best means available without stopping to be reasonable.   It may be objected to the suggestion just made—to the effect that this demoniac was a Jew—that Jesus tells him to go home[1] and tell his friends, whereas in verse 20 we read that ' he began to publish in Decapolis,' &c. ; so that it looks as if either he did not go home at once, or his home

[1] Mark v. 19.

was in Decapolis, not in Galilee.   But the nearest Jewish
territory to Gerasa would not be Galilee, but Perea.   If
the man were a Perean Jew, he would pass through part of
Decapolis on the way home, and would, of course, talk
about his cure.

Our Lord's relish for ' character ' is brought out by Mark
with perfect naturalness : Jesus loves to come across a case
in which a quick-witted brain is at the disposal of a loving
heart.   In ii. 5, indeed, it would seem, on a casual reading,
that a man's sins are forgiven for the sake of the faith of
the four friends who brought him through the roof.   All
three Synoptic evangelists agree here, so that we must take
this statement, ' And seeing their faith, He said to the
paralysed man,' very seriously.   But the subject can best
be handled when we come to discuss the nature of ' faith '
in this Gospel (pp. 103 ff.).   It need only be noticed here that
the man could not speak for himself ; he was young—in
Mark [1] he is addressed as ' child ' ; in Matthew[2] still more
tenderly, ' Take courage, child '—his seizure the result of
sin ; hence in this instance soul-cure comes first.   We may
take it that the utterly dejected look in the young man's
eyes told Jesus something of his story ; the painstaking
ingenuity, the desperate perseverance of his friends told
Him more.   ' Seeing their faith,' He makes a rapid estimate
of the lovableness and the misery of the friend they had
gone so far out of their way to bring to Him ; then, turning
to the sufferer at His feet, He reads in his eyes the secret of
their love, and says, ' Thy sins are forgiven.'

So when a Gentile woman will not be discouraged by an
apparent rudeness, but retains coolness enough to make
a witty retort, He says, ' On account of this word go thy
way.'[3]   The rudeness, by the way, was not so great as it
sounds to us, for Jesus says, ' It is not meet to take the
children's bread and cast it to the puppies.'   ' Puppy '
was a pet name for a child in those days outside the
borders of Palestine.   Horace, Martial, and Juvenal
all use ' puppy ' in somewhat the same way as we
use the word ' kitten ' or ' kiddie ' of children ; and
Jerome writes to Paulla, addressing her as ' My puppy.'
The ' puppy-dogs ' are members of the household as well
as the children, though not perhaps quite on the same

[1] Mark ii. 5.   [2] Matt. ix. 2.   [3] Mark vii. 29.

footing. She was a Gentile woman, and understood at once, answering like a flash, ' Yes, sir ; but the puppy-dogs under the table eat of the children's crumbs.' Where children eat there are often more crumbs on the floor than on the table ! She might have been offended at the Lord's seeming flippancy, but we can dismiss from our minds any thought of rudeness. If she had been a Jewess it would have been different. The remarkable thing about this woman was that the more desperately in earnest she was, the more command she had over her native wit, her readiness of mind and speech ; and Jesus, as always, will throw her upon her own resources and bring her out. In much the same way He exults in the ' faith ' of the chival-rous and soldierly centurion[1] ; this story, strange to say, does not occur in Mark.

Jesus was the conscious and recognized Master of the soul ; when once the reserve of shyness or pride was broken He could do with men and women what He would. The atmosphere in the background of Mark's picture of his Lord is one of ' sovereign sway and masterdom,' so easy and assured as to inspire fear as well as wonder. Nine times in this Gospel the crowds listening to or watching Him are said to have been lost in wonder ; in fact, Mark has no fewer than three strong words all denoting violent astonish-ment, and in none of them is the idea of fear wholly absent. Five, or perhaps six, times he describes the disciples them-selves as afraid of their Master. In regard to the last and most doubtful of these—for the original Mark, as we have seen, breaks off just when he is about to tell us of what the women-followers of Jesus were afraid—Jacoby says, ' Though the end is accidental, it admirably reflects the feeling with which Mark stands before Jesus ; Jesus is to him the sacred mystery of humanity.' The other occasions upon which the followers of Jesus are said to have been afraid of Him are as follows : when He stills the storm,[2] when He comes to them ' walking upon the sea,'[3] on the mountain of Transfiguration,[4] on His first explicit prophecy of the Passion,[5] and—the clearest case of all—when He turns to go to Jerusalem for the last time.[6] Two observa-tions are worth making in regard to these references. In

[1] Matt. viii. 10 ; Luke vii. 9.   [2] Mark iv. 41.   [3] Mark vi. 50.
[4] Mark ix. 6.   [5] Mark ix. 32.   [6] Mark x. 32.

the first place, the tendency to be afraid of Jesus seems to have grown upon the disciples as they got to know Him better ; in the second, the wonder of the people was not simply dependent upon sensational works of power ; it was not *mere* excitement. 'They were stricken dumb by His teaching'[1] before He healed the demoniac in the synagogue at Capernaum, and the same expression is applied to the people at Nazareth, where 'He could do no mighty work.'[2]

Jesus must have been a great popular preacher. In the language of later Judaism 'He has authority'[3] would mean 'He is plainly commissioned by God.' His words were commands ; they had hands and feet to carry a man away with. So[4] a Roman soldier talked to Him as if this very unmilitary Jew were his commanding officer ! He could make a Galilean crowd, thirsting for miracles, listen to a sermon they could not understand.[5] In Mark 1. His miracles cause so much excitement that He has to slip away to get a chance of preaching.[6] ' I came out ' means naturally ' I came out of Capernaum,' though Luke[7] has ' I was sent '—from heaven. But after a time He emerges easily master of the situation, though those turbulent politicians, the Galileans, must have felt that they were being offered sermons instead of leadership. Personal magnetism was a determining factor in His power as a preacher. The people were used, like many modern audiences, to sermons full of quotations ; His ' I say unto you ' was novel and startling. As men listened to Him they felt instinctively that He had a right to speak as He did ; His attitude was always ' This is true, and you know it,' and you did know it ; for the time at least you were quite convinced.

But to those early hearers His sway over the demons was the most amazing feature of His ministry ; Mark emphasizes this fact at every turn. What we should call mind-cure was practised by the Pharisees and taught by them to their pupils.[8] They probably dealt with easy cases by hypnotic methods. But their results were secret and dubious ; His were visible, and could be tested by everybody. And He was amazingly cool about it ; He talked

---

[1] Mark i. 22.　[3] Mark i. 27.　[5] Mark iv. 1 ff.　[7] Luke iv. 43.
[2] Mark vi. 2–5.　[4] Matt. viii. 8.　[6] Mark i. 38.　[8] Matt. xii. 27.

to them colloquially—compare what was said above about the winds and waves. We must remember the enervating climate of the lakeside, six hundred and eighty feet below sea-level ; the lack of sanitation and of hospitals ; and the fact that the insane roamed about the streets at will, only dangerous cases, like the Gerasene demoniac, being removed to lonely places, chained up and left to perish. The terror caused by sights and sounds met with daily in the Galilean lanes and streets must have led by suggestion to the spread of mental disease, and no one knew who would be the next victim. ' A new teaching ! With authority ! Even the unclean demons out and away at a word ! '[1] We can hear the very cries of the crowd. Jesus Himself seems to have thought but little of His exploits in this direction ; indeed, the fact of His cavalier treatment of the demons—as of the winds and waves—may suggest that to Him they, like the storm, were merely natural effects of natural causes (cf. i. 25 and iv. 39). This consideration perhaps gives us the clue to a difficult passage,[2] in the course of which Jesus replies to the charge that He cast out the demons ' by Beelzebub, the prince of the demons '—in other words, by the practice of unhallowed magic—the idea being, apparently, that the prince of darkness had a secret arrangement with this arch-enemy of his, by which Jesus was given a certain amount of power over some of the demons in return for mysterious services in other directions ; in other words, that this battle had been settled, as football matches are sometimes alleged to be ' squared ' beforehand, that Jesus had actually fallen down and worshipped the devil for a little brief authority.[3] Jesus answers by exposing first the absurdity of such a theory, then the criminal motives of those who framed it. If Satan were really compelled to make such terms with his foe, he must indeed be at his last gasp[4] ; such an accusation by itself proves that he has more impregnable fortresses at his command than the minds of poor mad people. If he had been ejected from any of his strongholds, it can only be by *force majeure* of One stronger than he.[5] Moreover, this accusation was not only absurd, it was insincere. If it had been a mistake, it might have been pardonable ;

[1] Mark i. 27.   [2] Mark iii. 23–27.   [3] Luke iv. 6.
[4] Mark iii. 26.   [5] Mark iii. 27.

D

as it was, it was a deliberate attempt to harness the superstitions of ignorant people in the service of a campaign
known to be infamous by the men who launched it.

A certain plausibility was lent, it would seem, to this
insinuation by the fact that the demons almost invariably
recognized Jesus as the Messiah ; this is made very evident
by Mark.[1] Upon this dark subject I can offer only two
suggestions. I suppose that lunatics have an uncanny
intuition into character ; this may possibly have a bearing
upon the strange phenomena repeatedly noticed in the
Gospels. We should also bear in mind that the prevailing
feature of life on the lakeside in those days was intense
nationalist enthusiasm (Galilee was a hotbed of political
unrest), and that in times of great popular excitement
unbalanced people tend to lose their reason altogether, and
in their mania to reflect in an exaggerated form the passions
of the times. We remember the demoniac obsessed by
the Roman legion. Probably the madmen who hailed
the Lord as Messiah felt the power of His personality
at once, and the subject uppermost in their crazed
minds was at once associated with this new influence.
The Lord seems to have regarded the testimony of these
fanatics as a kind of storm-signal, and, wherever possible,
to have suppressed it. This consideration, however, leads
us to the discussion of a larger question, which cannot be
treated incidentally.

For not only from the demons does Jesus refuse to allow
any public recognition of His Messiahship ; if He can help
it, He will not have the question openly discussed by
anybody. References to this studied reserve in Galilee
occur with very marked frequency in Mark's Gospel up
to ix. 30, when—with the journey to Jerusalem—they
cease altogether. They are as follows : i. 25, 34, 43 f., 45 ;
iii. 12 ; iv. 12, 34 ; v. 43 ; vi. 31, 45 ; vii. 36 ; viii. 10, 30 ;
ix. 9, 30. Apart from these more or less explicit intimations, we have such passages as ix. 25, where Jesus breaks
off His conversation with the father of the epileptic boy,
and disposes of the case rapidly, because the crowd was
running up again. Perhaps iv. 11 ff. is, of all the passages
referred to above, the most puzzling to Gospel readers.
Luke cuts the quotation from Isaiah[2] short in the most

---

[1] Mark i. 24, 34 ; iii. 11 ; v. 7.   [2] Isa. vi. 9, 10.

abrupt way, as if he were too honest to leave it out altogether, but could not conceal his uneasiness about it.[1]
Curiously enough, he makes, as it were, the *amende honor-
able* to the quotation at the end of the Acts,[2] giving it at
full length in Paul's address to the Jews at Rome. Matthew[3] gives us the passage from Isaiah in an extended form,
which is, in itself, something of an explanation. Roughly
speaking, the difficulty here is that Jesus seems to say that
the parables are meant to fence off the 'mystery of the
Kingdom' from all but His intimates. It is often said,
in alleviation of this hard saying, that the Greek conjunction
translated 'that' was in our Lord's day losing its meaning
as denoting deliberate purpose, and weakening down to
the idea of mere result ; so that we ought to render it here
rather 'so that' than 'in order that.' But this does not
carry us far, for foreseen consequence does not differ greatly
from purpose ; and it may be asked, 'If the parables were
not meant to reveal truth, why were they uttered ? ' May
not the motive of our Lord have been at once to set eternal
truths in unforgettable form, and at the same time to
discourage the curiosity of mere sensation-hunters—in a
word, to sift His congregations ? For the parables of
Jesus are by no means easy ; in some of the most human
and picturesque of His stories there is a kind of twist, an
unexpected turn of thought which really contains the point
in itself, but needs patient consideration. The 'parables
from Nature' are more difficult than His stories of human
life and character, for the former contain a history of the
Church and the Kingdom in small compass, while the latter
concern certain aspects of particular social, individual, and
national problems. In the Parable of the Sower, Jesus draws
a distinction to start with between hearers and listeners.
The quotation from Isaiah sets the Speaker at once in line
with the great prophets of Israel ; like Isaiah, He does not
begin on the 'wooing' note, but with an imperious claim
to be heard with serious attention, and an unfaltering survey
of the prospects of His message-rejection by the great
majority, but the ultimate triumph of the 'holy seed'
(compare Mark iv. 26 ff. with Isa. vi. 13).

When we further inquire as to the strategy underlying
this policy of reserve, various tentative suggestions can be

---

[1] Luke viii. 10.   [2] Acts xxviii. 26 ff.   [3] Matt. xiii. 14 f.

made. One of our Lord's temptations[1] shows us that the desirability of a great popular and sensational appeal had occurred to Him, but that the idea had been instantly rejected. Perhaps He was naturally sceptical of the value of such methods, but the references quoted above surely mean much more than this. In the first three Gospels Jesus never speaks of His miracles as 'signs' or as wonders' at all ; in the last His most marked reference is somewhat disparaging.[2] It is not true that He never spoke of their value as evidence of His mission,[3] but it is clear that He 'staked everything upon His moral claim.' As Dr. Gwatkin has said, ' The lazy search for infallibility runs through the religious history of mankind' ; Jesus never tries to dragoon men into a reluctant acquiescence by a display of His power. He combines with the distrust of popular enthusiasm noted above a consistent respect for the rights of the individual conscience, running like a thread of silver through all the miracles reported by Mark ; for the one thing that concerned Him was that the men and women with whom He dealt should get at the heart of the matter. This principle is enshrined for all time in one of the great sayings found only in this Gospel : ' The Sabbath was made for man, not man for the Sabbath '[4] (compare the Jewish saying, ' The Sabbath is holy unto you ; to you is the Sabbath given over, and ye are not given over to the Sabbath ' ; Jesus sides with a school of thought which dates from the Maccabean age[5] in Sabbatarian controversy.) The same kind of feeling is shown in the insertion found in Codex Bezae after Luke vi. 5 : ' On the same day, catching sight of a man working on the Sabbath, He said, Man, if thou knowest what thou art doing '—that is, if he could give a morally adequate reason for his conduct—' blessed art thou ; but if thou knowest not, thou art accursed and a transgressor of the law.' To these considerations there should be added the entire freedom from self-consciousness characteristic of Jesus in Galilee, as portrayed in Mark. He knows that He is giving, as Weiss puts it, ' expression to the last and highest demand of God ' ; but apart from this He has for the time being no further concern with His own personality, and is willing to make allowance for misunder-

[1] Matt. iv. 5 ff.   [2] John iv. 48.   [3] Matt. xi. 20 ff., &c.
[4] Mark ii. 27.   [5] Cf. 1 Mac. ii. 40.

Mark's Picture of Jesus and His Friends 53

standings which are purely personal.[1] This is brought out
more clearly by Luke.[2] The discussion of the name ' Son
of Man ' must be left to a later chapter (Part iii., chap. iv.) ;
but it is plain that it was chosen, as against ' Son of God,'
because it alone combined the ideas of highest exaltation
and utmost humility. It is noteworthy that Mark[3] has
' for My sake, and for the gospel's sake,' while Matthew[4]
has ' for My name's sake.' Other examples of this significant difference are to be given below, but this one is sufficient to show that, whereas in Matthew Jesus ' fills the
picture ' to such an extent that neither gospel nor Kingdom
are set alongside of Him, in Mark the Messenger and the
message go together. Our first evangelist's attitude to
his Master is very beautiful, but here perhaps Mark is
more faithful to the actual words of Jesus.

Bousset has suggested that our Lord was never quite
easy with the idea of Messiahship, that He could not enjoy
it with His whole heart, because it was inadequate to His
own conceptions of His Person and work. If we say,
' The idea as then understood,' we are justified in accepting
this statement. But it is not true that He never applied
to Himself Messianic titles. Apart from His constant
use of the phrase ' Son of Man '—there can be little doubt
that this was a recognized, though not by any means a
fashionable, name for the Messiah—we cannot help noticing
one strange fact about the references to the deliberate
secrecy of Jesus as enumerated above ; chapters ii. 1–iii. 6
give us a section wholly without them. Moreover, in
chapter ii. Jesus makes a great Messianic claim—' The Son
of Man has power upon the earth to forgive sins '—and
calls Himself the ' Bridegroom,' which can only mean the
Messiah[5] ; nor is there any attempt at suppression following
the healing of the man with the withered hand.[6] Some
scholars think that the conflicts with ' scribes from Jerusalem '—that is, scribes who had been taking their turn in
the service of the Temple, and belonged to priestly families
(cf. Luke i. 8)—described in this section, are out of their
proper place here, and should at least follow iii. 22, where
' scribes who had come down from Jerusalem ' are mentioned. But is it not perfectly natural that the Lord's

[1] Mark iii. 28.　　[2] Luke xii. 10.　　[3] Mark x. 29.
[4] Matt. xix. 29.　　[5] Mark ii. 10, 9.　　[6] Mark iii. 6.

attitude should be different, when He was challenged by educated sceptics, from that which He was compelled to assume by the embarrassing enthusiasm of the credulous crowd ? For after all the secret of the mysterious reserve of Jesus must be sought not in Himself, but in the times. In the next chapter we shall notice that He practised it only when He was actually staying in a certain dangerous area—the strip of densely populated country between the mountains and the western border of the lake ; and we have seen already that when He is met by a challenge from the outside world He is never slow in responding to it. In the Fourth Gospel Jesus is never, or very rarely, on the defensive ; but the Fourth Gospel is mainly concerned with His ministry in Judaea. It seems to me exceedingly significant that, in the Synoptics too, when Jesus leaves Galilee, He leaves His reserve behind, and even when He is in the danger-zone a breath from Jerusalem is sufficient to rouse Him to lay aside any attempt at secrecy. The narrow land where our Lord chose to work was seething with unhealthy excitement, for the nature of the people, like the soil upon which they lived, was volcanic. All the more notorious nationalist leaders of those days came from Galilee, and what Pilate thought of them is clear enough from the fact that he was glad to get rid of some of them by a dastardly massacre in Jerusalem.[1] Josephus estimates the population of Galilee at nearly three millions, and Sir G. A. Smith seems inclined to accept his figure. At any rate, at every crisis in Josephus, as in the Gospel, the crowd comes running up. In the first chapter of Mark the atmosphere is electric.

But we must leave the dramatic development of the story of the ' acceptable year '[2] in Galilee to the next chapter. We ought, however, to notice here the fact that the casting out of the ' unclean spirits ' would, in the popular mind, be associated with the coming campaign against the Romans. It was commonly believed that these ' unclean spirits ' really belonged to the heathen world ; compare the association of the Roman legion with the demons noted above. They had, it was supposed, come into Galilee with the Gentiles, and afflicted the people of God because of their infection by the looseness of pagan manners.

[1] Luke xiii. 1.   [2] Luke iv. 19.

That the demons were at last being cast out would be taken as proof positive that the ' redemption of Israel '[1] was coming, and that Jesus was indeed the long-expected Leader.

I can only refer to one other feature of Mark's Gospel very briefly. There is a tendency in this book to treat the apostles in a somewhat cavalier fashion, and we hear little about them except their failures and shortcomings. A list of passages, with references to Matthew or Luke, or both, in whose record any undue roughness in dealing with these faithful men is smoothed away, so far as a scrupulously honest treatment of their materials would permit, will make this clear.

Mark iv. 13 is made quite harmless in Matt. xiii. 18 ; Luke viii. 11.

Mark iv. 38 : The petulant note in the appeal ' Carest Thou not,' &c., is softened in Matt. viii. 25 to ' Lord, save, we perish ! ' ; while Luke viii. 24 has ' Master, Master, we perish ! '

Mark iv. 40 : ' How is it that ye have not faith ? ' ; Matt. viii. 26, ' O ye of little faith ! ' ; Luke viii. 25, ' Where is your faith ? '

Mark vi. 51, 52 is contradicted in Matt. xiv. 33, which must come from another tradition.

Mark viii. 17–21 is much sharper than Matt. xvi. 8 ff. ; in Mark viii. 21 we have ' Do ye not yet understand ? ' ; in Matt. xvi. 12, ' Then they understood.'

In Mark viii. 27 ff., 33 no praise is awarded to Peter's confession ; on the other hand, he is called ' Satan ' in verse 33, or perhaps simply ' adversary ' ; this would explain Matthew's ' Thou art my hindrance ' (xvi. 23). Matt. xvi. 17 ff. 23 gives us both praise and blame ; Luke ix. 20 ff. neither praise nor blame.

Mark ix. 6 : ' He did not know what reply to make.' Peter here is made to say something, because he did not know what to say. We all do that sometimes, but such talk for the sake of filling up a pause has little value. The disciples are in the same position in Gethsemane ; compare Mark xiv. 40, which both Matthew and Luke omit. The insinuation is dropped by Matt. xvii. 4, 5 ; and is altered by Luke ix. 33 to 'not knowing what he is saying '—a very different thing !

Mark ix. 9 ; Matt. xvii. 9 : Here Matthew agrees with Mark that Jesus enjoined silence about their vision for the time being ;

[1] Luke ii. 38; xxiv. 21.   Acts, i. 6.

Luke ix. 36 suggests that they did not need to be told to be quiet.

Mark ix. 33 : The twelve dispute about their leadership behind the back of Jesus, and are silent when He charges them with their behaviour. Matt. xviii. 1 ff. puts a much better complexion upon the incident, for according to his account the disciples bring a straightforward request for information upon the general question, ' Who is greatest,' &c. Luke ix. 46 mentions the argument, but says nothing as to its origin.

Mark x. 13, 14 : Both Matthew and Luke omit the displeasure of Jesus, while Luke xviii. 15 ff. softens ' rebuked ' into ' were for rebuking.'

Mark x. 32 is quite altered in Matt. xx. 17 ; Luke xviii. 31.

Mark x. 35 : James and John bring their own request ; according to Matt. xx. 20, ' the mother of the sons of Zebedee ' takes the initiative, though Jesus replies to the sons, not the mother. Moreover, ' Teacher, we want You to do whatever we ask ' is tempered into the vaguer ' asking something from Him.' Luke leaves the story on one side altogether.

Luke xxii. 45 : In addition to the omission noticed above as common to Matthew and Luke, Luke xxii. 45 has a kindly excuse for the sleepy disciples : they were ' sleeping after sorrow.'

Dr. B. W. Bacon thinks that Mark was a Pauline pamphleteer, with something of an animus against the original disciples of the Lord. In view of the very strong traditions as to Mark's Petrine connexions, it is more reasonable as well as more charitable to suppose that Peter, who, as we know from his portrait in the Gospels, did nothing by halves, habitually obliterated himself in his preaching, so that his Master might stand out the more, and that the later evangelists are only doing these men bare justice when they hint that Peter and the others were not quite so black as they have painted themselves. But it is clear that this somewhat ruthless treatment of the apostolic circle, in a Gospel which must have emanated from that circle, is a strong evidence for its authentic character, and should be taken along with Schmiedel's ' pillar-texts'— to be discussed in a later chapter (see p. 99)—as sufficient proof that this Gospel at least cannot have been an invention. The founders of an esoteric religious cult —as, according to Mr. J. M. Robertson, the apostles were—

would scarcely have made themselves cut so sorry a figure
in their own book, in a story worked up for the purpose of
propagating the cult, for the permanent success of the cult
would surely have depended upon the glamour with which
the author of the cult-book had surrounded the hero and
his first followers.

IV

THE ORDER AND ARRANGEMENT OF THE GOSPEL

ORDER has not generally been considered a strong point in Mark's Gospel, but it cannot fairly be called disorderly. It will be remembered that Papias quotes ' John the presbyter ' as his authority for the statement that Mark wrote down all that he remembered of Peter's preaching ' accurately, yet not in order.' Possibly he meant to suggest rather incompleteness than disorder, for in the whole Gospel we have a complete account of forty days only in our Lord's ministry, all told. Under these circumstances it is all the more noteworthy that we can trace a development which is at once intelligible and probable.

In chapter i. 1–15 we have a very brief and rapid prologue. The ministry of Jesus begins with the consciousness that He is the Messiah, an inward certainty verified by His Baptism. From the first the distinction between the preaching of John the Baptist and that of Jesus is made clear. Jesus says, ' The time hath been completed ; repent and believe in the good news.'

Chapters i. 16–iii. 6 depict for us a ministry Galilean in interest and limitation, carried on indoors. We cannot tell how long it lasted, for in chapter i. a specimen day in the life of Jesus is described ; there are five miracles and five teachings in this section, and we have at first popular enthusiasm, then Pharisaic opposition, the section closing with a conspiracy perhaps engineered by scribes who had lately come from Jerusalem—they are not mentioned till we come to iii. 22.

In iii. 7–vii. 23 regions as far apart as Idumaea in the far south, Tyre and Sidon in the north, come into the range of our Lord's influence ; the relatives of Jesus become concerned for Him, and wish to put Him under constraint

It is not actually said who suggested that He had gone out of His mind,[1] but we may conjecture that the scribes from Jerusalem condescended to approach the relatives of their new and formidable Rival with a view to His removal. Evidently Jesus had little or no sympathy in His own home or among His own relatives.[2] The other evangelists tend rather to slur this fact over, from a natural desire to shield the mother of Jesus ; but John vii. 5 explicitly tells us that at this stage the brothers of the Lord did not believe in Him.   From Mark vi. 4, Matt. xiii. 57 cuts off ' and among His relatives,' while Luke iv. 24 omits not only this clause, but ' and in His own house ' as well. We cannot blame the mother of Jesus even upon the basis of Mark's account of the matter ; without doubt her motive in the attempt to bring Him back home was that He had not time to take proper meals.[3]   In view of developing opposition, Jesus proceeds now to organize His forces. He chooses twelve out of a more or less loosely attached circle of disciples, and in chapter vi. we have a very brief account of their first missionary tour, i.e. probably typical of many such preaching expeditions (cf. Luke ix. x.). In the course of this section we watch a double change ; Jesus deserts the synagogue for the open air, and at the same time begins to speak in parables.   The change to field-preaching may simply have been due to the size of His congregations, but it seems to suggest a break with official religion.   The coming of the scribes from Jerusalem, with instructions from head quarters—for we may be sure that the Sanhedrin had already the new movement under observation—would almost certainly result in an embargo upon this dangerous preaching on church premises.   The reason for the adoption of the parabolic method of teaching has been discussed already.   At the same time the training of the twelve begins, private explanations being vouchsafed them, and the desire for retirement in their company becoming more pronounced.[4]   Significant incidents in this section are the rejection at Nazareth, and the rousing of a sinister interest in Jesus in the mind of Herod.   It is at this period, too, that Jesus renounces the Pharisaic tradition, and thus makes His final break with popular

[1] Mark iii. 21.   [2] Mark vi. 4.   [3] Mark iii. 20.
[4] Mark iv. 34, &c.

religious ideas ; henceforward hostility between the Lord and the Pharisees strengthens and deepens.

Chapters vii. 24–x. 31 : A period of wandering, each incident occurring at a different place.   Tyre and Sidon, the Decapolis, Bethsaida, the neighbourhood of Caesarea Philippi, and Perea, all figure in this section, some of these places being outside Palestine proper, nearly all outside Galilee.   A glance at the map will show that vii. 31 describes a most extraordinary proceeding.   Jesus is in the vicinity of Tyre, and sets out from thence to the lake, which lies to the south-east.   He goes *north* to Sidon ; then, apparently via Caesarea Philippi and the eastern bank of the Upper Jordan, to the Decapolis, a district which lies at the south-eastern end of the lake—and the whole tour is hurried through in one verse !   After the feeding of the four thousand He goes northward again, before the tidings of this new wonder has had time to get back to Galilee, and at viii. 27 is back at Caesarea Philippi !   It is obvious that the omission of the second miraculous feeding would get rid of an awkward salient in the narrative ; Luke leaves the whole section out.   On the face of it, it would seem unlikely that, after the unhappy sequel to the first feeding, Jesus would go out of His way to meet the crowds again, or risk the repetition of such a scene.   At the same time, if we reject this, we shall find ourselves obliged to cancel a good deal more.   Chapter vii. 31–37 is closely attached to the story of viii. 1 ff., and viii. 20 will have to go.   On the whole we had better leave the passage where it stands in both Mark and Matthew, noting by the way that the diction of the second story is more formal and sacramental in tone, and that vii. 36 implies that Jesus is once more very near the danger-zone.   In the course of this period public preaching ceases altogether, and the prophecies of the Cross become more definite.

Chapter x. 32–the end : From this time forward the story is told in greater detail.   Jesus suddenly throws secrecy to the winds, and openly declares His Messiahship. Here we have the Triumphal Entry, the Cleansing of the Temple, the Parable of the Vineyard—all of which have their share in hastening the final catastrophe.   We have already seen that Jesus became aggressive even in Galilee when critics lately from Jerusalem were present, dropping

back into His habitual reserve when they were gone.   There
is certainly no avoidance of excitement now, and the
Galileans, so often disappointed at home, are wild with joy.
The twelve, too, whose spirits had sunk almost to zero under
the repeated prophecies of His own humiliation and death,
begin to pluck up heart again.   There is a great contrast
between the atmosphere of x. 48, where the followers of
Jesus, who seem to be in what we should call a ' nervy '
condition, try to keep one blind beggar quiet, and that of
xi. 7 ff., where caution is flung to the winds, and all conspire
to make a very joyful noise.   Something, it has been inferred,
must have happened in the interval to change their mood
from grim foreboding to this unrestrained exuberance of
delight.   Was it the raising of Lazarus ?   We must recognize the presence of gaps in the Marcan outline ; but it is,
we must confess, not easy to see how so decisive an event
came to be omitted even in an incomplete Gospel ; stranger
still, Mark is followed by Matthew and Luke in this serious
omission.   Peter was perhaps away at the time, for in John
xi. 16 Thomas takes the lead ; it may be argued that Peter
would not have been quiet if he had been there at all.   One
ingenious critic has hazarded the speculation, in view of an
old reading in Luke x. i.—' seventy-two ' instead of
' seventy '—that Peter and Andrew may have gone with
the ' seventy ' of Luke x. to look after the young men !
However, that reading can easily be accounted for.   Luke
has seventy-two generations of Jesus ; seventy-two was
the traditional number of the nations of the world, as well
as that of their guardian angels.   To Eastern readers the
temptation to make seventy into seventy-two would be
almost irresistible.   In any case, Peter's momentary
absence will not explain an entire silence upon this subject
in his preaching, if silence on his part there was.

But it is worth noticing that a curious reserve in regard
to the family at Bethany is consistently maintained by the
first three evangelists.   Luke mentions the names of
Martha and Mary, but calls their home ' a certain village '[1]
though he names Bethany in another context.[2]   Mark
has the story of an anointing at Bethany,[3] but Mary[4] is
simply called ' a woman,' and the scene of the incident is

[1] Luke x. 38.   [2] Luke xix. 29.   [3] Mark xiv. 3 ff.
[4] John. xii. 3.

' the house of Simon the leper ' ; in both these points he is followed closely by Matthew. Luke omits this story altogether ; this is all the more remarkable because he is everywhere else concerned to emphasize whatever redounds to the honour of a woman. It is true that he has a story of anointing, but it is in Galilee, at the house of ' Simon the Pharisee,' the heroine on this occasion being ' a woman who was a sinner in the city.' Ramsay thinks that Mark and Matthew have confused two separate incidents, one of which took place at the house of Simon the Pharisee,[1] perhaps in Galilee ; the other at the house of Mary and Martha in Bethany.[2] Mark, he argues, had heard fragments of both, though he did not know that there were two ; from one he gathered that the anointing took place at the house of a Simon ; from the other that it happened at Bethany. He knew of a Simon at Bethany who had been a leper, and he jumped to the conclusion that this Simon was the host in question ! John, however, seems to imply that Lazarus was not the host, in spite of the fact that Martha was waiting at table ; for it would hardly be necessary in that case to mention that he was among those present. There is no necessary contradiction here.

The solution of the riddle may possibly be found in John xi. 2 ; for it is significant that the fourth evangelist refers to an anointing b Mary, the sister of Lazarus, before he comes, in the order of his narrative, to the incident at Bethany. All sorts of explanations of this fact may be given, as, for instance, that this is a note anticipating events a little for the sake of clearness. But may not this verse just as well refer back to the story—presumably known to his readers—told in Luke vii. 36 ff. ? If so, the most reasonable explanation of the facts would seem to be that there was some special reason for this reserve on the part of the first three evangelists, and that when the Fourth Gospel came to be written such caution was no longer necessary. The reader is never allowed in the Sypnotic Gospels to locate the family, Luke[3] omitting the name of the village in which they lived, when he does mention the sisters' names ; while Matthew and Mark agree in dropping out all reference to the sisters or their brother. If Mary of Bethany was also the sinful woman of the Galilean town,

[1] Luke vii. 36 ff.   [2] John xii. 1 ff. ; xi. 2.   [3] Luke x. 38.

and can be identified with Mary of Magdala, who first
appears immediately after the story of the Galilean anointing,[1] the puzzling fact that Mary of Bethany disappears
so unaccountably after the second anointing is explained :
the ' other Mary ' of Matt. xxvii. 61, xxviii. 1, is almost
certainly Mary the ' mother of Joses.'[2] It may be that the
evangelists have been more careful of Mary's reputation
than she was of her own, when she re-enacted her first
penitence, and that there has been a deliberate attempt to
keep readers from tracking the family down to the village
where, perhaps, relatives still lived.[3] It is only fair to say
that another explanation is possible, if no great weight is
attached to the argument from John xi. 2 ; Mary of Bethany
may have heard of the golden deed of her fallen sister in
Galilee, and wished to show that she loved the Lord quite
as much as any woman had ever done.   But the idea of a
competition in the display of love seems to rob the story of
some of its beauty.

These considerations scarcely afford a satisfying explanation of so serious an omission as that of the raising
of Lazarus.   All that we can say is that there is something
mysterious about this family, and also that there is an
obvious gap in the Marcan narrative, precisely at the point
at which the fourth evangelist inserts the great miracle
at Bethany.   The real difficulty is that John makes the Raising of Lazarus the immediate occasion of the fatal collision
between Jesus and the Sanhedrin[4]; while in Mark its place is
taken by the Cleansing of the Temple, which John omits here,
though he narrates a similar incident at the opening of
the Lord's ministry.[5] We must recognize the fact that
the Marcan scheme does present us with a number of effects
without an adequate number of causes.   No clear account
is given us of the development of Pharisaic hostility, and
the calling of the apostles is introduced into the record
very suddenly.   Matthew keeps back his first statement

---

[1] Luke viii. 2.   [2] Mark xv. 47.
[3] A weak point in this theory may be found in the fact that there appears
o be no evidence that ' seven demons ' (Luke viii. 2) meant that Mary of
Magdala had been, in the technical sense, ' a sinner.'   It may just as well
stand for hysteria.   The Rev. W. Bradfield suggests that it was because
this Mary had hysterical tendencies (cf. the reading of the ' Lewis ' Syriac in
Luke xxiv. 11, ' As if they had spoken out of their wonder,' i.e. hysteria)
that the risen Lord appeared first to her ;   He was afraid of a relapse !
[4] John xi. 47 ff.   [5] John ii. 13 ff.

of the Pharisees' extreme bitterness to xii. 14, though it is
true that he has previously[1] told us of the accusation of
wizardry. It is more likely that they would try to under-
mine the influence of Jesus and get Him out of the way by
less drastic measures before resorting to murderous conspiracy with those who, under normal conditions, were
their declared enemies. Very important is the fact that
Matthew leaves out ' the Herodians ' at xii. 14, and even
so late as xxii. 15 makes it clear that Pharisees and Sadducees are acting in separate groups. From xxii. 16 it
would appear that the ' Herodians ' formed a kind of middle
party between the two extremes ; the Court party would,
of course, be interested in questions of taxation, and so
might be used on this occasion to embarrass Jesus, if
the ' Herodians ' were a separate party at all. We
may say with some confidence that the Sanhedrin, made up
as it was of Pharisees and Sadducees (cf. Acts xxiii. 7),
only acted as one body in the final scene.

Yet, when all is said, the Marcan order retains its wonderful clearness and dramatic force. In the first chapter the
mission of Jesus begins with a glorious sweep of success ;
the coming of the ' good news ' rushes down upon the sultry
lakeside towns like a strong clean wind, leaving the crowds
rocking in breathless excitement. In chapter ii. forces
momentarily scattered by the first sudden onset have found
time during the withdrawal of Jesus[2] to rally in the instinctive reaction of officialism against anything which threatens
the established order. When the Preacher appears in
Capernaum again, murmurs of criticism are heard ; but
they are soon drowned[3] in the rising tide of popular
expectation. But the Pharisees have now been drawn in,
and every step carries them farther on the road which leads
from antipathy through intrigue to murder. They try to
trade upon the universal repulsion felt for the ' publicans,'
with whom already Jesus had come to be associated, and
seek to involve Him in a heresy hunt.[4] Foiled in this,
their instinctive antagonism takes the deeper hue of
unscrupulous intrigue. ' Scribes from Jerusalem,'[5] with
a commission from head quarters, appear upon the scene,
and a new campaign is launched. The attack takes shape

---

[1] Matt. ix. 34.   [2] Mark i. 39ff.   [3] Mark ii. 12.
[4] Mark ii. 7 &c. ; cf. vv. 16, 18, 24.   [5] Mark iii. 22.

in two directions ; on one hand the family of Jesus is induced to take measures for His removal, and on the other the sinister suggestion is made that Jesus is really a dangerous magician. Both attempts are frustrated, and the Lord is left free to resume His popular appeal. But already one of the factors in the final tragedy has taken its place in the movement of the gospel ; professional jealousy is at work, and does not cease to be active until, uniting with other forces antagonistic to the Hero, it has encompassed its prey.

Meanwhile another tragic element in the situation has been slowly unfolding itself. So early as the first chapter the danger of popular misunderstanding is present already. The crowd can scarcely wait till the Sabbath is over ; ' As soon as the sun was set '—the Sabbath ended at sunset on Saturday evening—the whole town was gathered at the door.'[1] After a busy evening Jesus at last retires, but He has seen enough to convince Him of perilous possibilities at Capernaum. Accordingly He slips away to the hills before the others are stirring.[2] When ' Simon and those with him ' follow Him to His retreat, He tells them to their dismay that He intends to make an extended tour over ' the whole of Galilee '[3]—this according to Mark ; while Luke,[4] though his language is vague, seems to be aware of a ministry covering a still wider area : ' He was preaching in the synagogues of Judaea '—corrected (?) to ' Galilee ' in the later MSS., represented by our A.V., to conform with Mark. Probably, in accordance with Luke's general usage, Judaea here means the whole of Palestine, including Galilee (cf. xxiii. 5) ; but it is conceivable that the third evangelist had heard of an actual mission in Judaea proper at this juncture. If so, we should have a possible bridge between the Synoptic Gospels and that of John. Perhaps the Galilean disciples did not accompany Jesus upon this journey.

' Some days afterwards '—Mark's phrase is indefinite— He is again[5] in Capernaum, and a period follows when He appears to have been less anxious to suppress excitement, perhaps because the scribes lately from Jerusalem had brought with them a new atmosphere of challenge. The

[1] Mark i. 32, 33.   [2] Mark i. 35.   [3] Mark i. 39.
[4] Luke iv. 44.   [5] Mark ii. 1.

E

respect in which these great men were held would naturally distract the minds of our Lord's hearers from their dreams of revolt under the leadership of the new Prophet ; a fresh issue had been raised, and the volatile Galileans watched with intense interest the contest between their latest Hero and the authorities.   Thus the danger of the gospel being submerged in a riot becomes for a time less menacing.   The atmosphere of chapter iv. is quieter ; Jesus is Master of the situation in both directions.   His enemies have been baffled, while the Galileans, with a new respect for their Hero's powers, settle down to listen to what He has to say. But His manifesto, outlined in chapter iv., is disappointing to His audience, and from this time forward His success as a popular preacher begins to wane.   When evening comes Jesus crosses the lake.   His sleeping in the storm tells us something of His condition : physically He is weary, but His heart is still at rest.   After a short stay upon the eastern shore—notice that he makes no attempt to keep the Gerasene demoniac silent about his cure,[1] the reason, of course, being that He is not now in the danger-zone—He is soon back again,[2] but we hear no more of preaching in Capernaum.   A tour in the highlands follows, with a visit to His old home.[3]   From the upland country He begins to ' send out ' His twelve ' two by two,'[4] while He dis-appears from view, either going to Judaea or to His quiet retreat in the hills.   With this crisis the first year of the ministry comes to an end.   The outlook was not hopeful ; neither by the lakeside, nor in His own highland country, nor yet at Jerusalem, was there any room for His message. In face of these foreshadowings of the cross, He sends His twelve away, partly perhaps because He felt the need to be alone to think and pray, partly because they could for the time being do the straightforward propagandist work of the Kingdom more effectively than He.

During this veiled period several things conspired to give a keener edge to the patriotic passions of the Galilean populace.   Mark, significantly enough, fills in the gap with his account of the murder of John the Baptist.[5]   If the massacre of Galilean pilgrims by Pilate[6] took place also at this time, we can understand how it was that the people,

---

[1] Mark v. 19.   [2] Mark v. 21.   [3] Mark vi. 1 ff.
[4] Mark vi. 7 ff.   [5] Mark vi. 14 ff.   [6] Luke xiii 1 ff.

discouraged by the disappointingly spiritual character of
the Lord's first great pronouncement, would begin to dream
of Jesus again.   The disciples themselves have been infected
by the passions of their congregations, and have come back
in a mood of morbid excitement.   If proof were needed,
their report is enough to reveal the state of public feeling.
So again Jesus retires, this time across the lake, and in
company with His disciples.   Matthew and Luke both
seem to imply, though neither of them asserts directly,
that the leading motive for this retreat was the murder of
John, while Mark ascribes it [1] to the need for rest after their
exciting experiences ; they certainly wanted steadying in
more ways than one.   But, John being gone, the desire of
the Galileans that Jesus should take his place and avenge
his death on Herod and the Romans has been fanned into
a flame.   Passover-time has come round, and those who
had gone up to Jerusalem have left instructions that this
tantalizing Prophet should be found and followed at all
costs ; when Jesus arrives at the eastern shore, the poor
leaderless folk are there before Him. [2]   But as all the men
who were fit to go were away, and He is out of the feverish
atmosphere of the lakeside towns, Jesus feels Himself free
to indulge them.   His own thoughts are full of the Cross
which already He had come to see next Passover-time
would bring ; He will entertain them all to the paschal
supper.   But the day ends with another disappointment.
After the wonderful meal the excitement of the crowd can
be restrained no longer.   When once their hunger has been
relieved and they begin to feel better, the hopes with which
they had entered their quest for the lost Leader
reassert themselves.   It is now or never ; the Master gathers
from their ominous whisperings that they are plotting
' to take Him by force and make Him a king.' [3]   Even the
disciples cannot be trusted just now.   Mark draws a veil
over this scene, but seems to hint that the twelve were
involved, for they were ' *constrained* to embark ' again. [4]
Jesus sends them one way home and the crowd another,
while He goes up into the hills to pray.   Mark vi. 46, be
it observed, implies a definite abandonment of the Lord's
public ministry in Galilee—' He bade them a regretful
good-bye.'   Soon He rejoins His disciples, knowing

[1] Mark vi. 31.   [2] Mark vi. 33.   [3] John vi. 15.   [4] Mark vi. 45.

how much they needed Him, for their terror at the Apparition on the water tells us something of the state of their nerves. Work is resumed for a short time at the north-west corner of the lakeside, but is apparently confined to healing. In the interval the disciples recover their confidence, disturbed as it had been by their Leader's refusal to take His proper place as King. So the second element in the tragic movement has revealed itself ; we may call it political prejudice.

In the seventh chapter the two factors, already separately developed, are seen to be in combination, and make any public ministry in Galilee impracticable. ' Scribes from Jerusalem ' again appear,[1] emboldened by what they think to be palpable evidence of diminishing confidence on the part of Jesus. Henceforth they follow Him about and challenge Him openly. He replies by a strong attack and an attempt to free the misguided Galileans from their dominance. Specially noteworthy in this connexion is vii. 14, ' Summoning the crowd to Him again ' ; Jesus is trying to break up the unnatural alliance between the unthinking passions of the people and the cynical men who are managing them for their own purposes. When this attempt fails He leaves Galilee, striking north-west, and only returning to the lake by a long détour in Gentile territory.[2] When at last He arrives in the Decapolis there are again scenes of enthusiasm ; but Jesus now extends His policy of reserve to the eastern shore, probably for the reason that the whole of the lake district is by this time aflame with curiosity about His strange doings, a curiosity made all the livelier by His long retreat and sudden reappearance.[3] It is too late for privacy, however, and the crowd gathers again. After the second miraculous feeding Jesus crosses the water once more to Dalmanutha, wherever that was. Matthew [4] has ' the region of Magadan ' according to the best reading, a site which is equally unknown. Dr. Harris has suggested that the expression ' to the region of Dalmanutha ' is simply a copyist's mistake[5] ; for ' dalmanutha ' is very near the Aramaic for ' to the parts of.' The real name has been lost, and ' to the parts of ' has been repeated

---

[1] Mark vii. 1.   [2] Mark vii. 31.   [3] Mark vii. 36, 37.
[4] Matt. xv. 39.   [5] Mark viii. 10

by inadvertence. At any rate, it is clear that Jesus is still studiously avoiding Galilee; John vi. 25 is ambiguous, while John vi. 59 suggests that discourses delivered on two distinct occasions have been combined in this chapter. Notice ' began ' in viii. 11, ' The Pharisees went out and began to dispute with Him ' ; as often in Mark, ' began ' denotes a fresh development. The Pharisees have taken the withdrawal of Jesus at a critical moment as a sign of weakness, and hope to complete His humiliation by pressing a demand which they had reason to think would embarrass Him ; the refusal to comply with it would, they surmised, discredit Him finally in the eyes of a wonder-loving public. For a ' sign from heaven,' technically known as ' the daughter of a voice,' was regarded as the only real guarantee of real prophetic inspiration. It was the voice from heaven which convinced John the Baptist,[1] and reassured the disciples on the mountain of Transfiguration [2]; we remember, too, what a sensation the voice from heaven made in Jerusalem.[3] A clap of thunder at least was expected from any one claiming to be the Messiah. Each outburst of popular appreciation is now followed by a counter-attack, and Jesus ' sighs in spirit,'[4] wearied by the conflict with the mountains of suspicion and prejudice which barred His way to the people's hearts for whom He had come to live and, if need be, die.

Meanwhile Mark has made yet another complication clear. It is in this section that Jesus addresses most of those reproaches to the twelve which have been discussed already. By omitting the praise with which Peter's confession was welcomed, Mark may have allowed his master to paint himself into the picture in colours which do him less than justice ; at any rate, he does succeed in showing us that there was a real peril even in the devotion of the twelve. In Mark viii. 30 the confession is followed simply by a command to ' say nothing about it to any one.' J. Weiss thinks that the Lord read in the speaker's eyes and in the tone of his voice the note of political fanaticism, and so met his declaration by a chill prophecy of failure and death ; ' Seeing His disciples '[5]

[1] Mark i. 11.   [2] Mark ix. 7.   [3] John xii. 28, 29.
[4] Mark viii. 12.   [5] Mark viii. 33.

—they were all of one mind—' he rebuked Peter.' Whether
that is so or not—and, in face of Matt. xvi. 17 ff., it is
difficult to accept the statement unreservedly—there can
be little doubt that, even while He gladly welcomed His
followers' confidence, He did see danger ahead ; the grave
words which in the First Gospel, as in the Second, follow
hard on the heels of warm commendation prove this.
Throughout this period the whole attention of Jesus is
taken up by the persistently renewed effort to accustom
His twelve to the idea of the cross. At the same time
He reassures them first by a promise,[1] then by a visible
foretaste,[2] of the coming glory, followed yet once more
by an injunction to secrecy. The same dread of popular
excitement is manifest in ix. 25 ; this miracle must have
taken place somewhere at the north-east corner of the
lake, for after it Jesus is able to travel about in Galilee
and finally arrive in Capernaum without attracting public
attention. Apparently the crowd has now been effectually
shaken off, and He is able quietly to set out upon His
fateful journey to Jerusalem.[3] But by this time another
current has been encountered in the movement of the
story ; the Hero is to be isolated from His friends, who
are still faithful, but whose bewilderment now deepens
into misunderstanding. Our third section has left the
preparation for the culminating scene nearly complete ;
we began it with the union of calculating hatred and
unthinking prejudice in enmity to Jesus, and we end it
with the wavering of His friends.

In all other tragedies, whether in literature or life, the
hero himself fires the train, because the march of events
brings out some flaw in his own moral fabric. This divine
tragedy is more poignant still, for it is no hidden weakness
in the Hero, but the uttermost exercise of His virtue,
which sets the final process in motion. We are never
allowed to be sorry for Jesus ; He is almost encircled now,
but He can always break through, and is Master of the
situation to the end. At any moment He can call upon
His Father to send ' twelve legions of angels,' or without
them[4] can cast His assailants to the ground by the unveiling
of His Majesty ; but He will not burst through the cords of

---

[1] Mark ix. 1.   [2] Mark ix. 2 ff.   [3] Mark x. 1.

[4] Matt. xxvi. 53 ; John xviii. 6.

death in this summary fashion. At the beginning of the
fourth section Jesus has escaped the net spread for Him in
Galilee, and is on His way to Judaea by the eastern route
across the river. He is well known in Perea already,
perhaps through previous visits or the talk of Galilean
pilgrims ; if, as we conjectured, the demoniac of chapter v.
was a Perean Jew, his testimony would increase public
curiosity. Once outside Galilee Jesus resumes His habit
of public preaching,[1] and the Pharisees become active again.
This time they try to involve Him in trouble with Herod,
whose dominion included Perea as well as Galilee. They
seek for a pronouncement upon the divorce question, with
the case of Herod and Herodias in view. Plain words upon
this subject had led to the murder of John ; surely Jesus
will not be less courageous than he. If the ' Lewis ' Syriac
is right in putting x. 12 in front of x. 11, the defiant attitude
of Jesus becomes yet more unmistakable ; He never feared
that ' fox.'[2] So—following the suggested change—we see
that He makes His meaning absolutely plain by setting
the woman's case first ; Herodias had divorced her husband
to marry Herod. The Pharisees are powerless either to
embarrass Him or to deflect His course. His set face, His
undeviating progress towards Jerusalem, the very seat of
the hated government, soon rouse old dreams of some
great revolutionary stroke, and once again Jesus becomes
a popular Hero. Children are brought to receive the
blessing of the Messiah, and a local member of the Sanhedrin[3]
offers his services, hoping, by the use of his wealth and
influence in the sacred cause, to obtain eternal life. As for
the disciples, they are more bewildered than ever, for they
cannot yet forget His dismal prophecies of failure and
humiliation ; if their Master's studied discouragement of
enthusiasm in Galilee had been surprising, His almost
reckless defiance of consequences now was more amazing
still. In Galilee He was sure of strong support ; but here
He was challenging the authorities in the very seat of their
power, unarmed and almost alone, and this after having
deliberately alienated those who might have helped Him !
Jesus and they, it will be observed, have exchanged rôles.
In Galilee He had discouraged popular excitement ; now
they are nervously anxious to keep the crowd quiet. This

[1] Mark x. 1.   [2] Luke xiii. 32.   [3] Luke xviii. 18.

consideration explains their attempt to keep the children away, as well as their endeavour to suppress the incon-venient clamour of Bartimaeus.[1] They were further bewildered by the drastic terms offered to the young man, whose wealth and influence, they imagined, might have been useful in an emergency ; moreover, the Lord Himself did not seem to take a more cheerful view of the prospects before Him. References to the Resurrection ' after three days '—a proverbial phrase meaning ' very soon '—only confused them more at this stage.

When they arrive at Jerusalem their mood has changed again. A possible reason for this swift reaction from nervous timidity to vociferous enthusiasm has been found already outside Mark's Gospel ; but if we confine our attention to this book considered by itself, we may suggest that the request of James and John[2] proves that at least two of the three who had witnessed the Transfigura-tion had by no means lost all hope of the speedy setting-up of the Kingdom—the others evidently regarding the demand made at that juncture as being ill-timed as well as in bad taste—and also that the company of pilgrims from Galilee, who had followed the progress of Jesus through Perea, were delighted at the Master's change of demeanour, soon infecting His disciples with their own easily kindled revolutionary passions. Then follow the Triumphal Entry, with its demonstration allowed, if not encouraged, by the Hero of the day, and the still more challenging Cleansing of the Temple, by which the pilgrims were enraptured, for was it not a fulfilment of Messianic prophecy ? Apart from Pharisees and Galileans, Jesus has now to reckon with the vested interests of entrenched bureaucracy, and He throws down the gauntlet at once. Cattle reared by these monopolists on their estates in the neighbourhood of the city were sold at exorbitant prices to would-be wor-shippers within the Temple precincts, and only their agents were allowed to do business there. If John[3] is right in his statement that this scandal had been exposed once already by our Lord, the fact that even so violent an action went even now unchallenged becomes at once intelligible. It was a notorious abuse, intensely unpopular with the public, and only continued because no one but Jesus dared

[1] Mark x. 13, 48.   [2] Mark x. 35.   [3] John ii. 14 ff.

forcibly to interrupt it. The Lord's language on this occasion is stronger than before. In John ii. 16 we read, ' Make not My Father's house a shop ' ; now it is, ' Ye have made it a den of thieves.' Little wonder that there was no need of a ' whip of small cords '[1] this time ! When Gentiles, incensed beyond endurance by the exactions of these licensed thieves, who filched away from them their part of the ' house of prayer designed for all nations '[2] only to use it as a cover for further robbery, threatened their persecutors with violence, the Jewish trader would leap, we are told, over the barrier, beyond which his victim could not pass on pain of death,[3] and from that point of vantage defy his pursuer. All self-respecting Jews hated this organized robbery, which made of the Temple a mere brigand's cave, to which these licensed highwaymen could carry their spoils, and from the shelter of which they could securely challenge their pursuers to do their worst. So it came about that there was at first no overt opposition to the Lord's high-handed action ; at the same time it brought into line the most deadly of the enemies of Jesus, and they proceed at once to treachery. The ' cursing of the fig-tree,'[4] which comes in here, gives us, with tragic clearness, the Lord's own view of the situation. Taken in conjunction with the parable of the fig-tree spared yet one year longer[5] (see Part ii., chap. i.), it shows us that Jesus is losing hope for His own people.

For the Cleansing of the Temple was not simply a protest against a gross abuse : it was the last appeal of a Patriot. Jesus is re-enacting the part of Jeremiah in these first days of Holy Week. That Matthew at least was conscious of this is proved by the fact that his account of the trial scene is persistently reminiscent of a somewhat similar crisis in the life of our Lord's greatest forerunner. Jesus and Jeremiah are alike in this—in that both are aware that their own martyrdom will inevitably bring political ruin upon the nation for which they are dying, and, further, in that their attitude to the Temple was the chief count in the indictment argued against both of them. Meanwhile two of the parties who are plotting the death of Jesus are seen to be in association ; scribes and chief

[1] John ii. 15.   [2] Mark xi. 17   [3] Eph. ii. 14.
[4] Mark xi. 13 f.   [5] Luke xiii. 6 ff.

priests approach Him upon His arrival next morning with
a question artfully designed to involve Jesus with the
government.   They make no comment upon His proceedings yesterday ; they only ask for information.   Clearly
He is making a bid for the rôle of Messiah ; will He tell them
plainly if that is so ?   They are quite willing to discuss
His pretensions on their merits.   The people prick up
their ears, eager to catch His answer.   They are sure that
their Leader, who has been so much less disappointing
since He came south, will take this opportunity of making a
public statement.   But He refuses to reply directly, only
countering His assailants with a question which is as
difficult for them to answer as they had hoped theirs would
be for Him.   It is evident from Matt. iii. 7 that ' many of
the Pharisees ' and even ' of the Sadducees ' had in a half-
hearted kind of way tried to patronize John the Baptist's
revival movement ; probably the more highly placed
officials had discreetly kept away, as John could not have
been to their taste.   John was now the idol of the people,
and any refleection upon his memory would instantly have
raised a storm.   Perhaps the Lord's question was a quiet
reminder addressed to some of His interviewers of days
when their minds were still open to good impressions, an
appeal to the better men among both Pharisees and
Sadducees at the eleventh hour to save themselves from
this unnatural alliance with the shameless monopolists
with whom they could have nothing in common except
their hatred of Himself.   At the same time Jesus is appeal-
ing to those who meant to be His friends not to allow themselves to be duped by the sinister intrigues of men who,
they must see, could not be working together for any honest
purpose.   They had been divided on the question of John ;
they would have been divided still, if they had been
honourable or even consistent men.   Lest there should be
any doubt as to His own position, He proceeds forthwith
to define it, and to expose the designs of His worst enemies,
the high-priestly clique, whose maladministration of their
sacred trust He had already so ruthlessly disturbed.   In
this parable His enemies recognize that Jesus has
thrown down the gage of battle ; but for the time being the
Lord is protected from their rage by the crowd, delighted
by His undisguised claim to the title of Messiah (' the

Beloved Son '—that is, ' only Son '—Mark xii. 5, 6), eagerly awaiting and perhaps arming for the next move, which, they thought, must surely be an open challenge to the government. Their final disappointment explains, on the human side, all that follows.

Meanwhile the Pharisees take the next step by themselves ; their public association with the chief priests they now see to have been a blunder, and this time they come alone. They are noticeably polite, but are bent on mischief. One particularly ominous feature of the situation now is that all parties in the Sanhedrin are working together behind the scenes, for the mention of that elusive party, the Herodians,[1] shows that there is an attempt to use Herod, who is up at Jerusalem for the feast, against Jesus. The compliments upon His fearless even-handedness, as displayed in the Cleansing of the Temple yesterday, with which they open the encounter, are meant to disarm the suspicions of the crowd, roused by the appearance of some of their number along with the hated priests earlier in the day. They are really playing a double game. On the one hand, they are anxious to make Pilate and Herod uneasy about the latest developments ; on the other, to suggest to the Galileans that they—the Pharisees—are only seeking to help on the revolution by inducing their strangely backward Leader to make the pronouncement which might be a signal for revolt. They are too clever to believe that even now Jesus intends to lead the revolutionary movement ; but their purpose is either to lead Him on to a position from which there can be no retreat, or to induce Him once and for all to disclaim any intention of nationalist leadership, and so incense the mob against Him. We must remember all through that the turbulent crowd of pilgrims hold the key to the situation, for Pilate and Herod are merely anxious to get this dangerous week over without trouble. If once the crowd can be turned against Jesus, they can trust them to do the rest, for they still hold their trump-card, Bar-rabbas, till now a popular hero, and only for the moment submerged in the tide of enthusiasm for Jesus. The Lord sees ' their hypocrisy ' at a glance, and by His answer refuses to commit Himself either way for their

---

[1] Mark xii. 13.

convenience, at the same time propounding an eternal principle.

The Sadducees, who come next, are more clumsy ; they seem to be trying to score a point at the expense of their new allies, the Pharisees. The question of immortality had, it is true, become at this time almost a political matter, for one of the things which most deeply divided the Romanizing party from the patriots was the passionately held Pharisaic doctrine that martyrs in the cause of Israel had a special place in the Resurrection. The popular conception of the Messiah's kingdom, says Dr. Charles, was that of the first thirty-six chapters of the Book of Enoch, according to which its members, including the risen right-eous, were to enjoy every good thing, and each have a thousand children. They thought to place Jesus upon the horns of a dilemma, and oblige Him to confess either that there was no resurrection, or that polygamy and polyandry would be practised in the Kingdom. The conception embodied in our Lord's answer tallies almost exactly in thought and partly in word with that described in Enoch, chapters xci.-civ.—the resurrection is to be one of spirit, and the risen righteous are to rejoice as the angels of heaven.[1] This incident is valuable for our immediate purpose in two respects : it casts a clear light upon the minds of the men who could ask so crude a question—They were ' much mistaken '[2]—and at the same time goes far to explain the comparative failure of our Lord's attempts to win the common people, who could and did entertain such crudely materialistic ideas.

It is clear from the next few verses—peculiar this time to Mark—that the appeal made just before to the Pharisees had not altogether missed fire. Some of them did respond to His plea for moral sincerity. The next question was no mere trap. Matthew[3] puts a sinister interpretation upon this inquiry as upon the others, while Luke[4] contents himself with the remark that some of the scribes applauded the discomfiture of the Sadducees ; but not all the scribes were blinded by prejudice to the rightness of the Master's teaching so far as its main outlines were concerned. Jesus welcomes the ready appreciation of His own reading of the law shown by this intelligent man with evident relief ;

[1] Matt. xxii. 30.   [2] Mark xii. 27.   [3] Matt. xxii. 34 f.   [4] Luke xx. 39.

he, at least, unlike the Sadducees, was 'not far astray from the kingdom of God.' His enemies are for the moment silenced ; so far from being outwitted, He has forced them to fall back in confusion.

A passage follows, the obscurity of which we must frankly admit. Jesus is teaching in the Temple. Scribes and priests alike have retired, and He is free to address the crowd without interruption. Evidently the purpose of the question reported in Mark xii. 37 is to expose the fallacy inherent in commonly held views of the Messiah's office. It is difficult to believe that Ps. cx. can have been written by David, the opinion prevailing among scholars being that it is the work of a Court poet, composed in honour of Simon the Maccabee, who was the first to be anointed both king and high-priest. It is not necessary to infer that our Lord Himself accepted the popular theory of its authorship, nor need we suppose, as some have done, that He is denying His own descent from David. He is concerned with a much more vital matter. The materialistic conception of the world to come so obstinately clung to by the common people proved at last a fatal barrier between our Lord and the men of the country, where ' most of His mighty works had been done,' with whom He had so much in common ; the nationalist passions which met Him at every turn in Galilee were bound up with this false idea of the nature of the Kingdom, this in its turn with the tradition that the Messiah was to be a descendant from David, and therefore a conqueror like him. If only He could show them how little foundation there was for these crude notions of theirs even in the Old Testament ! The people clearly do not understand, but His teaching still exerts its old charm, and they listen to Him quite willingly as He proceeds to attack those of the scribes who lived in popular favour and public honour on the strength of a display of piety and learning, while they traded upon the superstitions of pious widows and other ignorant people anxious for a share in the life of the world to come, of which they painted such alluring pictures.

Full discussion of chapter xiii. would be out of place here. It contains a discourse on the subject of the ' last things ' delivered in private to the disciples. Many scholars think that this section should be separated from the main body

of the Gospel, as it appears to contain a ' fly-sheet ' at first
published by itself—perhaps in A.D. 68, the date at which,
according to Eusebius, a revelation came to the Christians
of Judaea, warning them to flee from the Holy City before
its fall—but afterwards incorporated in one of the later
editions of Mark's Gospel.   Luke is widely divergent here,
while Matthew follows Mark very closely, though not
exactly.   If Luke saw the first draft, and the compiler
of the First Gospel the second — after the addition
of the ' fly-sheet '—the facts easily explain themselves,
the principal argument for the ' fly-sheet ' theory being
found in the words ' Let him that readeth understand.'[1]
Most critics would not deny that the ' fly-sheet ' contains
some authentic words of Jesus, and from our present point
of view this impression is deepened by the fact that some
prophecy of the future uttered at this juncture helps us to
understand a change of mood in the disciples which becomes
apparent as Passion Week goes on.   At the Triumphal
Entry they are leading the acclamations of the Galileans
with a disregard of consequences which is in the strongest
contrast with their timidity when they are passing through
Jericho.   Apparently they have almost forgotten their
Master's predictions of failure and death, and the old
Galilean spirit of gay rebellion has caught them by contagion from the noisy crowd of pilgrims, eager to pay off old
scores with the government now or never.   Jesus must have
said something in His private talks to discourage their ill-
grounded hopes ; the discourse of chapter xiii. would do
that effectually.   For His public actions so far would
rather tend to increase their confidence than diminish it ;
at last He has decisively assumed Messianic prerogatives.
Later on in the week they are in possession of weapons[2] ;
this suggests previous preparation for revolution.   When
the Lord spoke not of swift upheaval, but of persecution
and long struggle, with the end ' not yet '[3] in sight, His
words must have chilled His followers, and brought
back into their minds the dark prophecies which He
had uttered before, but which they had set aside so
lightly.
     All this brings us face to face with the mysterious figure

[1] Mark xiii. 14 ; Matt. xxiv. 15.   [2] Mark xiv. 47 ; Luke   xxii.38.
[3] Mark xiii 7.

of Judas 'the traitor.' Dr. Wright has lately made the interesting suggestion that he was a not altogether unsuccessful candidate for the leadership of the twelve. He bases his argument partly upon Mark xiv. 10, where Judas is—in some early MSS. at least—spoken of as 'the one of the twelve '—that is, he says, 'the first of the twelve,' just as Christians called Sunday 'the one day of the week.'[1] Dr. Harris (*Expositor*, July, 1917) has shown that there is some doubt about the reading of that verse, and also quotes the Book of Enoch as evidence that 'the one of' does not always mean 'the first of.' At the same time he goes on to prove that Judas did originally hold a higher place in the list of apostles than he does in our Gospels, and that is enough for our purpose. Again and again Judas is called 'one of the twelve '—perhaps once 'the one.' Was he also the 'one of His disciples'[2] who asked the question about the Temple? If 'Iscarioth' really means 'man of Kerioth '—Dr. Harris thinks it stands for 'of the tribe of Issachar '; Dr. Cheyne emended to 'man of Jericho '—he was possibly the only Judaean in the apostolic circle, though we cannot be sure of this, for 'Simon the zealot' may very well have been a Judaean too. The rivalry between Judaea and Galilee had, perhaps, something to do with the heart-burnings among the disciples. Was there a Galilean trio at one wing of the twelve, a Judaean at the other? If Judas was a Judaean, he would be specially interested in the Temple, and very much taken aback at our Lord's prophecy of its complete destruction. Then we must take into account the story of the anointing at Bethany which follows.[3] Mark does not tell us which of the fellow guests of Jesus it was who passed a harsh criticism upon Mary's gift[4]; at any rate Peter had nothing to do with it. Matthew[5] says that the disciples, John[6] that Judas was responsible. As Mark associates the visit of Judas to the chief priests directly with the supper at Bethany, we have good reason for our acceptance of the Fourth Gospel's testimony upon this point. The fact that Judas went straight off to the conspirators after his Master's rebuke looks like sudden pique, but we should hesitate to attribute his action to any such trivial grounds. It is unthinkable that a chosen

[1] Mark xiv. 10. [2] Mark xiii. 1; cf. John xii. 4. [3] Mark xiv. 3 ff.
[4] Mark xiv. 4, 5. [5] Matt. xxvi. 8. [6] John xii. 4.

apostle of Jesus—chosen, it may be, from a large circle of Judaean disciples for the closest intimacy—could have been mean enough to betray his Master to His bitterest enemies simply because he had been rebuked. He must have been secretly mutinous long before. Moreover, it is difficult to believe that the price paid for the disclosure which led to the arrest of Jesus can have been either the only or the chief consideration even to one who had an excessive regard for the value of money and the things that money can buy. With John xii. 6 I hope to deal later. Matthew says that the chief priests doled out to Judas ' thirty pieces of silver,' about £4 16s. of our money ; but we cannot be sure of the exact sum paid, for the passage quoted[1] is one of many where our First Gospel has been influenced by the text of the Old Testament.[2] We gather that it was not a large amount. If Judas was a poor man, thirty pieces of silver may have seemed a considerable sum to him ; but, if the money had been his sole consideration, he would surely have driven a better bargain. Probably, being an Oriental, he did try to do so ; the only point which we are concerned to press here is that a greedy man with valuable information to sell, and able to haggle at his leisure, would have disposed of his goods at a dearer rate. What, it may be asked, did he actually disclose ? Some have thought that it was what they call the ' Messianic Secret ' ; but surely that was no secret by this time ! We should have assumed that it was simply the time and place at which the arrest could be carried out without fear of interruption, if it had not occurred to us that the conspirators would already have accurate know-ledge of the habits of Jesus. The only piece of information sufficiently important to induce Pilate to issue a warrant for the arrest would be the news that the followers of Jesus were arming. Possibly at the same time Judas told the chief priests something about the words Jesus had used in regard to the Temple, for this scent is followed keenly at the trial before the high-priest.[3] Indeed, the whole manner of arrest seems needlessly elaborate. Jesus Himself exclaims at the ' swords and staves ' of the armed rabble who advance against Him, as if He were a ' robber '—that is, a revolu-tionary leader.

[1] Matt. xxvi. 15.   [2] Zech. xi. 12.   [3] Mark xiv. 58.

The truth, perhaps, is that this is just what, since the report of Judas, they had come to think He was. Jesus[1] asks them why they had not seized Him when He was teaching in the Temple. They were afraid to do so, partly because He was still the Hero of the crowd, partly because they had reason to believe that His followers were arming. This information they took to Pilate, who immediately orders the arrest, but insists upon absolute secrecy. We have little light so far upon the motives of Judas, and must proceed by the aid of more or less probable surmise. We must first examine the money motive ; for that is the generally accepted explanation of his behaviour. On this matter we have to reckon with two great difficulties. If Judas were really so bad a man as to betray his Lord to torture and death for money, it is almost unthinkable that Jesus should have chosen him ; it is still less credible that he should have been smitten with utter remorse so quickly afterwards. In reference to this last point, I am aware that we have in the New Testament two accounts of the end of Judas, which cannot be forced into harmony. Matthew[2] tells us that when he ' saw ' that ' He '—this might mean Judas, but reads more naturally as ' Jesus '—was condemned, he repented, and turned over the thirty pieces of silver to the ' chief priests and elders ' ; in the Acts,[3] on the other hand, Peter informs the other apostles that Judas himself—not the chief priests, as Matt. xxvii. 6, 7—bought a small estate with the money, and afterwards ' swelled up and burst in the middle,' whereas, according to Matthew, he hanged himself in desperate remorse. Apart from our natural desire to think as well as possible of the chosen friends of Jesus, there are more substantial reasons for preferring the Matthean account. Papias preserved a story according to which Judas swelled up to a huge size and was crushed by a passing carriage. We can easily explain such traditions. One of the books which both our Lord and His apostles knew was *The Story of Ahikar*—for evidence of their acquaintance with this widely diffused Eastern fable see App. I. (printed at the end of Part iii.)—in which the villain of the piece, Nadab by name, betrays his uncle Ahikar. When his treachery is brought home to him, he swells up immediately, becomes blown up like a

[1] Mark xiv. 48.　　[2] Matt. xxvii. 3 ff.　　[3] Acts i. 17 ff.

F

bladder, and dies in agony. The other apostles, looking
back upon the whole tragic business, would think no end
too bad for the traitor, and would not inquire too closely
into the origin of a story current shortly after the Resurrection, while the treachery of one of their own number
was still fresh in their minds, to the effect that Judas had
followed to the end the model appropriate to all traitors.
The real truth would only come out slowly, and we are
consequently fairly safe in taking the more charitable view
open to us, in spite of the fact that Matthew's account also
has been influenced—in language at least—by a parallel
Old Testament story, that of the suicide of Ahithophel. [1]

Let us try, then, to construct a theory upon the wider
basis. The chief remaining obstacle is likely to be the
Fourth Gospel, with its very definite statements—that
Jesus spoke of Judas as ' a devil ' at a comparatively early
stage in His association with him ; and, further, that Judas
was a mere pilferer, using for his own purposes the contents
of the common purse. [2] I do not intend to attribute these
declarations solely to what may be called retrospective
bias, though the possibility that bias of this kind has
coloured such accounts of the character of Judas as have
come down to us must not be left out of view. ' One of you
is a devil ' may mean no more than that Jesus saw dangerous tendencies in Judas, just as—about the same time—
He addressed, or seemed to address, Peter as ' Satan.' [3]
It may well have come out afterwards that Judas had used
the contents of the purse for other purposes than poor
relief. But if he had been simply spending the money
upon himself, we are compelled to ask why, in the first
place, did Jesus expose him to temptation by putting the
bag in his hands, and then, when He had observed this
most unworthy trait in his character, why did He still
entrust such money as there was to him, as He was thought
to be doing so late as John xiii. 29 ? We are driven to the
conclusion that there is more behind. Matt. xxvii. 3
makes it plain that Judas did not expect Jesus to be
condemned, and so acquits him of the worst imputation ;
at least he, like the other enemies of Jesus, did not know
what he was doing. Let us suppose that Judas was a man
of some practical ability, chosen by Jesus as the steward of

[1] 2 Sam. xvii. 23.   [2] John vi. 70 ; xii. 6.   [3] Mark viii. 33.

His company of disciples—a really able and, at that time, a genuinely good man. As a Judaean he is a little inclined to look down upon his rough Galilean comrades. His parts soon win him some sort of leadership; but, to his chagrin, Jesus persists in His favour to the Galilean fisherman Peter. He tries to assert his claims behind the back of Jesus; for it is significant that Peter complains of constant offences committed by his 'brother.'[1] Hence follow unseemly discussions as to precedence, which the Master rebukes, telling Judas in effect that, if he wishes to be first, he must go on making himself useful to the others in all sorts of quiet ways; he must be at the service of them all. When Jesus appoints Peter steward of the new Kingdom,[2] Judas takes fresh offence, for he thinks himself the man in possession. Perhaps the Parable of the Unjust Steward[3] bore originally upon the case of Judas; his best plan would be to 'make friends' of the others while he had some precarious hold upon his office, instead of alienating them by his scarcely concealed scorn. Another clue is offered by the Lord's use of the word ' comrade ' in three places in the First Gospel. Ps. lv. 13 suggested the use of the word 'comrade'; this was the great testimony passage (see below Part iii.) on the betrayal. Arguing back from the last of the three occurrences, where Jesus,[4] shrinking from the traitor's kiss, calls him ' comrade '—' do what you are here for '—may we infer that Judas is meant by the ' comrade ' of Matt. xx. 13; xxii. 12 ? Nowhere else in the Gospels does the word ' comrade ' occur. We may, if we will, imagine that the glance of Jesus passed from the open countenance of Peter, who, at any rate, associated himself with the others—' We have left all '[5]—to a darker face, shadowed by a bitter jealousy. He said ' to *one of them* '; may not this be Judas, ' *one* of the twelve ' ? If Peter was ' this last,' need Judas be jealous because the Lord chose to be specially generous to such as he? What was he doing in the happy company without the ' wedding-garment of love ' to his Lord ? It was about this time that the dangerous elements in his make-up became specially prominent, with the result that Jesus

[1] Matt. xviii. 21.   [2] Matt. xvi. 19.   [3] Luke xvi. 1 ff.
[4] Matt. xxvi., 50.   [5] Matt. xix. 27.

warns him in so many words that he is giving himself over to the devil.

What was the devil-inspired plot that was slowly taking shape in the mind of Judas? Evidently, like his Galilean comrades, he was, after his own fashion, a patriot; his name speaks for the fact that he came from a thoroughly Jewish family. But he despised the visionary enthusiasm of these Galilean fanatics. *His* attachment was to more substantial things than any Kingdom in the clouds; he loved the city and the Temple. As the rivalry between himself and Peter became, to his thinking at least, more embittered, he begins to notice that Jesus is directing His watchful gaze upon him more and more often; and at this he is the more aggrieved. Peter and the others were ambitious too, but they followed the Master more for His own sake than for what He could promise them. With Judas other considerations, partly patriotic, partly ambitious, came first, real love for Jesus only second. We have seen some reason to believe that the seed of rebellion had already been sown in his heart in his jealousy of Peter, and we may guess that he was at the bottom of the protest of the ten against the request of James and John. We can perhaps trace a shadowy kind of prominence for Judas in the probability that Jesus washed his feet first on the evening of the supper. ' He comes then to Simon Peter '[1] seems to hint that the Master had been to some one else first, and Judas has been mentioned already.[2] He had forced himself into a primacy amongst the distraught Galileans, which the evangelist is anxious to forget. The others are tossed this way and that by wild hopes and desperate fears; Judas shows no trace of hesitation or of shame, in spite of the urgent and repeated warnings of Jesus, nor do his colleagues suspect him.[3]

Some readers have thought that Judas was deceived by the chief priests, who persuaded him that Jesus would suffer no harm at their hands, and that if the result of the arrest proved that there really was a strong popular backing for the revolution they would throw into it the weight of their own influence, thus assuring its success. This theory requires us to assume that the traitor was excessively

---

[1] John xiii. 6.　　[2] John xiii. 2.
[3] Mark xiv. 21; Matt. xxvi. 25; John xiii. 23, 24.

simple-minded, specially when we remember that he brought to the garden an armed body of Temple attendants, and, according to the Fourth Gospel,[1] a cohort of Roman soldiers. Two possibilities remain: Judas may have thought that, in the last resort, his strangely dilatory Master would be constrained to assert Himself, and, supported by His disciples, who are armed for the purpose, to throw back His mob of enemies. In that case the most unnecessary kiss, attested by Matthew, Mark, and Luke, becomes at once intelligible ; it is meant as a kind of signal to them and to Jesus Himself. The word ' safely,' which, as we noticed above, is peculiar to Mark, should then be taken ironically: ' Take Him away safely—if you can ! '[2] Certainly the kiss could not have been necessary to identify Jesus ; it was a moonlit night, and He was well enough known. Otherwise interpreted, it involves an additional touch of hatefulness, with which we would gladly dispense. But, if this plot failed, Judas had another string to his bow. Even if his Lord was taken safely away, he still trusted to popular clamour to make Pilate's position impossible. For if these clumsy Galileans were not to be trusted in delicate manœuvres, they could be relied upon to make a most effective uproar. Anything was better than this endless talking while the precious days were passing ; a few days or hours, and the feast would be over, and these riotous Galileans gone. What a hero Jesus would be if His trial became the occasion of a glorious victory against the power of Rome in face of all the intrigues of those hateful parasites of Rome, the chief priests ! He, Judas, would use them for other purposes than their own. After such services even Peter could not refuse him his rightful place, as first minister in the new Kingdom.

It must be confessed that the scheme was a plausible one. Pilate's position was precarious. The enemies of Jesus, with a little management, might be set against one another ; for, by all their traditions and professions, the Pharisees were pledged to the nationalist side. Here we may notice two perplexing elements of the situation already hinted at. For one thing, Jesus knew the direction in which the thoughts of this strange follower of His were moving ; yet He never tries to check him, except by verbal warnings,

[1] John xviii. 3.   [2] Mark xiv. 44.

and at the last He says, ' What thou doest, do more quickly.'[1]
We simply refuse to believe that Judas was taken into the
circle of close friends of Jesus, and kept there to the end,
merely because it was ordained that treachery should
play a part in the Passion of the Son of God.   All that we
have learned of the Saviour cries out against the suggestion
that Jesus could use the soul of a man as a pawn, even for
the most sublime of purposes.   But if Judas was not quite
so bad as that, and if Jesus saw that the only way for this
tragically obstinate man to find out his terrible mistake
was the way of remorse and despair, which he was so soon
to tread ; if, moreover, the Master knew that He was to be
betrayed, having come to this conclusion in lonely reading
of His Father's will in Scripture[2] and in prayer, we can
dimly perceive that, though there came a time when it
would have been better for Judas ' that he had not been
born '[3] to this long delusion and sudden despair, he is not
beyond the mercy of God, and was not left out of the prayer
of Jesus when He said, ' Father, forgive them, for they know
not what they do.'   The other disciples, it should also be
observed, were quite unaware of his treachery ; they do
not suspect him, and, though ' the disciple whom Jesus
loved ' is allowed to identify the traitor, the information is
given in a whisper.[4]   Peter, though it was he that asked
for it, cannot have been told, or he would have made an
attempt to prevent Judas from leaving the room.   Matthew seems to imply that all were told,[5] or at least that
Judas was directly charged in the hearing of all ; but John[6]
informs us in so many words that they did not then guess
why Judas was going out ; Luke[7] suggests that the subject
was submerged in a discussion upon the old subject of
' Who was the greatest ? ' in which Judas succeeded in
floating the conversation past the awkward question.
We may infer that of the company only Jesus knew all,
and He did not choose to interfere.   If the theory advanced
here has any foundation—and, of course, it is highly
speculative—the mystery surrounding the financial record
of Judas is also explained.   The money was being used as
the nucleus of a revolutionary war-chest.   The lavishness
of Mary's gift annoyed her critic, because the money would

[1] John xiii. 27.   [2] Mark xiv. 49.   [3] Matt. xxvi. 24.   [4] John xiii. 26.
[5] Matt. xxvi. 25.   [6] John xiii. 27 ff.   [7] Luke xii. 23, 24.

have been useful to him ; the most practical way, he would argue, helping 'the poor ' would be to bend all their energies to the consummation of the revolution.   It may be said that we are, in this somewhat elaborate theorizing, ignoring the fact that disappointed ambition will, in some not naturally bad men, lead them to the direst treachery in a merely wrecking spirit, and that the sudden remorse of Judas is quite in keeping with an equally sudden resolve to destroy what he could not direct.   All I can say in answer is that the whole tone of the Gospels suggests a long-premeditated plan (cf. John vi. 70), that the betrayal was not the mere result of a bitter mood.   Judas is either a strangely cool conspirator in what would seem, in view of its outcome, an aimless act of treachery, or he was, as I have tried to prove, unashamed almost to the last, because his intention seemed to him to be good.

But, as the event proved, Judas understood neither his Master nor the resources of the men who used him for their own purposes.   They could not fathom Jesus ; all they knew was that they were more afraid of Him than they cared to confess.   But they could manage men of the Judas type, and they were immensely relieved when they got him into their power.   In the meantime, while the air is full of conspiracy, the commanding self-possession of Jesus is more wonderful than ever.   With perfect coolness He makes arrangements for the celebration of the Paschal meal with His friends.   Evidently He has disciples in Jerusalem whose identity is unknown to us.   The friend who provided the ass upon which He entered the city, the owner of the house with the upper room, the young man who dared to follow when the rest forsook Him ; they flit across the scene like shadows in an atmosphere of secret passwords and understood signs, and we feel that Judas had something substantial to go upon when he staked his soul upon a great *coup d'état*.   How far they were privy to such designs as his we cannot tell ; but we see in Jesus the only figure moving with mastery in the hourly-shifting scene.   That the chief priests are the victims of all kinds of morbid terrors is proved by the behaviour of their underlings at the arrest,[1] and their elaborate preparations for the seizure of one unarmed man.   They obviously expect resistance, and

[1] John xviii. 6.

have secured a whole cohort of soldiers from Pilate.[1]　At
this stage the Pharisees are submerged in the Sanhedrin,
but we cannot acquit them of complicity in the plot by
which Judas was lured to his doom.　Most reconstructions
of the life of Christ (e.g. ' Philo-Christus ') suggest that
Judas had for some time been intriguing with the Pharisees.
There is no direct evidence of this, but it is doubtful whether
the traitor would ever have approached the chief priests
unless the Pharisees, whom he reckoned upon as secretly
his allies, had been with them.　Neither Matthew nor
Mark[2] mention that the scribes were present when Judas
made his offer ; but everywhere else, up to the end, chief
priests and scribes are acting in concert, for neither Judas
nor the riotous Galileans could have been used and managed
without the help of the moral prestige which at critical
moments the Pharisees were able to contribute to the
conspiracy.　As for the Galileans, we feel what an uncertain
quantity they were.　If our theory of Judas be correct,
he would surely have been moving among them, pleading
for their support, and raising their expectations of armed
revolt, connived at, if not directed, by Jesus.　They must
not allow themselves to be deceived by the passivity of the
Leader to whom they are all looking.　If He is not at last
going to act decisively, why had He come to Jerusalem at
all, why enter the city in triumph, why set about the
Messiah's work so promptly ?　He is only quiet now because
secrets must be kept, and as one of those who know, he
can assure them that arrangements have been made for a
consummation within twenty-four hours !　Let them be
ready early to-morrow morning.

But more restless and distracted than all the others are
the eleven.　Their questions, as reported in the Fourth
Gospel, reveal to us their utterly bewildered condition :
' Why cannot I follow Thee now ? '　' How has it come
about that Thou wilt reveal Thyself to us, and not unto the
world ? '[3]　If only He would take them into His confidence,
and let them die, if need be, to make Him King of the world,
they would at least know what to think and do.　If He did
not intend to lead them any longer, why had He brought
them up from Galilee ?　They are entirely loyal, willing

---

[1] John xviii. 3.　　[2] Mark xiv. 10 ; Matt. xxvi. 14.
[3] John xiii. 37 ; xiv. 22.

to follow Him to prison and to death; but why should He persist in talking as if the issue were settled beforehand? Since they had come to Jerusalem, surely prospects had brightened; He had only to raise His hand, and earth as well as heaven was at His command, for He was great and strong enough for anything. But, to their dismay, He talks less like a revolutionary leader than ever. They had expected this last supper to be the scene of a solemn swearing of allegiance to Him and to each other. Instead of that, He says that they are not to 'follow Him now,' prophesies that they will all desert Him. Why should He reflect upon their loyalty now, when they had been so faithful? They never loved Him more, and never understood Him less. By-and-by they move from the room into the open air, and all but Peter, James, and John are left behind; while Jesus, with His favoured three, enter the garden, to which He and His friends have a right of entry at all hours. Once there, and forbidden to come too near, an intolerable weariness creeps over them. They can see dimly the outline of His prostrate form, perhaps hear His sobbing. They dare not approach Him, and yet—alas for their promises of faithful attendance!—they cannot endure the strain of this awful suspense, and soon fall asleep. In a little time He wakes them, but leaves them again to sleep out the time. I have already tried to trace the course of the Master's inward passion; what I am anxious just now to make plain is the dramatic setting of the tragedy. We are drawing near to the crisis now; all the currents are running together. The Pharisees are central, joining hands with the chief priests on one side, the Galileans on a second, the disciples, whose misunderstanding of their Lord finds its representative in Judas, on a third. For the Pharisees were the party who made it all possible upon the human side. They are using, as they alone are able to use, as their instruments the chief priests, the Galileans, the obstinacy of Judas, the weakness of Pilate, for the end upon which, in the Second Gospel, they have been set almost from the first appearance of Jesus in Galilee. Jealousy, the worst of sins when tested by the gospel standard, has now harnessed in its service the minor rivalries of the apostolic circle, the shameless greed of the high-priestly families, the unthinking bigotry of the

Galileans; 'the unclean spirit' cast out from these respectable pietists has now returned, bringing with it 'seven other spirits worse than itself.'

When Judas appears again with his motley band of Temple guards and Roman soldiers, the eleven are utterly unready to fight effectively, if they had been allowed to do so. Jesus comes into the centre of the stage, and quietly takes charge of the proceedings. Never did He show Himself so completely Master of men and things as on that last night. A look is enough to hurl His enemies to the ground, and all, friends and foes alike, watch Him with a fascinated wonder which is more than half fear as He calmly gives Himself up to His powerless assailants, Judas, we may be sure, most amazed of all. They are paralysed, but by-and-by Peter comes back to his senses, and fumbles nervously for the sword which[1] he had understood his Master to have told him to bring. Then, blindly and with trembling fingers, he strikes at the nearest man, and only succeeds in cutting off his right ear. Luke tells us that Jesus stopped to heal the wounded man[2]; Matthew that Peter is sharply reproved for his attempt to fight, though only John[3] informs us that it was Peter; Mark[4] simply gives us the one dramatic fact : 'They forsook Him, and fled,' Judas among them. We can imagine that, in their bitter humiliation, they turn upon Judas and drive him away, scattering afterwards in different directions, Peter and 'the disciple whom Jesus loved' alone following; while an unknown 'young man' appears only as swiftly and inconsequently to disappear again.[5] Mark tells us of only one trial at night, before an informal meeting of the Sanhedrin, hastily convened at the high-priest's house. According to the Fourth Gospel, on the other hand, Jesus is taken before Annas first. Though Caiaphas was high-priest, his father-in-law, Annas, was chief of the family, holding the reins of power in his hands, and perhaps occupying the official residence. Luke[6] makes it clear that there were two trials, one in the high-priest's house, the other before the full Sanhedrin in the morning. But the verdict in such a court is settled beforehand. In spite of the absence of trustworthy evidence, they all sentenced their

[1] Luke xxii. 36.   [3] John xviii. 10.   [5] Mark xiv. 51.
[2] Luke xxii. 51.   [4] Mark xiv. 50.   [6] Luke xxii. 54, 66.

Victim to death. It is noteworthy that the onus of the charge lay in our Lord's attitude to the Temple. Apparently Judas was not to be found, but witnesses did come forward with a mangled version of one of the sayings of Jesus about the Temple. Mark implies that the evidence forthcoming was false ; John that it was true in essentials, but that it did not mean what the enemies of Jesus thought it meant.[1] In any case a verdict of ' blasphemy ' is duly brought in and confirmed at a meeting of the Sanhedrin convened at dawn. The whole business had been grossly illegal. The midnight meeting, the hasty sentence, the search for hostile witnesses, and the browbeating of the Prisoner, all conspired to make a travesty of justice; but most disgraceful of all was the shower of blows, taunts, and insults in which the long-suppressed devilry hidden in the hearts of these worst enemies of Jesus at last found satisfaction.

Meanwhile the scene shifts to the court outside the high-priest's house, where Peter is seen with the firelight on his face. There are various small discrepancies between the Gospels at this point ; but, if Mark is Peter's Gospel, we shall do well to follow his guidance here. How did Peter come to disown his Master ? It has been argued that an Oriental would consider himself justified in withholding the truth when he was taken at a disadvantage. To him it would be a mere matter of reasonable self-protection, for truth, according to old-world ideas, is due to friends, not enemies. There is much in this contention ; but an examination of what may, by justifiable inference, be surmised as to Peter's state of mind tells us something more. For though love was uppermost, ambition had never been absent from Peter's thoughts, if only the ambition of being signally serviceable to his Master. His association with the Lord had been so strangely begun, and in its course had been marked by so many special favours, that some distinguished post of honour and of danger must surely be reserved for him in the new Kingdom. Peter never left out the claims of others, as Judas habitually did, and James and John, or their mother for them, had once done ; but a real ambition it was all the same.[2] But ever since, in strangely stern answer to a well-meant piece of advice,

[1] Mark xiv. 56 ff. : John ii. 21.   [2] Mark x. 28.

Jesus had called, or seemed to call, him 'Satan,'[1] he had
lost his sense of easy intimacy with his Master. When he
has to complain of the exasperating conduct of Judas
he must 'come up' to Jesus.[2]   He has fallen back
to a level with the rest, the proud day when he made
the great confession and received that greatest of all
compliments from the lips of Jesus almost forgotten in the
pain of this terrible rebuke. After a time he almost
disappears in his own Gospel. We hear of his intervention
at the Transfiguration,[3] of a diffident reminder ('Peter
began to say'[4]) that the disciples had some claim to the
confidence and regard of their Lord ; but never again does
Peter 'take' Jesus and venture to 'rebuke' Him. Even
the fact, recorded only by Luke,[5] that he was one of the
disciples selected to arrange for the Paschal supper is
suppressed in his own Gospel, and on the last week he only
appears to make a seemingly trivial remark about the
fig-tree which his Lord had cursed.[6]   Was he still thinking
of that awful reproof, wondering how near it had been to a
curse, and if his life was withering at the roots, like the
fig-tree, under the rebuke of Jesus ? Why was Jesus so
unlike Himself sometimes ? All the while, along with this
growing uneasiness, there underlay his thoughts and
moods a disappointed ambition, not strong enough to
poison his loyalty, but rendering a man of his passionate
temperament more than usually susceptible to what may
be called cold fits of depression. As to his faithfulness, he
was quite sure of that ; he had of late had many self-accus-
ing thoughts, but his loyalty no one had ever doubted.
Probably he had scarcely the least idea why his Master had
rebuked him so sternly ; he did not know what he had
done to deserve his relegation to a place so far away from
the confidence of Jesus. There is something very pathetic
about his protestations in the upper room. To Peter in
these last days everything else had seemed to be slipping
away. His old dreams, his feeling that he understood his
Lord better than anyone else—a feeling that had become
so strong and sure at Caesarea Philippi, and had been so
rudely shattered directly afterwards—were things of the
past. The others could cry aloud for joy when Jesus

---

[1] Mark viii. 33 (see, however, page 55).   [2] Matt. xviii. 21.
Mark ix. 5.   [4] Mark x. 28.   [5] Luke xxii. 8.   [6] Mark xi. 21.

entered Jerusalem. Peter is not prominent then, because he could not so easily forget those forebodings that had brought the clouds across his sky. As the week went on, and the darkness deepens about the Master, we may imagine him taking refuge from uneasy thoughts in quiet preparation to defend Jesus with his life, if it came to that. From the beginning of his association with Jesus we can trace in Peter a curious and very pathetic tendency to take charge of his Lord. It appears at the Transfiguration, and most obviously of all in Mark viii. 32, where he ventures to 'rebuke' Jesus, his reproof recoiling swiftly upon his own head : ' Peter, taking Him aside, began to *rebuke* Him . . . and He turned, and *rebuked* Peter.' Now he is subdued and quiet, but is sure that his Master will soon need his trusty follower, whose proffered services He had pushed aside so curtly.

At last the evening comes, and Master and disciples alike feel that the day of destiny has arrived. In the upper room Peter is more bewildered than ever. He feels very far away from Jesus, for when he wants information he is compelled to ask the ' beloved disciple,' who now has the place that Peter had thought was his. Even then he is not told who the traitor is.[1] His suspense is beginning to tell upon him ; he is unaccustomed to the close atmosphere of the city rooms and streets, and the last strain upon his endurance comes when he is taken into the garden, but is told not to come too near.[2] There he can see his Lord in agony. If only he could do something, go up and whisper words of encouragement ! But he dare not, for he is afraid of another rebuke. Worst of all is this intolerable weariness that is creeping over him. Do what he will, he cannot hold up his head. He had always lived in the open air, and his nerves had never been subjected to such a strain before. In a few moments, in spite of his sense of imminent danger and his desperate desire to stand by his Lord in the crisis of His fate, he is asleep ; in so healthy a man Nature will not be denied. Then, in what seems to him a moment, it is all over. He is wakened to see Jesus standing over him, strangely calm now, and excusing their inability to keep awake. Scarcely have they got away from the shadow of the trees when they are confronted by Judas and his armed

[1] John xiii. 27 ff.   [2] Mark xiv. 34.

band, and instinctively Peter's hand feels for the sword hidden beneath his cloak. But it would seem that Jesus is not going to need his help after all, for look ! by His mere majesty He has hurled His assailants to the ground ! It is amazing, and Peter's hand drops away from his sword. What follows must have seemed, when he could think with some degree of calmness, not amazing only, but incredible. That, after such a manifestation of power, Jesus should have allowed these cowardly enemies of His to lay rude hands on His sacred Person was more than Peter could bear, and, in blind fury, he lashes out with a hand that he cannot keep steady at the nearest man. In his own preaching he drew a veil over the incident and its sequel, not from any fear of exposing himself, but because any courage he showed then was not worthy to be compared with what he would have described as his most miserable behaviour just afterwards. In Mark xiv. 47 the would-be defender of Jesus is simply ' one of those who stood by,' not deserving on that night to be called even a disciple of the Lord. From Matthew xxvi. 51, where Peter is spoken of more tenderly as ' one of those with Jesus,' we learn that he was sharply told to put his sword back ; from Luke[1] that Jesus healed the injured ear ; only from John[2] that it was Peter. Thereupon ' they all forsook Him, and fled.' If they were not to fight, what could they do for Him now ?

By-and-by Peter turns and creeps stealthily towards the light in the courtyard of the high-priest's house. After all he may still be of some use ; at any rate he will stay and see the end [3] before he goes back to try to take up the thread of the old life again and forget his dreams. On the way he is thinking hard. Why had Jesus led them to Jerusalem, only to dismiss them as if they were no further use to Him now ? Why had He told them to take a sword with them if they were not to use it ? It is easy for us to see the beauty of the Lord's surrender, but we must remember that it would seem to those simple-minded men a real surrender, not only utterly unnecessary, but a surrender betraying a failure of nerve. Why had his Lord collapsed so lamentably as He had done, or seemed to do, in the garden ? Long-stifled resentment begins to rise in his mind, not so high as to drown his loyalty, but still

[1] Luke xxii. 51.   [2] John xviii. 10.   [3] Matt. xxvi. 58.

dangerously high.   After all he had loved Jesus, and would gladly have died for Him ; but to be told to go without a word of explanation or of thanks !   No, he did not want thanks ; but he did feel bitterly the withdrawal of confidence, which had cast a gloom over his life during the last few months.   For the life of him he could not think what he had done to deserve it.   Peter was the kind of man who must be doing ; the energy of mind which finds vent in action turns in upon itself when the opportunity for action is denied him.   So by the time he reaches the house his brain is in a fever.   He is admitted into the courtyard, in the centre of which a fire is burning, on the strength of his acquaintance with the ' beloved disciple,' who is ' a friend of the high-priest ' ; and he sits over the fire, trying to cloak his nervousness by joining in the chatter of the servants.   We need not go over the scene which follows, for it is painful to dwell upon the humiliation of a brave man.   Perhaps Peter's thrice-repeated denial was partly meant as a measure of defence ; but surely there is something more.   May he not in some measure for the moment have meant what he said when he exclaimed, ' I know not the man ? '   Was he not in the position of a man vainly trying to break through a net, to pretend that what had been had not been, to wash his hands of the history of the last few years and be a fisherman again ? Already in the upper room he had asked the Master to wash not his feet only, but his clumsy hands and puzzled head, to obliterate the history of the last months.   Jesus had no use for him now !   But he could not break away, for the chain held tight.   Jesus had prayed for him,[1] and, though he did not think of it then, not all his cursing and swearing could avail against the prayer of Jesus, or make Peter feel as Simon used to feel, before he first met his Lord. Nothing can ever wash out the mark that the Lord leaves upon the man with whom He has once had dealings ; he may become a renegade, but he can never be as though these things had not been.   His very dialect betrays him !   Only a look is needed to bring him to hand again. Putting John i. 42 and Luke xxii. 61 together, we see that it was the same penetrating glance with which Jesus had first greeted Peter.   In those two looks are written

[1] Luke xxii. 32.

the history of Peter's soul. Broken at once, he ' sets to '
' and begins to weep.' [1] There we must leave him, and
take up the main thread of the action again.

In the morning Jesus is found alone, face to face with
His triumphant foes. The chief priests have informed
Pilate, the procurator, whose sanction they require before
He can be put to death, that this man is a leader of sedition,
and that His disciples are arming for revolution. There
will, they assure him, be serious rioting if drastic measures
are not taken at once. The crowd too have heard of
the arrest, and are in a dangerous humour. When they
see Jesus a bound Prisoner, they are visibly taken aback,
and in their murmurs of dismayed surprise the parties
hostile to Him see their opportunity, taking advantage,
according to Matthew,[2] of a well-meant attempt to save
the Prisoner on the part of the governor's wife. They
could see disappointment with Jesus written upon the
faces of the Galileans. ' The chief priests,' we read—
' and the elders,' adds Matthew—' persuaded the crowd
to ask by preference for Bar-rabbas.' The name of this
' son of a Rabbi,' according to some authorities, was also
' Jesus.' He was a real revolutionist, who had been
involved in a street riot, in which blood had lately been
shed. For a little time he had been the hero of the crowd,
but now had been forgotten by all but the Pharisees,
to whose number his father or teacher probably belonged.
Here was a chance indeed, for they can make capital
out of the fact that Pilate is so obviously anxious to
release Jesus, and is counting upon the people clamouring
for their latest Champion. The very fact that the intensely unpopular governor is favourably inclined to his
Prisoner is enough by itself to turn the crowd against
Him ; but it is clear that they were as anxious as Judas
had been to bring the feud between people and governor
to an issue then and there. Judas had told the ring-
leaders of the Galileans that he had every reason to hope
that Jesus would be Master of the situation by morning.
Now Judas has vanished, the Jesus in whom they had
trusted is helpless, and rumour has it that He gave Himself
up without a struggle ! Is it true that Judas, one of this
man's followers, arranged for His arrest last night ? ' It

[1] Mark xiv. 72.   [2] Matt. xxvii. 19.

looks as though,' we can hear them whispering to one another, 'it has all been concocted beforehand to keep us quiet ! They knew what we were out for this time. That is why we were fooled by that procession the other day ! There is the governor's wife. If He were really the people's man, would all these great folks be so anxious to get Him off ? The scribes who told us not to trust Him were right after all. Do you remember what trouble we had with Him in Galilee, and how cautious He was about the taxes the other day ? He has betrayed the people, sold us ! And now they think that we shall not see through their precious plot ; shall shout for Him to be discharged, and go quietly home ! ' It is just when discontent has reached this point that the chief priests intervene with their suggestion about Bar-rabbas, and so fire the train. At least Bar-rabbas has done something. As for this man, He is a traitor to the cause, and if Pilate chooses to stand by Him, so much the worse for Pilate ! By the time the governor's wife, or her messenger, has retired, the mischief is done. A wild shout greets him, as he turns to face the crowd again : ' Not this man, but Bar-rabbas ! ' The few friends of Jesus are soon silenced, and the Lord Himself forgotten in the excitement of the long-expected struggle with Pilate. The procurator's manifest embarrassment adds fuel to the flame, for, to Galilean thinking, the partiality of the governor proves the Prisoner's guilt. We shall not follow all the futile shifts to which Pilate has recourse. Matthew adds the last touches to the tragedy, but I will reserve the notice of his contribution to a later chapter.

In Mark's picture of the Cross, however, there is one illuminating verse which does more to explain the inner meaning of the Passion than any other in the Gospels. In xv. 23 we read of ' myrrhed wine.' Here we must notice the primary importance of this detail as an element in the dramatic movement of the Gospel. This tragedy differs from others in that its Hero is undrugged all the way through. In all the others the tragic hero, in spite of his virtues, is in some degree a party to his own destruction, through some weakness or ignorance of his own. Here the Master does play a part in precipitating the catastrophe, but it is an active part. He knows beforehand

G

the rôle that Peter, Judas, the Galilean pilgrims, are to
take ; He is never merely drifting, or letting things happen
because He cannot prevent them. He is Master of His
fate, as the noblest tragic hero never is, for He lays down
His life ' of Himself.'   Thus it is that He is able to extricate
His friends, as they cannot.   Hamlet draws Ophelia down
with him, as King Lear Cordelia ; whereas Jesus, going far
deeper than they into the abyss of tragic passion, is still
strong enough, on the very edge of His despair, to carry
those who have followed Him clear away from the vortex—
able to the last to save others, where He would not save
Himself.   So the drama becomes one not of tragic defeat,
but of tragic victory, and the Resurrection no mere happy
ending, rather a necessity, the only thinkable sequel to
such a story.   In the other great tragedies a faint gleam
of hope at the end is perhaps enough—the ' flights of
angels ' singing Hamlet to his rest, the tremulous ' she
lives ' of the dying Lear—because we can, through the
sorrow and confusion of catastrophe, trace a kind of fitness,
a rough justice which, along with a hint of something
better than the wasteful process of the present moral
order, leaves us not altogether sad or unsatisfied.   We
can at least see that it must have come to this, and hope
that eternity will repair the ravages of time.

   But in this tragedy—the supreme tragedy not merely
of literature, but of life—no gleam of sunset-light can
ever be enough.   From our knowledge of the working
of evil in our own lives, the course followed by the men
who brought Jesus to His death is horribly natural ; but
it can never be natural that such a Soul as His should
succumb to it.   For the Personality of Jesus is not less
but more vivid than that of the great figures in Sophocles
or Shakespeare.   No serious student of the Gospels with
even a glimmer of imaginative insight could ever bring
himself to believe that such a portrait could be painted
except from memory.   This tragedy, indeed, is not merely
like life ; it is life's master-secret, and makes the rest
bearable.

V

THE GREAT NOTES OF THE GOSPEL

IT remains for us to gather up some features of the Gospel according to Mark which have a bearing not only upon history, but upon theology. For one thing Mark gives us a very candid statement of the limitations both to the power and the knowledge of Jesus in the days of His flesh. All the passages which Schmiedel in his famous article on 'Gospels' in the *Encyclopaedia Biblica* called the 'pillars' of the gospel need not be enumerated here. Three of them are very important. They are Mark vi. 5, 6; x. 18; xiii. 32: 'He could not do any mighty work there . . . and He was surprised at their unbelief'; 'Why callest thou Me good?' &c.; 'Of that day or that hour knoweth no man, not even the angels in heaven, nor even the Son.' Two of the three are, it should be noted, sayings of the Master Himself; the other might be an indiscretion of the writer's, but the reference to the fact that the Lord was baffled is too sustained to warrant the suggestion of a mere slip. There were, then, some things that Jesus did not know, some things He could not do. Schmiedel calls such texts 'pillar-passages,' because they not only vouch for their own authentic character, but carry a good deal else as well. Granted that the Gospels were written by worshippers of Jesus to prove that He was the Son of God, no statement would have found its way into the records which seemed to detract from His power and knowledge unless it was based upon fact. 'He *could* not do any mighty work there ' in the passage quoted from Mark is altered in Matt. xiii. 58 to 'He *did* not do many mighty works there '—a very significant change, showing that the difficulty of reconciling Mark's bold declaration with the divine power of Jesus

99

was already felt when our First Gospel came to be published.
Luke's omission of this feature in his much fuller account
of the visit to Nazareth points in the same direction, and
both Matthew and Luke delete all reference to the surprise
of Jesus at the unbelief of the Nazarenes. Similarly,
the inconvenient question put by Jesus to the rich
young man in Mark x. 18 is altered in the oldest MSS.
of Matt. xix. 17 to ' Why askest thou Me concerning the
good ? '—though Luke in this case agrees with Mark ;
while the best texts of Matt. xxiv. 36 omit the words ' not
even the Son,' which come from Mark xiii. 32.

Of course, these ' pillar-texts ' do not contradict our
belief in the real Divinity of our Lord. It might be
argued, indeed, that ' Why callest thou Me good ? None
is good except One—God ' is an affirmation rather than
a denial of a perfection of character more than human.
Evidence from contemporary literature goes to prove
that ' Good Master ' was simply a courteous form of
address, equivalent to our ' Be so good as to tell me.'
If so, our Lord's sharp interruption gains fresh point :
' good ' is too great a word to be degraded to the service
of mere politeness ; if the young man meant anything
more than this, let him consider what such a tribute
implies. If this suggestion seems too subtle, we may say
that our Lord is making a protest against the casual use
of a great word. Exactly the same process has for a
long time been going on with the word ' good ' in our own
language ; but it has gone farther, for ' my good man '
has become a very effective way of expressing something
like contempt. In any case no possible doubt of our
Lord's perfect freedom from the consciousness of ever
having sinned can reasonably be based upon this passage.
My own interpretation would be that this quick question
tells us what was going on in the Speaker's mind. Just
then He was very much occupied with deep thoughts
about Himself and His commission. ' Why was He so
different from others ? Why this barrier, which lately
He had felt more than ever, widening and deepening
between Himself and the rest of His Father's children,
so that when He spoke of things which He had always
taken for granted He seemed to be speaking in a language
strange even to the men whom He had sought to make

His friends? Why did men call Him good? Why were
they so much drawn to Him, and yet so often would
not let Him do for them what He could do, what
must be done, if they were to be saved? Why were they
so near, and yet so far?' We have the evidence of the
First Gospel to show that the question was found embarrassing by young Christians. It was not that it really
reflected upon our Lord's perfect goodness, but that
it seemed to do so, and a quite honest man, such
as the compiler of our First Gospel was, preferred
another reading of the Aramaic original, giving a less
dangerous sense. Behind the three passages already
mentioned lies a greater, omitted by Luke, but common
to the first two Gospels; and in this case we know from
sources outside our Gospels that the text in question
caused difficulty and offence. It is the cry of despair
upon the cross: ' My God, My God, why hast Thou forsaken
Me?' Very many Christians of the first centuries could
not believe that Jesus was God when He uttered these
words. Some thought that a phantom suffered upon
the cross, or that the Holy Spirit, which had come down
upon Jesus at His baptism, had now deserted Him; others
that Simon of Cyrene was crucified by mistake for the
Lord Himself. Perhaps it was to show the absurdity
of this last suggestion that Simon's sons, Alexander and
Rufus, are mentioned in Mark xv. 21. Rufus may possibly
be identified with the Rufus of Rom. xvi. 13, and, if earlier
editions of the Gospel had given rise to dangerous specula-
tions about Simon, the writer or editor of the Gospel as
we have it may have thought it wise to put them out of
court by a reference to the sons of Simon, one of whom
was a well-known member of the Church at Rome. For
the same reason Simon disappears altogether in the
Fourth Gospel, and Jesus is said to have carried His own
cross. [1]

If, as some suppose, the Gospels were a concerted attempt
to elevate a mere man to divine rank, how do these extraordinary statements come into them? They seem to
defeat their own purpose. The very fact that some of
them caused difficulty soon after they were published
shows us that they could not have been allowed to stand

[1] John xix. 17.

unless they had been irrefutably true. We may draw
two inferences : one to the effect that the basis of Mark's
Gospel is the history of a real Man, who was sometimes
perplexed and surprised, angry and depressed ; the
second, that the evangelists were genuinely honest men,
for we must remember that not all the ' pillar-passages '
are found only in Mark. The fact that Matthew and Luke
alter or omit some of them proves simply hesitation as
to the correctness of their source rather than contradiction.
This very hesitation, it should be observed, makes our
argument all the stronger, as it testifies to the fact that
the writers were worshippers of Jesus, and represented
average Christian opinion in finding so frank a statement
of the limitations of Jesus hard to digest.

The other outstanding feature of Mark's Gospel in this
region is its very individual and practical interpretation
of the meaning of the ' faith ' so highly valued by Jesus.
Something like a definition of faith is given us in our
Lord's saying as reported in Mark xi. 22, 23, where the
words ' Have God's faith '—as perhaps they should be
translated— . . . ' in his heart, but believes that what
he talks of is happening,' are peculiar to this Gospel.
' Have God's faith ' may mean either ' faith that rests
upon God ' or ' faith of divine quality.' Even a grain
of faith with the mustard-seed's vital potencies (cf. iv. 31)
could remove mountains. In this passage, however,
the main stress seems to be upon concentration of purpose
and desire, ' is not distracted in his heart, but believes.'
Another note is that of assurance, for we are to rest assured
that our prayers are being answered while we pray ;
compare the present tense in Mark ii. 5, ' Child, thy sins
are being forgiven.' But Mark's interest does not lie
in definitions, but in instances. It will be worth our while
to enumerate them. They are as follows :

ii. 5 : ' Seeing their faith, He said to the paralytic man,' &c.

iv. 40 : ' How is it that ye have not faith ? ' (R.V. ' Have ye not
yet faith ? ').

v. 34, 36 : ' Daughter, thy faith hath saved thee : go in peace,
and be cured of thy complaint. . . . Overhearing ' (or ' not heed-
ing ') ' the matter talked about, He says to the synagogue president,
Be not afraid ; only go on believing.' This is altered by Luke

to a phrase which looks Pauline: ' Only believe '—one act of
faith—' and she shall be saved.'

vi. 6 : ' He was surprised at their unbelief.'

vii. 29 : ' On account of this word, go.' The word ' faith
does not occur here, but its idea is implied, and Matthew [1] has,
'O woman, great is thy faith ! '

ix. 23, 24 : ' And Jesus said to him, Oh that *if* Thou canst !
All things can be to him that believes. Immediately the father
of the child cried out, and said, Lord, I am believing ; help Thou
mine unbelief.'

x. 52 : To blind Bartimaeus : ' Go thy way ; thy faith hath
saved thee.'

Chapter ii. 5 may be thought of as unique in this
respect, that a man's sins are—apparently—said to be
forgiven for the sake of other men's faith. All three
Synoptic Gospels agree upon this point (cf. Matt. ix. 2 ;
Luke v. 20), so that there can be little question of a mere
slip. Of course we need not limit the scope of the word
'their' to the stretcher-bearers ; we may say 'The faith
represented by the group'—including the sufferer, who
may well have been a party to the transaction ! But
before we come to the discussion of this particular
instance it is perhaps advisable to sum up the characteristics common to all our examples. In each case,
where signal faith is exercised, we notice that either
the sufferer or his friends are very persistent, and will
not be discouraged by any obstacle whatever. Bartimaeus
will not be gagged ; the woman with the haemorrhage
must elbow her way through the crowd to get to Jesus ;
while the synagogue president, to whom the delay had
made just all the difference, is bidden, in spite of all, to
keep on believing. It is the same with the negative
instances—those of lack of faith. The men of Nazareth
are side-tracked by the first objection against Jesus which
occurs to them ; the disciples wake their Lord directly
they get into trouble upon the lake. The example quoted
from ix. 23, 24 is specially illuminating. The father's
' if ' reveals to Jesus a momentary faltering which might
prove fatal to a complete cure ; his patience is almost
exhausted by the failure of the disciples to help him, and

[1] Matt. xv. 28.

a further effort is needed.   When this effort is forthcoming,
doubtful and wavering as it is, it is enough for Jesus, and
the cure is carried through.   There is, however, a suggestion
of strain and difficulty, as in the cases noticed above
from vii., 31 ff. ; viii. 22 ff.   The healing is gradual,
and the demon ' tears ' its victim ' much,' so that
' he became like one dead.'   Luke softens this part
of the story,[1] and Matthew [2] makes the cure quite easy
and instantaneous ;   Mark, as in several other examples,
is much fuller and more suggestive than either.   Evidently
we are concerned here with a more than usually noxious
form of demon-possession ; ' This kind,' says Jesus, ' goeth
not out except by prayer.'   Did Jesus Himself need to
pray when called upon to heal desperate diseases ?   John [3]
seems to imply that He did, but that it was not His habit
to pray, as we do, in great emergencies ; rather that He
armed Himself for all emergencies by a life of prayer.
The disciples had been successful before with less serious
cases, but the more severe test betrayed their prayerless-
ness.   Difficulty may also have been caused by the fact
that there was a necessity here for what may be called
vicarious faith.   A greater degree of persevering earnestness
would appear to be needed in order to carry a blessing
to another, from whom, either because of youth or the
prostration of sickness, little effort on his own behalf can
be expected, than where only oneself is involved.   In
ii. 5, vii. 29 we find two other instances of vicarious faith,
in both of which the faith of those who sought a blessing
for another is easily triumphant.   In each of these cases
faith is inspired and fortified by a great love, as it was in
the father of the epileptic boy ; but while *he* was perhaps
the kind of man whose anxiety flusters him, they became
more alert and self-possessed the more desperately they
were in earnest.   In the story told in ii. 1 ff. the ingenuity
of the lovers of their friend pleases Jesus ; the idea of
letting him down through the trap-door (see pp. 28, 29) was
a stroke of genius—the genius that is willing to take great
pains.   In vii. 25 ff. the Gentile mother's refusal to take
offence and her ready wit earns His delighted approval.
In both instances, as in the story of the centurion who
loved his slave, told by Matthew and Luke, ' faith ' almost

[1] Luke ix. 42.   [2] Matt. xvii. 18.   [3] John xi. 41.

amounts to what we call ' character,' brought to its highest perfection by unquestioning trust in the power and the bounty of God in Jesus, and a self-forgetting love to the one on whose behalf help is sought.

But the first example upon our list—that quoted from ii. 5—demands a fuller discussion, for very great questions are involved. The apparently unique thing in this story is that it is not a mere matter of bodily healing, but of the saving of a man's soul by the faith of his friends. Something has already been said in mitigation of this difficulty (p. 103). We say that the man must have been penitent, but we have to put that into the narrative. All we can do is to state one or two of the problems raised by this story. Did Jesus always heal the soul of His patients first ? He did so in this instance. Is it really unique, or was it regarded by Him as an illustration of His methods ? Did He heal the man's soul that He might use the new confidence which must have followed upon the conscious removal of guilt to co-operate with its own power in the healing of the body ? Clearly, when the man was bidden to get up and carry the mat upon which he had been lying, he was called to make a venture of faith. Would he have been capable of such an effort of will if he had not received already that inward reinforcement spoken of here as the forgiveness of sins ? Probably Jesus did not make any sharp distinction between body and soul. (To Him salvation meant the healing of the whole man); in many cases the whole man was set right together. But here there is an unmistakable order, and the ' soul ' comes first. This man may have been so utterly helpless that he could not speak or think for himself. If so, we can understand that he needed restoration to self-command before the Lord could hold any personal relations with him.

We have already noticed that only in the case of the Gerasene demoniac does Jesus deal directly with the victims of demon-possession themselves. We infer that He treated those who were still capable of an effort of will in one way ; those who were completely prostrate in another. This shows us that Jesus was not dependent upon the co-operation of His patients even when the bestowal of spiritual blessing was concerned, and guards us against hasty generalization. Yet He does seem to

H

have been able to do more for men and women when they were ready to take a hand themselves; He was glad to have the support of ' faith ' either in the patient or the patient's representatives. ' He could not do any mighty work there because of their unbelief ' certainly suggests that an unsympathetic atmosphere did most seriously limit the Lord's power. This consideration perhaps explains the comparative dearth of works of healing during the last weeks of His ministry, as it gives us His reason for taking Peter, James, and John into Jairus's house [1]; He was making sure of the right atmosphere for the accomplishment of a difficult work beforehand. He could dispense with it, if need were; but it cost Him more to work, so to say, in a vacuum. When the woman with the hæmorrhage [2] tried to steal relief without the ordeal of an interview with her Healer, ' power went out of Him '; when there came before Him a deaf and dumb man, to whom He could neither talk nor listen till the cure was wrought, He ' sighed.' [3] Even at Nazareth He did lay His hands upon a ' few sick folk,' but anything further was out of the question. We should be glad to know what the evangelist meant by a ' mighty work.' I imagine that *Jesus* would use the term of the saving of the soul, the whole man. (Our conclusion must be that, according to the evidence of this Gospel, any kind of deliberate contact with Jesus resulted in the healing of the body. On the other hand, such evidence as we have is rather against the theory that soul-healing was always an indispensable preliminary to bodily cure. In specially pitiful cases Jesus did sometimes ' forgive sins,' when the dumb misery of the patient was his only appeal. Even then He was greatly helped by the resolute and resourceful affection of the patient's friends.)

It remains for us to examine a little further into the nature of ' faith,' and then to make one or two practical deductions. Is faith in God, or faith in Jesus, or a union of the two, meant by the expression as used in this Gospel ?

If xi. 22 be translated ' Have faith in God,' we have an answer ready to our hand. On the whole, when we take into account the emphasis which Jesus everywhere places upon the personal relations of His clients with Himself,

---

[1] Mark v 37.   [2] Mark v. 27-30.   [3] Mark vii. 34.

we shall perhaps most safely define the Marcan faith on this side as trust in God as revealed in Jesus ; but it is no merely passive surrender. Mark describes for us a very active and indeed business-like faith, and, incidentally, gives us a necessary balance to the Pauline idea—what may be called a comment upon his master's doctrine in terms of the practical man. So he becomes the true bridge between Paul and James. and we can understand how he could make himself useful both to Peter and Paul, for he was evidently a man of all parties and of none. Faith, as illustrated in Mark's Gospel, may be defined as a painstaking and concentrated effort to obtain blessing for oneself or for others, material or spiritual, inspired by a confident belief that God in Jesus can supply all human need.

As to our practical deductions, our material certainly warrants a much bolder attitude towards problems of what is called ' faith-healing ' than is usually taken by moderate Christian opinion. Abuse has often crept in where too much stress has been laid upon merely human media. The whole question of healing cannot be avoided by Christian preachers much longer ; but the story of the disciples' failure in a serious case [1] when the Master was away should warn us that we avail nothing either for ourselves or for others unless we give the central place in all our teaching upon the subject of the Christian law of health to the conviction that not merely God, but *God in Jesus*, is, since the Lord came, the sole source of healing for body and soul. There is a great future before Christian healing, but the less we hear about our part in the matter the better. It is true that we read of ' gifts of healing ' in the early Church, but they died away when the consciousness of the presence of the risen Lord with His Church became faint. Nor need we discountenance the use either of medical science—for this also is a revelation of the grace of God in Christ, and many of the methods of Jesus, we may be sure, would not have been used, as they would not have been necessary, if that revelation had been available then—or of ' suggestion,' for the evidence of the Gospels goes to show that Jesus Himself employed such means in several instances ; but, at any rate, in

[1] Mark ix. 18.

more serious cases we shall do well to point each other and hold ourselves to the Living Christ, and leave to Him the task, too delicate and dangerous for our ignorance, of dealing with the secrets of the soul. There is no reason for believing that every sick person who crossed the path of our Lord was healed, and we need not expect that any certain and wholesale method of healing will ever be forthcoming ; but we may be permitted to hope that, with a new consciousness of the reality of the Saviour—it is the chief work of the Christian teacher in this generation to arouse and quicken into assurance this consciousness —there may also come to us a revival of the gift of healing, our almost complete lack of which is the most ominous sign of our failure to make the treasure of His grace our own. The cure of the paralysed man,[1] already discussed, reminds us, too, that it is dangerous to dissociate bodily from spiritual healing.

[1] Mark ii. 10, 11.

PART II

THE GOSPEL ACCORDING TO LUKE

SYNOPSIS OF PART II

CHAPTER I

THE TEACHING OF JESUS AND ITS METHOD

A system of opposite, though not opposed, paradoxes—Illustrations—Bad motives and good intentions—Losing and finding oneself
—Self-judgement and toleration—Privilege and responsibility—
The Kingdom and the demand of Jesus. Other examples of two-sidedness : (1) In sayings : The coming of the consummation—
The things that must be given and the things that can never be
given away—The unwritten sayings—Reckless speech and cowardly
silence—The inevitableness of good and evil—The preacher's
obligation and his reserves—The duty and danger of anger—Two's,
three's, and one alone—' Raise the stone '—Asking and giving—
Twin sayings—A bridge between them—Sayings about salt and
light—Conscious and unconscious advertisement—The Father in
heaven and in secret—Some differences between Gospels accounted
for by this consideration—Specially difficult instances—The fig-tree
and the mountain—Yes and no, with a sidelight from Paul—The
disparagement and recommendation of force—Buying swords and
perishing by the sword—The correlatives sometimes placed side by
side—The group of sayings about Jonah and Solomon—Strong-man's house—The homeless Homegiver—Two aspects of purity—
The improved repetitions of Jesus; (2) The parables : Veil, but
unveil—Jesus, the Finder and the Found—Our attitude towards Him
and His towards us—The Prince's wedding and the rich man's
feast—Where twin parables have run together—Talents and pounds
—Two parables about the far country, about stewards, about waiting
for the Bridegroom, about the rich man and the one on whom he
shut the door, about two sons, about seed sown in the night—Jesus
the Sower and the Seed, the Shepherd and the Door, the Vinedresser
and the Vine—Two parables about two debtors, about the growth
of the Kingdom, about lost things, about different kinds of shame-lessness in prayer—Two sayings about the adversary—About

persistent prayer—The unneighbourly neighbour and the neigh-
bourly stranger—The sparing and the cursing of the fig-tree—The
Gerasene swine—The traces of the same process in the Fourth
Gospel—Inferences.   (pp. 117–133.)

CHAPTER II

GENERAL PURPOSE OF THE WRITER OF THE THIRD GOSPEL

The Gospel and the Acts by the same hand, a companion of Paul
and his doctor—' Theophilus '—Luke an Antiochene—His opportunities of getting at the facts—Something like a scientific history
for educated people, especially the governing classes—John and
Jesus, Bethlehem and Nazareth—Development insisted upon, and
the friendly relations between Rome and the Christians of the first
generation brought out—His sources—Mark, Q, Mary the mother
of Jesus—The ' Travel-document '—Its unique features—Was
Joanna his authority here, or Manaen?—Knowledge of Herod
and his Court—Possible contributions of Paul.   (pp. 134–144.)

CHAPTER III

LUKE THE PHYSICIAN : HIS POINT OF VIEW

A man of the larger world—Omits matters of purely local interest, and smooths away vulgarisms—His difficulties with Mark's
vocabulary—A careful scholar, anxious to exculpate the Roman
Government—Sometimes hazy about geographical detail—Tends
to replace Oriental by Greek expressions—Uses language current
in society and commerce—Allusions to imperial history of the times
—Grace and charm—The beauty of forgiveness and penitence—
Employs Pauline words with a non-Pauline colouring—The courtesy
of Jesus—Greek proverbs in Luke and Acts—A ready writer—
Use of athletic terms—His passion for precision, stress upon reason-
ing faculties—Manners for ministers—Medical colouring of his
writings—Doubts about demoniac possession—' Convalescent,'
malaria, ' examine,' nervous disease, the ' power ' of Jesus, epidemic
disease, and chronic complaints—The doctor's needle, the ' infant's
swaddling-clothes '—Studies in the habit of ' talking to yourself '—
Further illustrations of the way in which the writer's profession
peeps out—Jesus the Healer—Did He watch His patients after cure?
                                                          (pp. 145–158.)

CHAPTER IV

THE SAME SUBJECT CONTINUED

Socialistic tendencies in the Gospel—The sermon ' on the level place'
a public manifesto—Relation to Q—Contrast with Matthew—Sense
of social wrong and of the inhuman humiliation of hunger—Property

out of place in the Kingdom—The unjust steward and the practicability of the Lord's teaching on the use of perishable goods—
Making friends—No hope of ' independence ' in this life or the next
—Parables and the ' how much more ? '—Parable of talents illustrates equality of reward, that of pounds equality of opportunity—
The devil and material property—Jesus condemns the whole social
and economic order of His time without argument—The Pharisees
and money—Sympathy with the poor—Luke's ascetic tendencies—
The Baptist's meat—Diet—Fatlings and the fatted calf—Fasting
in the Birth story, not in the main body of the Gospel—The power
of the devil—Love of simplicity and discipline—No slippers for the
house, no change of clothes—The two kinds of supper at Bethany—
Energy in self-discipline—Living by fits and starts—The tower-
builder and the King—The power to do and bear—Digging—Worry
a kind of dismal intoxication—A touch of sinister irony—Prejudice
in favour of celibacy illustrated : reasons for believing that some
exaggeration here. Luke's interest in feminine characteristics and
concern to emphasize the fact that women were, upon the whole,
friendly to Jesus—His portrait-gallery of women—His Greek sensibility—Weeping in this Gospel—Its homeliness, pathos, and pitiful
tenderness. Also the Gospel of exuberant joy : first solos, then a
chorus of praise, to God, to Jesus, to God in Jesus—Wonder and
fear. The Gospel ends as it began, with peace and blessing—Jesus
the Hero of the crowd all through—Exultation, leaping, dancing,
merriment—The philosophy of Christian revelry—The great fifteenth
chapter.   (pp. 159–179.)

CHAPTER V

OTHER FEATURES OF THIS GOSPEL

Emphasis upon prayer—Prayer at the Birth, the Baptism, choice
of twelve, multiplying of loaves, Transfiguration—For Peter, for
His murderers—The mountain and the garden—Parables on prayer
—The forbearance of God—Light and shadow chase each other over
the Master's mind—Not dependent upon human persistency—We
pray, Jesus prays ; we agonize, and He was in agony ; we 'dig,'
and He digs about us ; we turn, and He turns first—Repentance—
Need for thoroughness—The lost son rises from physical distress
to penitence—How the Lord takes the will for the deed—So must
we—The wrong kind of repentance—The Pharisee's self-entangled
prayer—What different men see in themselves—Zacchaeus—The
dying thief—The people's belated remorse—Hearing and taking
in : the distinction illustrated. Luke and the Pauline vocabulary :

'justify,' 'believe,' and 'salvation'; 'peace' also a favourite
word. From Jesus the Healer to Jesus the Mediator. Doctrine
of the Spirit in Luke—Never uses the phrase 'the Spirit of God'
—The Holy Spirit—Jesus Himself takes the place of 'the Holy
Spirit' as the Gospel proceeds. The Passion central—The cloud at
the Transfiguration. Before the Cross He is the 'Chosen,' afterwards the 'Appointed.' The way to the Cross—Its milestones—The
shadow of Jerusalem over the travel-narrative—The word 'accomplish,' 'visit'—The thrusting forward of the cry over Jerusalem—
Luke looks first forward, then backward to the Passion—Eschatology and history—Luke tends to interpret prophecies as referring
to historical events—God and Satan—The Second Coming in Luke—
A quotation from a lost wisdom-book—'This,' not some future
catastrophe, the crisis of history—The Session at God's right hand
dates from the Passion—Pentecost and the Second Coming.

(pp. 180–195.)

CHAPTER VI

THE GOSPEL OF CATHOLIC HOPE

Prejudices of Luke—Dislike of crowds—Pharisees from the crowd
—The people and the crowds—Jesus and the crowd. His sympathy
with (1) old-fashioned Jewish people—Influence of the Old Testament—Jewish technical terms. (2) Gentiles—In the framework
of world-history—The pedigree of the Saviour—Roman soldiers and
John—'Launch out into the deep.' (3) Pharisees—Their overtures
to Jesus—The Sabbath question. (4) Samaritans—The seventy—
Reprisal for Samaritan inhospitality—Breaking with ceremonial
law as to clean and unclean foods—Matthew has 'Come,' Luke 'Go'
—Luke's omissions—The grateful and the Good Samaritans—The
universal meaning of the story of the prodigal and of Dives and
Lazarus—The Book of Jonah and its influence upon Jesus—'These
stones'—'Redemption' and 'ransom'—'Father, forgive them'—
Luke's universalism really universal—Hope of Israel and full tide
of the Gentiles—'Hypocrisy' in the wider sense of the word had
been the despair of Jesus, came to be the foundation of His hope—
How Paul appropriated it to his own case. In all three Gospels the
'Kingdom' figures less, the 'Son of Man' *more*, prominently as the
story goes on—The adventure of Jesus—That He was 'classed
with lawless men' means that hope has been carried even to the
outer darkness by the visitation of the Son of God—What Jesus
dreaded in death He has told us in the story of Dives and Lazarus—
Has 'Father Abraham' the last word?—'If One go to them from

the dead '—Jesus holds two worlds together when He prays ' Yet
not My will, but Thine, be done '—His consecration to the fellowship of lost souls and His consequent victory—The sinner may be
forgiven, and yet the memory of sin live on. Does the Lord
Himself figure in the parables of the travel-narrative?—Not
mentioned, but everywhere suggested—Key-notes of the Third
and of the First Gospels. (pp. 196–211.)

I

THE TEACHING OF JESUS AND ITS METHOD

IN J. F. Clarke's *Legend of Thomas Didymus*—a fascinating reconstruction of the life of Jesus—the sentence occurs (p. 312), 'But to Him every question was like a globe, having an infinite number of sides, and He saw them all.' Whenever we try to penetrate below the surface of the Master's teaching, we come upon a system of opposite though not opposed paradoxes. To take a general instance to start with, the Sermon on the Mount lays great emphasis upon the importance of motive. To wish to hurt is morally as questionable as actual murder, the lustful look equivalent to adultery. Yet we are to know the tree by its fruits, and the whole discourse finds its climax in *doing* : ' He that heareth My words, and doeth them.'[1] You will not do unless you want to do ; but it is not enough to *want* to do good. Bad motives which shrink from action are no better for that reason ; indeed, they are positive sins. But good motives which are not carried into deed—'thoughts hardly to be packed into a narrow act '—are not positive virtues ; they must find their way into practice, or die, for virtuous aspiration is a less hardy plant than evil desire.

Again : ' What shall it profit a man if he gain the whole world, and lose himself ? Or what shall a man give in exchange for himself ? ' Yet ' he who is bent upon saving himself shall lose himself, and he who loses himself in love for Me shall find himself.' In this case we can see a little way round the ' globe.' A man's own self is the only thing which is altogether his own, nor is it worth his while to be ever so rich or successful if to gain the treasure

[1] Matt. vii. 24.

or the plaudits of the world he must cease in any measure
to be himself. At the same time, the way to be truly
himself is not to be specially concerned about his own
faculties or appropriate sphere at all ; he will never be his
own master until he has learnt to forget himself in some
high service of love. The dignity of the man who never
thinks about his dignity, the utter disregard of his health
shown by the perfectly healthy man, the self-discovery
which follows self-forgetting, when a man falls in love or a
woman has borne a child, above all the Saviour's own
passing through a voluntary loss of peace to a peace
unassailable for ever, are all examples of this greatest of
all truths. Yet the truth remains a paradox, or rather
is to be found in the drawing together of two paradoxes,
which at first sight seem to be far apart or even contra-
dictory, but as we follow them up can be seen to bend
together, till they meet in Him who is the Truth. Here
is another ' pair ' : ' He that is not with Me is against
Me,'[1] and ' He that is not against us is on our side.'[2]
Our attention is at once drawn to the difference between
' Me ' and ' us ' ; but it is clear that while both sayings
agree in declaring the non-existence of moral neutrality,
the one contains a law of self-judgement, the other the
principle of toleration.

But wherever one dips into the teaching of Jesus as
embodied in the Gospels, the same two-sidedness leaps
to the eye. ' To him that hath shall be given '[3] ;
' Every one to whom much hath been given, from him
shall much be sought in return '[4]—privilege and responsibility go together, each giving birth to the other. ' Why
call ye Me Lord, Lord, and do not the things that I say ? '[5] ;
and yet ' By thy *words* thou shalt be justified, and by
thy *words* thou shalt be condemned.'[6] ' Every plant
which My Father hath not planted shall be rooted
up '[7] ; ' Let both grow together till the harvest.'[8] Of
course, we have in this case an implied harmony in
the words ' to the harvest,' but there is a difference
in outlook. The Kingdom is present already, and yet is
still to come ; it spreads like the leaven, grows outwardly

---

[1] Luke xi. 23 ; Matt. xii. 30.   [2] Luke ix. 50 ; Mark ix. 40.
[3] Matt. xiii. 12 ; xxv. 29 ; Mark iv. 25 ; Luke viii. 18; xix. 26.
[4] Luke xii. 48.   [5] Luke vi. 46.   [6] Matt. xii. 37.
[7] Matt. xv. 13.   [8] Matt. xiii. 30.

like the mustard-tree. Jesus Himself makes only a light demand upon those who come to Him,[1] yet He calls His followers to cross-bearing, to toil, shame, and death, to a temporary parting from all other desirable things, to a final loss of nothing good.[2] He is a Suitor, gentle and pleasant, but His beloved does not know where He will take her, and at first, it may be, is not sure whether she can trust this tremendous Lover ; once the walk is begun she finds all toils easy, all journeys homeward-bound, if only she loves enough.

So far we have been dealing with cases of what we may call antithetical or antiphonal paradox, the solution of which follows hard upon their statement. Did the mind of the Master work in this way ? Many discrepancies between the Gospels lose any difficulty they may present when due weight is given to the many-sidedness of His teaching. One or two more examples may be given before we proceed to our examination of the parables from this point of view. ' Seek, and ye shall find ' ; but there is a time coming when ' many shall seek to enter in, and shall not be able.'[3] ' Knock, and it shall be opened unto you ' ; but some day men shall stand outside and knock at the door—in vain.[4] The door is always open, yet not wide open[5] ; it is hard to enter for all, and may become impossible for some. The coming of the consummation is as certain as the approach of summer, will be as clear as the process of the seasons or the growth of the green blade for those who have eyes to see[6] ; yet it will come upon men before they know it, like ' a thief in the night '—it draws near gradually, and swoops down at last.[7] ' Give to every one that asketh thee,' but ' give *not* the holy thing '—the signet-ring (see Part iii., ch. ii.) 'to the dogs ' ; ' From him that would borrow from thee turn thou not away,' but there are some things that a man can neither lend nor borrow : ' Give us of your oil, for our lamps are going out—not so, lest there should not be enough for us and for you.'[8] Love for the Bridegroom cannot be passed on from one to another, or borrowed ready-made at a moment's notice !

---

[1] Matt. xi. 30.   [2] Mark x. 30. [[3] Luke xi. 9 ; xiii. 24.
[4] Luke xi. 9 ; xiii. 25.   [5] Matt. vii. 13.   [6] Mark xiii. 28 ; iv. 28.
[7] Mark xiii. 36 ; Matt. xxiv. 43.   [8] Matt. v. 42 ; vii. 6 ; xxv. 9.

When we call in what are known as the 'unwritten sayings' of Jesus—sayings, that is, which are not found in the Gospels, but are attributed to Him in the writings of the Fathers and elsewhere—we find that they very often fit in with some such scheme as this. 'Every word that a man shall not speak, he shall give an account thereof in the day of judgement'—a saying reported in the Palestinian Syriac version of the Gospels—obviously answers to 'Every idle word that a man shall speak'[1]; compare also 'Good must needs come'—ascribed to Jesus in the *Clementine Homilies*—with 'It must needs be that offences come' (Luke xvii. 1, &c.). Another saying found in Ephrem's *Commentary upon the Diatessaron*, Tatian's *Harmony of the Four Gospels* (see App. III.)—' He who does not preach commits a sin '; in a fragment of Irenaeus's *Letter to Victor*, ' When a man is able to do good, and doeth it not, he is alien from the love of God '; as well as in Justin Martyr (*Dialogue with Trypho*, 73), and underlying Jas. iv. 17 and 1 Cor. ix. 16,—provides a perfect balance to ' Give not the holy thing to the dogs.'

In one or two places in Patristic literature 'Be ye angry, and sin not,' &c.,[2] is quoted as a saying of Jesus, and it pairs off with Matt. v. 22, ' Whoever is angry with his brother.' ' Where two or three are gathered together in My name, there am I in the midst of them ' is found in Matt. xviii. 20 ; compare the saying found in the famous Oxyrhynchus papyrus, and restored by Blass as follows : ' Wherever there are two, they are not without God, and where one is alone, I say, I am with him '—so making the requisite two. Perhaps the most natural and satisfying explanation of the words which follow the sentence just quoted, ' Raise the stone, and you shall find Me ; cleave the wood, and there am I,' can be found in the suggestion that Jesus is here pronouncing His blessing on the lonely missionary, church-builder, and pathfinder, parted by the very conditions of his pioneer work from Christian fellowship. In any case it provides us with the counterpart of Matt. xviii. 19, 20. Another ' unwritten saying,' this time to be found in Acts xx. 35, ' It is more blessed to give than to receive,' affords us a bridge from ' Ask, and it shall be given you, . . . for every

[1] Matt. xii. 36.   [2] Eph iv. 26 f.

one that asketh receiveth ' to ' Give, and it shall be given you ; good measure, pressed down, shaken together, and running over, shall they give.'[1]   Here again is another pair :   God gives for asking ; God and men alike give to the man who is willing himself to give.

Going back to the material supplied by the Gospels, we can trace two sayings about salt, and two about light, perhaps indeed two pairs.   Salt is used for two purposes, for preserving and for seasoning.   An illustration taken from its preserving qualities is found in Matt. v. 13, while the other member of the pair is extant in Mark ix. 50 (cf. Luke xiv. 34) : ' Have salt in yourselves, and be at peace with one another ' (the reading of ix. 49 is discussed in Part i., p. 33) ; ' The wisdom that cometh from above is first pure, then peaceable.'[2]   ' Salt ' in this connexion answers, it would seem, to that saving common sense, that ' clubbable ' quality, which keeps men and institutions together.   Two of the companion sayings about ' light ' may be found together in Luke xi. 33 ff.   The first gives us the effect of the Christian's radiant spirit upon visitors— ' those who come in from the road ' ; the second upon his own home circle (v. 36).   Luke ix. 26 and xvii. 22 also balance one another.   The one tells us that some *shall* see ; the other that others, no matter how much they long to do so, *shall not* see, the coming of the Kingdom, for ' spiritual things are discerned by spiritual people.'   We are to let our ' light shine before men, *that they may see* ' our ' good deeds '[3] ; on the other hand, we are not to do our ' righteousness *to be seen* of men.'[4]   Our Father is in heaven, but He is also ' in secret.'[5]

The same kind of explanation may account for the difference between Matt. vii. 22 f. and Luke xiii. 26, for Matt. has, ' Have we not prophesied in Thy name ? ' ; Luke, ' Have we not eaten and drunk in Thy presence ? ' ' However much you think you have done for Me,' says Jesus in the First Gospel, ' However much I have done for you,' He declares in the Third, ' your salvation is not *ipso facto* guaranteed.'   Mark xi. 25 implies, ' Where two of you are disagreed, nothing good is *possible* ' ;   Matt. xviii. 19 asserts that where

---

[1] Luke xi. 9 ; vi. 38.   [2] Jas. iii. 17.   [3] Matt. v. 16.
[4] Matt. vi. 1.   [5] Matt. vi. 6, 9.

'two of you are agreed, nothing good is *impossible*.' Matt. xviii. 21, 22 corresponds to Luke xvii. 4, the one saying dealing with the case of the constant offender; the other with that of that even more trying person, the man who is for ever apologizing, only to offend again.   Luke vi. 37 (Matt. vii. 1), '*Judge not*,' may be set over against Luke xii. 57, '*Why do you not* of yourselves *judge* what is right?'; compare '*Judge not* according to appearance, *but judge* righteous judgement'[1]—another bridge!   Matt. ix. 16, 17, taken with Luke v. 38, 39, provides us with an interesting case.   The last sentence in Luke looks like a putting of the other side in the great argument, for Jesus is radical and conservative in one.   In Matt. x. 25 we have a more difficult instance, for Luke vi. 40 is something like it, and yet strangely different.   The words in question are —in Matthew, 'It is enough for the disciple to be as his Teacher, and the slave as his Lord'; in Luke, 'Everyone who is perfected shall be as his Teacher.'   Both sentences are introduced by the words, 'The disciple is not above his Teacher,' while Matthew has also 'nor the slave above his Lord.'   The best explanation seems to be that these are not identical, but companion, sayings. The meaning in the First Gospel is, 'You are not to be over-ambitious, or think either in the range of your influence or the manner of your reception to surpass your teacher'; whereas in the Third Gospel the maxim becomes positive, 'Let your ambition be, when your training is complete, to become as your teacher.'   Matthew emphasises the gentler, Luke the more energetic, aspects of the Christian character; each is true to type, and both strains must have been present in Jesus.   In the Fourth Gospel the thought is carried a stage further: 'Greater works than these shall ye do, because I go to My Father.'[2]

A surprising difference between Matthew and Luke is to be found in Matt. xvii. 21, Luke xvii. 6.   I cannot bring myself to believe that these are not separate sayings; at any rate, two distinct traditions would seem to be involved.   The 'fig-tree'—it is almost certainly a fig-tree, not a black mulberry—might be taken to mean Jerusalem, which was proving itself so great an obstacle to the coming of the Kingdom; compare what is said below of the

[1] John vii. 24.   [2] John xiv. 12.

cursing of the fig-tree (p. 130). One (Matthew) might be thought of as referring to a natural obstacle ; the other (Luke), to a positive cause of mischief. In one case at least Matthew and the Epistle of James—the latter is no ' Epistle of straw,' as Luther labelled it ; it is our best authority for the teaching of Jesus outside the Gospels— give us a very suggestive pair.[1] According to Matthew's version, if we wish to say ' Yes ' or ' No ' emphatically we must be content with a repetition of the simple ' Yes ' or ' No ' ; according to the Epistle, when we say ' Yes ' we are to mean ' Yes '—we must learn to say ' Yes ' and ' No' unreservedly, and have done with it ; when we begin to explain that our affirmation or denial is to be inter- preted in such and such a way, we are in for trouble (compare Paul's reference to some such saying in 2 Cor. i. 18). The Matthaean saying is directed against un- wholesome over-emphasis, the ' correlative ' in James against diplomatic reservations and evasions.

The principle enunciated above—to the effect that Matthew tends to report sayings which illustrate the gentler aspects of Christian character, while Luke is attracted by its more forcible and striving elements— will perhaps help us in the exposition of a much more difficult and elusive discrepancy—that, namely, between Matthew and Luke at Matt. xi. 12, Luke xvi. 16. The First Gospel has, ' From the days of John the Baptist until now the kingdom of heaven has been suffering vio- lence, and violent men have been carrying it by storm. For all the prophets '—the prophets come first as in Matt. xxiii. 34—' and the law prophesied up to John ' ; the Third Gospel, ' The law and the prophets found their climax in John : from that time forward the kingdom of God is preached (as good news), and every one gets into it by violence.' In this case the saying reported by Matthew appears to imply that the days of violence ended with John the Baptist (' until now ') ; in other words, violent methods are repudiated, as being out of date. This meaning is clearly in keeping with the whole argument of the section, which deals with the contrast between John and Jesus. Luke's version is more obscure ; it seems to mean, " You will have to use violence '—

[1] Matt. v. 33 ff. ; Jas. v. 12.

upon yourself presumably—' if you are to get into the Kingdom.' Putting the two together, we interpret thus : ' You must not use violence upon others, but you will have to put pressure upon yourselves, if you are to enter the Kingdom.' John carried his converts by storm ; Jesus used gentler means, but this does not mean that mere softness and good-nature are the order of the day under the new dispensation, for Jesus employs what is really the more forceful method of evangelism : (He induces men to put pressure upon themselves.)

The case is clearer in two other passages, occurring, in Matthew and Luke respectively, in the garden scene. In Luke xxii. 35 ff. Jesus recommends His followers to buy swords at any cost, and in v. 50 we find that they have taken Him at His word, and are anxious for the fighting to begin. In Matt. xxvi. 52, on the other hand, we have a decided repudiation of the use of the sword : ' All who take the sword shall perish by the sword.' Reconciliation here is not difficult ; Matthew reports a general maxim, which is profoundly true, though it does not of necessity mean that the sword is never to be used, for it may be right sometimes to risk destruction in defence of the truth. In this context its application is obvious : to try to defend Jesus by force would be useless, for it would only involve the disciples in His fate, a consummation which the Master was determined to avoid. On the other hand, they might, if they stayed with Him much longer, have to defend *themselves* ; in any case they must be ready for a day or two to rely upon their own resources. It is plain that Jesus saw both sides of the ' force ' question. He came, He had said, to ' cast,' not ' peace,' but a ' sword '[1] (Luke xii. 51 explains as ' division ') ' upon the earth ' ; yet it was not in vain that the angels had sung of ' peace on earth ' at His first coming. For a somewhat similar variation compare Matt. vii. 21 ff., Luke xiii. 24 ff. (see p. 119).

Luke xii. 8 ff. gives us an example of a different process, for the two correlatives are here placed side by side. The passage is as follows : ' But I say unto you, Every one who confesses Me before men, the Son of Man also shall confess him before the angels of God ;

[1] Matt. x. 34.

but he that denieth Me before men shall be denied before the angels of God. And every one who shall say a word against the Son of Man, it shall be forgiven him ; but to him who has blasphemed against the Holy Spirit it shall not be forgiven.' Luke has here an altogether satisfactory collocation, for the second saying is plainly a modification of the first. There is an opposition between the negative idea of ' denying ' and the positive ' speaking against.' The Son of Man is the eternal Judge—our attitude to Him decides our destiny ; not necessarily, however, our attitude towards any particular phase of His earthly ministry—in this case genuine misunderstanding is possible—rather our attitude towards the spirit which obviously animated Him. The same idea colours the Johannine saying, ' If not, believe Me for the mere works' sake.'[1]

A curious group of sayings is found in Matt. xii. 6, 40, 41, 42 (cf. John ii. 19). There were, it may be suggested, in the original tradition two pairs of sayings, one dealing with Jonah and Solomon, the other with the Temple. The members of the first pair may be found in Matt. xii. 41, 42 ; those of the second in Matt. xii. 6, John ii. 19. In a later chapter evidence is offered in support of the conclusion that Matt. xii. 40 does not belong to the authentic text of the First Gospel. The process by which the tradition became confused is not hard to make out. The first member of the first pair (Matt. xii. 41) ended with the words ' a greater than Jonah is here,' while one of the members of the second pair (Matt. xii. 6) ended with the words ' a greater than the Temple is here.' In the other member of the second pair the phrase ' three days ' occurred (John ii. 19). ' Jonah ' was already associated with the same group of sayings, and Jonah at once suggests the prophet's imprisonment in the fish for ' *three days* and three nights ' ; so the gloss (Matt. xii. 40) has arisen, and has perhaps taken the place of the authentic saying found in John ii. 19, and alluded to in Mark xiv. 58, Matt. xxvi. 60, 61—possibly also in 2 Cor. v. 1. It is noteworthy that the First Gospel does not say in so many words that there was nothing in the report of the two ' false witnesses,' and that both Matthew and Mark imply that Jesus did not deny the imputation ; while John says, in effect, ' Yes, He did say it, but you did not know what He meant.'

The differences in point of view between Luke xi. 21, Matt. xii 29, and Mark iii. 27 are at least suggestive. I doubt whether Luke, with his historical conscience, would of his own motion add such phrases as ' fully armed,' ' equipment,' ' in which he had trusted,'

[1] John xiv. 11.

K

or the characteristically socialistic clause 'distribute his spoils.'
In Matthew and Mark the interest is all with the Invader of
the strong man's house ; in Luke the saying has almost become
a parable dealing with false confidence in material treasure.
Matt. xi. 28, 30, taken along with viii. 20 (Luke ix. 58), supplies a
striking paradox—the homeless Homegiver ; and in Matt. xi. 11,
v. 19 we have two complementary sayings about 'the least in the
Kingdom.' In Luke viii. 21, xi. 28, there are, again, two sayings
concerned with those who hear and keep (or do) the word of God.
Luke xi. 28 suggests that we need not desire earthly kinship with
Jesus (cf. 2 Cor. v. 16), but must be content with simple obedience ;
Luke viii. 21 that, if we are obedient, we are, as a matter of fact,
spiritually akin to Him. We do not claim the honour, but He
gives it to us, without our asking. For the same kind of difference
see below on Luke xvii. 7 ff., xii. 37. Another pair of sayings upon
the subject of purity may be found in Luke xi. 40, Mark vii. 19
(R.V.). The one tells us what purity does, the other what it does not,
consist in. Sometimes the second member of a pair is a revised
and improved version of the first. Like all good preachers, Jesus
often repeated Himself ; but, like all good preachers, He never
merely repeated Himself. Matt. x. 29, taken along with Luke xii.
6, Matt. x. 35 f. along with Luke xii. 52 f., are examples of this
process ; but, as I have dealt with these cases in a later chapter,
I will pass at once to the parables.

For it is precisely in the parables that this principle
finds its most striking illustrations. A very instructive
case may be discovered in Matt. xiii. 44, 45. These parables,
which are obviously a pair, are treated by Trench and other
commentators as merely parallel. I cannot imagine what
is gained by seeking thus to reduce our Lord's meaning
to its lowest terms. Why should one parable convey
only one truth ? Is it likely that two parables should
mean exactly the same thing ? We are warned, in the
common Synoptic tradition [1] (this again is balanced
by Matt. xiii. 35—the parables veil, but they also unveil
the truth), that the parables were not intended to be easily
assimilated by the average intellectual digestion ; that,
indeed, they were framed to rouse protest and, through
protest, further inquiry. Surely it is merely stupid, in
the interests of a barren simplicity, to chain the reader

[1] Mark iv. 11 f. ; Matt. xiii. 13 ff. ; Luke viii. 10 ; cf. 2 Cor. iv. 3.

down to one point. These great pictures were meant for all time, for men in all stages of critical culture and of all degrees of mental curiosity ; we should use the microscope in our study of them as we do with the marvels of Nature. In this case it is not fanciful to see in the second of these twin-parables that the whole conception is turned round. In the first of the two the kingdom is the object found ; in the second it is the Finder. In the first the Kingdom is the supreme discovery of life ; to make it his own, every man in his turn has to forgo possession of everything else. In the second, according to a conception equally typical of the First Gospel, the King is Himself the Kingdom ; the ' pearl of great price ' is the man whom He finds ; to make him His own, He has, in His Incarnation, already given up all that He had. On the contrast, see an article by Dr. G. G. Findlay in the *Expositor* (7th series, vol. v., p. 158). A somewhat similar instance is discoverable in the Third Gospel, in which we find at xii. 37 what is virtually a parable depicting faithful Christians as slaves upon whom their Master waits ; but at xvii. 7 ff. Jesus speaks as though it were unthinkable that the Master should wait upon His slave, no matter how hard his work has been. In each of these ' pairs ' one ' parable ' gives us our Lord's feeling about us ; the other, the attitude due from us to Him. Luke xii. 37 is exquisitely illustrated by the ' foot-washing ' in John xiii.

Sometimes the First Gospel gives us one member of a pair, the Third the other. In Matt. xxii. 1 ff. we have the parable of the Prince's wedding ; in Luke xiv. 16 ff. the story of the man who made a great feast. In each case formal invitations are sent out beforehand ; in each case the guests who have accepted the first invitation excuse themselves at the last moment. But the chief point in the Lucan story is to be found in the kind of guests who came in, whereas the climax of the parable in Matthew comes when one of them is cast out. Later on I shall suggest that the parable as reported by Matthew was really addressed to the disciples. My own conviction is that in the First Gospel the twin-parables have run together. There were two stories current, both originally told by Jesus, one dealing with a rich man's

supper, the other with a Prince's wedding. Matt. xxii.
4, 5, 8–10 comes from the first (it is parallel to Luke xiv.
16–24), but Matt. xxii. 6, 7, 11–14 are fragments of the
other, addressed to the disciples. The evangelist did not
know that there were two distinct stories, and so has
made the whole bear upon the royal marriage. A very
curious case of difference may be observed in the parable
of the ' talents ' (Matt. xxv. 14 ff.) as compared with that
of the ' pounds ' (Luke xix. 11 ff.). The latter is complicated by certain topical references, of which some account
is given later, but one or two clearly marked differences stand out when Luke's introductory matter is left
on one side. In the story of the ' talents ' the slaves
start with *unequal* chances, but those who are successful
end with an *equal* reward (Matt. xxv. 21, 23) ; in that of
the ' pounds ' the slaves are given *equal* opportunities,
and obtain a reward *strictly according to relative merit*.
The Lucan parable is admirably socialistic in outline,
whereas the First Gospel here as elsewhere (see especially
the parable found in Matt. xx. 1 ff.) illustrates an idea
upon which I shall dwell with relish later on, to the effect
that, in view of the inequalities of life as it is, the fairest
thing would be for all faithful people to come out in the
long run pretty much on a level. The introductory words
in Luke xix. 11 do not seem to fit the parable as a whole ;
I am inclined to think that this is another case of mixture,
Luke being responsible this time. Some reason will be
given in the sequel (pp. 207, 208) for associating vv. 12, 14, 27
with the story of the ' lost ' son.[1] If we can separate the
two seams of parabolic material in Luke xix. 11 ff., we can
trace two stories about slaves left in charge of his revenues
by their master, together with a fragment dealing with a
nobleman who went into a ' far country' (cf. Luke xv. 13)
to claim his kingdom. The true complement to the story
of Matt. xx. 1 ff. is perhaps to be found in that of the unfaithful husbandmen,[2] just as there are parables of an
unrighteous steward,[3] and of a faithful steward.[4] The
' vineyard,' it should be said, stands for Palestine, the
' harvest '[5] for the world.

---

[1] Luke xv. 11 ff.
[2] Mark xii. 1 ff. ; Luke xx. 9 ff. ; Matt xxi. 33 ff.[7]   [3] Luke xvi. 1 ff.
[4] Luke xii. 42.   [5] Matt. ix 37 ; Luke x. 2 (cf. John iv. 35)

In Matt. xxv. 1 ff. we have the parable of the 'ten virgins'; in Luke xii. 36 there are clear traces of its counterpart. In the one case the virgins are waiting outside for the time to go in to the Bridegroom's presence; in the other, as in Rev. iii. 20, the Bridegroom is outside and Himself knocks for admission. In the Third Gospel we find a study of the rich man's relation to God and his own soul in the story of the rich fool; his relation to his poor brother is set forth in that of 'Dives' and Lazarus. Both pictures are seen in the light of the future life. In Matt. xxi. 28 ff. there is a parable of two sons told from the point of view of their obedience or otherwise to their father's service; in Luke xv. 11 ff. we hear of two sons and their love or lack of love to the old home. In each case the younger, though seemingly less loyal, is vindicated at the expense of his elder brother. But in one case the elder son is polite, but disobedient; in the other he is obedient, but distinctly ungracious. In Mark iv. 26 ff. the good seed grows secretly while the farmer sleeps; in Matt. xiii. 24 ff. the weeds grow secretly while the farmer sleeps: in the parable of the 'Sower' the growth to the harvest is looked at from the side of the soil; in John xii. 24 from that of the Seed. In one case Jesus is the Sower, in the other the Seed, just as in the Fourth Gospel He is by turns the Good Shepherd and the Door of the sheep,[1] in Luke xiii. 7, 8 the Vine-dresser, in John xv. 1 ff. the Vine. Matt. xviii. 23 ff. gives us a parable of two debtors; while in Luke vii. 40 ff. the same theme occurs in a different setting. One bears upon the relative importance of our great debt to our Lord and our little debts to one another; the other on our relation as great or little debtors to our Lord. The parables of the leaven and the mustard-seed are obviously 'twins,' as are those of the lost sheep and the lost coin. It was perhaps habitual with Jesus to appeal to the women as well as the men in His audiences; compare the mustard-seed and the leaven, and what is said below of Luke xvii. 34, 35 (p. 173).

Perhaps Luke is right in giving us the parables of the unjust judge and the Pharisee and the publican together, for the one is concerned with the right, the other with the wrong, kind of shamelessness in prayer. Another possible

[1] John x. 7, 11.

suggestion comes from the word 'adversary,' which is found also in Matt. v. 25, Luke xii. 58. Where our grievance is trivial, we are to settle the matter as soon as may be ; where it is serious, we do well to leave it in the hands of God. One interpretation does not, of course, exclude the other, for the parables of Jesus put out shoots in all directions—'The trees of the Lord are full of sap.' There is one more link between the story of the unjust judge and another of the parables—that of the friend who came at midnight. Both alike furnish examples of persistent prayer. But in one we are concerned with prayer simply for ourselves ; in the other with prayer animated by a desire to help a friend ('A friend has come from a journey'). This last story can be set in very effective contrast to that of the Good Samaritan. One describes a neighbour who was not very neighbourly ; the other, one who was very neighbourly, but was not a neighbour.

In one case at least one member of a 'pair' has come down to us as a miracle, or parabolic miracle. The sparing of the fig-tree in Luke xiii. 6 ff. appears to correspond to the cursing of the fig-tree in Mark xi. 14, 20, Matt. xxi. 19 ff. When the 'fig-tree' was described as likely to be spared, Jesus had not lost hope for the Holy City, for which the 'fig-tree in the vineyard' stands. A little later He has come to see that, though Jerusalem would exist a little longer, she was yet doomed to barrenness, and His tragic despair expresses itself in the cursing of the fig-tree, after the failure of His last appeal at the Triumphal Entry. Later on still, after the agony in the garden, He breaks through to hope again, and prays, 'Father, forgive them.' Schweitzer thinks that the 'fig-tree' was threatened with barrenness in eternity, and compares an extraordinary saying, based upon materials taken from the Book of Enoch, and attributed to the Lord Himself by Irenaeus, and also in a Coptic encomium upon John the Baptist (see App. II.) giving a luscious description of the miraculous fruitfulness of corn-field and fruit-tree in the Kingdom. If this is a genuine saying of the Lord—and its attestation is fairly good—the parabolic miracle of Mark xi. 14 would be its counterpart (cf. Matt. xxvi. 29, ' *This* fruit of the vine ').

A more difficult instance is that of the Gerasene swine.

Matt. xii. 43 f., Luke xi. 25 f., give us a saying about the 'unclean spirit,' the last words of which are, 'The last state of that man becomes worse than the first.' In 2 Pet. ii. 20 we find practically the same words, and there follows what looks like a commentary upon this parable or something like it, while in v. 22 we have a reference to 'the true proverb' about a dog and a pig. The pig comes from *The Story of Ahikar*—rediscovered at Elephantine, and familiar to readers of Æsop and the supplementary *Arabian Nights*—certainly one of the books known to our Lord and His apostles (see App. I.). There a sow is taken to a luxurious bath, and afterwards proceeds to wallow in the nearest gutter, the reason presumably being that she is possessed by the unclean spirit associated by many Oriental peoples with swine and swine's flesh. Here—in the story of the demoniac—is a practical case. Jesus had said that the 'unclean spirit' when cast out of a man wanders through the world seeking a home. As there is a danger of his coming back again in greater force than ever (cf. Matt. xii. 45 and Mark ix. 25, 'Come out of him, *and enter no more into him*'), what more natural and seemly proceeding could there be than that he and his clan should be housed in the swine—according to popular belief, their native element? The evangelic values have already been dealt with in Part i. (chap. iii.). Meanwhile we have a cento of passages about pigs, which may be taken in the following order : Matt. vii. 6, 2 Pet. ii. 22, Luke xv. 16, Mark v. 13. The first means that some people behave like pigs, and should be dealt with warily ; the second that dirt sticks ; the third that, however much a man may look and act like a pig, he can never settle down to be one; the fourth that, when the Savour comes this way, the man becomes a man again, and the pig-spirit goes, no matter where, so long as it goes for ever. It is tempting to think that all four are connected, and that all come, directly or indirectly, from Jesus.

We may say, I think, with some confidence that Jesus loved to develop one theme from different points of view, to hang two pearls on the same thread. Confirmation is added to our theory when we notice that something of the same way of thinking is traceable in the Fourth Gospel too. Examples may be found in ' I judge no man : and,

if I judge,'[1] 'I do nothing of Myself,'[2] taken along with
'I lay down My life of Myself,'[3] 'If it were not so, I would
have told you that I am going to prepare a place for you :
and if I go and prepare a place for you.'[4] There are
several others. Our inference must be that the gospel
tradition is richer than has often been supposed, and
that it is scarcely ever right to reject either alternative
rendering of any of the Lord's sayings or parables. If
there had been one or two, or even half a dozen, cases of
such antiphonal paradoxes, we might have ascribed the
appearance of one in Matthew and the other in Luke to
accident or to the prejudices of the reporter. When the
same feature recurs so repeatedly that hardly a parable or
saying is left unpaired, we are driven to the conclusion
that these men are reproducing not merely the words of
Jesus, but something of the way in which their Master's
mind worked. Their peculiarities of temperament and
outlook have only made them the more eager to gather
together, the better able adequately to reproduce, that
particular aspect of the teaching and life of Jesus which
appealed most powerfully to them. In the four Gospels
we get not the lowest but the highest common measure of
four distinct personalities, each seeing part of the Truth
as it is in Him of whom they wrote, each focusing that
part all the more intensely because he could see no more.
Jesus Himself saw all sides of the truth together, and
with vividness more than equal to the sum of the particular
degrees of intensity with which His reporters caught their
share. To put the matter more simply, because He was
so passionate in all His universal thinking and feeling, He
could be rendered far more adequately by men who, in
their narrower circuit, thought and felt intensely, and,
as a consequence, had their own preferences and prejudices.
Four live men, who see one thing so clearly as sometimes to
fail to do justice to the others, are better fitted to give us
a complete picture of One who saw all things clearly than
would be any number of men who saw a good many things
not so clearly—at least, if the four look from a different
angle. It is in the providence of God that the four evangelists were real men, biased not only in favour of their

---

[1] John viii. 15, 16.   [2] John viii. 28.
[3] John x. 18.   [4] John xiv. 2, 3.

Subject, but of a particular view of their Subject, Himself the many-sided Truth. It is our task in these chapters to bring out what they saw ; and all will have been done in vain unless readers are led to feel that none of the three Gospels under immediate consideration is a mere bundle of ' sources.' Each of them is the work of a real man, a man whom we may know only less intimately than we know Him in whose favour they have, upon the whole, so completely suppressed themselves.

II

GENERAL PURPOSE OF THE WRITER OF THE THIRD GOSPEL

LITTLE doubt is left in the minds of most scholars in these days as to the identity of the writer of the Third Gospel. We know that Luke ' the beloved '—that is, in the language of the day, ' my own ' or ' my only '—' physician ' was a companion of Paul upon some of his journeys, and perhaps during his imprisonment at Rome.[1] The ' Acts of the Apostles ' and the Third Gospel profess to be the work of the same hand, and a careful comparison of the style and vocabulary of the two leads us almost inevitably to the conclusion that this was the case. In the Acts there are certain passages in which the word ' we ' takes the place of the conventional ' they ' in the narrative, and these passages bear the appearance of a diary of travels undertaken in Paul's company. They are evidently written by a doctor, for medical language abounds in all kinds of contexts. All that we need to do is to make these sections the basis of our study, and then carry through a comparison of their diction with that of the rest of the Acts and the Gospel. This has been done by Harnack most thoroughly, and his examination of the evidence lies at the disposal of English readers in *Luke the Physician*.[2] His verdict is that both books were written by a physician, and that he was that companion of Paul to whom we owe the ' we-sections.'

We are met upon the threshold of the Gospel by a sentence of faultless Greek prose—in striking contrast to the happy-go-lucky Greek of Mark—containing a dedication addressed to one ' Theophilus,' apparently an official

[1] Col. iv. 14 ; Philem. 24 ; 2 Tim. iv. 11.
[2] Crown Theological Library (Williams & Norgate).

of the Roman Government of some standing, for 'Most Excellent' is a complimentary title, appropriated by Roman officials of equestrian rank, and used of Felix and Festus in Acts xxiii. 26, xxvi. 25. It is not probable that 'Theophilus'—we cannot be sure that this was his real name—was as yet a Christian, though he had already received some information about the new religion, for Christians did not call one another 'Most Excellent' in those days, however distinguished the brother addressed might chance to be. Small reliance can be placed upon the statement of the *Clementine Recognitions*, to the effect that he was 'in a more exalted position than all the powerful people in Antioch,' or that he was a convert under Peter's preaching in that city ; still less to the later tradition that he was the third Bishop of Antioch. That Luke was himself an Antiochene is quite likely. Codex Bezae has in Acts xi. 28, ' And there was great rejoicing ; and when *we* were assembled,' &c. If this reading has any foundation, Luke is located at once at Antioch in Syria ; there are other signs that this was the case scattered here and there in early Christian literature.

In his preface the author tells us that he belonged to the second generation of Christians, but that he had enjoyed exceptional opportunities of getting at the facts which he intends to narrate. He had communicated both with eye-witnesses and their pupils ; ' ministers of the Word ' suggests at once Mark, for he is the ' minister ' of Barnabas and Saul in Acts xiii. 5. His claims appear to be well founded, for he had been at Jerusalem,[1] had stayed with Philip the deacon at Caesarea,[2] and may well have known Mary, the mother of Jesus. He does not profess to be the first to attempt a history of ' the things that have come to their fulfilment amongst us ' ; his, he modestly tells us, is but one of many accounts, whether oral or in writing, all purporting to give a continuous record of the life of Jesus. He had tested the narratives of his predecessors by the oral tradition of ' original ' disciples,[3] and had carried his studies back to the first beginnings ; this may be a hint that he intends to go further back than Mark had done, as he does in the Birth story, a feature of the Third Gospel conspicuous by its absence in Mark.

[1] Acts xxi. 17.   [2] Acts xxi. 8.   [3] Acts xxi. 16.

This Gospel is, then, the first Christian book directly addressed to the governing classes. It is noticeable that Luke is the only New Testament writer to mention a Roman emperor by name.[1]   He is seeking to write something like a scientific history for the benefit of educated people, and with his book the gospel makes its first appearance upon the stage of the great world. For instance, the relations between the families of John the Baptist and Jesus are described with some minuteness as accounting for the association of the two prophets afterwards, and the unusual character of John's birth prepares the way for the greater miracle of the birth of Jesus.   We are also told how it came about that Jesus was born at Bethlehem, and yet was called ' Jesus of Nazareth.'   Still, chronological order does not seem to have been a supreme consideration with Luke ; there is no specific mention of the date or the fact of John's imprisonment at the point when Jesus begins His work in Galilee.   But development in the broader sense of the word is strongly insisted upon.[2]   The history of John, which he has recorded so much more fully than Mark, is suddenly dropped at iii. 20, though he does figure once more in vii. 18 ff., in much the same way as, in the Acts, Peter disappears almost entirely soon after Paul comes upon the scene.   The knowledge of John's execution is assumed in ix. 7–9, but the fact is never related.   The visit to Nazareth appears to be pushed forward out of its place, for Jesus is already known to have worked miracles at Capernaum, and yet Capernaum has not yet been mentioned.[3]   Frequent instances of vagueness as to *place* may perhaps be accounted for when we bear in mind that Theophilus would not be much interested in local details. Luke's purpose is to show the governing classes that the empire had nothing to fear from Christianity ; in this particular he faithfully reflects the standpoint of his master Paul, who was often personally friendly with Roman officials,[4] and felt certain of a measure of justice when he appealed to the emperor.   He labours the fact that Pilate acquitted Jesus, as he loves to tell how imperial officers found nothing worthy of death in Paul.   In the trial scene before Pilate the charge of treason brought against Jesus

---

[1] Luke ii. 1 ; iii. 1 ; Acts xi. 28 ; xviii. 2.   [2] Luke ii. 40 ; ii. 52.
[3] Luke iv. 23 ; cf. v. 14.   [4] Acts xix. 31.

is made quite explicit,[1] and the governor's testimony to the
Lord's innocence is strongly emphasized.[2] Bar-rabbas,
on the other hand, was actually guilty of 'sedition and
murder.'[3] One of the 'transgressors' with whom 'He
was reckoned,'[4] it is further pointed out, in the hour of
death solemnly acquitted Him of any participation in
crime against civil law.[5] In the Acts also, Luke is careful
to show that the imperial government had nothing directly
to do with the persecution of the apostles. Stephen is the
victim of false witnesses,[6] and Herod puts James to death
and arrests Peter *to please the Jews*.[7] Paul appeals confidently to his Roman citizenship, and once makes the
local officials apologize for their treatment, while Felix
only prolongs the latter's imprisonment at Caesarea because
he was subservient to his Jewish wife and the Jews generally,
he himself being a notoriously corrupt official.[8]

In regard to Luke's relation to Mark, we have, in the first place,
a much fuller account of John's preaching inserted between Mark i.
6–7.[9] John seems to have been interesting to Luke for his own
sake, partly perhaps for a reason suggested below (see p. 159), partly
also because followers of the Baptist were active from Alexandria
to Antioch at the time when these books were written,[10] and ' Theophilus ' may well have been aware of their propaganda. But the
subordination of John to Jesus is made clear by the Baptist's
sudden departure from the stage when Jesus appears. After the
thrusting forward of the visit to Nazareth—to which we do not
come in Mark's Gospel till chapter vi.—Luke returns to the outline
provided by his predecessor in Luke iv. 31–44, stopping by the way
to give his own account of the call of Peter,[11] a story which he may
have obtained from the oral tradition to which he had access. It
is certainly curious that this narrative of Peter's call does not occur
in Mark. The fact that this section is very closely parallel to
John xxi. 1–14 has led many scholars to the conclusion that this
passage is out of place, our evangelist having confused the record
of the second call of Peter by the lake with that of his original appointment. They observe that the nature of the miracle is, with slight
variations, the same on both occasions, as the place of its performance
is the same ; and they lay stress upon the penitent cry of Peter,[12]

[1] Luke xxiii. 2.   [2] Luke xxiii. 13–16.   [3] Luke xxiii. 19–25.
[4] Luke xxii. 37.   [5] Luke xxiii. 41.   [6] Acts vi. 13.   [7] Acts xii. 2, 3.
[8] Acts xvi. 37, 38 ; xxiv. 26, 27.   [9] Luke iii. 7–14.
[10] Acts xviii. 25.   [11] Luke v. 1–11.   [12] Luke v. 8.

which, they urge, is much more easily intelligible after his fall than before it. On the other hand, the first commission is not the same as the second, for feeding and tending sheep and lambs is not the same thing as catching men alive; and while we must beware of a needless duplication of miracles—always an easy and therefore dangerous way out in apologetic—there is here a real development from the missionary call to that of the pastor, from Peter's outspoken and passing penitence to the self-control and humility of John xxi. 15–17. Omission in Mark's Gospel can possibly be accounted for by the tendency, everywhere observable in that Gospel, to call attention away from Peter's own performances. It is quite as easy and almost as dangerous, when two narratives look alike, to cancel one without further reflection, as it is for the apologist to fall back at every turn upon the convenient theory that it must have happened twice.

After this interruption the Marcan thread is carried on as far as Luke vi. 11,[1] when our author reverses the position of the call of the twelve and the beginning of the Lord's wider ministry.[2] Mark iv. 1–25 is substantially reproduced in Luke viii. 4–18, while viii. 19–21 picks up Mark iii. 31–35, and viii. 22–56 follows Mark iv. 35–v. 43. The parabolic teaching, however, found in Mark iv. 26–29, 33–34, is left on one side, and the material of Mark iv. 30–32 is not used till xiii. 18, 19. In ix. 1–9 Luke returns once again to Mark, and his predecessor is followed on the whole in ix. 10–17[3]; then he omits Mark vi. 45–viii. 26, except Mark viii. 11–13 and viii. 14–21, which are caught up in reverse order in Luke xi. 29–32 and xi. 53–xii. 1. He follows Mark viii. 27–ix. 8 in ix. 18–36, leaving out Mark ix. 9–13 as concerned with a question not interesting to ' Theophilus ' and Gentiles generally, and with fair closeness in ix. 37–50.[4] Mark ix. 42–48 reappears in abbreviated form in Luke xvii. 1, 2, but vv. 49, 50 are dropped, like Mark x. 1–12— again as only intelligible to a Jewish public. Not till Luke xviii. 15–34 does he resume the Marcan scheme,[5] while Luke xviii. 35–43 corresponds to Mark x. 46–52. The narrative of the last days of the ministry follows Mark very closely, though there are other elements to be reckoned with here. Luke omits the story of the cursing of the fig-tree,[6] as also Mark xiii. 21–23, 33–37, and xv. 16–20, and reverses the order of Mark xiv. 18–21,[7] and xiv. 22–25.[8]

---

[1] Mark iii. 6.
[2] Luke vi. 12–16 ; Mark iii. 13–19 ; Luke vi. 17–19 ; Mark iii. 7–12.
[3] Mark vi. 30–44.   [4] Mark ix. 14–41.
[5] Mark x. 13–34.   [6] Mark xi. 12–14, 20–22.
[7] Luke xxii. 21–23.   [8] Luke xxii. 15–20.

Scholars are agreed that at least one more document underlies this Gospel, containing either sayings of Jesus, or incidents which gave rise to them. Its original form would be that of the papyrus recently discovered at Oxyrhynchus in Egypt, which consists of a number of sentences purporting to come from the Master, each introduced by the words ' Jesus says ' (see Part iii.). Opinions differ as to whether Q—the sign, German in origin, used by scholars when referring to this lost document—was a Gospel in the full sense of the word, whether Mark made use of it, and whether Luke and the author of our First Gospel had access to it in the same form. Variations between Matthew and Luke are so considerable, even when they are running in parallel lines, that many scholars feel themselves compelled to think of Q as existing in two editions or of two Q's, just as they suppose Luke and Matthew to have seen separate editions of Mark, each of them different from the Gospel as we possess it. We shall be safe in assuming that Luke and Matthew did use a collection of the sayings of Jesus in one form or another.

Our evangelist's intimate account of the birth of Jesus may well have come from Mary herself, as also the story of His boyhood, and the detailed report of the visit to Nazareth.[1] The twice-repeated statement that ' Mary kept these sayings in her heart'[2] seems to imply, ' She kept them for me.' That some strongly Jewish source underlies chapters i. and ii. is evident from their Hebraic cast, remarkable in a book expressly meant for a Gentile, and from their suffusion with the language and the spirit of the Old Testament. The little circle of old-fashioned people who received the newborn Messiah supplied their Gentile friend with his information here. It is noticeable that at vii. 13, x. 1, xi. 39, xii. 42, xiii. 15, xvii. 5, 6, xviii. 6, xix. 8, xxii. 61, and perhaps in xxiv. 3, as in John iv. 1, Jesus is called ' the Lord ' in narrative. Mark xi. 3 is evidence that this was what the twelve called Jesus when talking to outsiders; may we take it that the use of the title in narrative is a sign that we are dealing in these passages with fragments of *oral* tradition ?

But perhaps the most interesting section of this

---

[1] Luke iv. 16–30.   [2] Luke ii. 19, 51.

Gospel is the great block of material, most of it
peculiar to Luke, which extends from ix. 51 to xviii. 14.
This has been called the 'Travel-document,' because
its contents are all crowded into the narrative of the
last journey to Jerusalem. The march from Galilee
begins very early, it will be observed, in Luke's Gospel ;
in Mark we do not hear of it till we come to x. 32.
According to the Third Gospel, on the other hand, it
must have been a leisurely journey, for into it is pressed
a wealth of material, which adds incalculably to our knowledge of Jesus, but can scarcely all have come in then.
This section contains the parables of the Good Samaritan,
the importunate friend, and the shrewish widow ; sayings
about many and few stripes, about the slave upon whom
his lord waits, the slave who would not dream of his
master waiting upon him ; references to the massacre
of Galilean pilgrims by Pilate, and the falling of the tower
of Siloam ; specimens of the table-talk of Jesus, and His
advice to guests and host ; parables of the rich fool, of
'Dives' and Lazarus, the lost coin, the lost son, the
unjust steward, the fig-tree spared another year, the
Pharisee and the publican ; the healing of the woman bent
double, of the man with the dropsy, and of the ten lepers,
with the return of one of them ; the refusal of Jesus to
decide the rival claims of two quarrelsome brothers, and
the warning given to Him by the Pharisees of the intentions of Herod, with His contemptuous reply ; the exclama-
tion of the sentimental woman[1] ; and the home scene with
Mary and Martha. In this section, too, we have our only
account of the sending of seventy disciples 'before His
face.' All these passages we owe to Luke, and it is possible
that his authority was ' Joanna, the wife of Chuza, Herod's
steward,'[2] who accompanied the Lord upon this journey.
Even where Matthew has parallel sayings or parables—for
instance, the Lord's Prayer and such passages as xi.
14 ff.[3], xi. 29 ff.[4], xi. 34 ff.[5], xi. 37 ff.[6], xii. 3–6[7], xii. 22 ff.[8], xii.
33 f.[9], xii. 35[10], xii. 42 ff.[11], xii. 51 ff.[12], xiii. 22 ff.[13], xiv. 16

---

[1] Luke xi. 27 f.   [2] Luke viii. 3.   [3] Matt. xii. 22–30 ; 43–45
[4] Matt. xii. 38–42.   [5] Matt. vi. 22, 23 (cf. v. 15).   [6] Matt. xxiii. 1–36.
[7] Matt. x. 26–33.   [8] Matt. vi. 25–33.   [9] Matt. vi. 20, 21.
[10] Matt. xxv. 1 ff.   [11] Matt. xxiv. 45 ff.   [12] Matt. x. 34–36.
[13] Matt. vii. 13, 14.

ff.[1], xiv. 25 ff.[2], xiv. 34[3], xv. 1 ff.[4], xvi. 13[5], xvi. 16[6], xvi. 17[7], xvi. 18[8], xvii. 2[9], xvii. 3, 4[10], xvii. 6[11], xvii. 21[12], xvii. 24[13], xvii. 31[14], xvii. 35[15], xvii. 37[16], xviii. 14[17]— they are all so differently placed and introduced in the two Gospels, often also so differently worded and motived, as to raise the question which has been discussed already— whether Luke and Matthew are really reporting identical sayings.

It has been observed above that one of the sources for this Lucan matter may be found in the little band of women, in whom our author would appear to have been greatly interested, who accompanied Jesus upon His last journey[18]. Luke has special information about Herod and his Court, and omits the story of Salome's dancing. Herodias's daughter, Salome, according to Josephus, was then a married woman ; and if the incident has any foundation in fact, it is probable that the popular tradition, as reported by Mark and Matthew, has mistaken ' girl,' meaning ' slave-girl,' for ' girl,' a colloquial expression for ' daughter.' Luke was evidently inclined to disbelieve the whole account; if he was acquainted with Joanna, his omission ought to lead us gravely to suspect a story which has always attracted morbid people. Other passages about Herod are, on the other hand, inserted only by Luke. Jesus, warned of the tyrant's intentions, called him a ' fox.' Herod himself did not, Luke informs us, think that Jesus was John the Baptist risen from the dead, as Mark[19] seems to suggest. Our Lord Himself was tried before Herod[20], who mocked Him, dressing Him up like a puppet-king, and as a result of their common difficulties with Galilean patriots and their uncomfortable Prisoner on that day, Herod and Pilate became fast friends. In these details Luke is probably right ; he should also be treated with respect when he refrains from speaking of the Herodians. They appear in Mark iii. 6, xii. 13 ; Matthew only mentions them on the second of these two occasions[21] ; Luke drops them out

---

[1] Matt. xxii. 1 ff. [2] Matt. x. 37, 38. [3] Matt. v. 13.
[4] Matt. xviii. 12–14. [5] Matt. vi. 24. [6] Matt. xi. 12, 13.
[7] Matt. v. 18. [8] Matt. v. 32 ; xix. 9. [9] Matt. xviii. 6, 7.
[10] Matt. xviii. 15. [11] Matt. xvii. 20 ; xxi. 21. [12] Matt xxiv. 23.
[13] Matt. xxiv. 26, 27. [14] Matt. xxiv. 17, 18. [15] Matt. xxiv. 40, 41.
[16] Matt. xxiv. 28. [17] Matt. xxiii. 12. [18] Luke viii. 2, 3.
[19] Mark vi. 16. [20] Luke xxiii. 8 ff. [21] Matt. xxii. 16.

L

altogether. Josephus speaks of 'partisans of Herod, but not of 'Herodians.' Probably Herod posed as a blasé spectator of the turmoils of Jewish politics, and left the task of dealing with revolutionaries to the Roman governor.

Another suggestion has been made by the Rev. J. A. Robertson (*Expositor*, March, 1919) ; the information about Herod and his Court underlying parts of the 'Travel-document' as well as its tendency to make as good a case as possible for the Pharisees, may come, he thinks, from Manaen (Acts xiii. 1) who was a member of the church at Antioch, and had been brought up along with Herod the tetrarch. He was the grand-nephew of an older Manaen, an Essene (that is, super-Pharisee), who resided at the Court of Herod the Great.

A more interesting question comes into view when we approach Luke's special contribution to our knowledge of the history of Passion Week. The late Dr. J. H. Moulton made the tentative suggestion some time ago that our evangelist owed to Paul much of his material in this section of his Gospel. He argued that Paul had seen Jesus in Jerusalem, and that one or two signs of his presence may be detected, even before the last week, in the Third Gospel. As one of his instances he quoted the phrase 'God forbid,' which occurs in Luke xx. 16, and is found nowhere else in the Gospels—a phrase habitual with Paul, and not specially characteristic of any other Jewish writer. If Paul was at that time a pupil of Gamaliel in Jerusalem, it is almost certain that he would have been there at Passover-time. It is also worthy of notice that Luke here introduces the word meaning 'look through,' upon which something has been said already (Part i., chap. iii.). The same word is used of the Lord's first glance at Peter[1], His searching look at Peter when that ardent loyalist had disowned Him,[2] and His interested survey of the young magistrate's face as he came up[3] to Him. We gather that the word is employed to express a kind of glance characteristic of Jesus when He is watching actual or possible disciples going through a crisis ; if Saul led the cry of shocked dissent on that day, what must have been the thoughts of Jesus as He looked into the angry face of the young man who was to be

[1] John i. 42.   [2] Luke xxii. 61.   [3] Mark x. 21.

His greatest apostle? To him the Lord was then a mere 'stone' of stumbling; one day Saul would fall over it, and would be 'broken,' to be moulded anew, and built into the framework of the Church, 'Jesus Christ being the chief Corner-stone.' Paul himself, using probably the Book of Testimonies (see Part iii., chap. ii.), becomes, in Rom. ix.–xi., the expounder of the very parable which, when it was first uttered, roused his furious resentment.

Luke's contributions to the actual story of the Cross consist of three sayings of Jesus: 'Father, forgive them, for they know not what they do '[1]; 'Verily I say to thee, To-day thou shalt be with Me in Paradise '—this is introduced by the story of the dying thief[2]—and 'Father, into Thy hands I commend My spirit.'[3] 'Father, forgive them' would, one thinks, most naturally be interpreted as referring to the (presumably) Gentile soldiers who nailed the Saviour to the cross; but all the patristic testimonies agree in applying it to the Jews, who really crucified Him. The apocryphal 'Gospel of Peter' actually makes them, with Herod, repudiate a share in Pilate's washing, and Dr. Rendel Harris founds a strong plea for the retention of Luke xxiii. 34—which Westcott and Hort reject for textual reasons—in the text of the Gospel, on the ground that its omission in important MSS. can be accounted for by the anti-Judaic prejudice brought to its highest pitch by the tendency, so manifest in Luke and Acts, to put all the blame for the murder of Jesus upon the Jewish people. If it does refer to the Jews, it must stand, for it could not have been inserted in a Gentile Gospel like this unless it had been really uttered; indeed, our instinctive desire to make it apply only to the Roman soldiers may well be a relic of the same unworthy prejudice—a prejudice little to the credit of a people who 'were not beautiful enough among the nations to have His mother born among us, and would have crucified Him in one year instead of three.' If the testimony to this most divine of the Lord's sayings came from Paul, we have at once a connexion with such passages as 1 Tim. i. 13, 'I did it in ignorance,' as well as with the hopeful tone of Rom. xi. 26 (cf. also Rom. x. 2, 'not according to knowledge'), and of the earliest Christian preaching (Acts iii. 17). It is still more tempting to

[1] Luke xxiii. 34.   [2] Luke xxiii. 40 ff.   [3] Luke xxiii. 46.

conjecture that the story of the 'penitent robber came from Paul, for does he not implicitly set himself alongside of this malefactor when he says, ' I have been crucified with Christ ' ?[1] He too had been swept from Calvary to Paradise.[2] The third saying, which gives us the self-committal of Jesus, is closely parallel with Acts vii. 59, except that what the ' Father ' is to Jesus, Jesus Himself is to Stephen. When we notice that the appeal for the pardon of his murderers was also repeated by Stephen,[3] and that Saul was present on this second occasion,[4] we see reason for suspecting that he was responsible for the clear emphasis upon this obvious parallel in his friend's Gospel. As to Luke's account of the Last Supper, it is established that the words of Institution have been transferred to the Gospel from 1 Cor. xi. 24, 25.

[1] Gal. ii. 20.
[3] Acts vii. 60.
[2] 2 Cor. xii. 4.
[4] Acts vii. 58.

III

LUKE THE PHYSICIAN : HIS POINT OF VIEW

OUR author is evidently the nearest approach to a man of
the world—the phrase is used without prejudice—amongst
the evangelists. The 'sea of Galilee' becomes merely the
'lake of Gennesaret' in his Gospel; nor is he so clear as to
local conditions as is Mark. In v. 19 the men who brought
their paralysed friend to Jesus let him down 'through
the tiles '—for an explanation of this see above (Part i.,
chap. ii.) ; Luke is thinking of a superior middle-class villa
in the Roman style, not of the Galilean cottage. He traces
the genealogy of Jesus back to God, and outside the Birth
story all references to purely Jewish questions tend to be
deleted. He softens harsh metaphors and laboriously
corrects Mark's vulgarisms; for instance, the phrase 'fishers
of men ' of Mark i. 17 becomes 'thou shalt be a catcher
of men alive,'[1] and the decorous word 'money' is substituted
for the colloquial 'brass' of Mark vi. 8 in Luke ix. 3.
He does not quite know what to call the 'stretcher' in
v. 18 ff. First it is a 'bed,' then a 'little bed 'or ' pallet,'
then—as if in despair—' the thing on which he was laid.'
Mark uses a more homely word, which we may translate,
if we will, ' mat '; it is used by Luke himself in Acts ix. 33,
but for some reason studiously avoided here. 'The thing
on which he was laid ' looks like a dictionary phrase, and
the most reasonable explanation of these variant translations is that Luke is seeking a more exact rendering of the
Aramaic word which Mark had translated 'mat'; or
perhaps our author has simply crossed out the objectionable
word 'mat' from the phrase 'the mat on which he was
laid.' He tries all the suggestions of his dictionary
in turn, without satisfying himself ; then, when the same
tiresome word turns up again in the (also possibly Marcan)

[1] Luke v. 10.

stories of Peter in Acts i.–xii., he relapses in despair
upon the homely ' mat.'   There are signs of something like
the same process in Luke xiv. 12, where there is no Marcan
basis.   ' When thou makest a breakfast or a supper,'
we read ; but there is no meal in the East corresponding to
our erstwhile substantial English breakfast, so that the word
here (as also the related verb in John xxi. 12, 15, and in the
Western text of Luke xv. 29—see below, p. 177) should
be rendered a ' banquet,' ' to have a dinner '—that is, any
meal to which invitations are issued.   In the next verse
a third alternative translation is introduced, ' When thou
makest a party.'¹   Here, then, are three Greek words for
the same idea once more.   It should be observed that this
instance does not decide whether Luke is using in this
part of his work a written document or a fragment of oral
tradition ; all it does tell us is that he is translating into
Greek from Aramaic.   The word which I have rendered
' party ' also occurs in Luke v. 29, where it is used of Levi
the publican's ' at-home.'   We must be careful not to
exaggerate Luke's Greek culture ; if he came from
Antioch, he would know something of Aramaic at first
hand, for North Syrian Aramaic was spoken in the country
districts round Antioch.   His preface may have been a
specially polished exercise in Greek prose composition ;
elsewhere he scarcely comes up to the standard, say, of
the Epistle to the Hebrews.   In v. 36, 37 he cobbles up
Mark's figure most laboriously, and in v. 39 takes care to
point out our Lord's sympathy with the connoisseur's point
of view.
    On the whole he is a careful scholar, according to the
measure of those days.   He catches accurately the real
cause of offence in vi. 1.   ' Rubbing ' the corn ' in their
hands ' was a transgression of Sabbath law, because it was
a kind of threshing ; if you were hungry, you could pluck
the ears of corn, so long as you did not leave the path, but
you must not rub them out in your hands.   It has been
pointed out already that Luke avoids Mark's apparent
suggestion that the disciples left the path.   Similarly,
he explains the mysterious ' Cananaean ' of Mark iii. 19 as
meaning ' zealot ' or political fanatic, so giving us a useful
hint of the company that Judas kept in those days.   We

¹ Luke xiv. 13.

noticed above that he is particularly anxious to exculpate the Roman Government ; in this connexion
he makes it plain that, so far as he knew, there were no
Roman soldiers in the band which arrested Jesus,[1] and
he drops out all reference to the mocking of our Lord by
Pilate's guard.[2] The same motive comes out in ‘wishing
to release Jesus,’[3] ‘whom they were asking for,’[4] both
Luke only (cf. Acts iii. 14). In vi. 47 ff. he adapts a parable[5]
to less purely local conditions ; Palestinian scenery
provides the details in Matthew's version ; while the
imagery in Luke's rendering answers to conditions in the
great river-valleys of the North.

Under these circumstances it is not surprising that Luke
is sometimes a little hazy about the geography of Palestine
proper. Chapter iv. 44 gives us, in the best MSS., ‘and
He was preaching in the synagogues of Judaea.' Does this
mean the Roman province of Judaea, or is it a general
territorial name for the whole country, including Galilee ?
It is Luke's normal practice to employ territorial names,
and we have ‘Judaea’ again in vii. 17, where Galilee must
surely be meant ; while xxiii. 5 is even more remarkable,
‘teaching in all Judaea, beginning from Galilee.' I suggested above (Part i., ch. iv.) that there may be a hint here of
a journey southward at this point, but the evidence goes to
show that we cannot lay much stress upon Luke's use of
the name ‘ Judaea.' At first sight it would seem that our
evangelist thought of ‘ Decapolis ’ as a city, whereas the
name stands for a district held by ten Greek cities[6] ; possibly, however, the ‘ city ’ is Gerasa. He alters Mark's
‘ country-towns ’[7]—an exceedingly apt expression, used
by Josephus as specially characteristic of Galilee—to
‘ cities.' Here again it is quite likely that he wished to
suggest a tour not confined to Galilee, for Mark[8] has
‘ the neighbouring country-towns ’ ; Luke,[9] ‘ the other ’
(foreign ?) ‘ cities,' mentioning ‘ Judaea ’ immediately
afterwards. The outsider is evident in the substitution of
‘ the opposite side to Galilee ’ in viii. 26 for ‘ the other side
of the sea.'

---

[1] Luke xxii. 52 (cf. John xviii. 3).   [2] Mark xv. 16 ff.
[3] Luke xxiii. 20.   [4] Luke xxiii. 25.
[5] Matt. vii. 24 ff.   [6] Luke viii. 39.   [7] Mark i. 38.
        [8] Mark i. 38.   [9] Luke iv. 43.

Our evangelist also tends to replace Oriental phrases by more restrained Greek expressions. Matt. xi. 17 has 'ye did not beat your breasts,' but Luke prefers 'ye did not weep' (see below, p. 173); however, he retains the beating of the breast, along with weeping, in viii. 52, where Mark—one would fancy with a touch of contempt for so extravagant a display of grief—has 'weeping and making a great noise.'[1] Another strong Oriental gesture is toned down in Luke ix. 5, 'shake off the dust from your feet' (cf. x. 11, 'say, Even the dust that clings to our feet we wipe off against you ') ; Mark has 'shake out the earth beneath your feet.'[2] Luke's first expression merely implies that they were to shake the dust away by a kind of kick ; from his second all we should gather is that they should *say* that they were doing so. Mark makes the procedure quite clear ; they were to take off their sandals and shake out the dirt that had wedged itself in between sole and foot. 'One of the old prophets' is a frankly Gentile phrase.[3] The feeding of the five thousand is located at a 'city called Bethsaida '[4] ; if Luke is right here, we must place the miracle at the north end of the lake. On the whole it looks like a mistake, for Mark[5] and Matthew[6] have 'a desert place.' The feelings of a very much civilized townsman are reflected in viii. 27, where the misery of the demoniac is summed up in the words 'and for a long time he had not worn an upper garment ' (but see pp. 157–158 for an alternative explanation), 'and did not stay in a house.' Mark's crying and cutting himself with stones,'[7] which Luke, with his habitual restraint, leaves out, gives us a much more tragic picture of the madman ; Luke's tone is that of one Greek gentleman writing to another. The same feeling for the horror of a homeless life can be discerned in ix. 12, where the disciples are described as aghast at the prospect of the crowds not finding shelter for the night (that ' they may put up for the night,' Luke only). Is that the reason why he thought that the miracle must have taken place near a city of some kind, because Jesus could not have kept the people so late in **a**

---

[1] Mark v. 38.
[2] Mark vi. 11.   [3] Luke ix. 8, 19.
[4] Luke ix. 10.   [5] Mark vi. 31.
[6] Matt. xiv. 13.   [7] Mark v. 5.

lonely spot, without the possibility of a night's lodging ?
Again we feel that the emphasis is misplaced ; to stay out
all night would be no hardship for Galileans by the sultry
lakeside.   In xi. 29 he omits ' adulterous ' (? from Q, for
Mark viii. 12 has not got it), which is found in Matt. xvi.
4 ; it was a Jewish term for ' idolatrous.'   Luke also misses
the symbolism of the ' whitened tombs,'[1] having the much
vaguer phrase ' hidden tombs.'   Certain Jewish kings
had been buried close to the Temple precincts.   Later,
because of their association with ancestor-worship, they
were pronounced unclean or ' tabu '[2] ; but as it was not
always easy to detect the entrance to a sepulchre, they
were whitewashed afresh every spring.   But ' Theophilus '
would not know this, and any reference to ' whitewashed
tombs ' would bewilder him ; ' unseen sepulchres ' gives
the sense for all practical purposes, though Matthew's
version has an added touch of piquancy for those ' Christians ' who, whether at the Easter Communion or the
Covenant Service, are content with an annual whitewash-
ing.   Similarly, Luke softens the ' uncleanness ' of Matt.
xxiii. 27 into ' evil.'[3]
   In xii. 19 the rich fool addresses his soul after the
fashion of a comfort-loving Roman gentleman talking
to his ' genius ' ; Luke has ' think about the crows ' in
xii. 24—a Greek idea—while Matt. vi. 26 has ' look closely
at ' (our old friend, signifying a searching glance—see
Part i., chap. iii.) ' the wild birds ' ; in xii. 27 ' think about
the lilies,' where Matthew[4] gives us the humbler Jewish
' learn a lesson from the wild lilies.'   In xii. 51 he substitutes the explanatory word ' division ' for the ' sword '
of Matt. x. 34, and in xii. 58 he has ' before a magistrate '—omitted in Matt. v. 25—' court-officer ' (Matthew,
' attendant '), ' the last mite ' (½ quadrans) for ' the last
quadrans ' (⅛ farthing) of Matthew's version.   Luke xiii.
19 has the townsman's phrase ' in his own garden ' instead
of ' in his field '[5] or ' on the land '[6] ; xiii. 24, ' house door '
instead of ' city gate.'[7]   In the interests of completeness
Luke adds ' and north and south '[8] to the reminiscence of

[1] Matt. xxiii. 27 ; Luke xi. 44.
[2] Ezek. xliii. 7 ; Numb. xix. 16.
[3] Luke xi. 39.   [4] Matt. vi. 28.
[5] Matt. xiii. 31.   [6] Mark. iv. 31.
[7] Matt. vii. 13.   [8] Luke xiii. 29.

Isa. lix. 19 in Matt. viii. 11 (cf. Ps. cvii. 3). East and west are always the two chief points of the compass to the Jew, the course of whose history ran from eastern desert to western sea; but Luke came from the north himself, so very naturally north and south come in. Words current in the world of business are much more frequent in this Gospel than in the others; such are 'trade,'[1] 'made a profit of,'[2] and 'made'[3]—here Matthew has the less technical 'I gained'[4]—'I blackmailed'[5]; in this passage, as in iii. 13, the word is peculiar to Luke. The signet-ring and the 'first robe' in the story of the 'lost' son would be familiar ideas to the Syrian landowner of the period (for the signet-ring compare Matt. vii. 6, and above, p. 119); they stand for the restoration of the bankrupt boy to his share of the family inheritance.[6] Unless the suggestion made above is accepted (see p. 122), 'to this fig-tree'[7]—might look like a rationalizing of a difficult saying.[8] Matt. xxi. 34, 36 has 'slaves,' 'other slaves'; Mark and Luke[9] agree that the 'Lord of the vineyard' sent them one at a time. Matthew is nearer, as usual, to the Old Testament, in which the prophets come in groups; the others to the probabilities of the case—compare Matt. xxii. 3 with Luke xiv. 17, where precisely the same difference may be observed. Luke is the only one of our evangelists to mention the Roman military prisons.[10] In xxi. 29 he seems to be uncertain whether Mark[11] has got the right tree, for he adds 'and all the trees,' and in xxii. 25 he marks an allusion to Ptolemy Evergetes (the 'Benefactor'), a member of the famous Greek dynasty in Egypt. References to the imperial history of the times may be found in xiii. 1 ff., xix. 12 ff., as in ii. 1, iii. 1— all are peculiar to Luke. In xxiii. 47 we have 'righteous man,' where Matthew[12] and Mark[13] show 'Son of God.' Both phrases in the Jewish language of the time meant the same thing; but 'Son of God' was the specifically Jewish mode of expression, whereas 'righteous man'

[1] Luke xix. 13.
[2] Luke xix. 16.
[3] Luke xix. 18.
[4] Matt. xxv. 20, 22. :
[5] Luke xix. 8 (cf. iii. 13).
[6] Luke xv. 22.
[7] Luke xvii. 6.
[8] Matt. xvii. 20; xxi. 21; Mark xi. 23.
[9] Mark xii. 2, 4, 5; Luke xx. 10–12.
[10] Luke xxi. 12; xxii. 33.
[11] Mark xiii. 28.
[12] Matt. xxvii. 54
[13] Mark xv. 39. :

is much more natural in the mouth of a Gentile centurion.

It will be observed that this evangelist is very much of a Greek. He is fond of the word ' grace,' but he uses it in a distinctively Hellenic way. The beautiful phrase ' The words of grace' (Dr. Rendel Harris suggests ' charm ') in iv. 22 refers quite as much to the style and delivery as to the subject-matter of our Lord's sermon at Nazareth, and in vi. 32, ' What grace have ye ? ' we have an excellent foil to Matthew's very Jewish ideas, ' What do ye extra ? ' ' What reward have ye ? '[1] Luke is thinking of the Christian's bearing, Matthew of his positive achievement ; both are right, for the word of Jesus, we may be sure, included both in its scope. Words from the same root occur, and are found in Luke only, in vii. 42, ' He graciously forgave them both,' or, more literally, ' He did the gracious thing by both ' ; vii. 21, ' He graciously bestowed sight ' ; vii. 47, ' by grace of which I say to thee, Her sins, the many, are forgiven, because she loved much.' Though Luke was the friend and companion of Paul, his use of the great Christian word does not reproduce his master's idea. ' Grace ' to our evangelist is not all on the side of God ; there underlies his employment of words and phrases derived from ' grace ' a very sensitive appreciation of the beauty of penitence and gratitude in the forgiven soul, as well as that of free grace on the part of the forgiving God. Bad manners are rebuked in vii. 45, and in viii. 15 we notice a genuinely Greek expression, translated in our version ' an honest and good heart.' Perhaps that is as near as we can get to the meaning of the original in English ; the only other suggestion which I can make is ' in a will disposed to noble ends.' ' Honest and good ' is a rendering of the Greek idiom corresponding to our ' gentleman ' ; ' without *arrière pensée* ' is our nearest modern phrase. In ix. 62 we have a Greek proverb found in a more extended form in Hesiod, ' Who doing his work with diligence would plough a straight furrow, no longer glancing back after his companions ' ; in the same way, the Risen Lord appears to quote Pindar and Aeschylus to Saul on the road to Damascus.[2] Possibly some consideration of this sort has given rise to Hahn's

[1] Matt. v. 46, 47.   [2] Acts xxvi. 14.

theory that Luke himself was the would-be follower
addressed in ix. 62, and that he became one of the seventy,
of whose missionary journey he alone tells us. We can
well imagine that Jesus would become a Greek to the
Greeks, but we cannot be sure that, where a Jewish saying
reminded Luke of a Greek proverb, he has not instinctively
allowed the words to catch the Greek rhythm. That he
wrote quickly is suggested by ix. 53, where we read, ' His
face was going ' ; this appears to be a Hebraism incorrectly
used, and refers back to ' He set His face like a flint '
(cf. Isa. l. 7) ' to go to Jerusalem.' There may be a side-
glance in ix. 51 to Hazael's setting his face to go to Jerusalem,
for in the LXX the words are the same ; Jesus went to
save as deliberately as Hazael to destroy.[1]   Like other
ready writers, Luke sometimes calls into his service an
expression which slips from his pen twice in quick succession, and then never employs it again.   The Birth
story proves that he was very anxious to keep, as far as
possible, the Jewish atmosphere and setting of the story
in the main body of the Gospel ; this only makes the
obtrusion of his native Greek the more striking. Additional piquancy is given to the praise of ' shamelessness '
expressed in xi. 8, and implied in xviii. 5, by our knowledge
that the writer is here doing violence to his own instincts
of dignity and restraint. ' Fit '—in much the same sense
as that conveyed by our colloquial phrase—in ix. 62,
xiv. 35, is distinctly Greek, as it is athletic in suggestion ;
in Heb. vi. 7 and in the Greek versions of the Old Testament it bears a different meaning ; only in the *Targum*
of Onkelos[2] and in the saying of the Rabbis—' The worker
who proves himself fit in the work of the garden has
access also to the storehouse '—do we find anything like
the same sense.   For another athletic figure see xiii. 24,
where 'agonize' to enter may be translated ' Fight hard to
enter' ; here both the preliminary training for the games as
well as strenuous participation in them is implied—the
meaning is very nearly, ' Keep yourselves in fighting form.'
   The Greek passion for precision can be discerned in
i. 4 (' the certainty of the words about which you have
received instruction '), and the same note may be heard
in xi. 52, ' the key of *knowledge* ' ; Matthew[3] has ' ye close

[1] 2 Kings xii. 17.   [2] At. Ex. iv. 13.   [3] Matt. xxiii. 13.

the Kingdom '—the ' Lewis' Syriac of Matthew, ' ye hold
the key of the kingdom of heaven before men.'   In xi. 17
Luke renders ' thoughts,' where Matt. xii. 25 has ' passions ';
in ii. 35, v. 22 (cf. xxiv. 38) ' reasonings,' whereas Matt.
ix. 4 has again the word which I have translated ' passions.'
The Lord's charming courtesy is brought out in xii. 37,
and the charge to the seventy might be taken as the
nucleus of a handbook on manners for ministers.   Indeed,
if the missionaries on that occasion were sent to Gentile
homes, and were Jews, x. 8—' eat what is set before you '
—was a hard saying, anticipating Peter's Joppa vision
and the whole discussion of Gal. ii. 12 ff.   The value
of friendliness is vividly set forth in xvi. 9, and the story
of the Good Samaritan speaks loudly in praise of the
neighbourly spirit common to good sportsmen of every
class.   In xix. 40 we notice a rebuke to churlishness,
and the same commonness of mind is glanced at in xx. 23
(' low scheming ') ; Matthew[1] has a word corresponding
to the Old English ' naughtiness '—they were ' out for
mischief '—Mark[2] ' hypocrisy.'   The ' Highest ' is a
favourite phrase with our evangelist ; it is, of course,
a Jewish expression meaning ' God,' but it would be
specially attractive to a Greek (cf. Matt. v. 45 ;
Luke vi. 35).

That Luke was a doctor might be inferred from his books
without the help of Church tradition.   The peculiar
intimacy of the Birth story suggests that Mary would
tell a doctor more than she cared to confide to others.
Specially interesting from this point of view is iv. 23 ;
the doctor is painfully conscious that medical men are
not immune from criticism.   He is not quite so precise
in his descriptions of demon-possession as are the other
Synoptists ; there are traces of hesitation, if not of
scepticism.   In iv. 33 we find a strange expression, ' a
spirit of an unclean demon,' and in iv. 35 Jesus says,
' Come *out away from* him ' ; Mark[3] has ' an unclean demon '
and ' come *out of him.*'   Luke is not sure whether the
evil power is really inside the man or is only attacking
him from outside.   Luke viii. 27, again, is vaguer than
Mark v. 2—' having demons ' instead of ' in an unclean
spirit.'   When, however, the stronger statement appears

[1] Matt. xxii. 18.   [2] Mark xii. 15.   [3] Mark i. 23, 25.

in the words of Jesus Himself, he generally reproduces
it (e.g. xi. 26).

Going back to iv. 35, we observe that Luke says that
the demon did not injure the man, wbereas in Mark we read
that the demon ' tore ' him.[1]   In iv. 39 Jesus stands over
Peter's mother-in-law, as a doctor would, and in iv. 38
we have a medical term—' consulted Him about her.'
Interest in the details of the healing methods of Jesus
is manifest in iv. 40, ' laying His hands upon each one,'
and the incorrect word ' paralytic '[2] is replaced by ' paralysed man,'[3] ' whole ' by the cautious doctor's phrase
' convalescent.'   This last word is very common in the
Gospel ; it is translated ' safe and sound ' in xv. 27,
is frequently found in letters of the period—' I hope
you are pretty well '—but, apart from 3 John 2, only
occurs elsewhere in the New Testament of ' wholesome
doctrine ' or ' healthy ' spiritual life in the Pastoral
Epistles.   In iv. 38 our author uses the proper technical
term for malaria ; in Acts xxviii. 8 the word translated
' fever ' means ' gastric fever.'   Sick people in this Gospel
are always cured by the laying on of hands, demoniacs
by the word of exorcism.   In ix. 38 ' look at ' is another
doctor's word—' examine '—and Luke avoids the vague
term ' weakness,'[4] but uses the medical expression ' prostration ' in the curious phrase ' a spirit of prostration.'[5]
Does he mean to imply that this poor woman's prostration
was rather nervous than organic ?   It is clear that there
is no question of demon-possession here, rather of a lack
of spirit—in the other sense of the word.   Luke's avoidance
of Matthew's phrases ' torments' and ' tormented'[6] suggests
the observation that the first evangelist looks at the
case from the standpoint of the patient's suffering ;
the third from the doctor's point of view, laying stress
upon his medical condition.   ' The power ' of our Lord
to heal is quite a Lucan idea[7] ; in viii. 46 a reference
to the ' power ' is put into the mouth of Jesus, where
Mark[8] has only a statement of his own.   The fact that
Luke has ' powers,' in the sense of ' acts of power ' or
' mighty works,' only twice, on both occasions where

[1] Mark i. 26.   [2] Mark ii. 3, 5, 9.   [3] Luke v. 18, 24.
[4] Matt. iv. 23 ; ix. 35 ; x. 1.   [5] Luke xiii. 11.
[6] Matt. iv. 24 ; viii. 6.   [7] Luke vi. 19.   [8] Mark v. 30.

his reverence for the actual words of Jesus forbade alteration, as against six examples in Matthew and three in Mark, leads us to think that he preferred to think of the healing virtue of Jesus as uniformly exercised rather than of the comparative impressiveness of His particular achievements. In vii. 21 he gives us an interesting distinction between epidemic diseases and chronic complaints, and in vi. 40 ' every one who is duly certified ' is peculiar to this Gospel.

But illustrations of Luke's obtrusively medical phraseology abound on every page of his books ; his ' needle ' in xviii. 25 is a doctor's needle ; his descriptions alike of the swaddling-clothes of the baby Jesus and the first aid rendered to the man found ' unconscious '— another technical term—on the road by the Good Samaritan are delightfully medical ; the ' little children ' brought to Jesus, like the Holy Babe Himself, become ' infants ' (in the medical sense) in Luke xviii. 15 (cf. ii. 12), while in xxi. 11 ' epidemic diseases ' appear among the woes of the last times—in this Gospel only. The lost son ' comes to himself,' as a patient comes out of a swoon[1] ; did Jesus really mean that the boy had fainted away? while the Pharisee in his morbid pride and the rich fool in his self-absorbed complacency talk to themselves like sick men in delirium.[2]

I may mention at this point that there is a series of studies in the bad habit of talking to yourself in Luke's picture-gallery. Simon the Pharisee ' said within himself,' the rich fool ' reasoned within himself,' the prodigal ' came to himself,' the unjust steward, like the unjust judge, ' said within himself,' while the Pharisee in the parable ' prayed within himself.' Simon was talking to himself, when he should have been listening to Jesus, and so becomes the odd one out in the company. The rich fool is wholly absorbed in himself, and sets to work to be merry—an impossible task—by himself ; but by-and-by his uninvited guest—God—touches him on the shoulder, and he is summoned to join the others— ' They are asking for you.' The Pharisee in the temple gives us a still more ironical picture of fatuous self-importance ; he ' plants himself ' to pray—the same word is

[1] Luke xv. 17.   [2] Luke xviii. 11 ; xii. 17.

used of Zacchaeus, when he made his great declaration—
while the publican simply 'stands,' and the words that
we overhear give us the substance of his self-involved
thoughts. The unjust judge is concerned about his own
dignity; like representatives of the vested interests in
later days, he concedes a grudging justice to the oppressed,
because he is afraid that the lower classes may take the
law into their own hands one of these days. The lost
son and the unjust steward both wake up, as from a dream,
to find themselves stranded, and hasten to make friends.
The undernote in all these parables is the necessity of
fellowship for beings such as we are in such a world as
this, and emphasis is placed now upon the folly of those
who hold themselves aloof from others, now upon the
prudence of those who, finding themselves alone, make
up their minds at all costs to find shelter and a home, for
independence is a comfortless unreality. The elder
brother in the parable from one point of view, 'Dives' from
another, are also variations upon the same theme.

To go back to our main subject : the wastrel's life in
the 'far country' is described in language which reminds
us of the tones of a discreet and experienced doctor—
'living irregularly'—and is in strong contrast to the
elder brother's blunt assertion—'who has devoured thy
living with harlots.' A curious instance of Luke's loyalty
to his profession is to be found in his treatment of
the story of the woman with the haemorrhage. Mark,
who seems rather to have enjoyed a hit at the faculty,
says in the most sweeping fashion that she had 'spent all
her living' and had 'suffered many things at the hands
of many doctors'; that she got no better, but rather grew
worse.[1] In the later MSS. of Luke there has been some
harmonizing, but earlier and better copies have 'who
could not be healed by any.'[2] Here is a twofold insinuation:
Luke will not allow that she had been to a properly qualified
doctor, and at the same time suggests that the trouble
was not any lack of medical skill, but her own inability
to rally ; this, of course, only makes the Good Physician's
success the more wonderful. In viii. 55, 56 it should be
noticed that he reverses the order of Mark v. 43. With
Mark the primary interest is the general policy of reserve

[1] Mark v. 26.   [2] Luke viii. 43

consistently maintained by Jesus in the towns of the
lakeside ; Luke is thinking of the treatment of the patient.
He often tells us how long the sufferer had been afflicted[1]
—only Luke viii. 43 has a parallel in Mark—and in v. 12
he substitutes ' a man in an advanced stage of leprosy '
for ' a leper '[2]; this helps us to understand the anger of Jesus
(see above, Part i., chap. iii.) in this case, for the man was a
public danger in the crowded streets (Luke alone tells us
that the incident happened in ' one of the towns ').
The leper, who was afflicted with a very contagious form
of the disease, was disregarding all sanitary regulations
—that he should not come into town or village—and Jesus
sharply bids him obey the law in future.[3]   Chapter xvi. 24
is redolent of the sick-room, and in xxii. 44 we have
' clots of blood ' and ' as the pain became more intense,'
medical language in this verse going far to prove the
genuineness of this sacred passage, questioned as it is, for
textual reasons, by Westcott and Hort.

We are not surprised to find Jesus depicted in this
Gospel as Healer *par excellence.*   In ix. 1, 2 the healing
of diseases is emphatically included in the apostles' commission (cf. also ix. 6).   In Mark vi. 7, on the other hand,
only ' authority over unclean spirits ' is mentioned, though
we are told in Mark vi. 13 that they did heal ' many
invalids,' ' anointing them with oil.'   This last piece of
information, which reminds us of Luke x. 34, James v. 14,
is omitted here by Luke, perhaps because it was not inserted
in the copy of Mark's gospel which he saw (see Part i., chap.
ii.) or else because he preferred to think that the power of
Jesus transmitted to His disciples was enough without the
use of medicines.   In the charge to the seventy, moreover,
healing takes precedence even of preaching.[4]   ' Maimed
and halt ' figure in the parable of the Banquet,[5] whereas
in his parallel story of the Prince's wedding Matthew[6] only
refers to the ' bad and good.'   So, in ix. 11, Jesus teaches
and heals the crowd on the eastern shore of the lakeside ;
in Mark vi. 34 we only hear of His teaching.   Luke is
interested, too, in the fact that the Gadarene had not for

---

[1] Luke viii. 43 ; xiii. 11 ; Acts iii. 2 ;   iv.   22 ;   ix. 33 ;   xiv. 8.
[2] Mark i. 40.   [3] Luke v. 14.
[4] Luke x. 9.   [5] Luke xiv. 21 (cf. xv. 12).
[6] Matt. xxii. 10.

a long time been able to endure clothes on his body,[1] that the man healed on the Sabbath day at Capernaum had his *right* hand withered,[2] and he alone tells us of the healing of Malchus's *right* ear[3] ; he is careful to show that this was a surgical operation, for the ear had been taken clean off. Very significant also is the stately phrase ' accomplish cures ' in xiii. 32 ; does it mean that Jesus watched His patients after they were healed, to guard against relapse ? It is everywhere apparent that to this writer preaching and the healing of body and soul held an equal place in the mission of Jesus, whereas to Mark at least preaching and teaching, whether public or private, always came first, healing occupying a comparatively subordinate place.

---

[1] Luke viii. 27.   [2] Luke vi. 6.   [3] Luke xxii. 50, 51.

IV

THE SAME SUBJECT CONTINUED

IF Luke was not a Socialist in the modern sense of the term, he was an ardent social reformer. He dwells upon the social teaching of John the Baptist, perhaps because it was socialistic in one sense[1] ('He that has two vests, let him share with him who has none'), though not in another[2] ('Be content with your wages'). He would probably have resented the suggestion that the communistic experiment made at Jerusalem after Pentecost was a fiasco, for he describes the life of those early days with evident delight.[3] He has perhaps even exaggerated a little our Lord's dislike of money and all that money stands for. Does the Sermon 'on a level place'[4] really correspond to the Sermon on the mount, reported in Matthew, chapters v.–vii.? Matthew seems to have gathered up into one continuous discourse sayings which are scattered in Luke's Gospel through chapters vi., viii., xi., xii., xiii., xiv., xvi., xxi.; and in Luke's version the 'Woes' upon the rich, the satisfied, the well-fed, and the popular are peculiar to him. The direct address, moreover, maintained throughout the 'Sermon' in Luke vi. 20 ff., is in strong contrast to the series of generalizations reported by Matthew, according to whom the personal note only comes in at v. 11. But the outstanding difference consists in the fact that, whereas in Matthew Jesus, 'seeing the multitudes,' goes up into the hill-country, as though to get away from them, Luke tells us that Jesus had come down to the lower ground, though it is true that the beginning of the discourse is addressed to the disciples.[5] The 'Woes' upon 'you that are rich,' &c.,[6] can hardly have been meant to apply to the inner circle of His

[1] Luke iii. 11.   [2] Luke iii. 14.   [3] Acts ii. 44, 45, &c.
[4] Luke vi. 17.   [5] Luke vi. 17.   [6] Luke vi. 24.

followers, unless He was threatened with some patronage from rich people. On the whole, one is inclined to think of the ' Sermon ' in Luke as a relatively public manifesto ; of that reported in Matthew as a series of teachings meant for His closest adherents, leaving the question open as to whether or no the whole ' Sermon ' was delivered upon the occasion suggested by the first evangelist. Luke's arrangement can best be accounted for by the theory that he is following Q's order or lack of order, while Matthew appears to be systematizing here as elsewhere. The ' But ' of Luke vi. 27 is interesting ; it would seem that our author has left out the contrast with the older law, so strongly emphasized in Matthew, as not sufficiently relevant to his main purpose, that of reaching Gentile readers ; he forgot, however, to drop the ' But,' which depends for its force upon the section of Q which he had omitted. When Luke[1] has ' ye that are poor ' (Matt. v. 3, ' the poor in spirit '), ' ye that are hungry now '[2]— Matt. v. 6, ' those that are hungry and thirsty for righteous- ness'—' for the Son of Man's sake '[3]—Matthew first ' for righteousness' sake,'[4] then ' for My sake '[5]— probably Q had ' the poor,' ' the hungry, ' the persecuted,' &c. Polycarp has ' the poor,' the hungry,' ' the perse- cuted *for righteousness*' sake, for *theirs* (as Matthew) ' is the kingdom of God.' Matthew's ' poor in spirit ' and ' hungry and thirsty for righteousness ' are probably instances of his habit, to be discussed later, of explaining ambiguities for the benefit of young Jewish catechists. But the main line of difference is plain: Matthew tends to interpret the words of Jesus as bearing chiefly upon moral and spiritual distinctions ; with Luke social inequalities and their redress loom very large.

The saying reported in Luke vi. 34, 35 has no exact counterpart in Matthew ; evidence from papyri confirms the rendering ' despairing of nothing ' (better, perhaps, ' of no man '). More than once Luke, as he does here, adds (? from oral tradition) a third illustration of a general principle—compare Luke xi. 11, 12, where ' an egg ' and ' a scorpion ' come in, while Matthew[6] has ' a loaf ' and ' a fish ' only, with their ' substitutes,' ' a stone ' and ' a

---

[1] Luke vi. 20. [2] Luke vi. 21. [3] Luke vi. 22. [4] Matt. v. 10.
[5] Matt. v. 11. [6] Matt. vii. 9, 10.

snake.' In xii. 42 'rations' take the place of Matthew's 'food,'[1] and in xiv. 18, 19 property is regarded as a hindrance in itself to membership in the Kingdom (Matt. xxii. 5 is much vaguer). The same parable gives us the call to the poor[2]; Matt. xxii. 10 has simply 'bad and good.' The sense of social wrong dominates the parable of 'Dives' and Lazarus, and special sympathy with people who have to go short of food is evident here,[3] as well as in xv. 16 ; the humiliation of hunger kindles the writer's imagination, and he revels in the thought that the tables will by-and-by be turned. Or perhaps it would be truer to the facts to say that he eagerly caught and reported stories told by Jesus which brought out His compassion for those who have to do without. Jesus will have nothing to do with the disposal of property[4]; His disciples are to keep away from every kind of covetousness,[5] even when what the world calls their rights are concerned ; the rich fool was a fool because he talked of '*my* goods,' '*my* fruits,' '*my* soul.' In xiii. 27 Luke has 'workers of injustice,' where Matthew[6] has 'workers of lawlessness.' According to Luke, Jesus condemned by implication the whole social system. Property of any kind is 'the mammon of unrighteousness,'[7] as the 'judge' of xviii. 6 is 'the judge of unrighteousness '— in other words, the judge who was typical of an unrighteous social order. In xvii. 28 our evangelist adds (? from oral tradition) 'they were buying, they were selling, they were planting, they were building '; compare Matt. xxiv. 38 and Sirach xxvii. 2 : 'Sin will thrust itself in between buying and selling.' 'The steward of unrighteousness,'[8] like Zacchaeus,[9] saves himself by the sacrifice of material property.

In regard to the parable of the unjust steward, the practicability of our Lord's teaching should be noticed. In spite of the fact that He considers the economic basis of the social life of His own time as utterly unsound, and therefore transient (' My lord is taking from me the stewardship '), Jesus is willing to point the way of salvation to men who have still to subsist within the boundaries of

---

[1] Matt. xiv. 45.   [2] Luke xiv. 21 (cf. vv. 12, 13).   [3] Luke xvi. 21.
[4] Luke xii. 13 ff.   [5] Luke xii. 15.   [6] Matt. vii. 23, &c.
[7] Luke xvi. 9.   [8] Luke xvi. 8.   [9] Luke xix. 8, 9.

the present order. Stewards of Oriental estates, like many other officials, were not paid a salary, but were allowed to deduct part of the rents for their own maintenance. The steward assessed the tenants of the estate at as high a figure as he could make them pay, then sent a proportion of the money as it came in to the landlord, the rest being regarded as his own commission. This steward was not unrighteous, because he mismanaged the estate—indeed, the word 'was accused '[1] might mean 'was wrongfully accused '—nor because he kept part of the rents for himself (that was understood to be his rightful perquisite, nor would his master have 'praised' him[2] if he had himself been adversely affected by the interviews with the two tenants) ; but because the whole organization typified by the relation of landlord, steward, and tenants was radically wrong. What the steward did was to forfeit his own share of the rent, forgoing present advantage for the sake of future security. The tenants, to whose rescue he was able just then to come, in virtue of still holding his office—he was under notice, but not yet dismissed—were in difficulties, regarding him as having relieved them of an impossible situation, would, he calculated, give him employment, or at least hospitality until he could find employment, when his notice expired. This parable is of extraordinary interest, for it not only gives us an insight into the Master's economic and social teaching, but it also provides us with advice as to how to deal with money, a nuisance, it is true, but perhaps a necessary nuisance. It should be specially interesting to us in these days, when the present economic and social order appears to be under notice to quit. What are we to do? How provide for the new age? Insure by all means, says Jesus ; but not only nor chiefly in cash securities ; even the 'sons of this age' agree that friendship is the best investment, for friends never go out of circulation, while money, like health and time, does. The friends who will help you in the new world are those who, in the existing state of society, are more or less dependent upon you. Here, we observe, Jesus parts company from the worldly-wise. 'Make friends with those above you, if you can,' say they ; 'Make friends

---

[1] Luke xvi. 1.   [2] Luke xvi. 8.

with those beneath you,' says He. The next parable—
that of 'Dives' and Lazarus—enforces the same lesson
in reference to the life beyond the grave. If 'Dives'
had made friends with Lazarus in his prosperous days,
Lazarus might have done something for him in the world
beyond ; but he did not think it worth his while. He
was not simply lacking in generosity, he was also a great
fool. Like the other rich man who left God and death
out of his reckoning, he left his poor brother out of his
reckoning, and we are all so bound up in the bundle of
life together that we cannot afford to leave any one out
of account ; we are all parasites, and independence is
an empty word. If 'the whirligig of time has strange
revenges,' the wheel of God's eternal justice has yet
stranger ; 'the first' must be 'last,' and 'the last first,'
if there is justice in the universe of God ; for the poor
and the sick do very often learn to practise the virtues
of courage, patience, and self-denial, virtues which must
be rewarded in the eternal order. We are all stewards,
unjust stewards, stewards under notice of dismissal ;
while we have a little of the world's perishable goods,
money, health, time, we are advised to use them in the
service of people who are better than ourselves, but who,
under the inequalities of our present life, have not so
much of any or all of these as we. We are to 'show'
ourselves 'trustworthy bankers'—an unwritten but well-
authenticated saying of Jesus—for, like the modern banker
and the ancient steward, we are allowed to take a commission
for services rendered ; we have no absolute possession,
and we shall not be allowed even to take the commission
much longer.

It only remains to be said in regard to this
parable that, as in that of the unjust judge, a comparison between the shrewdness of the worldly man and
the perfect wisdom and knowledge of God is clearly intended. The unjust judge vindicates the widow when
his personal comfort and dignity are threatened ; the
unjust landlord praises that sly dog, his steward, for his
shrewdness. How much more will a just God 'avenge
His own elect ? '[1] How much more will the righteous
Lord of all take cognizance of kindness done to the 'least

[1] Luke xviii. 7.

of these His brethren,' not for the sake of present or future advantage, but out of the ready friendliness of a sympathetic heart.

Luke, it will be observed, shows a significant fondness for the word 'steward,' Matthew preferring 'slave.'[1] It is also interesting to notice that whereas in Matt. xxv. 14 ff. the successful slaves begin with unequal opportunities, but end with an equal reward, in Luke[2] they begin with equal opportunity, and end with unequal rewards (see above, p. 128). The ideal in the First Gospel is equality of reward, that in the Third equality of opportunity. In xvii. 31 we have 'goods' mentioned, where Matthew[3] and Mark[4] mention only the 'upper garment'; and the devil is closely associated with *property* in Luke xi. 21, 22, where 'fully armed,' 'his own mansion,' 'his property,' 'his equipment,' 'on which he had relied,' and 'distributes' are all peculiar to Luke (cf. Matt. xii. 29, Mark iii. 27). 'Distribute' is quite a Lucan word; it occurs also in xviii. 22, 'distribute to the poor,' where Matthew[5] and Mark[6] show simply 'give'; for Luke believes in a regulated and thoughtful charity. In xvi. 14 he charges the Pharisees with being 'lovers of money'; but, apart from the 'devouring widows' houses' of Mark xii. 40, Luke xx. 47, we have not much evidence that they were open to this particular accusation. One of their maxims was 'He that hath little business shall become wise' (Sirach xxxviii. 24), and it is likely that their regard for a life of cultured leisure might lead to an undue valuation of the means by which alone such leisure can be obtained; but this is about as far as we can go, for Matthew, who evidently had something of a bias against the Pharisees, does not refer directly to this charge. In xviii. 24 Luke has 'those that have money' (i.e. any at all), where Matthew[7] has 'a rich man'; Mark[8] agrees with Luke here. Chapter xi. 41 seems to mean 'Charities breed charity.' Sympathy with the lives of the poor shines upon every page of this Gospel. The parables of the lost coin, of the friend at midnight, with its picture of the one-roomed cottage

[1] Luke xii. 42 ; Matt. xxiv. 45, &c. [2] Luke xix. 13 ff.
Matt. xxiv. 17, 18. [4] Mark xiii. 15, 16. [5] Matt. xix. 21.
[6] Mark x. 21. [7] Matt. xix. 23, 24. [8] Mark x. 23.

where the family sleep together in the living-room, and of Lazarus are all found in Luke alone ; while Mark's ' one poor widow '[1] becomes ' a widow who had to work for her living.'[2]

Whether Luke was a Socialist or not, the tendency of his mind was strongly ascetic. He omits John the Baptist's meat diet ; it is curiously suggestive of the difference between old-world ideas and those of the present day that the fact, reported by Matthew[3] and Mark,[4] that John indulged in a meat diet, albeit a meagre one, caused serious difficulty to early readers of the Gospel. Tatian altered ' locusts and wild honey ' to ' milk and honey of the mountains ' ; others, by a dexterous change of a single letter, instead of ' locusts ' read ' parsnips.' Certainly, whether Luke was a vegetarian or not, the ' fatlings ' of Matt. xxii. 4 disappear in Luke xiv. 16 ff. ; but we are glad that our evangelist did not lay violent hands upon ' that fatted calf.' In the Birth story, as in the Acts, fasting has a prominent place[5] ; that references to the virtue of fasting do not occur in the main body of the Gospel is evidence that Jesus did not say much about it. In iv. 2 our author takes the fasting of Jesus in the wilderness to mean that He ' ate nothing ' ; Matthew's ' having fasted '[6] would be covered, if we think of a meagre and casual diet, like that of John. In iv. 6 we notice a tendency to give up civilized society as hopeless ; Luke is much more definite than Matthew about the power of the devil (cf. Matt. iv. 9). Both Matthew[7] and Luke[8] show themselves sceptical about Mark's ' but hath an end,'[9] but Luke alone has ' for a time ' or ' until an opportunity '—the Greek is capable of both meanings—in iv. 13 (cf. Matt. iv. 11) ; the devil is not so easily shaken off. Our evangelist also is our sole authority for the Lord's last sad saying at His arrest : ' This is your hour and the authority of darkness.'[10] Mark ii. 20 reads ' Then shall they fast in that day ' ; Luke v. 35, ' Then shall they fast in those days ' ; the observance of Lent is based upon Luke's version of this saying. The insertion of ' and (live) delicately,'[11] ' pleasures of life,'[12] and ' in

---

[1] Mark xii. 42.	[4] Mark i. 6.	[7] Matt. xii. 6. 2	[10] Luke xxii. 53.
[2] Luke xxi. 2.	[5] Luke ii. 37.	[8] Luke xi. 18.	[11] Luke vii. 25.
[3] Matt. iii. 4.	[6] Matt. iv. 2.	[9] Mark. iii. 26.	[12] Luke viii. 14.

endurance '[1] shows the same tendency, and it is significant that in this Gospel the twelve missionaries are not allowed to take ' a staff '[2]; Matt. x. 10 agrees here, though Mark vi. 8 has ' except a staff only.' This would seem to be clear evidence that Matthew's and Luke's account of this missionary charge came from Q.

The same love of simplicity and discipline may be observed in Luke's twice-repeated use of the phrase ' day by day,' where it is not found in the other Gospels. These words are peculiar to his report in ix. 23—' take up his cross daily '—and in xi. 3, ' Give us day by day our bread for the coming day.' Chapter ix. 62 we have noticed already, but in xvii. 32 ' Remember Lot's wife ' is also found here only, and enforces the same lesson. In the charge to the seventy a very bare simplicity is insisted upon.[3] Mark[4] tells us that the twelve were to be ' shod with sandals '; Luke[5] will not allow foot-wear of any kind (so Matt. x. 10). People wore sandals and carried shoes then, the shoes being put on after the foot-washing on arrival at the traveller's destination. The whole purport of these directions is that the itinerant preachers are not to 'affect the gentleman'; they are not, for instance, to carry slippers for the house. (Matthew, it may be observed, has no reference to ' saluting no one by the way'; he, as we shall see, is all for friendliness.) In the same spirit Luke has already translated a perhaps ambiguous phrase in the first of his two ordina-tion charges, ' They are not to have a change of vests '[6]; Mark vi. 9 apparently means, ' You are not to put on two vests at the same time,' as well-to-do people sometimes did, one vest being worn over the other, for the sake of warmth. The seventy, successful as they have been, are not to think highly of their achievements; they are to be content to be citizens—not necessarily officials— of the Kingdom.[7] ' A simple meal, or even one course,' is all that Jesus, or Mary, who understands His tastes, needs at Bethany, for Mary has ' chosen the best kind of dish,' and she shall not be compelled by her somewhat overbearing sister to worry about anything else just now.[8] The whole passage may be translated : ' Martha, Martha '—

---

[1] Luke viii. 15.   [3] Luke x. 4.   [5] Luke x. 4.   [7] Luke x. 20.
[2] Luke ix. 3.   [4] Mark vi. 9   [6] Luke ix. 3.   [8] Luke x. 41, 42.

for the double address in tender expostulation compare xxii. 31 on the lips of Jesus, viii. 24 on those of His disciples (both Luke only)—' you are making a great noise and worrying '—she was banging the plates down, and affecting to be very busy, as some good women will when they are ' getting at ' another woman, and are aching for a scene—' about making a great supper. We do not need much ; indeed, one dish will be quite enough ; Mary has chosen the best kind of meal (for all of us) and she shall not be dragged away from it '—the intimate ease of friends who understand one another too well to make a great display of hospitality. The best thing to do when Jesus came to your house was not to feast Him, or to make a fuss, but just to sit down and listen. This very charming home scene, in the rendering of which I have followed the best of the older MSS., we owe to Luke only ; it falls in readily with his own tastes, and at the same time carries upon its face the mark of essential truth. Luke xvi. 16 (cf. Matt. xi. 12) I have discussed already (see pp. 123, 124) ; if the theory put forward there be accepted, this saying gives us a recommendation of energetic measures in self-discipline, which harmonizes closely with the general drift of the Gospel.

The last clause of xii. 29 is a little difficult to translate, but the sense is fairly clear. At one time I was greatly drawn to our colloquial ' Don't get under the weather,' but evidence of any such meaning in the Greek of the period is wanting. The verb used here has certainly something to do with the weather or the air. Sometimes it means ' To get above oneself,' rather more often ' To be swayed by every wind that blows ' ; hence the rather tame translation ' Neither be ye of doubtful mind.' We may, if we will, adopt the rendering ' Do not get above yourselves,' as people who have plenty of food and clothes are apt to do ; this translation is quite safe, and the more piquant reading, other things being equal, is always likely to be right when the words of Jesus are concerned. On the other hand, the reference to ' worrying ' just before shows that Jesus is thinking of people who live by fits and starts, and come down as quickly as they soar up in their own conceits. In xii. 30 Luke omits the ' all ' which we find in Matt. vi. 33, and the first part of

xii. 33—'Sell your property, and give alms; make to yourselves purses that do not get old' (cf. xvi. 9, 'Make to yourselves friends')—is peculiar to this Gospel. In xiii. 24 we have 'Few shall be able to enter'; Matt. vii. 14 gives us 'Few shall find the way'; according to Luke's version all may find the way, but few can enter the door. Specially interesting in this connexion is the passage—found in this Gospel only in its complete form— beginning at Luke xiv. 28. Both the 'man' and the 'King' in this 'pair' of twin-parables (see above, chap. i.) are meant to represent the Lord Himself. The 'man' is building a 'tower,' the 'King' planning a campaign. The 'tower' stands for the Kingdom in its defensive aspects, as a tower of refuge and salvation; the campaign for the same Kingdom in its aggressive warfare against evil. Jesus will not recruit for His more adventurous service any one who is not prepared to go the whole way with Him, and 'bid a regretful good-bye' (cf. Mark vi. 46, 'bidding farewell' to the crowds) 'to all his possessions.' Similarly drastic is Luke's addition in xiv. 26, 'yes, and his own self also,' and xiv. 35 is more explicit than either Matt. v. 13 or Mark ix. 50; the 'salt,' when corrupted, is no use to the owner even for manure. It may be observed that the word translated 'fit' (see above, p. 152) recurs in this verse, and that the phrase 'to be able'—to do something hard—is a favourite with our evangelist. It occurs in xiii. 24—noted above—xiv. 30, 'was not able to complete it'; viii. 43, 'she could not be healed'; xvi. 3, 'I cannot dig'; and its compound is found in the best reading of xxi. 36, 'that ye may prevail to flee all these things.'

A closely related idea underlies the Lucan use of the word 'dig,' which occurs thrice in this Gospel, and is in all three cases peculiar to it. The instances are: vi. 48, 'who dug and went deep'; xiii. 8, 'that I may dig about it'; xvi. 3, 'I cannot dig.' To 'dig' is to go deeply into things. The 'Vinedresser' will make a searching examination of the condition of the fig-tree's roots; the house-builder puts into the disposition of his soul-home some hard thinking; the steward, on the other hand, feels himself too old to plan out his life afresh, and seeks for some kind of less strenuous activity. The same sense of responsibility is conveyed by the substitution of the word ' steward ' for ' slave '[1]; it is all the greater because our stewardship of Another's property[2] is to be taken from us ; our failure is certain,[3] and the ' true riches ' are set in sharp contrast with the ' unrighteous mammon.' In xxi. 19 we notice the word ' endurance ' —of hard conditions—again (cf. viii. 15, ' in endurance '), and xxi. 34 is much more explicit than Matt. xxiv. 49, ' eat and drink with the drunken.' Here we have ' in drunken nausea and debauch and worries about getting a living'; the association of ideas is startling, and reminds us of viii. 14, ' worries and wealth and pleasures of life.' Worry would appear to be a kind of dismal intoxication (compare the union of the notions of extravagant depression and hysterical exaltation in xii. 29—see above, p. 167). In xxii. 16 ' until it be fulfilled in the Kingdom ' takes the place of ' until I drink it new '[4]; Luke is disinclined to take the figure literally. A sinister irony can be discerned in xxiii. 11 (Luke only), where Jesus wears for the first and last time ' a splendid robe ' ; compare vii. 25 and xvi. 19— this last passage also Luke only—the rich man is described as ' clothed in purple and fine linen ' ; Jesus was ' with the rich,' and in kings' palaces only in His death.[5]

In harmony with the vein of asceticism perceptible in our evangelist is his prejudice in favour of celibacy. This comes out rather amusingly in the evident relish with which our evangelist describes the peremptory refusal of the married man to come to the banquet—' I am married to a wife, and therefore I cannot come.'[6] The other invited guests are at least polite ; they say, ' I pray thee, have me excused ' ; but for the much-married man the fulfilment of his engagement is out of the question. Another very curious case of detailed possible discords in the home life of married people is to be found in xii. 52, 53. Matthew's version[7] reproduces the Old Testament[8] almost exactly ; according to Luke, Jesus keeps in view the complexities of the imagined situation. ' There shall be hereafter five in one house divided, three against two and two against three, father against son

---

[1] Luke xii. 42 ; xvi. 1 ff. ; Matt. xxiv. 45.   [2] Luke xvi. 12.
[3] Luke xvi. 9.   [4] Matt. xxvi. 29 ; Mark xiv. 25.   [5] Isa. liii. 9.
[6] Luke xiv. 20.   [7] Matt. x. 35.   [8] Micah vii. 6.

and son against father, mother against daughter and
daughter against mother, mother-in-law against daughter-
in-law and daughter-in-law against mother-in-law.' The
mother-in-law, being the odd one out, has the casting
vote, and throws in her lot with her son and his daughter
against the daughter-in-law and her son! It is difficult
to believe that these delicately humorous touches have
not come from Jesus, for had He not lived in Peter's home,
where the mother-in-law question was not unknown?
We become a little more sceptical when we notice that
the 'wife' is twice included—by Luke alone—amongst
the possessions which are to be left behind for the Kingdom's sake.   In xiv. 26 (cf. Matt. x. 37, 38) there are two
points at which this added sharpness becomes perceptible ;
Luke has 'if any one hates not,' while Matthew gives us
simply 'loves more than Me,' and he also mentions ' *wife* '
as well as 'brothers' and 'sisters' in his list of those who
are to be ' hated.'   Probably Jesus said ' house ' or ' home,'
and our evangelist interpreted it as including ' wife ' ;
but it is just in such explanations that his predilections
come out.   In xviii. 29 we can compare Luke with Mark
as well as Matthew.   Luke has ' no one who has left house,
or wife, or brothers, or parents, or children ' ; Mark x. 29,
' no one who has left house, or brothers, or sisters, or
mother, or father, or children, or lands ' ; Matt. xix. 29
follows Mark here.   It might be suggested that Mark
left out the ' wife ' because Peter, his master, was known
to take his wife about with him.[1]   On the whole, however,
we are warranted in assuming that our third evangelist's
prepossessions have not been without influence here.   Our
suspicion is increased when we compare Luke xvi. 18 with
Matt. v. 32, xix. 9 ; the main purport of all three passages
is the same, but the emphasis is sensibly different.   In
Luke stress is laid upon the guilt of a second marriage ;
in Matthew upon the sin of breaking up the home ; Mark
x. 12 appears to give us a middle term.   But it is in
Luke xx. 34 that the case is clearest ; taken straightfor-
wardly as it stands, the sentence beginning ' The sons of
this age marry, and are given in marriage,' seems to imply
that those ' who are counted worthy to attain to that age,
and the resurrection from the dead, neither marry, nor

[1] 1 Cor. ix. 5.

are given in marriage' *in this life*; it will be observed that neither Matthew nor Mark[1] leave room for this inference. Luke has not changed the words, for he is clearly working upon a different tradition ; but the apostolic practice and its endorsement by Paul's approval, if not his imitation, in I Cor. ix. 5 lead us to think that Luke cannot be altogether right at this point. In xix. 10 ff. Matthew gives us what may be considered a more credible tradition of our Lord's pronouncements upon this question.

There are evidences upon almost every page of this Gospel of Luke's knowledge of and interest in women. The story of Salome's dancing is historically doubtful, but we are sure that Luke was glad to leave it out. In iii. 19 he puts the blame for the murder of John the Baptist upon Herod rather than Herodias, and he suppresses the fact, reported in Mark vi. 3, that the sisters of Jesus were present at the painful scene at Nazareth. The interest of the Birth story in this Gospel is all with Elisabeth and Mary, whereas in the First it alternates between Joseph and the Babe. Anna appears alongside of Simeon, and in ii. 48 it is Mary, not Joseph, who speaks to her Boy. 'As was supposed,' in iii. 23 gives Jesus over unreservedly to Mary, and in iv. 26 the contrast drawn by the Lord finds culmination in 'a woman that was a widow.' The pathetic situation of the widow of Nain is the leading motive in vii. 12 ff.; this passage is peculiar to Luke, as is also the vindication of a sinful woman in the presence of a callous man.[2] If the theory advocated in Part i. chap. 4 is correct, Luke's chivalry is set in a yet stronger light, for Mary is shielded, while her act is dwelt upon with a delicate appreciation which surely reflects the spirit of Jesus. In viii. 2, 3 our evangelist dwells with lingering pleasure upon the self-forgetting love of the women-friends of Jesus, who were well-to-do, and yet were true Socialists (cf. Acts iv. 36). One at least of these women, as we have seen, may well have become one of Luke's informants. In viii. 19 we discern the writer's sympathy with the mother who could not get at her own Son ' because of the crowd,' nor will Luke allow that Mary wished to interrupt the Lord's ministry ; she only wanted ' to see Him.'[3]

Chapter viii. 47, 48 directs our attention to the courage

---

[1] Mark xii. 25 ; Matt. xxii. 30.   [2] Luke vii. 36 ff.   [3] Luke viii. 20.

of the woman with the hemorrhage; 'before all the people' is found in Luke only. His knowledge of some types of feminine human nature is evident in the domestic drama in x. 38 ff.; Martha is sketched to the life in the words of Jesus to her, and in xi. 27 f. where we have the obtrusively mothering soul who, when she listens to Jesus, interrupts His discourse with a very audible wish that she were His mother. Chapter xiii. 11 ff. gives us a pathetic picture of an invalid woman; in xv. 8 ff. we have a parable which would appeal to women set alongside of that of the lost sheep; and in xviii. 1 ff. another kind of woman, this time the persistent and rather shrewish widow, is added to our portrait-gallery. 'Lest she weary me by her continual coming' is a misleadingly tame translation; the clause really means, 'Lest, if she keeps on coming, she should give me a black eye,' or, as modern slang has it, 'one under the eye.' The 'Lewis' Syriac version has 'Lest she take hold of me'; the judge is actually afraid, or pretends to be afraid, of assault and battery. 'Fastening her eyes upon him'[1] exactly describes the girl's cool stare at Peter; Luke (see Part i., chap. iii.) has deliberately changed Mark's 'looking searchingly' at him, because that word is kept for Jesus. Codex Bezae at xxiii. 2 mentions that Jesus was charged with 'leading astray women and children'; this reading conveys to us a sense of the scorn which the enemies of Jesus felt for feminine intelligence, and is an indirect tribute to the loyalty of the women to Him. Chapter xxiii. 27 again suggests the mutual sympathy which must have existed between Jesus and women, even when the men forsook Him; and in xxiii. 49 we are told that the friends of Jesus did not altogether forsake Him, least of all the women. Through the Resurrection story[2] the women who loved Jesus are even more to the fore than in the other Gospels, and there is a touch of resentment in xxiv. 11, 'and these words appeared to them like women's gossip'; the 'Lewis' Syriac has 'As if they had spoken out of their wonder,' a still more striking suggestion of hysteria. On the whole men do not come out well in comparison with women in this Gospel. In xi. 31, 'A queen of the south shall rise in the judgement with the *men* of this generation' (Matthew

[1] Luke xxii. 56.   [2] Luke xxiii. 55; xxiv. 11.

who puts the 'men of Nineveh' first,[1] while Luke gives the 'queen of the south' pride of place, has simply 'with this generation '), and xvii. 34, 35, where the men appear to be in bed while the women are working, are examples in point ; according to Matt. xxiv. 40, 41 all four are at work, the men on the land, and the women at the mill. It is well known that the story of the woman 'taken in adultery' found in John vii. 53–viii. 11 does not really belong to the Fourth Gospel. Papias, reported by Eusebius, tells a similar story which appears to come from the lost Gospel 'to the Hebrews,' but in the Ferrar group of MSS. it follows Luke xxi. 38 ; traces of Luke's hand have been found in the wording of the story, and it is certainly a passage after his own heart.

Our evangelist's Greek sensibility may account for several cases in which 'weeping' finds a place in this Gospel only. At vi. 21 we have 'Blessed are ye that weep now ' (Matthew, 'Blessed are the mourners '[2]) ; so also vii. 13, ' do not go on crying ' ; vii. 32, 'We lamented, and ye did not weep '— Matthew,[3] ' beat your breasts ' ; and in xix. 41 he tells us that when our Lord came in sight of Jerusalem ' He wept.' Touches of pathos and of a tender, generous spirit abound everywhere ; the anger of Jesus with a leper[4] disappears in Luke v. 13, and in vi. 36 'pitiful' takes the place of Matthew's 'perfect,'[5] as does 'graceless'—compare what is said on page 151 as to Luke's fondness for the word 'grace' and related expressions—that of 'evil' in Matt. v. 45. Active benevolence is suggested in vi. 33, where Matthew[6]— with his usual emphasis upon friendliness—has ' salute,' and vi. 38 with its note of lavish generosity is found only in this Gospel. Notice also the ' only son ' of vii. 12, and in vii. 15 'gave him to his mother ' ; compare viii. 42, ' only daughter,' ix. 38, ' because he is my only son,' and ix. 42, ' gave him to his father '—all three found in Luke only. Chapter vii. 40 ff. gives us the parable of the two debtors, one of the points of which is the charming way in which the debt was crossed off the creditor's books ; ' He graciously forgave them both.' In viii. 10 an uncomfortable quotation is begun, but dropped like a hot coal. In Acts xxviii. 26 ff., perhaps after further experience,

---

[1] Matt. xii. 41, 42.   [2] Matt. v. 4.   [3] Matt. xi. 17.
[4] Mark i. 41, 43.   [5] Matt. v. 48.   [6] Matt. v. 47.

N

Luke gives it at full length ; possibly he felt easier
about putting it into Paul's mouth than upon the
gracious lips of Jesus, but he is too honest to leave it out
altogether. Something of the same sort happens in xii. 10—
'shall not be forgiven'—for Luke's omission of Mark's
'guilty of an eternal sin'[1] gives us the impression that a
painful subject is passed over as quickly as possible.
Chapter ix. 43 gives us a great word, 'the greatheartedness
of God,' and in ix. 55 we have a sentence which, for reasons
that I cannot enter into here,[2] I regard as the true
reading of the passage : 'And He said, Ye know not of
what spirit ye are : for the Son of Man is not come to
destroy men, but to save them'; here the same broad
philanthropy is manifest.

This Gospel alone has 'son of peace,'[3] and in x. 18 we
can trace a generous estimate of the success of the seventy.
The parable of the Good Samaritan gives the watchword to
heroic rescue work in its whole conception, and most of all
in the verdict of the appreciative lawyer ('he who did the
merciful thing with the man') and in the answer of Jesus,
'Go thou, and do likewise.' The bearing of this great
story upon Christian neighbourliness has already been
emphasized. Luke's version of the Lord's prayer gives
us the significant word '*every one* who is in debt to
us,'[4] and in xi. 36 we have the gracious and homely picture
—that of the cottage lit up by the lamp's kindly flash ;
the Christian's social life is to be all welcoming
light. The same note in another tone sounds in
xi. 41, and in the next verse we notice 'the love of God'—
may we say 'love like God's'?—where Matt. xxiii. 23 has
'mercy and faithfulness.' 'I say unto you, My friends
(xii. 4) breathes the same spirit as xxii. 28—both peculiar to
Luke—and xii. 6 is very beautiful. Matt. x. 29 has 'Are not
two sparrows sold for a penny (literally a farthing, a
passing of our money)?'; Luke, 'Are not five sparrows
sold for twopence?'; Matthew, 'not one of them falls
to the ground without My Father'; Luke, 'not one is
forgotten before God.' Here again our evangelist would

---

[1] Mark iii. 29 (cf. Matt. xii. 32).
[2] See an article in the *L.Q.R.* of October, 1913, for a statement of the
case, and App. IV.
[3] Luke x. 6.　　　　　　　　　　[4] Luke xi. 4.

seem to have given us an improved version of a saying found in a simpler form in the first Gospel ; compare the 'five in one house' passage, above (pp. 169, 170). The added point—which must, I think, come from oral tradition—is to be found in the ' five ' and the ' twopence.' Sparrows were sold for consumption by the poor at two a penny and five for twopence, the odd one being thrown in as a makeweight with the rest ; with God the odd one counts full value, for He does not deal with His creatures in the wholesale and promiscuous way of commerce.   Pathos is added to the parable of the rich fool by the skilful use of personal pronouns, ' *my* goods,' ' *my* soul,' ' *thy* soul from *thee*,' and in xii. 32 ' little flock ' strikes once again a note of pitiful tenderness.

Particularly impressive in this connexion is xii. 37, 38, where the slave is waited upon by his master—for the contrast with xvii. 7 ff. see above, page 127 ; and in xiii. 6 ff. —also Luke only—we have the forbearance of God depicted (this again should be set over against the cursing of the fig-tree—see p. 130—which is not found in Luke).   The invalid woman of xiii. 11 ff. is a 'daughter,' as Zacchaeus is a 'son,' of 'Abraham,'[1] and Lazarus is 'carried into Abraham's bosom.'[2]   In xiv. 5 we might see the same tendency in ' son or ox ' (R.V.), if the juxtaposition did not seem excessively awkward ; in this verse we must accept Dr. Harris's emendation ' pig or ox '—' pig ' and ' son ' are written in identical Greek letters in the older Greek MSS., the word for ' son ' being only distinguished by a line over the top, and this was sometimes omitted. The haunting word ' lost ' resounds through chapter xv., binding all three parables together ; Matthew[3] prefers ' wandered.'   Chapter xix. 10, too, should be mentioned here ; it does not belong to the true text of Matthew.[4]   The irony of xx. 13 is heightened by Luke's addition of ' per-haps,' and a kindly excuse is made for the disciples in xxii. 45, ' sleeping after sorrow.'   In xxiii. 28 ff., 34, 40 ff., 48, Luke uses material peculiar to his Gospel to soften the picture of human wickedness presented by the Passion story as much as he can ; and xxiv. 17 ff., 39, 41 are all suffused with a spirit of pity for the disciples, as

[1] Luke xix. 9.   [2] Luke xvi. 22.
[3] Matt. xviii. 12–14.   [4] Matt. xviii. 11 (A.V.).

characteristic of Jesus as it is of this most large-hearted of his reporters. The ' Risen Lord ' breathes peace and blessing ; the ' blessing ' mentioned in xxiv. 30, 50, is found in Luke alone.

If the Gospel of Luke is marked by a less restrained note of pathos than the others, it is also characterized by a more exuberant joy and wonder. Elisabeth ' cries out with a great shout,' while her babe ' dances in her womb ' at the approach of Mary ; her song, the ' Magnificat '—for it should be dissociated from Mary, the best MSS. having ' and she said,' not ' and Mary said '—is a paean of triumph,[1] while the first thing that her husband does upon his recovery of speech is to ' talk, blessing God'; his song of praise follows, and begins with ' blessed.'[2] Then we have the angels' chorus,[3] and the shepherds are roused to ' glorifying and praising God '[4] (notice the two participles, and the confirmation supplied to the A.V. reading of xxiv. 53, ' praising and blessing God,' by this Lucan mannerism). The music passes to Simeon's lips in ii. 28 ff., and he in turn ' blesses God,' while Anna adds her tribute of praise.[5] Jesus too is ' glorified of all '[6]; it is no accident that a word used of God is now transferred to Him. ' Amazement ' follows praise in iv. 36, but now it is tinged with fear ; cf. what is said of Mark's Gospel in Part i., chap. iii. The element of fear is very noticeable in v. 9, 10, where we read that ' amazement had got hold of him (Peter) ' and Jesus answers, ' Be not afraid.' ' Ecstasy,' praise, and fear are blended in v. 26 ; God is ' glorified ' in ii. 20, Jesus in iv. 15 ; now it is *God in Jesus* who receives the homage of men. The paralysed man ' glorified ' God for his cure in v. 25 ; fear and praise join again in vii. 16 ; while the parents of the little girl restored at Capernaum are in ecstasy.[7] The admiration of ' the crowds ' is indirectly referred to in ix. 18—Luke only has ' the crowds '—and in ix. 43 ' *all* ' are smitten with wonder. Jesus discourages a merely personal tribute in xi. 27 f., and the note of praise to God is resumed in xiii. 13. His deeds of mercy compel a momentary shame even in 'those who are set against Him,' while ' all the crowd ' unrestrainedly rejoice at ' all the glorious things that were done by Him.'[8] The insertion

[1] Luke i. 46 ff.   [2] Luke i. 64, 68.   [3] Luke ii. 14.   [4] Luke ii. 20.']
[5] Luke ii. 38. :   [6] Luke iv. 15.   [7] Luke viii. 56.   [8] Luke xiii. 17.

of the story of the grateful Samaritan at xvii. 12 ff. enforces the duty of thankfulness ; and xviii. 43 also is peculiar to Luke ; our evangelist dwells again upon the silencing of the Lord's enemies in xix. 48, xx. 40, xxi. 15.   In xx. 19 the scribes and chief priests are afraid to arrest Jesus, for, as Luke insists, He is still the Hero of the crowd—compare also xx. 26 ; xxii. 6 ('without a crowd,' Luke only) and xxiv. 53 completes the Gospel upon the note set at the beginning.   On the whole Luke does not make the fact that Jesus was much less popular at the end of His ministry than He had been in the early Galilean days quite as clear as Mark does, perhaps because he was not so well informed as was his predecessor as to the state of parties at the time ; it must be remembered that Mark had grown up at Jerusalem.   He rather tends to ascribe the increasing loneliness of Jesus to the rigour of His demands—see especially xiv. 25 ff.   Jerusalem figures far more promi-nently in the Third Gospel than it does in either Matthew or Mark, the part played by the Galileans not being brought out so clearly as by its predecessor.

We can still further justify our reference to the ex-uberant joy characteristic of this book.   Words meaning 'exult' and 'exultation' occur at i. 14, 44, 47 ; x. 21—only elsewhere in the Gospels Matt. v. 12 ; John v. 35 ; viii. 56 ; in 1 Peter three times ; in Hebrews and Jude once each ; in Luke i. 41, 44, vi. 23, moreover, we have 'leap' for joy—in LXX Gen. xxv. 22 ; Ps. cxiv. 4, 6, but nowhere else in the New Testament.   The story of the lost son gives us 'music '—really the 'symphony,' now called in the east 'sampoon,' a musical instrument something like the bagpipes—' and dancing.'[1]   In this chapter too we have merriment in vv. 23, 24, 32.   On the whole I am inclined to accept the reading of Codex Bezae in v. 29, ' that I might have a dinner with my friends,' instead of ' that I might make merry with my friends ' ; riotous mirthful-ness is not in keeping with the elder brother's character. The Vatican MS. has ' a little kid,' the ' Lewis ' Syriac version 'that fatted calf ' ; both these lively readings suggest that the elder son had his eye upon *that* calf. The father, beaming all over because his boy has come home, is set in sharp contrast to the churlish elder

[1] Luke xv. 25.

brother—notice 'these many years I have been a slave
to thee' and the fact that while both father and servant
say 'thy brother,' the surly fellow will not own his brother ;
he says 'thy son.' An old Irish Latin version, we are told,
goes a stage further with 'this son of the devil.'

Our evangelist sets this heavenly gaiety alongside of
the mirthless revelry of the rich and well fed. 'Dives'—
or Phinehas, as he is called in the traditions of the Eastern
Church, Lazarus (Eleazar) being said to have been his
father !—succeeds in being 'merry and bright'—an
almost literal translation of xvi. 19—'every day' (compare
the *daily* simplicity and self-discipline of the Christian's
life[1]) ; that was because he did ask his five brothers in, while
the rich fool set to work to be merry by himself !—but the
rich fool can only 'try to be merry'—we may render the
delicate change of tense in xii. 19, 'I will say to myself,
"You ought to be settling down, old man. Have a
meal and a drink ; try to be merry."' The words
'rejoice' and 'joy' occur nineteen times in Luke's Gospel,
as against twenty-six times in the other Synoptics taken
together, or twenty-three times if the places where one of
these words is used in mockery are left out of consideration ;
'rejoice with' only in Luke xv. 6, 9 in all four Gospels.
The 'Shepherd rejoices' over the sheep, the 'woman'
over her recovered coin, but actual merriment or *home-joy*
comes in along with the less brightly coloured word only
when a lost son is concerned. There is, too, a rising note—
'joy in heaven' (v. 7), 'joy in the presence of the angels'
—a reverent Jewish way of saying 'in God's heart' (v. 10)
—merriment, social joy, in which God and we can join ;
you cannot dance or be merry without a partner. Why
have our Methodist hymn-book revisers preserved that
unimaginative corruption of Charles Wesley's hymn 'Ye
neighbours and friends, to Jesus draw near' ? In the
original version it began 'Ye neighbours and friends *of*
Jesus, draw near.' The whole point of the hymn, as in the
Gospel, is that *we* are the 'neighbours and friends' of
Jesus, and are invited to share His triumphs, the angels
being out of it in this matter. 'Laugh,' in the simple
form of the Greek verb, occurs here only in the New Testament ; it is the proper antithesis to the Lucan 'crying,'[2]

---

[1] Luke ix. 23 ; xi. 3.   [2] Luke vi. 23, 25.

The key-note of the Gospel is praise ; even the 'stones will shout' when Jesus comes to His own[1] (Luke only—cf. iii. 8). Pharisees, like the elder brother in the parable, disapprove of noisy hilarity in religion ; Luke is our principal witness to the fact that Jesus not only tolerates the gaiety of simple souls who laugh, dance, and sing boisterously when they are happy, but joins in, with a disregard of dignity which reflects the merry heart of God. The 'cultured' people who sing even ' My heart it doth dance at the sound of His name ' in a minor key and label as ' irreverent ' the happy tumult of a revival-meeting are grievously far away from the spirit of the Gospels. We have in this Gospel the true doctrine of Christian revelry ; the believer may and should dance if he feels like it, and when there is something worth dancing about, but not with strangers—all depends on the company, the time, and the reason for festivity.

[1] Luke xix. 40.

V

OTHER FEATURES OF THE GOSPEL

OUR evangelist is remarkable for his clear and strong emphasis upon prayer ; he tells us much about the prayers of Jesus, and to him we owe the prayer-parables.[1] ' All the people ' are ' praying ' at the beginning,[2] so that the coming of the Christ is itself an answer to prayer. While Jesus is praying—' and praying ' is peculiar to Luke— the Holy Spirit descends upon Him.[3] Luke v. 16 is more emphatic than Mark i. 35, and Codex Bezae adds ' and prayed ' to the ' blessed ' of ix. 16—it is while Jesus prays that the loaves are multiplied. Again, in ix. 18 solitary prayer precedes the great question ' Whom do the crowds say that I am ? ' and, while the Lord is praying—Luke only—His face assumes an unearthly glory.[4] After He had prayed[5] the disciples approach Him, asking Him to teach them to pray like that. Before His choice of the twelve He spends the whole night in prayer,[6] and in xxii. 45 the words ' rising up from the prayer ' are also peculiar to this Gospel ; prayer avails even in Gethsemane. Before we turn to the prayer-parables, we notice xxi. 36—Luke only in this form ; xxii. 32—the prayer of Jesus for Peter ; xxiii. 34—His prayer for the pardon of all the others engaged in the tragic business of the Cross. Very striking is the parallel between the Transfiguration and Gethsemane, so clearly brought out here. On both occasions Jesus is praying, while the disciples are asleep—in ix. 32 ' heavy with sleep ' and ' when they had awaked ' are Luke only. The subject of His prayer on both occasions is the same (ix. 31 also is peculiar to Luke) ; but upon the mountain His face shines, in the garden His sweat is ' like great clots

---

[1] Luke xi. 5 ff.; xviii. 1 ff., 9 ff.   [2] Luke i. 10.
[3] Luke iii. 21.   [4] Luke ix. 29.
[5] Luke xi. 1.   [6] Luke vi. 12.

of blood.'   In both cases heavenly support is forthcoming ;
Moses and Elijah upon the mountain, 'an angel from
heaven ' in the garden, 'strengthening Him.'   In Gethsemane ' pray ' stands by itself without the ' watch '
of Matthew–Mark.[1]
   The parables about prayer are exceedingly interesting,
but also a little perplexing.   The unjust judge[2] and the
churlish neighbour[3] alike only yield to pressure when it is
becoming a nuisance ; but the story of the importunate widow
leads straight up to a terrific problem—that of the ' forbearance of God '[4]—and ends upon a sombre note, almost as
though for once Jesus had lost heart.[5]   What strikes us in
both cases is that our Lord is letting Himself go in the
delight of story-telling ; He must have loved telling stories
for their own sake, apart from the ' moral.'   All the more
impressive is the reaction from the zest with which the story
of the shrewish widow is told to the haunting cry with which
it closes ; ' Only when the Son of Man comes shall He find
the faith '—faith of a genuine type—' on the earth ? '
Prayer, in Luke's Gospel, answers to the idea of ' faith ' in
Mark ; it is the expression of trust and expectancy, which
will not let itself be daunted by anything whatsoever.   For
it is true after all, in spite of the deep shadows which here
and there pass over this radiant Gospel, that its final
note is a great hope.   We are not dependent upon human
persistency ; where it fails, and those who should watch
are asleep, while men in their ignorance crucify Christ
afresh, we have an advocate with the Father,[6] who prays
for us and for them, as Jesus did for Peter and the others
when they were not equal to praying for themselves,
as He did for His murderers when, in their ignorance,
they nailed to the cross their only Hope.[7]   We must rest
in the prayers of Jesus, who by His passion became our
Advocate, as He became upon the cross the One Mediator
of Salvation.
   Equally emphatic is our evangelist's emphasis upon
repentance.   Luke loves to show us how men and women
were broken up and made anew when the Lord of souls
came their way.   A good example of this process, so often
dwelt upon in these pages, is the Lucan story of Peter's

[1] Luke xxii. 40.   [2] Luke xviii. 1 ff.   [3] Luke xi. 5 ff.   [4] Luke xviii. 7.
[5] Luke xviii. 8.   [6] 1 John ii. 1.   [7] Luke xxii. 32, 45 ; xxiii. 34.

first meeting with Jesus by the lake, and his flash of sudden remorse, ' Depart from me, for I am a sinful man, O Lord ! '[1] Luke also is our only authority for the explicit statement that Levi ' left all '[2] to follow Jesus. In v. 32 he has the explanatory words ' to repentance ' (Luke only). The passages in which the word ' dig ' occurs have been already mentioned (p. 163) ; does ' I cannot dig '[3] mean ' It is too late for me to start life all over again '? The abandon of the Magdalene's repentance is brought out in ' hath not ceased to kiss My feet.'[4] Though she drenches the feet of her Redeemer with her tears, and dries them with the unbound tresses of her hair, the Lord does not let her go without a hint of the greatness of her sin—' Her sins, *which are many*, have been forgiven.' It is only a hint, but it brings her back in deepened thankfulness to His feet. She loves because she is forgiven ; she is not forgiven because she loves. The proverb[5] (Luke only) about driving the furrow straight reminds us of the builder who dug and ' went deep '[6] (again Luke only), and in xiii. 1 ff. we have a section, peculiar to Luke, dealing with the necessity of universal repentance ; it finds its climax in the parable of xiii. 6 ff.—notice especially v. 8, until I can *dig* about it, and give it a basketful of manure,' the last clause I reproduce in the vivid form found in Codex Bezae. The Vinedresser will seek to drive our shallow penitence deeper, and see if there is yet in Jerusalem a ' place of repentance.'[7] The word ' agonize' (see p. 152) is peculiar to Luke[8] ; the Lord's ' agony' in the garden—mentioned explicitly by Luke alone[9] —carries us through our less severe soul-struggles, as His prayers give weight to our fitful petitions. We cannot pray as we ought, but He prays for us. We cannot ' dig ' or ' agonize ' as we ought ; He ' digs ' about the roots of our lives, and is in ' agony ' for us. In xiv. 26 the phrase ' yes, and His own soul '—or, as we should say, ' himself '— ' also ' should be considered in this connexion. Chapter xiv. 33 expresses the same idea in material form— ' possessions ' instead of ' self '—and throughout chapter xv. ' repent ' is the key-word (vv. 7, 10, 19, 21). The

---

[1] Luke v. 8.   [2] Luke v. 28.   [3] Luke xvi. 3.
[4] Luke vii. 45.   [5] Luke ix. 62.   [6] Luke vi. 48.
[7] Heb. xii. 17.   [8] Luke xiii. 24.   [9] Luke xxii. 44.

'repentance' of the prodigal deepens as the action
goes on ; at first it is prompted by the memory of
better days and the humiliation of hunger. If 'when
he came to himself' is not interpreted in the medical sense
suggested on page 155, it will mean something like the self-
despising of xiv. 26 ; for the penitence of the prodigal
becomes less self-regarding, as appears from the little
speech composed in view of his meeting with his father—
'I am not worthy to be called thy son ; make me as one
of thy hired servants.' We see that the dread of this
terrible hunger is still uppermost in the boy's thoughts ;
it is as though he said, ' Only give me enough to eat ' ;
but the deeper note is present all the same. Perhaps the
most absolutely beautiful thing about the story is the fact
that, according to the best MSS., the last part of the
speech is never uttered, for it is smothered in a kiss. He
stops, or is stopped, dead at ' I am no more worthy to be
called thy son.' ' While he was yet a great way off, the
father saw him, and ran ' ; even in this exacting Gospel, God
in Jesus is ready to take the will for the deed. This
thought carries on the idea which we are bringing to light
again and again ; we are to do what we can for ourselves ;
the rest is done for us by God revealed in Jesus, and it is
the greater half.

But the grace of God is never allowed to submerge
altogether the need for exertion upon our side, for ' every
one enters ' the Kingdom ' by force '[1] (in this form Luke
only) ; though ' the Kingdom of God is within you '[2] (also
Luke alone), you must force your way in. Chapter xvi.
30, 31 casts a sombre light upon the difficulty of repentance for gospel-hardened people, while xvii. 4 gives us
the other side again—you, like God, are to be willing to
take the will for the deed, however often you have been
disappointed. It may be that God is more patient with
men and women who ' come out ' afresh in every mission-
service than we are inclined to be. In xvii. 32 (cf. ix. 62),
on the other hand, we have the wrong kind of repentance,
which keeps one eye upon salvation, while the other longs
to be back ; and in xviii. 9 ff. we are presented with a study
in true penitence in contrast with the shameless complacency of the Pharisee. Did the Pharisee really pray

[1] Luke xvi. 16.   [2] Luke xvii. 21.

'to himself'? 'Within himself'[1] might mean that; a more moderate interpretation would be to the effect that his spoken words were much more decorous, but we are allowed to overhear what he was all the time saying *to himself.* In any case we have another suggestion here as to our proper attitude to ourselves : the prodigal comes ' *to himself,*' and is utterly depressed by what he sees there ; the Pharisee surveys himself, and is vastly impressed by what he sees there. With these two instances should be taken the self-absorption of the rich fool, who, like the Pharisee, is too comfortable to be severe with himself ; ' he reasoned *in himself.*'[2]

With xviii. 13 the two other pictures of repentance[3] (all three peculiar to this Gospel) should be compared. Even though we have a good record, we are still to be penitent (xvii. 10—Luke only—reading 'We are slaves,' without ' unprofitable,' which has slipped in here from a memory of Matt. xxv. 30). In xix. 8, 9, repentance is very practical. The question has been raised as to whether Zacchaeus is not simply declaring what had always been his practice; but ' this day ' and the reference to Abraham, who became the father of the faithful because he broke with his past, ' not knowing whither he went,' incline me to the traditional interpretation. Chapter xxii. 32 foreshadows the repentance of Peter—' when thou hast turned ' (compare John xxi. 20—' Peter, having turned, sees the disciple whom Jesus loved ' ; one of the signs that Peter had found the right way was that he now began to think of other people). The actual turning took place when ' the Lord turned ' and looked searchingly at Peter (xxii. 61—Luke only) ; each turns to the other, but the Lord turns first. As Jesus prays for us when we cannot pray for ourselves, ' digs ' about us when we cannot ' dig,' is ' in agony ' for us when we are not ready to ' agonize,' so now He turns to us before we turn to Him. The climax of the series of studies in penitence, which we owe to our evangelist, comes in xxiii. 40 ff., but at xxiii. 48 Luke completes his picture of the people who crucified Jesus, not knowing what they did, by a reference to their belated remorse ; compare the apocryphal ' Gospel of Peter,' according to which they said :

---

[1] Luke xviii. 11.   [2] Luke xii. 17.   [3] Luke v. 9 ; vii. 38.

' Woe upon our sins ! The judgement hath drawn near, and the end is at hand ! '

With this strong teaching on the need for repentance another feature of this Gospel may be connected. Luke is fond of calling attention to the difference between mere ' hearing' and what we should call 'taking in.' Mary, the mother of Jesus, is twice over said to have ' kept these things laid up in her heart.'[1] Notice also ' in your ears,'[2] ' as they heard these things'[3] (the wrong kind of hearing) ; but the man who hears the words of the Lord ' and does them' is like a builder who' dug and went deep.'[4] In viii. 8, after the parable of the Sower, Luke makes the saying ' He that hath ears,' &c. (also Matthew–Mark), yet more emphatic by prefacing it with ' As He said these things, He cried ' ; and in viii. 15 he alone has the suggestive words ' hold it down.' ' Take heed how ye hear ' also is peculiar to Luke,[5] as is the phrase ' those who hear ' in viii. 21. ' Set these words in your ears '[6] is only found in this Gospel ; in x. 16 we have ' He *that heareth you heareth Me*' (Matt. x. 40, ' He that receiveth you receiveth Me '), and Mary enjoys the ' best dish ' when she listens to her Lord.[7] ' Those who hear and keep '[8] strikes the same note ; in xviii. 6 we have another call to attention—' Hear what the unjust judge saith ! '—and in xix. 48 the breathless listening of ' all the people ' (Luke only ; Mark xii. 37, ' the common people heard Him gladly,' is much less graphic). Chapter xxi. 38 also is peculiar to this Gospel.

It is natural that the companion of Paul should show traces of his master's influence ; it is more noteworthy that he scarcely ever uses Pauline words in the full Pauline sense. ' Justify ' in this Gospel means something quite different from Matthew's ' righteousness ' ; Luke i. 75 is the only place where the First and Third Gospels approach one another in their employment of these great words, but it is almost equally remote from Paul's idea. The verb occurs four times in Luke's Gospel. The most striking case is found in vii. 29, ' the publicans justified God ' ; if this reading is right, the sense is that of Ps. li. 4. But the 'Lewis' Syriac reads much more naturally, for its

---

[1] Luke ii. 19, 51.   [2] Luke iv. 21.   [3] Luke iv. 28.
[4] Luke vi. 48.   [5] Luke viii. 18. : ?   [6] Luke ix. 44.
[7] Luke x. 39.   [8] Luke xi. 28.

text shows 'the publicans justified themselves to God.' In the corresponding passage in Matthew[1] we find 'precede you into the kingdom of God'; compare Luke xviii. 14, 'justified *rather than* the other.' In xviii. 14 'justified' is practically equivalent to 'saved,' and cannot be said to be used in the specialized Pauline sense. In viii. 50 Luke has 'only believe, and she shall be saved,' where Mark[2] shows 'only go on believing.' Here it would almost seem that our author has let himself be carried on by a familiar association of ideas (cf. Acts xvi. 31) to a well-known formula. Chapter viii. 13 gives us in Luke alone 'who for a time believe' (Mark iv. 17, 'are for a time'; Matt. xiii. 21, 'is for a time'). In x. 29 we meet with 'justify' again—'he, wishing to justify himself'; this reminds us of the old Syriac reading of vii. 29, and further confirms it; compare also xvi. 15, 'ye are they which justify yourselves.'

At xii. 46 Luke has 'unbelievers' or 'unfaithful' where Matthew[3] has 'hypocrites.' His ideas upon the mission of Jesus are simple and straightforward, for he is not a theologian. The Lord came to set men free from all ills, bodily, social, and spiritual (cf. iv. 18; xiii. 16—both Luke only). In vii. 50 there is no physical miracle, as there is in Mark where the same words are used ('Thy faith hath saved thee'—e.g. Mark v. 34; x. 52); in xvii. 19, too, the words refer primarily to spiritual blessing, which the Samaritan receives quite apart from the cure wrought before his return. 'Salvation' appears in Luke i. 69, 71, 77—defined in the last of these verses as consisting 'in forgiveness of sins'—as well as in xix. 9—only elsewhere in the four Gospels at John iv. 22. 'Peace' is another favourite word; in xix. 42 we have 'the things concerning peace.' Not very much can be made of the contrast between 'peace on earth,'[4] and 'in heaven peace,'[5] for we must reckon with the fact that both 'Peace' and 'Glory,' as well as 'the Highest,' like 'in the presence of the angels,'[6] 'Heaven,' and 'the power' (Mark xiv. 62), were Jewish expressions used in order to avoid the unnecessary utterance of the name of God; whatever may be said of the angels' song, the cries of the

---

[1] Matt. xxi. 31.	[2] Mark v. 36.	[3] Matt. xxiv. 51.
[4] Luke ii. 14.	[5] Luke xix. 38.	[6] Luke xii. 8; xv. 10, &c.

crowd at the Triumphal Entry may only imply a repeated invocation of God. ' Go in peace ' means ' God be with you ' ; cf. the salutation characteristic of the Risen Lord, ' A son of peace ' is a righteous man (see p. 150), and the whole passage may be interpreted 'Say, "God be with this house." And if there be a righteous man there, your blessing—" God be with you "—shall rest upon him ; if not, it shall come back to you.' In the Acts there is a progress easily perceptible from ' faith in God '—which is perhaps the Marcan idea (see Part i., chap. v.)—to 'faith in Christ.' The phrase'the faith which is through Him'[2] may be called the line between the two puttings of the case, but it is clear that the Lucan picture of the Good Physician is the real channel of transition. The supreme instance in the Gospel where Jesus is Himself the object of faith and prayer is that of the 'dying thief'; when the Saviour is on the cross, he does not say, ' Jesus, commend me to God,' but ' Jesus, remember me.'[3] In His atoning passion, the Lord becomes for ever the One Mediator of salvation.

Luke's doctrine of the Spirit is also easy to trace. It is a striking fact that he avoids the words ' Spirit of God ' ; compare Matt. xii. 28, 'in the Spirit of God,' with Luke xi. 20, 'the finger of God.' He often speaks of (the) 'spirit' and ' the Holy Spirit ' : i. 41, 67 ; ii. 26, 27 (' the Spirit') ; iii. 22 ('in bodily form') ; iv. 1 (' full of the Holy Spirit ' and 'led by the Spirit ') ; iv. 14 ('in the power of the Spirit ') ; iv. 18 (' the Spirit of Jehovah '—a quotation from the Old Testament) ; ix. 55 (' of what kind of spirit ') ; xi. 13 (' the Holy Spirit ' ; Matt. vii. 11, ' good things ') ; xii. 10 (for once both Mark iii. 29 and Matt. xii. 32 agree with Luke, but Matt. xii. 31 has ' blasphemy of the Spirit,' then in v. 32 ' against the Holy Spirit ') ; xii. 12 (Matt. x. 20, ' the Spirit of your Father ' ; Luke, ' the Holy Spirit,' but in a similar passage at xxi. 15 ' *I* will give you a mouth and wisdom '). The same emphatic ' *I* ' comes in again at xxiv. 49 : ' *I* am sending the promise of My Father upon you . . . power from on high ' (that is, 'from God '). To these passages—all, except xii. 10, peculiar to Luke, so far as the introduction of the ' Holy Spirit ' is concerned— we ought perhaps to add the Marcionite reading (see App. IV.) of the Lord's prayer at Luke xi. 2, as it bears all the

[1] John xx. 19, 21, 26.   [2] Acts iii. 16.   [3] Luke xxiii. 42.

marks of Luke's style—'Let Thy Holy Spirit come upon
us and cleanse us.' The most interesting feature of this
list of examples is that they occur so much more often in
the first half of the Gospel than in the second. In the
Birth story the ' Holy Spirit ' is distinctly the Spirit of God,
though Luke avoids that expression, and the case is the
same in the majority of instances up to chapter xii. ; after
that point Jesus Himself becomes the Inspirer of His
disciples, as at the end of the Gospel He is the Mediator
of salvation—' I will give you a mouth,' ' I am sending the
promise.' There is no contradiction here, but there is an
unmistakable change of emphasis. Our survey of Luke's
Gospel lends support to the suggestion that in the Acts,
as perhaps to the average Christian of those early days, the
Holy Spirit came to be regarded as primarily the Spirit of
Jesus ; Acts xv. 28, ' to the Holy Spirit and to us,' reads
very much like ' the Master with His disciples.'

In Luke's Gospel the Passion is altogether central ; it
is the perfecting of Jesus. The Transfiguration looks
forward to Gethsemane (see pp. 180–181) and the Cross. The
subject of conversation upon the mountain is ' the exodus
which He was about to fulfil in Jerusalem ' (Luke only).[1]
The ' cloud ' appears in all three Gospels, but in Matthew[2]
it is ' a shining cloud,' and only Luke[3] tells us that the
disciples ' were stricken with fear as they entered into the
cloud.' Matt. xvii. 6 says ' they were much afraid,' but in
his account it is of the glory of Jesus that they are afraid ;
in Luke they are afraid of the cloud. The ' cloud ' is the
shadow of the Passion, casting a chill over the disciples
as they enter into the last phase of their companionship
with Jesus, the cloud which never quite lifted again till
Easter morning. Jesus is ' the Chosen '[4]—compare xxiii.
35 ; the word is in both cases found only in Luke, chosen
for suffering, as we are chosen[5] to receive the blessing
won by His suffering ('elect ' of Christians also in Mark xiii.
20, 22 ; Matt. xxiv. 22, 24). After the Passion Jesus
is 'the Appointed' (Acts x. 42 ; xvii. 31—cp. 'as hath been
appointed,' Luke xxii. 22; this word is not found outside
Luke, Acts, and Hebrews, in the New Testament). Prophecies of the Passion made by Jesus receive special

[1] Luke ix. 31.   [2] Matt. xvii. 5.   [3] Luke ix. 34.
[4] Luke ix. 35.   [5] Luke xviii. 7.

emphasis ; ' Set in your ears these words '[1] is a phrase attached to one of them here only, and the journey to Jerusalem is, as we have seen, thrown forward. The stress laid upon the way to the cross cannot be mistaken ; observe the succession of ix. 51, 53, 57 ; x. 1, 38 ; xii. 50 (Luke only) ; xiii. 22, 33 (also Luke only) ; xvii. 11 ; xviii. 31, 35 ; xix. 1, 11, 28, 37, 41. Each stage of the approach to the city is reverently marked out, and our evangelist labours to make plain what Mark implies, that Jesus is once again the cynosure of all eyes, the object of unbounded curiosity and wonder (xi. 14, 29 ; xii. 1 ; xiv. 1, 25 ; xv. 1 ; xviii. 36, 43 ; xix. 3, 37, 48 ; xx. 19, 26, 39, 45 ; xxi. 38). Jerusalem casts her shadow over these chapters (ix. 31, 51 ; x. 30 ; xiii. 4)—Jesus transfers the subject of conversation from the Galileans to Jerusalem, which herself is symbolized by the fig-tree in the vineyard, in the parable which immediately follows[2] ; xiii. 22, 33, 34 ff. ; xvii. 11 ; xviii. 2 (Codex Bezae, ' *the* city') ; xviii. 10 (the Temple), 31 ; xix. 11, 28, 41 ff.–xiii. 34 ff. is the only one of these passages to which we can find a parallel in the other Gospels. Jesus Himself is the Good Samaritan travelling on a business journey up the Ascent of Blood ; notice the word in x. 33, ' journeying '— that is, ' travelling,' in the commercial sense, while the priest passes that way by mere chance, and so had more time to stop, if he had chosen to do so (v. 31).

In this connexion Luke is specially fond of words like ' accomplish,' ' make perfect ' (xiii. 32, ' accomplish healings ' . . . ' I am perfected' ; xii. 50, 'till it be perfected' ; xviii. 31, 'shall be brought to an end '—this phrase is not found in Mark x. 32 ; Matt. xx. 17–xxii. 37, ' the things concerning Me have come to their end'), all Luke only. The words ' visit ' and ' visitation' become, in the later chapters of this Gospel, pregnant with tragedy ; ' visit ' is used in i. 68, 78, as in vii. 16, with an altogether happy meaning ; but in xix. 44 the idea has taken a darker hue—only elsewhere in the Synoptic Gospels in Matt. xxv. 36, 43 in a much less specialized sense. Like the journey to Jerusalem, the great cry of pity and regret over the city is thrust forward, so that, whereas in Matthew[3] it comes after the Triumphal Entry, and the last words must refer to a second coming, in Luke[4] it comes

---

[1] Luke ix. 44.   [2] Luke xiii. 6 ff.   [3] Matt. xxiii. 37 ff.   [4] Luke xiii. 34 ff.

before, and consequently the words with which it closes must be taken as pointing to the entry itself with its sequel (see also below, p. 193). The same concentration of interest upon Passion-week is perceptible in xxi. 22, '*these* are days of recompense, that all the things written (in Scripture) may be fulfilled ' (Mark xiii. 19, '*those* (future) days shall be affliction '; Matt. xxiv. 21, ' For there *shall then* be '). Luke always prefers to report sayings which refer to the present rather than the future ; instances of this tendency can be found in xxii. 15—Luke only, for xxii. 16 has parallels in Mark and Matthew, not xxii. 15–xxii. 37—also Luke only, *this*, not some future, calamity is the crisis of history ; xxii. 53, ' this *is* your hour, and the authority of darkness '—Luke only ; xxii. 69, ' from the present moment,' Mark xiv. 62, ' ye *shall* see,' Matt. xxvi. 64, ' henceforward '; xxiii. 5, ' beginning from Galilee *up to this point* '—Galilee is the starting-point of Jesus, as Jerusalem[1] was to His apostles ; xxiv. 6, 7, ' while I was still in Galilee '—notice the reference back to the Passion, as formerly forward, in *v.* 7 ; xxiv. 26, 46. It is quite in keeping with the general movement of the Gospel that the last appearance of Jesus is in the neighbourhood of Jerusalem, for the book begins and ends there, as the Acts begins at Jerusalem and ends in Rome.

Readers will already have perceived that some of the passages quoted reveal what may be thought of as a bias against eschatology, and tend to make the interest of the Gospel rather historical than prophetic. The first message of Jesus is omitted,[2] though Luke iv. 18, 19 may be regarded as equivalent, with, however, a more definite application to the practical aspects of the mission of our Lord. When the words ' the kingdom of God hath drawn near ' come at last to be inserted,[3] they are saved from reference to anything but the present by the addition of ' to you.' Luke omits the twin-parables of the wheat[4] and the tares[5] growing while men sleep, probably because both were so definitely connected with Jewish eschatology—see especially Mark iv. 29, with its quotation of Joel's ' harvest ' of wrath. On the other hand, he retains the parable of the Sower, which admits of no such reference. Chapter vi. 46 is quite different from Matt. vii. 21 ; it is plain either that Luke has been using another ' source,' or that he is anxious to avoid any suggestion of ' that day '[6] On the whole it seems probable that Matthew has joined two distinct sayings in an eschatological framework, for in Luke xiii. 24 ff. we come

[1] Luke xxiv. 47. [2] Mark i. 15 ; Matt. iv. 17. [3] Luke x. 9.
[4] Mark iv. 26 ff. [5] Matt. xiii. 24 ff. [6] Matt. vii. 22.

to what is apparently a variant version of the second of the sayings in Matthew. But here again the words 'in that day' are absent, and if we are right in going straight on from Luke xiii. 24 to v. 25, reading 'shall seek to enter in, and shall not be able, after the time at which the Master of the house shall arise,' the whole context is removed from the 'last things' to an imminent spiritual crisis. The Master will not shut the door so much because the people outside are too late, as because they are not able to make up their minds to push their way in while they can (cf. xvi. 16 and the shutting of the door to would-be followers in xiv. 25 ff.). Our evangelist employs the phrase 'the judgement'[1] and 'that day,'[2] where his sources allow of no other interpretation; but he avoids the expression 'the day of judgement,'[3] for 'judgement' tends with him to become rather a process than a set occasion. From this point of view Luke provides us with a transition to the ideas characteristic of the Fourth Gospel. Chapter x. 18 may be taken in an eschatological sense, but even in xi. 2 f. there is a variant reading—'Let Thy Holy Spirit come upon us and cleanse us'—which clearly explains 'Thy kingdom come' not of a future, but of a present and altogether spiritual kingdom. Luke retains 'then hath the kingdom of God come upon you unawares' —as Matt. xii. 28—in xi. 20, but there is a significant change in xii. 5 (cf. Matt. x. 28); Matthew gives us 'Fear Him who can destroy both soul and body in Gehenna'; Luke, 'Fear Him, who after killing *hath authority* to cast into Gehenna.' The reference in Matthew might be to God or to Satan—probably to God (cf. Jas. iv. 12, 'to save and destroy'); whereas in Luke Satan must be meant, for 'authority' always means '*delegated* power,' and God's power cannot be delegated to Him. Of course, it is open to us to think that both may be right—that there were two sayings, one dealing with the fear of God, the other with fear of the power of evil; but it is more likely that we have here alternative renderings of the same saying. Luke is thinking in his translation of the power of Satan in the present world-order; Matthew of a future judgement. Along with this passage should be taken such references to Satan as in xiii. 16; xxii. 32, 53; and especially iv. 6 and x. 18. All of these are peculiar to Luke, except iv. 6, and even in this case the words 'this authority and their glory, because they have been given over to me, and to whomsoever I will I give it' are found only here. In the light of these passages, and of such other New Testament allusions

[1] Luke x. 14; xi. 31, 32.   [2] Luke x. 12.   [3] Matt. x. 15; xi. 22, 24.

to the power of Satan as Rev. xii. 12, we ought perhaps to interpret Luke x. 18—' I was watching Satan falling like lightning from heaven '—as commemorating rather the triumph of the power of darkness upon earth than his defeat. While His disciples had been enjoying their easy victories over ' all the power of the enemy,' Jesus had been wrestling with a deeper and darker problem alone. They did not know it, and He ' exulted in spirit '[1] that they could see what was given them to see ; but it was only possible to reap as they were doing, because He had been sowing, and when sowing ' the word ' did not suffice, would sow Himself.[2] Meanwhile they must not think, because of successes here and there, that the devil's power was broken, for, though they might make raids upon the enemy's lines, He alone could break through, and He by no other way than the Cross.

Coming back to our attempt to trace the main current of the Third Gospel, we notice that Luke omits the reference to the Second Coming found in Mark viii. 38,[3] and also leaves out ' is guilty of an eternal sin,'[4] if he is using Mark here, and not rather Q. If Q is his authority, he renders the saying in a much less precise and threatening form than Matt. xii. 32.[5] Chapter xii. 36, however, does seem to point to the Parousia, though here too the *mise en scène* is less clearly outlined than in the parable of the ten virgins[6] (see above, p. 129). The outline-parable which follows[7] also implies a Second Coming, but xii. 56—' this time '—seems to draw attention to present facts, considered in their moral meaning, rather than as omens of the future[8] (if the passage in Matthew is genuine—' signs of the times '). The Jewish parable of the two ways[9] is omitted, and the cry ' Jerusalem, Jerusalem,'[10] is set in this Gospel before the Triumphal Entry. Harnack has proved that the quotation from a lost Wisdom-book begun at Luke xi. 49—' Therefore I' (that is, 'Wisdom') 'will send to them '—includes the sentence upon Jerusalem (cf. Matt. xxiii. 34–39), so that Luke has divided the quotation into two parts, and is responsible for a disarrangement of Q at this point. The cause of this displacement is perhaps the ' Blessed is He that cometh in the name of the Lord ' found in Mark xi. 9. There is no reason for doubt as to whether Jesus can have quoted from Wisdom-sources not extant now ; but it will be noticed that, if

---

[1] Luke x. 21.   [2] John iv. 37, 38 ; xii. 24.   [3] Luke xii. 8, 9.
[4] Mark iii. 29.   [5] Luke xii. 10.   [6] Matt. xxv. 6.
[7] Luke xii. 37 ff.   [8] Matt. xvi. 3.   [9] Matt. vii. 13 f.
                 [10] Luke xiii. 34 ff.

Harnack is right, no argument as to previous visits to Jerusalem can properly be based upon this passage, for the ' how often ' would then refer merely to the visits of ' Wisdom.' In Luke xiv. 15 ff. there is a manifest rebuke to complacent explanation of the Messianic feast ; the guest who, in order to relieve the tension, changes the subject to the future life, is sharply reminded that the great feast when it comes may not be to the taste of such people as the Lord's fellow guests had proved themselves to be. Probably the ' fatlings'—if indeed the parable is the same as that reported in Matt. xxii. 2 ff. (see pp. 127–128)—are dropped out partly because they seemed too much in keeping with the crude material notions prevalent as to the nature of the feast, at which, according to a curious tradition, 'Leviathan' and 'Behemoth' were to be food for the pious. Luke xvii. 20–22—except in v. 21, ' Look ! here it is ! ' or, ' There it is ! ' all in this Gospel only—is very important in this connexion. Rab Zera said, ' There are three things which come unexpectedly. What are they ? The Messiah, treasure-trove, and a scorpion.'[1] Three Syriac versions have, in v. 21, ' the kingdom of God is among you ' (already) ; but Ephrem, the Syrian father, has ' in your heart.' The ' Oxyrynchus ' sayings of Jesus (see App. II.) in which it is equated into ' know yourselves ' is decisive for ' within you.' It is plain that the habit of looking forward, to the neglect of present facts, is discouraged here. Chapter xvii. 22 might be taken to mean ' days shall come ' (cf. v. 35) ' when you shall long to have a share in one of the Messiah's festal days, and shall not be able,' if it were not that this mournful prophecy was addressed to ' the disciples '; we infer that Jesus is speaking here of a regretful looking backward to the days of His flesh, as in Luke v. 35, rather than of disappointed hopes of His Second Coming. Luke avoids the phrase ' the coming of the Son of Man '[2] in xvii. 24, 30, while xix. 43 obviously refers to the historic siege of Jerusalem.

We have already seen that the interest of xx. 35 is transferred from the future life to this (pp. 170–171) ; the words ' those who are counted worthy to attain that age and the resurrection from the dead' take the place of ' in the resurrection '[3] and ' when they rise from the dead.'[4] The declaration ' The time hath drawn near ' is put into the mouth of the *false* prophet in xxi. 8, and in v. 9 we notice ' the end is not (coming) immediately ' for ' the end is not yet.'[5] Chapter xxi. 20 ff., 25, 26 follow an altogether different

---

[1] Matt. xiii. 44 ; Luke xi. 12.   [2] Matt. xxiv. 27, 37, 39.
[3] Matt. xxii. 30.   [4] Mark xii. 25.   [5] Mark xiii. 7 ; Matt. xxiv. 6.

tradition from that of the fly-sheet (see Part i., chap. iv.) reproduced in Mark-Matthew (cf. Matt. xxiv. 15 ff. ; Mark xiii. 14 ff.) ; divergences are so glaring here that explanations upon the basis of various renderings are out of the question. This is perhaps a fragment of oral tradition, dealing with our Lord's prophecies of the fall of Jerusalem ; Luke, as we see also from passages like xxiii. 28 ff., was specially interested in this subject. Chapter xxi. 31 omits ' at the doors ' from Mark xiii. 29,[1] and our evangelist has no reference to the great saying of Jesus reported in Mark x. 45 ; Matt. xx. 28 : ' the Son of Man is not come to be served, but to serve, and to give Himself a ransom for many.' It is true that at xxii. 27 we have the words ' I am in the midst of you as He that serveth '—the same word ; but there is nothing anywhere in this Gospel at all corresponding to the ' ransom for many.' Our inference must be that the whole section of Mark beginning with the request of James and John[2] was left out by Luke at this point as needlessly mystifying to his Gentile readers. It does not follow, of course, that he doubted its genuineness, still less that we need do so ; but it does imply that he interpreted the words ' a ransom for many ' eschatologically—as meaning, that is to say, to redeem ' many ' from the troubles which were to precede the Second Coming. Luke himself puts the word ' deliverance ' (see p. 202) into the mouth of Jesus[3] ; his difficulty cannot have been with the general idea. We might refer back to Isa. liii. 10— ' when His soul shall make an offering for sin ' ; but the LXX version is altogether different, for it has ' if ye give a sin-offering.' It should be observed that Luke has cancelled Mark's phrase ' on behalf of many '[4] (Matt. xxvi. 28, ' for many ') in his account of the Eucharist. If Luke xxii. 20 is part of the original Gospel, we have ' that is poured out on your behalf ' ; but textual critics, for very good reasons, suspect the authenticity of that passage. We gather that he rejected the clause ' to give Himself a ransom for many,' because he read ' ransom ' in the eschatological sense explained above, and also because ' for many ' seemed to him to imply ' not for all.' Chapter xxii. 29 f. is unmistakably eschatological, but Luke avoids the word ' regeneration,' which has a prominent place in the corresponding saying in Matt. xix. 28. ' Until I drink it new '[5] (Matt. xxvi. 29 adds ' with you ') is softened to ' until it be fulfilled '[6] ; and xxii. 69 is shorter and less realistic than either Mark xiv. 62 or Matt. xxvi. 64. The Session

---

[1] Matt. xxiv. 33.   [2] Mark x. 35 ff.   [3] Luke xxi. 28.   [4] Mark xiv. 24.
[5] Mark xiv. 25.   [6] Luke xxii. 16.

at God's right hand is to date from the Passion—Luke has ' from the present moment shall be ' ; Mark, ' and ye shall see.' In Acts vii. 56 Jesus is seen *standing* at the right hand of God, for He has risen to welcome Stephen ! We have noticed xxiii. 28, 29 (Luke only) already ; more striking still is the transition from future to present in xxiii. 42, 43. The ' dying thief ' says, ' Jesus, remember me when Thou comest in Thy kingdom ' ; Jesus answers, ' *To-day* thou shalt be with Me in Paradise.' ' The promise of My Father '[1] is not the Second Coming, but Pentecost ; the distinction is made clear in the Acts. [2]

---

[1] Luke xxiv. 49. [2] Acts i. 7, 8 ; ii. 17, 18.

VI

THE GOSPEL OF CATHOLIC HOPE

THE greatest contribution which this large-hearted evangelist has made to our knowledge is to be found in his
strong statement of the universal meaning of the mission
of Jesus.   Luke has his prejudices, it is clear, one of them
being his characteristically Hellenic dislike of a mob.
'The crowds,' not Pharisees and Sadducees specially, are
addressed as 'offspring of vipers'—that is, 'children of
the devil'—by John the Baptist[1] (cf. Matt. iii. 7).   In v.
15, 16 Jesus withdraws from the pressure of the crowd ;
according to Mark i. 35, He got up 'early in the morning,
while it was still dark,' before the crowds were stirring.
Matt. xii. 23, 24 tells us of the 'ecstasy' of the crowds,
and attributes the accusation of witchcraft to the Pharisees (see also Matt. ix. 34), as Mark[2] to 'Scribes from
Jerusalem ' ; Luke has merely 'some of them '—that is,
of the crowd.[3]   The crowds 'choke' Jesus[4] (Mark v. 31
has 'pressing upon Thee together '), and in xi. 29 it is
'when the crowds were gathering to Him ' that the Lord
says, 'This generation is an evil generation ' ; Matt. xii.
38 makes it plain that the 'Scribes and Pharisees ' provoked this declaration.   Chapter xiv. 25 gives us the
stern words of Jesus to the crowd, and Luke will not have
it that it was 'the greater part of the crowd '[5] (Mark xi.
8, 'many ') that acclaimed the Lord at His Triumphal
Entry ;   he writes 'the whole company of the disciples.'[6]
Even when Pharisees are the culprits, they are sometimes
described as 'Pharisees from the crowd.'[7]   Our evangelist
is probably right here ; at any rate, his reminder is useful
that the Pharisees were not an exclusive circle of educated
men, but formed the great majority of middle-class religious

---

[1] Luke iii. 7.   [2] Mark iii. 22.   [3] Luke xi. 15.   [4] Luke viii. 45.
[5] Matt. xxi. 8.   [6] Luke xix. 37.   [7] Luke xix. 39

people. When Luke has anything good to say of the rank and file of the hearers of Jesus, he calls them 'the people'[1]; in xii. 1 the words 'Meanwhile, when the countless numbers of the crowd were gathering together, so as to trample upon one another, Jesus began to say to His disciples first' are all peculiar to his Gospel. That our evangelist did not think highly of the wisdom of mass-meetings is clear from Acts xix. 32; but he is careful to show that Jesus did not feel in quite the same way about the crowds, for the words 'welcoming them' in ix. 11 are found here only.

But such traces of aristocratic feeling as can be discerned in this Gospel, along with the vein of pessimism and of revolutionary theory already observed, only serve as a most effective background for its shining spirit of catholic hope. Though himself a Gentile, Luke shows strong sympathy with the little circle of old-fashioned Jews— the Israelites indeed—who welcomed into their arms the newborn Messiah, and he succeeds in reporting their evidence in their own language, in their very tones. Everywhere as the story goes on he gives proof of a desire to do justice to its Jewish atmosphere; indeed, he is more deeply influenced by the language of the LXX—the Greek version of the Old Testament accepted as authoritative and used by Christians—than either Matthew or Mark. In xx. 11, 12 we have the words—peculiar to Luke— 'added to send'—I render literally to bring out the Hebraism—twice over. The phrase 'before His face' occurs twice in the Gospel,[2] apart from the Old Testament passage, which Luke has in common with the other evangelists[3]; 'His face was going'[4] (cf. 'He set His face' in ix. 51) we have noticed already. Chapter i. 66, 'the hand of the Lord'; xi. 20, 'the finger of God'; xvi. 22 (cf. iii. 8, xiii. 16, xix. 9), 'Abraham's bosom'; xxii. 15, 'with desire I have desired'; xxiii. 43, 'Paradise,'— should also be mentioned; they are all peculiar to Luke.

At the same time, Luke everywhere softens the peculiarly national aspects of the mission of Jesus. Chapter iii. 1 sets his story in the framework of world-history, and in iii. 5, 6 the quotation of Isa. xl.—dropped at v. 3 by Mark[5]

---

[1] e.g. Luke xx. 19, 26; xix. 48; xxi. 38.   [2] Luke ix. 52; x. 1.
[3] Luke vii. 27; Mark i. 2; Matt. xi. 10   [4] Luke ix. 53.   [5] Mark i. 2, 3.

and Matthew[1]—is continued, till in v. 5 the universal note
is sounded—' and all flesh shall see . . .' In iii. 14
Roman soldiers as well as Jewish publicans (iii. 13) come
to John for advice, and in iii. 38 the pedigree of Jesus is
traced back to Adam and to God.   Chapter iv. 24 ff. gives
us what may be called a foreign missionary address from
the lips of the Lord Himself ; we have already mentioned
the ' other cities ' of iv. 43.   ' Launch out into the deep '[2]
gives us the key to the story in which it is found as well as
to very much of Peter's history (cf. Matt. xiv. 29 ; John
xxi. 18, 19 ; Acts x. 15).   Allowance for conservative
prejudice is made at v. 39, and at vii. 3 ff.   Luke
is careful to give us a welcome instance of friendship
between Jews and Gentiles.   ' Wisdom is justified of *all*
her children ' (Matt. xi. 19 has ' works ') is a noble assertion
of the principle of tolerance.[3]   There is no contradiction
between our evangelists here, for to the Eastern mind
children are a kind of ' works,' and ' works ' a kind of
children, for a man is known by his works, or ' fruits,'[4] as he
is known by his children,[5] and for the same reason.   Luke
says what he can for the Pharisees, mentioning that they
sometimes asked Jesus to dinner,[6] and that they warned
Him of the designs of Herod[7] ; he leaves it an open question as to whether they were really animated by friendly
motives in either case.   It is possible that, when they asked
Him to their houses, they wished merely to patronize Him
and snub Him at the same time ; indeed, His table-talk,[8]
and the calculated rudeness of Simon[9] leaves us little option
in the matter.   This impression is softened, however, by
the magnanimous words of Jesus.   ' He frankly forgave
them both,' so the Pharisee was forgiven too !   Evidently
Jesus took the overtures of the Pharisees at more than
their face value.   At any rate, Luke gives us the fact
that Pharisees did make advances to Jesus, whatever
they were worth.

The same sinister interpretation may be put upon the
intervention of the Pharisees in xiii. 31, for Jesus replies
curtly—they were probably scheming to get Him out of
their neighbourhood.   But it cannot be an accident that

---

[1] Matt. iii. 3.　　　[2] Luke v. 4.　　　[3] Luke vii. 35.　　　[4] Matt. vii. 16.
[5] Sirach xi. 28.　　[6] Luke vii. 36 ; xi. 37 ; xiv. 1.　　[7] Luke xiii. 31.
[8] Luke xi. 37 ff. ; xiv. 7 ff.　　[9] Luke vii. 44 ff.

we have in this Gospel the only clear statement of
the Pharisaic point of view upon the Sabbath question.[1]
If the case was one of extreme urgency, the Rabbis would
agree that healing was no desecration of the Sabbath ;
but, on this occasion, the synagogue president would argue
that it was not ; the woman might well wait till
to-morrow ! Jesus, on the other hand, preaches the
doctrine that the Sabbath is not meant for mere inertia,
or even only for worship, narrowly interpreted, but for
beneficent activity ; He does not say, ' The better the
day, the better the deed,' but ' The better the deed, the
better the day '[2] (cf. John v. 17). It is not merely
lawful ' to do well on the Sabbath-day '[3] ; it is our moral
obligation to worship God in the way of service (' Ought
not ? '). In something of the same spirit, our evangelist
underlines, so to say, the miracles wrought outside the
borders of Palestine proper,[4] and he agrees with Mark
v. 19, 20 that Jesus bade the cured demoniac preach
in the Decapolis[5] ; this command is omitted in Matt.
viii. 34.

Equally noteworthy is Luke's feeling for the Samaritans.
In ix. 52 ff. we have a sharp rebuke to James and John
for their bigoted resentment of Samaritan churlishness ;
the only reprisal for inhospitality in one place being that
Jesus moves on to another (also presumably Samaritan)
village, and goes out of His way shortly afterwards to tell
the story of a very neighbourly Samaritan.[6] Matthew[7]
sets the incidents recorded in Luke ix. 57 ff. on the eastern
shore of the lake of Galilee ; Luke—apparently—in
Samaria ; and it is from Samaria that the Lord sends
out His seventy missionaries ' into every city and place
where He was to go.' This fact—that they were to visit
others than Jews—sets x. 8 in a strong light. ' Eating
and drinking what they have to give ' and ' Eat what is
set before you ' would be no mere instruction to observe
the rules of etiquette to a Jew likely to visit Gentile or
Samaritan houses, for obedience would involve breaking
with traditional prejudices which had become second
nature ; we can almost hear the accents of Paul.[8] The

---

[1] Luke xiii. 14.   [2] Luke xiii. 16.   [3] Matt. xii. 12.
[4] Luke viii. 26 ff.   [5] Luke viii. 39.   [6] Luke x. 33 ff.   [7] Matt. viii. 18 ff.
[8] 1 Cor. x. 25 (cf. Gal. ii. 12 ff.).

'Woes' against the lakeside towns were also, according
to Luke, uttered during this journey[1]; this implies a
comparison with our Lord's experiences in Samaria.
Matthew[2] places them in Galilee. In ix. 60—at this
point Matthew[3] is closely parallel in substance—Luke
has 'Go away and proclaim the kingdom'; Matthew has
'Follow Me.' In Matthew Jesus says, 'Come'; in
Luke, 'Go.' We are not surprised to discover that Luke
leaves upon one side Matthew x. 5, 6, vii. 6, x. 23; but
one would have thought that the story of a Gentile woman's
quickness and courage, told in Mark vii. 26 ff., Matt.
xv. 22 ff., would have appealed to him. Perhaps he did
not appreciate the distinction between 'dogs'[4] and
'puppies'[5] (see Part i., chap. iii.); more probably he was put
off by the story, as many people have been, rather needlessly, since. But there is another possibility, which
will come up for discussion later on (pp. 206–207).

If the suggestion of a Gentile or partly Gentile or
Samaritan mission of the seventy is justified, it is possible
that x. 21 (' babes ') refers primarily to those who were
not Jews; this interpretation gives more force to the
last clause of x. 22—' to whomsoever the Son wishes
to reveal Him.' The relevancy of the story of the Good
Samaritan to this context need not be urged again; its
chief point is that the neighbourliness does not depend
upon neighbourhood. Both ' Father ' and ' Our Father '[6]
would be ' Abba ' in Aramaic, but Luke's choice of ' Father '
is due to his dislike of the limiting suggestion of ' our.'
In viii. 16, xi. 33 our Gospel gives us ' that those *who
enter in* may catch sight of the light ' (xi. 33, ' the shining ').
Mark iv. 21 does not show the clause at all; Matt. v.
15 has ' it shines for all in the house.' The room of the
Christian soul is to be lighted for the benefit of visitors
in the Third Gospel; for the enjoyment of the home-
circle in the First. The placing of this saying in xi. 33
should be emphasized; it follows immediately after
references to such open-minded Gentiles as the Queen
of Sheba and the Ninevites.[7] Chapter xii. 47, 48 is
peculiar in substance to Luke, and may well be taken

[1] Luke x. 13 ff.   [2] Matt. xi. 20 ff. (cf. xi. 1).   [3] Matt. viii. 22.
[4] Matt. vii. 6.   [5] Matt. xv. 26.   [6] Luke xi. 2 ; Matt. vi. 9.
[7] Luke xi. 30 ff.

as referring to Gentiles, as xiii. 25 ff. is clearly pointed against Jews—'We have eaten and drunk in Thy presence, and Thou hast taught in our streets' is found in Luke alone. Still more striking is Luke's addition of ' whence ye are ' to the ' I know you not ' in xiii. 27 (cf. Matt. vii. 23) ; we should translate ' It does not matter to me where you come from.'

In regard to the story of the lost son,[1] we ought to keep in view the fact that it is founded upon the last two chapters of the book of Jonah, the classic plea for universalism. In both cases the younger brother—Nineveh in the older story—repents and comes back to the father ; in both he is warmly welcomed ; in both cases the elder brother protests,[2] and the father argues with him upon his brother's behalf. It follows that we must not leave the Jew and Gentile question out of our interpretation of the parable, though the coming of the publicans to Jesus was its occasion. At xvi. 16 we notice the phrase ' every one forces his way in,' and in xvi. 28 the ' five brothers ' are Jews, for they have ' Moses and the prophets.'[3] Nothing could be more pointed than the last clause of xvii. 16—' and he was a Samaritan'; the emphasis upon his alien origin is made yet more distinct by the words ' except this foreigner.'[4] The catholic atmosphere of the passage which follows is unmistakable[5] ; the Kingdom is not ' here or there,' but everywhere, and its final coming will flash upon the four quarters of the world at once.[6] At the hands of ' this generation ' of Jewish people the Son of Man must suffer, and in the judgement the heathen world shall rise up to condemn them.[7] Luke completes the compass in xiii. 29, and xix. 40 is conceived in the same spirit—' the stones will cry out ' (cf. iii. 8, ' God is able *of these stones* to raise up children to Abraham '). Chapter xx. 16 ff. is equally emphatic, but we have already commented upon this passage, with its possible reference to Paul. In xxi. 21–24 the directions to leave Jerusalem are heavily stressed, and at xxi. 28 we notice that '*your* deliverance' is implicitly contrasted with ' redemption for His people,'

---

[1] Luke xv. 11 ff.   [2] Jonah iv. 1 ; Luke xv. 28.   [3] Luke xvi. 29.
[4] Luke xvii. 18.   [5] Luke xvii. 20 ff.   [6] Luke xvii. 23, 24.
[7] Luke xvii. 25 ff.

'the redemption of Jerusalem,' 'to redeem Israel.'[1]
I have avoided the use of the word ' redemption ' in my
translation of xxi. 28, because Luke avoids the simpler
form of the Greek root where the broader Christian hope
is meant, employing by preference a compounded form
which carries with it rather the general sense of ' deliverance' than the specific idea of ;ransom-price'; compare
what is said above (p. 194) of Luke's omission of 'a ransom
for many '[2]; he keeps the simpler and narrower expression when he wishes to convey to our minds the hopes
of faithful Jewish people. Chapter xix. 14—here only—
taken along with v. 27, gives us a glimpse of the sterner
aspect of universalism ; Luke's individual record of
prophecies of the fall of Jerusalem (e.g. xix. 41 ff., xxi.
24 ff., xxiii. 28 ff.) is a sufficient commentary upon this
feature of the parable, but we may notice in passing
the reference to the ' far country ' (cf. xv. 13, and below,
p. 207).

But our most dramatic instance of our evangelist's
catholic tendency comes, as we should expect, in his
summing-up of the scene at the cross. In xxiii. 34 ff.
we read, ' But Jesus said, Father, forgive them ; for they
know not what they are doing '—this refers to the Jews
(see p. 143). ' And parting His garments, they '—the
Gentile soldiers—' cast lots, and the people stood beholding.'
The Jews look on—as Jonah, their agelong type, ' waited
to see what would become of the city '[3]—while Gentiles
divide between them the garments of the Messiah ; spectators then, they have been fated to be mere spectators
of the world's history ever since, but in these days they
seem to be coming into the current again, for ' the times
of the Gentiles ' are being ' fulfilled '[4] (cf. Rom. xi. 25,
27 ff.). For the universalism of Luke is really universal.
It does not simply turn the tables upon the Jews ; if
it did, it would be untrue to the spirit of Jesus. The
Jews repent[5] (Luke only)—too late, it is true, to undo
the mischief of their act, but not too late for mercy, for
had not the Lord already prayed for and won forgiveness
for them ? In the Birth story Luke has shown us his
power of appreciating and rendering the point of view

---

[1] Luke i. 68 ; ii. 38 ; xxiv. 21.   [2] Mark x. 45 (cf. Matt. xx. 28).
    [3] Jonah iv. 5.   [4] Luke xxi. 24.   [5] Luke xxiii. 48.

of people who differed *toto caelo* from himself (i. 54, 68, 71 ff.; ii. 25, 38; cf. xxiv. 21; Acts i. 6; xxiii. 6; xxiv. 15; xxvi. 6; xxviii. 20). His Gospel moves away from this standpoint as it proceeds, but it closes upon a note of harmony and catholic hope; in the Acts he completes his demonstration that after all the 'hope of Israel' and the 'full tide of the Gentiles' is essentially the same. Jesus hoped for His people, then He lost hope[1]; in the garden and upon the cross He won back to hope again.[2] So the wheel has come full circle, for the redeeming agony of the Son of Man made possible a new birth of hope beyond the doom which by the murder of their King 'His own' people were bringing upon themselves. In the logic of history there could be but one outcome for such perversity as theirs and ours; but there is something greater than the moral law revealed in history, for the Lord's 'strong crying and tears' have availed, we know not how, to pull the helm of the world's destiny hard round, and we may hope that the first, having become last, may in the consummation come to be first again.

Does the redeeming prayer of Jesus warrant us in going any further? In the discussion of the meaning of the word 'hypocrisy,' reserved for a later chapter (Part iii., chap. vi.). it is pointed out that in the Semitic idea underlying our Lord's use of the word, unconscious as well as conscious insincerity or unreality is included. If that is so, it is more than interesting to observe that, if this half-realized hypocrisy was the greatest hindrance and bewilderment incident to the ministry of Jesus, He would seem in the course of His Passion to have found in it His hope; when He prayed, 'Father, forgive them; for they know not what they do,' the range of His prayer extended to the Pharisees; indeed, Paul, the Pharisee, makes it his ground of hope in 1 Tim. i. 13, &c., ' I did it in ignorance'; compare Acts iii. 17, where Peter definitely associates the 'rulers' with the people of the Jews in this extenuation. Recognition of this fact is vital to us, for we are much more like Pharisees than publicans.

The Lord's use of the title 'Son of Man,' to be discussed in detail later on, means that the kinship of the Son of God with *every man* was part of the

---

[1] Luke xiii. 8 (cf. Mark xi. 14, and above, p. 130).   [2] Luke xxiii. 34.

instinctive consciousness of Jesus. His incarnation implies that God and man, as God made him, are one in Christ; His Atonement, that man, as he has made himself, is not and cannot be altogether severed from God. May we say that Jesus made a tremendous venture? He had seen the opening of the 'great gulf,' which, if allowed to widen still further, could never be bridged.[1] Neither mercy nor wrath availed to save the men who barred His way to their hearts; there was but one thing left—Himself. In all four Gospels alike, whereas the use of the words 'the Kingdom' almost disappears with the last phase of our Lord's ministry—except xiv. 25 x. 25 is its last occurrence upon the lips of Jesus in Mark, and He drops the words 'in . . . glory'[2] from His answer to James and John—the phrase 'the Son of Man' tends, if anything, to become more frequent as time goes on (twice in Mark ii., then twice in chapter viii., thrice in chapter ix.—then six times to the end of the Gospel; in Luke four times to the end of chapter viii., then nineteen times; in Matthew four times to end of chapter xi., then twenty-two times). The earlier examples, moreover, generally lay emphasis upon His exaltation, the later upon His suffering; of course there are exceptions to this rule, as one would expect. Did Jesus learn by experience, by the 'things that He suffered,' all that 'obedience' to His vocation as 'Son of Man' involved?[3] These men were coming to be alien from Him in all but the one fundamental fact, that they were men. He would stake everything upon that; would take His place with us, even if it meant such severance from God and hope as He had seen impending over His enemies. It was a real risk. Pure and sensitive souls have allowed social evils so to prey upon their minds that they have come to feel themselves tainted, and some have seemed to die in despair through mere association with sinners. In Jesus there was a sensitiveness and a power of getting outside Himself as unique as was His purity. We ought to translate Luke xxii. 37—a fuller discussion of this haunting passage in the Saviour's soul-history is attempted elsewhere—quite fearlessly, 'He was numbered with lawless men . . . for it is all over with Me' (cf.

[1] Luke xvi. 26.   [2] Mark x. 37-40.   [3] Heb. v. 8.

Mark iii. 26). The 'lawless men' are His murderers (cf. Acts ii. 23, &c.) ; them and their like He had threatened with banishment from His presence. Of them He had said, 'Let them alone'[1] ; now He could not find it in His heart to leave them, or any of us, to our fate. The 'Son of Man,' becoming 'Son of Man' indeed, did not cease to be 'Son of God,' but found a way back to the peace which had been His, not ours *from our end*. In this fact we find our one sure ground of hope that the 'outer darkness' cannot be the final doom of any soul of man, for His finished work must avail for all worlds where men can be.

If, as is suggested in the course of the next paragraph, Lazarus in the parable of 'Dives' and Lazarus stands for Jesus Himself, it will be seen that its closing words, 'if one go to them from the dead,' &c., cast a strong light upon the thought of Jesus as to death and its issues. Here was this spiritually rich and self-contained Jewish people, symbolized in the parable by 'Dives' and his five brothers, with the door shut upon Jesus and Gentile 'dogs' alike. 'Dives' and Lazarus are close together every day, for did not the Lord teach in their streets, did they not eat and drink in His presence ? By-and-by death will intervene and carry Lazarus away to Abraham's bosom; for Himself He had no fears, for 'He came from God and was going back to God,' but what of them ? All Father Abraham—who stands for the orthodox eschatology of His day and of ours—could say was that after death the barrier already between them would widen to a great gulf ; 'Dives' would not come to the help of Lazarus now, Lazarus could not pass over to 'Dives' then. We cannot simply turn down this terrible doctrine, for we can see it at wo.k in life as we know it ; the gulf does tend to grow wider and deeper, does seem to become impassable, nor could the Saviour Himself storm His way through the unbelief of man. But this parable is not the last word of Jesus upon the doom of the unrepentant ; and He alone can pass the final judgement upon this darkest of all mysteries, on which theologians have dogmatized so callously. His last word here was, 'Father, forgive them.' Could He have prayed as He did upon the cross if He had altogether lost hope for

[1] Matt. vii. 23 ; xv. 14.

P

His people, for all lost souls ? The agony in the garden is the strongest evidence, stronger than all His dark and terrible words, for the stringency of the moral law ; never before could we imagine Him having to say, 'Not My will, but Thine, be done.' He is as one struggling to keep a footing in two worlds that are every moment drifting more widely apart. His prayer ' Not My will, but Thine, be done ' is His consecration to the fellowship of lost souls, in whatever separation from His Father that fellow-ship may involve Him. Since He took all the risks and yet came through victoriously, and with all fear gone, may we not dare to hope that the drop of water has been carried by the One who did go to them from the dead, to cool the tongue of those who are in anguish in the quenchless flame of remorse ? Even for those who have obstinately refused the fellowship of the Son of God in the likeness of a poor brother, surely there are alleviations, and there is hope to make life endurable. If Jesus could still be Son of God when He utterly resigned Himself to be ' numbered with rebels,' can God and rebellious man ever be parted without hope of a return and a reconciling ? We may think that some people are not worth keeping, or we may think that life consumed by the ' worm that dieth not ' is worse than extinction ; as long as man is man, and He is Son of Man, there cannot but be some stirring of the life of God in every soul of man, wherever there is a man ; and it may be that even when the prodigal, after his long wandering, is gathered home, and remorse is overwhelmed in love, a sense of something lost may live on in the soul of the wanderer, who ' never can ' himself ' forgive.' For all we know the memory of man may be as eternal as the love of God, and love and remorse may live on together in heaven itself ; God may forgive us much more readily than we shall be able to forgive ourselves. So there may be sins which cannot be forgiven in this world or the next, while the sinner is fully and freely and for ever forgiven.

Jesus, as we noticed above, becomes more central as this Gospel proceeds. Only once, in a story taken from Q, does He heal any one without seeing them.[1] Another case, which perhaps did not seem to Him to rest upon quite

---

[1] Luke vii. 10 (cf. Matt. viii. 13).

such high authority, is omitted in his pages.[1]   The Lord is
the sole Channel of healing power, as He is the one
Mediator of salvation.   In many of the later parables,
however, the Saviour Himself has no obvious place; in those
of the Good Samaritan, the lost coin, the lost son, the unjust steward, 'Dives' and Lazarus, neither King nor
Kingdom figure.   In another parable where Luke is
clearly parallel to Matthew,[2] whereas Matthew mentions both King, Prince, and Kingdom, Luke has simply
' a certain man '; in Matthew the connexion with the
story that goes before the parable of the ' talents ' gives
us 'The Kingdom is likened unto a man '; Luke has
only ' a certain nobleman.[3]'   Nevertheless, all these
stories suggest Him in one way or another.   ' Lazarus '
(Eleazar) means almost the same thing as ' Jesus.'
According to the Syriac versions, Lazarus was not a
' beggar,' simply a ' poor man '; compare the Moslem
saying about Jesus (quoted at length by Dr. Rendel
Harris in the *Expositor*, August, 1918), ' No form of address
was more pleasing to Jesus than when any one said to
Him : " O poor man."'   Moreover, the words ' If one
go to them from the dead ' point to One who did.   The
business journey of the ' Samaritan '—in John viii. 48
Jesus is called a ' Samaritan '—up the Ascent of Blood
reminds us of another commercial traveller (cf. Matt.
xiii. 45) who went the same way, not ' by chance,'[4] and
who will come again to repay those who carry on His
work of rescue.[5]   The unjust steward brings to our mind
the faithful Son,[6] who was willing to forfeit more than
' the unrighteous mammon ' to ' make friends ' with
His tenants[7]; while the churlish elder brother is a foil
to that Elder Brother who followed the prodigal to the
' far country ' (cf. xix. 12) ' to get Himself a kingdom.'
The ' citizens ' He leaves at home rebel against Him in
the spirit of the elder son's complaint against his father,
because their influence is threatened by the new state of
affairs.   The link between these two parables is stronger
than any merely verbal association.   The difficulties,
in the second of the pair especially,[8] are greatly relieved

[1] Mark vii. 30 ; Matt. xv. 28.   [2] Luke xiv. 16 ff. ; Matt. xxii. 2 ff.
[3] Matt. xxv. 14 ; Luke xix. 12.   [4] Luke x. 31.   [5] Luke x. 35.
[6] Heb. iii. 6.   [7] Luke xvi. 9.   [8] Luke xix. 14 (cf. xv. 15).

when we read them together ; indeed, the section of the
parable of the ' pounds ' dealing with the purpose and
the result of the visit to the ' far country '[1] seems almost
pointless until we do so. Jesus is calling in the actual
visit of Archelaus to Rome ' to get himself a kingdom '
as an illustration ; but He would not have adduced the
case of this worst of the Herods unless He had something
quite different in mind.

These considerations tend to modify our first impression
that Jesus has not quite so central a place in the Third
Gospel as He holds in the First ; but we cannot fail to
see that here He is depicted rather as the Mediator of
salvation than Himself the Saviour. The name ' Jesus '
(' Jehovah saves ') is interpreted in Matthew[2] as meaning
' He *Himself* shall save His people.' This development
our Gospel—the second in order of time—does not so
clearly show, for Luke dwells rather upon the range than
upon the intrinsic nature of the Lord's salvation; in ix.
55, xix. 9, ' salvation ' stands for the salvage of individual
lives. On the cross the redeeming power of the prayers
of Jesus assumes a cosmic significance, but still His word
is ' *Father*, forgive them.' The key-notes of this Gospel
of hope may be found in ' I will arise and go to my Father,'
passing on into ' Father, forgive them ' ; in Matthew the
key-note is simply ' Come unto Me.'

Indeed, the word ' Go,' set over against the Matthaean
' Come,' might be taken as characteristic of the Third
Gospel in a larger sense ; it is the Gospel of the Road,
and Jesus is the Pioneer, the Roadmaker. He must
' walk to-day and to-morrow,' and ' on the third day '
will come to His goal. It is no accident that when we
have passed ix. 5, milestones and guide-posts are scattered
over the face of the narrative so freely (ix. 51, 53, 57, 62 ;
x. 1, 9, 11, 33, 38 ; xi. 53 ; xii. 35 ff., 45, 49 f., 58 ; xiii.
22, 24 f., 26. 32, 34 f. ; xiv. 26 ff. ; xvi. 16 ; xvii. 11 ;
xviii. 7, 31, 35 ; xix. 1, 11, 28). Everywhere is the note
of urgency ; there are no aimless journeys, for it is now
or never, both with the Lord Himself and the men of His
generation. He is for ever ' going out'—away from home
to be baptized, from baptism to temptation, from the
people of His own country to the lakeside, from Capernaum

[1] Luke xix. 12, 14.   [2] Matt. i. 21.

to Jerusalem, from the upper room to Calvary, always
a passer-by with nowhere to lay His head till He arrives
at the cross. ' How constrained I feel till I get it over,' He
cries. In Mark's Gospel the influence of the times, of the
outward constraint upon the course of the Lord's ministry, is
depicted ; in Luke's story emphasis is rather placed upon
the *inward* constraint laid upon Him. In the First Gospel
we have a serener picture ; there Jesus is not so much
studied as being moved (as in Mark), or as moving (as in
Luke) but as standing all the day long with outstretched
arms. In Mark we are told what men felt about Him,
in Luke what He felt about men, in Matthew what He
was in Himself. In Mark we see Him acting and being
acted upon, in Luke we see Him as the Messenger of God
not so much to individuals as to the life of His day and
of all times, with an appeal to be forced home quickly
and a mission to be accomplished within a given time ;
in Matthew He stands before us, in all His beauty to be
looked and wondered at, a tragic figure ' despised and
rejected of men,' God's ' Man of Sorrows,' the shedding
of whose ' innocent blood ' is the decisive fact in the
history of men and nations.

Luke's Gospel, the message of which we are trying to
summarize now, gives us the story of the founding of
the fellowship of the Catholic Church, the universal mission
of Jesus. For the sake of the greater He leaves behind
Him the narrower circles of influence—His family, His
first mission-centre—and, last of all, the men who had
become ' His brothers, and sisters, and mother.' As the
Gospel proceeds we watch the smaller, more self-contained
fellowships rent asunder : He lies down at the tables
of men, and the company breaks up too soon, for He
must hurry away ; even at Bethany, as on the Mountain
of Transfiguration, the talk is of the ' exodus ' which He
must shortly accomplish. To give Himself altogether
to the few is to exclude the many, and He can never forget
' the many.' Over all the later parables there broods a
great shadow, the fear of an eternal separation ; we hear
of a ' far country,' of a ' great gulf,' of a closed door where
men are knocking and a hand waves them away, of a Son
cast out of the vineyard and slain, of a cup of good
fellowship refused, and another cup of forsakenness drained

to the dregs ; last of all of One who finds His place among criminals, and is glad to think He will have a condemned malefactor with Him in Paradise. After the Cross the threads which have been snapped one after another, as the Lord broke away from those who would keep Him to themselves, begin to be gathered up again ; He can ' abide with them ' now, and though at last He is parted from them, they can sit quietly in Jerusalem, waiting till He shall come, quite sure that He is theirs, because they have learnt not to try to keep Him.

As for the Master Himself, so for His followers, there can be no rest till the work is done, if they are still to follow Him. They must not stand still, must not even look back, till the furrow is ploughed ; they must not stop to bring away the things or say good-bye to the people at home; they must not cling to parents or wife, but must say farewell to all that has made life worth living up till then. If they would ' go and preach the kingdom of God ' they must ' launch out into the deep,' and make the joint adventure fearlessly, for no one who is not prepared to do violence to his own tastes and inclinations can force his way into the Kingdom in strenuous days such as those are when Jesus sets the pace. Hard thinking, deep and instant repentance, drastic dealing with themselves, is what He demands of them ; and the speed grows greater till He outstrips His most willing followers, for His work cannot wait their leisure. Thus, as we draw up to the Cross, He is left more and more alone, for He is pressing on to regions never visited before by the foot of living man ; for a moment He Himself hesitates, and there is an hour of agony ; but He goes on past all our power to follow Him even in thought, and by-and-by comes back with blessing upon His lips and unshadowed peace upon His face. When He left His friends behind, He told them at least to be ready, with 'loins girt up and lamps burning,' for His return. That He did come back, that there was something in His demeanour when He came which quieted all their fears, and made them strong enough to be left, is proved not only by the change in the tone of His words, by the new serenity which breathes upon us still as we read them, but still more by the change which came to them. Up till now they had cowered in a room with doors shut for fear of the Jews ; after Pente-cost, the consummation of Easter, even prison walls cannot hold them in, and they, like Him, are borne out and out and out, till they cover the wide world with the message He had brought them.

PART III

THE GOSPEL ACCORDING TO MATTHEW

SYNOPSIS OF PART III

CHAPTER I

NATURE AND PURPOSE OF THE GOSPEL

Papias on Matthew's logia—Reconstruction of—Its date—Papias and the living voice—The book of Testimonies—Matthew the monk —Five divisions of the Testimonies and five sections of the Gospel— Why it was called the Gospel of Matthew—Words of Jesus recorded first—Q and the Fourth Gospel. Matthew gives us teaching of Jesus in its primitive Jewish form—His purpose and his explanations—The meaning of the first and fourth beatitudes—Additions to the Lord's prayer taken from other prayers of Jesus—Other illustrations of our author's method—His love for threefold and fivefold rhythms—His use of Mark—The great non-resistance passage—The Christian's absent-mindedness, off-handed generosity, friendliness—Church and meeting-house—The power of the keys— Nationalist sympathies of the evangelist—The lost sheep of the house of Israel—Devotion to his country's past, coupled with despair for its future—Dogs and swine—The limitations of the ministry of Jesus emphasized, but its ultimate universality made equally clear— Is Paul the ' enemy ' ?—Respect for legal sanctions—Teaching upon divorce—Love of Old Testament Scriptures—The sign of Jonah— Two beasts at the Triumphal Entry—Mixed quotations accounted for by the arrangement of the Book of Testimonies—Their universal colouring—Some felicitous quotations—The preferences of Jesus in the Old Testament—Zechariah son of Berechiah—The use and abuse of the Old Testament—Jesus thought in its language—Can the old law be reconciled with the new?—Jesus says it can.

(pp. 219–245.)

CHAPTER II

FURTHER CHARACTERISTICS OF THE FIRST GOSPEL

Bias against the Pharisees illustrated—Matthew's scrupulous honesty—His respect for the twelve—Peter in this Gospel—His walking on the water, the Lord's high commendation of him at Caesarea Philippi, with notes on Peter and Paul in Acts, and the

suggested difference between Petros and petra—Peter and the temple-
tax, with an inference as to the dealings of Jews and Christians in
Palestine in the first century—Peter seen in a thoughtful mood—
Matthew's gentleness towards Judas—The Sermon on the Mount
addressed to the inner circle—How Matthew got his name—Two
or three publicans among the twelve—The Lord's tenderness for
His own men—The spreading of His hands—His friends the light
of this world and the next—They are His discovery and He is
theirs—Fellowship with them His pearl of great price, our ring and
pearls—The company of Moses and Elijah left for that of Peter,
James, and John—How to keep old friends and make new ones—
The fellowship of true lovers in prayer—Two are better than one
and three than two—' O that the Lord would count me meet to wash
His dear disciples' feet '—Judas to the last the comrade of Jesus—
From ' God with us ' to ' I with you '—The ' disciple-gospel.'

(pp. 246–262.)

CHAPTER III

JESUS THE SON OF GOD

His Messiahship—The star and the wise men with their symbolic
gifts—' Where the Babe was '—The Babe and other children—
Macrobius on Herod's son—Only publicans and children come to
Jesus, others, friends and enemies alike, approach Him as into the
royal presence—Wonder growing to worship—Teacher, Master,
and Lord—Jesus the great light—Men wonder at Him, not He at
them—The disciples do not ' take' Him, they fall in behind Him—
He does not need to look round or make inquiries—His self-determination—Gospel and kingdom alike fade out of sight behind the
dominating figure of Jesus—His deliberate speed—The temple and
the city doomed when He leaves them behind—' Come unto Me '
and ' Depart from Me '—The sign of the Son of Man—' With you,'
' with Me '—The broken fellowship—The mastery of Jesus in Pilate's
hall—Where they had to go to find a man—Every scene in the
Gospel ends with Jesus only—The sombre irony of the Passion-
story—Jesus and Jeremiah—The light breaking through the clouds
—The curse becomes a blessing. The claims of Jesus—' I say unto
you '—The Master, the Householder, the King and the Prince—
' All are too mean to speak His worth '—The works of the Christ—The
call to the working people, and its older models—' Come unto Me '
runs through the Gospel like an undertone—To be worthy of
Jesus—What it means to find Him—A surprise on both sides—He
sets us making fresh discoveries of Himself and of each other—

Jesus the ' Wisdom of God '—The source of the ' Logos-doctrine ' not Philo but the self-consciousness of Jesus—The slave will not argue with his Master—To come to the rescue of His little brothers, is to come to Jesus. (pp. 263–287.)

CHAPTER IV

JESUS THE SON OF MAN

The Son of Man in Daniel and Enoch—Coming ' upon,' or ' with ' the clouds of Heaven—The Son of Man elsewhere in the Old Testa-ment—Was the ' Son of Man ' a popularly-accepted Messianic title ?—Almost only found in reference to Jesus on His own lips— He accepts other titles, but prefers this—His tenderness and humility illustrated—The Sabbath a day for such human service as can properly be called humane—He makes the best of weak and little things and people-healing and curing—Women and children at the picnic parties—No sermon that day—He ' carried ' our diseases— In what points Jesus differed from Pharisaic doctrine, with which He had certain affinities—His pity for the hungry sheep and His understanding advice to them—They are to live a day at a time, work in a team, and learn how to trust by His example—The in-valid and the drudge—Bread for the coming day, daily strength to bear daily trouble—The breathless music of the people's wonder— The amazing graciousness of Jesus—The religion of all poor devils— The parable of the tares, some of which might not be tares after all— The little ones and hindrances—How Jesus identifies Himself with them—Thrown, flung, and sunk—Better dead and better never born—The angels of the little ones—The eunuchs that man has made—Temporary inequalities to issue in an ultimate equality— Just to be there is reward enough—The solution of inevitable frictions—Mutual hindrance and mutual prayer—The mother of the sons of Zebedee—Jesus and disillusioned people.

(pp. 288–305.)

CHAPTER V

THE GENTLENESS OF THE CHRISTIAN DISCIPLE

Originality combined with gentle-hearted reverence—He loves to call himself a slave—The risk of walking on the water only to be faced when it is with Him—Losing yourself to find yourself—The cure of self-consciousness—The intrusion of our interpretations of Jesus an impertinence—Let Him speak for Himself—The rich young man who came to Jesus to be ' finished,' and was ordered down to the bottom class—The Christian disciple an expert in making friends because his heart at leisure from itself—The great Sermon and generally accepted maxims of conduct—Close to the common heart of man—The union of uncanny cleverness with love untiring as God's—Jesus will not allow His disciples to defend Him— Force no remedy—The children's charter.   (pp. 306–319.)

CHAPTER VI

' HOW SHALL WE ESCAPE, IF WE NEGLECT SO GREAT SALVATION ? '

Jesus, the last word of God to men—Throws down the gauntlet of mortal conflict—History and eschatology—Apparent contradictions in His authentic words regarding the future may be due to misunderstanding on the part of His reporters, or to varying moods of hope and fear in His own mind—An agelong progress to the ideal of the Kingdom by evolution culminating in a series of revolutions—The early hopefulness of Jesus followed by deepening disappointment—How natural His hopefulness was—His experiments in fellowship—The darker thoughts—Gehenna, fire, darkness, destruction—The man who is no use to anybody, the man whose presence destroys the fellowship—Is there any cause in nature for these hard hearts ?—The ' hypocrite '—What hypocrisy means on the lips of Jesus—The falseness which makes fellowship impossible— The one thing He could not understand—How He met it, and found on its other side His hope—The double voice of the Gospel—Only in Him can hope triumph over the logic of the observed facts of life.   (pp. 320–334.)

CHAPTER VII

THE SECRET LIFE OF THE CHRISTIAN AND ITS FRUITS.

The little extra, the fruit of the hidden life—The Christian, like his Master, keeps his sorrows and struggles to himself—Anger, contempt, and abuse—Sense of the sacredness of human speech— Words speak louder than actions—The ' idle word '—What swearing really consists in—Sincerity—The moral realism of the First Gospel —The three measure of meal—How the yoke becomes easy— ' From your hearts '—Difference between east and west illustrated from the parable of the two sons—Jesus the meaning of life—The Son of Man and the being of God—Meets us in young dreams and old despairs, in nature and conscience—The love of Jesus the master-key.   (pp. 334–351.)

I

NATURE AND PURPOSE OF THE GOSPEL

OUR discussion of the Gospel according to Matthew must begin with a quotation from Papias, reported by Eusebius. It is as follows : ' Matthew then, in Hebrew speech ' (that is, in Aramaic), ' compiled the logia, which each interpreted according to his ability.' The generally accepted theory in explanation of this rather obscure statement is to the effect that the Apostle Matthew was thought to have had something to do with a collection of the sayings of the Lord. Most scholars are agreed that some such compilation underlies the non-Marcan matter common to our First and Third Gospels. It is by no means clear, however, that both used the same book, and we have seen reason to believe that Luke had access to a rich vein of oral tradition. Harnack reconstructs Q as follows : It contained, he suggests, the preaching of John the Baptist with the baptism of Jesus, the Temptation, fragments of the Sermon on the Mount (Matthew) or the level place (Luke)—four beatitudes, ' Love your enemies,' ' Judge not,' the ' Golden rule,' the ' Lord's Prayer ' (in an undeveloped form), ' Ask, and it shall be given you,' ' the mote and the beam,' the wise and foolish builders—the saying about faith enshrined in the story of the centurion, hard sayings to would-be disciples, directions to the twelve, John's message to Jesus and our Lord's discourse about him, woes upon Chorazin, &c., the saying about the ' babes ' and the verse that follows (' All things,' &c.), the reply to the charge of magic, parables of mustard-seed and leaven and the lost sheep, some woes upon Pharisees, a saying or sayings dealing with the suddenness of the Son of Man's coming and the duty of watching, on cross-bearing, and ' Ye who follow Me shall sit upon twelve thrones.'

Sayings about the 'hairs of your head,' food and clothing, and the wild lilies and birds, about the sparrows,
and 'Fear not those who can kill the body,' &c., should
be included in this list. Other scholars (e.g. Canon
Streeter) are inclined to make the range of Q much wider,
accounting for the omission of some of the sayings included
in their reconstruction from the First or the Third Gospel
by the special interests of the evangelists. But if we
content ourselves with Harnack's minimum, we have a
fairly satisfactory basis for the study of the Teaching of
Jesus. Harnack agrees with most other scholars in
believing that Q did not include narratives as well as
sayings, the only exception he allows being the healing
of the centurion's servant recorded by Matthew and
Luke, but not by Mark. Even if Q did contain that
story, its point cannot have been the story, but the saying
to which it gave rise. That Q did not tell the story of
the Passion can be inferred from the fact that Matthew
follows Mark closely when he comes to Holy Week, and
that Luke and Matthew scarcely ever agree against Mark
in their records at this point. Ramsay thinks that Q
was a document actually contemporary with the life of
Jesus, accounting for the omission of the Passion story
in this way. The divergences between Matthew and
Luke, even when they appear to be running on parallel
lines, are so great that we shall do well not to make our
reconstruction of Q too rigid ; we must allow for a large
mass of authentic oral teaching floating about among
the Christians of the first and second generations. At
the same time, our evidence does not justify us in leaving
out of account the probable existence of a collection or
collections of the sayings of the Lord, written down at
least at a very early period after the Resurrection, possibly
even before it.

A careful study of Luke's preface[1] leaves us doubtful whether
there was, when he began to write, any *authoritative* record of the
sayings of Jesus, purporting to come from an apostle of Matthew's
standing (see Bartlet in *Hastings B.D.*, art. ' Matthew '). Papias
is reported to have said that he resorted to the ' living voice ' of
such ' disciples of the Lord ' as Aristion and John the presbyter,

[1] Luke i. 1-4.

because he preferred oral testimony to the colder written word. Professor Burkitt (*The Gospel History and its Transmission*, pp. 126, 127) has transformed the whole situation by his suggestion that what Matthew the publican really collected was a series of proof-texts or 'testimonies' about Christ from the Old Testament. Dr. Rendel Harris[1] has, I think, turned that suggestion—to which he had arrived independently—into what may be called, with fair security, a demonstration, founded upon a large body of evidence from Greek and Latin fathers, and culminating in his calling into court a MS. from the monastery of Iveron on Mount Athos, which Professor Lambros assigns to the sixteenth century, called 'Of Matthew the monk: A collection against the Jews, without a title (or summary of contents), in five books.' As we shall see in detail presently, Matthew is exceedingly rich in quotations from the Old Testament Scriptures, and there are many signs that one of the two earliest Christian books (the other being Q) was a collection of 'Testimonies' repeated in much the same order by writer after writer from Justin Martyr downwards, the succession corresponding roughly to the list of Testimonies from the Old Testament edited, under various headings, by Cyprian, the North African father, and appended to his writings in patristic collections. Dr. Harris suggests that this book was published in Aramaic, accounting in this way for the fact that our Matthew's version of the quotations which he gives does not always answer exactly either to the Hebrew Bible or any known Greek translation. The 'logia' mentioned by Papias will then become not sayings of Jesus at all, but texts of Old Testament Scripture used by early Christian apologists in their polemic against the Jews. We may notice here that our Gospel of Matthew has five clear divisions, in so far as its record of the Teaching of Jesus is concerned; their boundaries can be traced in the five-times repeated 'When Jesus had finished,' &c (vii. 28, xi. 1, xiii. 53, xix. 1, xxvi. 1). For the full presentation of Dr. Harris' argument, consult his "*Testimonies*."[2] Our conclusion must be that the First Gospel was called 'The Gospel of Matthew' because its outline was provided by Matthew's collection of 'Testimonies' from the Old Testament Scriptures, illustrated by sayings and parables which came from Q or from oral tradition to which our author had access, and the story of the life and death of the Messiah, already at his disposal in one or other of the editions of Mark's Gospel (see p. 26), adapted and revised to fit in with the first evangelist's scheme.

[1] Both were anticipated by the late Dr. Gregory.
[2] Part I., Camb. Univ. Press, 1916.

We need not be surprised that the words of Jesus were recorded before a connected biography was attempted; for they possess a self-evidencing quality, and are coined from one mint. Even in the very diminished record furnished by Harnack's reconstruction of Q we have such great teachings as that God does not deal in round numbers,[1] that He is touched by the feeling for our infirmities, that we must seek to live up to Him in faith and love, and, finally, that Jesus is Himself the link between God and man, for it must not be forgotten that the lofty claim made by our Lord in Matt. xi. 27, Luke. x. 22, is acknowledged to have come from Q. This is one of the points at which the First and Third Gospels are nearest to one another; here, if anywhere, they would appear to be using the same source. Moreover, this passage approaches as closely to the spirit of the Fourth Gospel as anything in the Synoptics; in this great declaration the earliest and the latest traditions of our Lord's sayings join forces. This point has been well put by a modern scholar : ' A son may reveal his father in two ways—by being like him (John), by trust and obedience (Q)'; Jesus fulfils both functions.

Even if Matthew's Gospel is by no means the first of the four in order of time, it is clear that it contains much of the earliest matter of teaching in its primitive Jewish form. So far as we can gather, the *raison d'être* of its publication from its contents, we should say that it was written for Greek-speaking Jewish Christians of Palestine with the special purpose of arming young catechists against objections current in Rabbinic circles. Many divergences from Luke, especially in the great Sermon, can best be accounted for by the need for explanation ; but such explanations can generally be justified by the double meaning of the Aramaic word used by the Lord Himself. A good example of the process involved may be found in Matt. v. 3—' poor in spirit '—where Luke vi. 20 has ' the poor.' We may infer that Jesus said ' poor ' employing the word ' ebionim '—that is, the ' poor ' or the ' pious '—a title perhaps arrogated to themselves by Pharisees in the Lord's day, as well as by Jewish Christians of the next generation. Q—we shall see

[1] Matt. x. 29 ; Luke xii. 6,

reason for believing presently that this book was published
in Greek—translated this by a Greek word which means
' poor in pocket.' But ' ebionim ' is much nearer ' lowly '
or ' poor in spirit ' than is either this Greek word or its
English equivalent. Matthew's version renders for us
the essence of the saying more faithfully than a barer
translation would have done. So with ' hunger and
thirst *after righteousness* '[1] ' Seek ye His kingdom
(Luke xii. 31, and Justin) *and His righteousness* '
(Matt. vi. 33) ; such clauses as ' that ye resist not the
evil one '[2] (see below, p. 227) and ' if any one will go to
law with thee ',[3] and the additions to the shorter Lucan
version of the ' Lord's Prayer.' Some of these clauses,
as is certainly the case with the doxology found in late
MSS., as in our A.V. at the close of the prayer (' Thine
is the kingdom,' &c.), may have found their way into
the text through the liturgy of the Palestinian Church ;
but in any case ' Thy will be done,' &c. is a real explanation of ' Thy Kingdom come,' and it has the additional
recommendation that it is based upon the prayer of Jesus
Himself in Gethsemane,[4] while ' but deliver us from the
evil one ' reminds us of another Lord's prayer[5] (' that
Thou shouldst keep them from the evil one '). Matthew's
version is rhythmical, while Luke's version (' Father, hallowed be Thy name : Thy Kingdom come : give us daily
our bread for the coming day : and forgive us our sins,
for we also ourselves forgive every one who is in debt to
us : and lead us not into temptation '—we are following
here the older MSS.) is in prose.

Turning to Matthew's Gospel as a whole, we are impressed at
once by the fact that it is Jewish in its arrangement. Even more
obviously than the Third Gospel, this book is influenced, both in its
order and its language, by Mark ; but, like Luke, our author im-
proves the style of his predecessor, reducing, for instance, very
considerably the number of ' ands.' From iii.-iv. 22 he follows
Mark's order closely, but afterwards he diverges sharply. He only
mentions our Lord's synagogue ministry somewhat vaguely—at
iv. 23 and ix. 35—while iv. 23-25 is substituted for Mark i. 21, being
based freely upon Mark i. 39 and 6, 6 b. Not till xii. 9 ff. does he

[1] Matt. v. 6.   [2] Matt. v. 39.   [3] Matt. v. 40.
    [4] Matt. xxvi. 42, &c.   [5] Jn. xvii. 15.

give an incident in the synagogue, and the impression created,
according to Mark, in the synagogue at Capernaum is made to
follow the Sermon on the Mount.   One of the topics of the
' Testimony ' Book was to the effect that the Christ was to be the
Lawgiver of a loftier state ; the statement of Christ's authority
is here dissociated from the Jewish constitution and attached to
His giving of a new law.[1]   After the cure of the leper,[2] Matthew
gives us, instead of an exorcism in the synagogue,[3] the healing of
a centurion's servant in the town,[4] probably because he preferred
the authority of Q to that of Mark.   For a line or two he now reverts to the Marcan order,[5] rounding off three cases of healing—
leprosy, paralysis, fever—one asks, a second is asked for, the third
receives without asking—with a prophetic quotation from the
Testimony Book.[6]   Then Jesus crosses the lake, and the stories
given in Mark iv. 35 ff, v. 1-20 follow—with important variations,
some of which will be noticed later—in Matt. viii. 23-34.   In
ix. 1-17 our evangelist comes back to Mark ii. 1-22, and then
forward again to Mark v. 21-43 in ix. 18-26.   Mark's short account
of the choice and mission of the twelve is expanded into a long
discourse by the aid of sayings taken from Q.[7] culminating in
xi. 1, one of our five landmarks (see above, p. 221).   This discourse
serves to illustrate another section of the Testimony Book : ' Christ
is Commander-in-Chief.'   Jesus is Commander of men (viii. 4),
disease (viii. 8, 15), demons (viii. 16, 21), winds and waves (viii. 26),
has authority to forgive sins (ix. 8), and commands instant
and complete allegiance (viii. 20, ix. 9, xi. 1) from His disciples.
In chapter xi. Matthew forsakes Mark, but for the conflicts between
Jesus and His opponents recorded in xii. 1-16 he reverts to the
substance of Mark ii. 23—iii. 12, closing with his usual quotation
from the Testimony Book (vv. 17-21).   Mark iii. 20, 21 he omits—
see below—in xii. 22, 23 he adds another miracle, then with the
help of Q he expands Mark iii. 22-30, following it up with Mark iii.
31-35[8] and an enlarged version of Mark iv. (Matt. xiii.), with
additional matter from Q and the Testimony Book, but omitting
Mark iv. 26-29.   He passes at once to Mark vi. 1-6 a in xiii. 53-58,
and after that never quite drops the Marcan thread, though he
embroiders it with more reminiscences of the Old Testament,
specially in the Passion story.

[1] Matt. vii. 29.   [2] Mark i. 40 ff. ;   Matt. viii. 2 ff.
[3] Mark i. 23 ff.   [4] Matt. viii. 5 ff.
[5] Matt. viii. 14-16 ;   cf. Mark i. 29-34.   [6] Matt. viii. 17.
[7] Mark iii. 13-19, vi. 6-13 ;   Matt. x.   [8] Matt. xii. 24 ff , 46-50.

Chronological data tend to be vague. The mission of John the Baptist is placed in the days of Archelaus,[1] and Matthew is very fond of the somewhat unsatisfactory word 'then,' which links several paragraphs together;[2] sometimes, however, its reference is more clearly defined (e.g. iii. 5, iv. 1, ix. 14, &c). In xii. 1 we read 'at that period' without any clue to the exact time meant; the disciples are back from their tour, and the place is Capernaum, but we are left to infer these facts. On the whole, our evangelist prefers rather to abbreviate Mark's matter than to leave it out, as Luke often does—notice the abbreviation of the story of the epileptic boy in xvii. 14–21, Mark ix. 21–24 being 'cut' altogether. He sometimes mentions names, where Mark has none—e.g. Caiaphas[3]; most of all is this true of the beloved name 'Jesus,' which occurs, on a rough computation, 114 times in this Gospel (Mark 60., Luke 71); at i. 21 he explains the meaning of the name for the believer. 'Jesus Christ' is found perhaps thrice[4] (only elsewhere in the Synoptics, Mark i. 1).

'If,' says a French writer, 'Matthew did not possess the art of the painter, like Luke, or that of the engraver, like Mark, he had, all the same, his own faculty, that of good workmanship; his was the constructive imagination of the architect.' Certainly he manifests a genius for orderly arrangement. The Birth story is divided into three sections (i. 1–17, the Lord's pedigree; i. 18–25, His birth; ii. 1–23, His childhood). Each step in the narrative is marked out by a Testimony (i. 22 f.; ii. 5 f., 17 f., 23 —the last presents a difficulty, for 'He shall be called Nazoraeus' is not found in the Old Testament; Jerome cites Isa. xi. 1, 2, 'a shoot out of the stem of Jesse, and a branch' (nazer), suggesting that Matthew has substituted 'Nazoraeus' for 'Nazarene' in order to glance at this passage, which was certainly quoted in the Testimony Book. The genealogy has perhaps been compiled by the author himself; it is arranged, for mnemonic purposes, in three sets of fourteen generations, a curious feature in the list of ancestors being the inclusion of three women of irregular life —Rahab, Tamar, and Bathsheba. Our evangelist has in view the Jewish slander against Mary, and he makes a twofold retort; he hints that the Davidic lineage was not free from blemish higher up, and at the same time makes it plain that Joseph's suspicions were set at rest by an angelic visitor. The text of i. 16 is not finally

---

[1] Matt. ii. 22, iii. 1.
[2] Matt. iii. 13, xii. 22, 38, xv. 1, 28, xix. 13, xx. 20.
[3] Matt. xxvi. 3, 57.   [4] Matt. i. 1, 18, xvi. 21 (in some MSS).

settled yet, for there is a cloud of various readings here, the simplest of which is that of the 'Lewis' Syriac version : ' Jacob begat Joseph ; Joseph, to whom was betrothed Mary the Virgin, begat Jesus who is called Christ.' Even this early reading does not involve disbelief in the Virgin Birth, for ' begat ' refers to legal kinship, not necessarily to physical parentage (Burkitt). Such modifications as are introduced into later copies are designed to reset or sharpen reference to the Virgin Birth, not to insert what was not already in the text.

The whole Gospel is almost mathematically arranged. In the first two chapters there are five testimonies and five dreams, just as in the Gospel as a whole there are five landmarks, built of testimony-material (see above for the divisions). There are three temptations,[1] there is a threefold description of the Lord's early ministry[2] (teaching, healing, preaching), five times ' Ye have heard that it was said . . . but *I* say unto you ' resounds like a hammer-stroke through the ' Sermon on the Mount ' (v. 21, 22, 27–28, 33–34, 38–39, 43–44). In vi. 1–18 we have three topics—alms-giving, prayer, fasting—our duty to our brother, God, ourselves (vv. 1–4, 5–15, 16–18). After the invocation the ' Lord's Prayer ' divides itself into two groups, each containing three petitions, and we go on to ' Ask, seek, knock,'[3] and—a little lower down—to ' Have we not prophesied . . . cast out demons . . . done many mighty works ' ?[4]; while in vii. 25, 27 we have ' the rain came down, and the rivers rose, and the winds blew.' Chapter viii. 1–15 gives us three miracles of healing, viii. 23, ix. 8 three more miracles, ix. 18–34 another group of three. ' What went ye out for ' ? is repeated three times in xi. 7–9—compare xii. 50, ' My brother and sister and mother '—and the Pharisees make a threefold attack upon Jesus.[5] There are three parables of sowing ;[6] three times ' Verily I say unto you '[7] is repeated, for in the best MSS. there is no ' verily ' at v. 19 ; there are three kinds of ' eunuch,'[8] and in xx. 19, as in xxi. 9, there is a threefold rhythm. In xxi. 28–xxii. 14 we have three parables, in xxii. 15–40 three questions to Jesus, in xxiii. 13–16 three woes. Chapter xxiii. 23 has ' mint and anise and cummin,' ' justice and mercy and faith ' ; xxiii. 34, ' prophets and wise men and scribes '—this arrangement corresponds to the three divisions of the Old Testament, but the ' prophets ' come first, the order being that favoured by the ' Higher ' critics !

---

[1] Matt. iv. 1–11.   [2] Matt. iv. 23.   [3] Matt. vii. 7.
[4] Matt. vii. 22.   [5] Matt. xii. 2 ff, 10 ff., 24 ff.   [6] Matt. xiii. 1–32.
[7] Matt. xviii. 3, 13, 18.   [8] Matt. xix. 12.

In the parable of the 'Talents' there are three men, in that of the 'Virgins' five wise and five foolish. Jesus prays thrice in Gethsemane,[1] as Peter denies Him thrice,[2] and Pilate thrice questions the people about Him.[3] There are three mockeries,[4] and three women at the Cross;[5] the apostles are to make disciples, baptize, and teach.'[6] Chapter x. 8 gives us a fivefold rhythm, x. 9, 10 a threefold movement within a group of five (' gold nor silver nor copper '—' gold,' &c., ' a wallet,' ' two vests,' ' shoes,' ' staff '). So with the numbers seven and ten : there is a sevenfold woe in chapter xxiii.—compare also xii. 45, xv. 34, 37, xxii. 25 ff., xviii. 21 ; there are ten testimonies in i. 1–iv, 11, in viii. 1, ix. 34 ten miracles. But the fact that there are only nine beatitudes —or eight, if vv. 10, 11 are counted as one—proves that our evangelist did not carry out his scheme in defiance of tradition.

All this is very Semitic. The fact that this Gospel is so unmistakably Jewish in construction as in atmosphere should give us confidence in its interpretation of the Lord's teaching, for His moral teaching is the most thoroughly Jewish thing about Him. Certainly we have in Matthew our most vivid presentation of the topical preaching of Jesus ; the famous passage about non-resistance may be taken as an example.[7] ' Ye have heard that it was said, Eye for eye, tooth for tooth '—Polycarp in his version adds ' slap for slap,' and he must be right, for, in Matthew, slapping comes in directly afterwards. ' But I say unto you, that ye resist not the evil one '—that is, ' the devil '; compare vi. 13, ' rescue us from the evil one,' and specially v. 37—just before— ' whatever is more than this comes from the evil one '; Jesus does not traffic in meaningless abstractions, for there is nothing ' good ' or ' evil ' apart from persons. ' But whoever slaps thee on the *right* cheek, turn to him also the other ; and whoever will go to law with thee, and is awarded thy vest, let him have thine upper-garment too ; and whoever shall conscript thee to go a mile, go *with him* two more ' (I follow Codex Bezae here). The passage is packed with topical allusions, all the more obscure to us because they would so readily be appreciated by the audience then. First, as to ' resist not the devil ' :

[1] Matt. xxvi. 36–44.   [2] Matt. xxvi. 69 ff.   [3] Matt. xxvii. 17–22.
[4] Matt. xxvii. 39–44.   [5] Matt. xxvii. 56.   [6] Matt. xxviii. 19, 20.
[7] Matt. v. 38 ff.

I have already (p. 223) suggested that this clause is an expansion inserted by the evangelist himself; in any case, it is quite in the spirit of the original saying, and is a real explanation. We are not to venture into the ring, so to say, with the devil; compare Eph. iv. 27, 'make no room for the devil'—this also, along with iv. 26, if we may trust the evidence of the dialogue of 'Adamantius' (the pseudo-Origen) against the Marcionites, was held in some quarters to be at least a reminiscence of a saying of Jesus; for in that dialogue, 'Be ye angry and sin not,' &c., is quoted by the Marcionite debater as a saying of the Lord Himself, and the orthodox disputant would not have let the reference pass if he had thought it a blunder. We are to fear the devil; by insisting upon our rights at every turn, we give the devil an opening, and challenge him to do his worst. On the other hand, we are rather to overlook small personal wrongs, to be only too glad to escape from a position which lays a man open on his most vulnerable side to the enemy of souls. Special piquancy is given to the first illustration of this wisely forbearing spirit by the phrase 'right cheek' ('right,' Matthew only); for a blow struck by a right-handed man would fall on the left cheek, unless it was delivered from behind, or with the back of the hand. The Rabbis made a shrewd distinction between a blow struck with the palm and a contemptuous flick with the back of the hand; the former was an injury, the latter an insult, and an insult is more to be resented than an injury. Jesus says, 'On the other hand, you are not to waste time in avenging insults; you are to pocket your dignity.' In case of serious injury you do well to seek the right kind of satisfaction[1]; but an insult is nothing, if you do not stoop to notice it. You are to be so busy with great things that you have no time to worry about little things, and must cultivate a beatific absentmindedness. Then, if any one chooses to insult you, he will soon give it up, for his purpose is to provoke you; to go calmly on, without stopping to brush the fly from your cheek, is the best way to tire him out, and at last perhaps to make him thoroughly ashamed of himself, so you may 'heap coals

[1] Matt. xviii. 15 ff.

of fire upon his head.'[1]   It is clear that, so far from its being impracticable or lacking in virility, the spirit inculcated here is characterized by a shrewd common sense, as clean and bracing as the wind on the heath.

The second illustration of this great-hearted spirit passes, as we should expect, from negative to positive, from mere refusal to compete with churlishness to an audacious generosity.   The Christian is not to go to law, if he can help it (cf. v. 25 ; 1 Cor. vi. 6) ; but ' if any one insists upon going to law ' with him, and the case is decided in his opponent's favour, with the result that he has to pay damages into court, rather than pay up grudgingly, because he must, he is to throw in the little extra.   That is the principle, but the setting in the law court provides us with a delightfully humorous picture, quite unique in literature.   The defendant is so poor that, when the case goes against him, all he can do is to offer one of his two garments, and as he can, for obvious reasons, do without his under-garment with least public inconvenience, he takes that off, and presents it to his triumphant opponent.   Then it occurs to him that, while he is about it, he may as well do the thing handsomely ; to the amazement of everybody, he proceeds to divest himself of his sole remaining garment and make his friend the enemy a present of this likewise !   One could scarcely imagine a course of action better calculated to turn the tables on the oppressor !   But the leading idea of this lively illustration does not concern the details of the picture, but its atmosphere and colouring.   The large free gesture of the poor man playing the gentleman with his scanty wardrobe pleased, we may be sure, our Lord's fancy ; He is describing no mean truckling to social wrong, rather a bearing, a way of doing things, such as at once lifts a man out of a miserably humiliating position above those who seek to degrade him.   The behaviour of the Lord Himself at His trial, when His enemies ' received Him with slaps '[2] and stripped Him of His garments, is our best commentary upon these verses.

The third illustration—given this time in Matthew only—is more startling, for it unmistakably contains the dangerous word ' conscript '—for State purposes :

[1] Rom. xii. 20 ; Prov. xxv. 22.   [2] Mark xiv. 65.

R

' If any one *compel* you to go one mile '—the milestone
on the Roman road—' *go with him* two more ' (see above).
The situation imagined here is not difficult to make clear.
Private passengers were often compelled in those days
of unrest to lend a hand to the courier who carried the
letters or dispatches. If the State imposes upon the
Christian the performance of a laborious or dangerous
public duty—a duty such as the one mentioned might
involve fighting with your own countrymen—he is not
to do as little as he can, with the idea of getting it over,
but he is to show his goodwill to the not very gentle official
who has commandeered his services by accompanying
him farther than he need. At the end of the first mile,
as Dr. Orchard has wittily said, he is to thank his friend
for the pleasure of his company, and tell him that he
cannot part with him just yet, for he is ' just beginning
to like him ' ; and this with no ironical or affected courtesy,
but because he has succeeded in really getting interested
in that somewhat unattractive person, a bullying N.C.O.
in a subject-country ! To say the least of it, that will
take the wind out of his sails ! The deeper note sounded
here—that of the triumphant friendliness of the Christian—
is to be brought out presently. Meanwhile we
must remember, in our estimate of this last saying, that
the Government to which our Lord commands so cheerful a submission was intensely unpopular ; the Sermon
at this point must have gone absolutely counter to the
wishes and tastes of His most attached disciples. According to the ' Sayings of the Jewish Fathers ' (iii. 18), Rabbi
Ishmael said something of the same kind : ' Be pliant
to a chief, and yielding to impressment, and receive
every man into cheerfulness.' Christians must recognize
to the full the God-given advantages of stable government, and give a shining example of true citizenship
generously interpreted. This may well have been the
most unpopular thing that the Master ever said ; He is
always consistent, but He here expounds His own maxim
—' Render unto Caesar the things that are Caesar's '
—in the broadest possible way. The Roman Government was, upon the whole, exceedingly gentle in its
treatment of Jewish susceptibilities, for, in Judaea at
least, they went so far as to issue a special coinage, in

order to avoid the constant reminder of their servitude,
which the imperial coins with the emperor's head upon
them would obtrude upon a suspicious and high-spirited
people. It was insisted only that the taxes should be
paid in Roman money ; that is the reason why in Matt.
xxii. 19 we have ' Show Me the tribute-money ' instead
of ' Show Me a penny.'[1] But the habitual patience of
the Government broke down with the Galileans, and it
was precisely to a Galilean audience that Jesus gave this
most unwelcome advice ! Pilate was nettled into some
flagrant acts of oppression by the opposition of Herod's
turbulent charge, and was finally recalled by the Emperor
Vitellius after a complaint on the score of his excessive
severity lodged by the Samaritans. Even if there were
oppression, the suggestion made here is that the wisest
way to put an end to it is so loyally to comply with all
lawful exactions as to leave no possible justification
for it.[2]

There is a silver thread running through this whole
section of the great Sermon ; Jesus is preaching a noble
carelessness about the Christian's own rights, along with
a generous recognition of the rights of others. So far
from involving a recommendation of a tame submissive-
ness, which 'lays itself down for any fool to tread upon,'[3]
the Lord's teaching insists that His disciple is to be above,
not beneath, taking offence ; he is to be ' too proud to
fight '—in his own quarrel. At the same time, he is to
be thoughtful in little things, and can find time to be
endlessly considerate, because he need not worry about
himself. We must go to the First Gospel for our com-
pletest rendering of the ethical teaching of Jesus in its
finer shades.

Reverting to the main subject of this chapter, we
should notice that behind the ' Church ' of xvi. 18, xviii. 17
—both Matthew only—lies the ' synagogue ' ; in xviii. 17

---

[1] Mark xii. 15.

[2] In Matt. v. 41, it should be said, there is no question of conscription
for directly combatant service, for the Jews were exempted from service
in the Roman conscript armies ; the modern counterpart is rather in-
dustrial conscription. In days of unrest like those in which Jesus lived,
however, the possibility of having to fight in defence of the State was not
excluded, for dispatches were carried by an armed guard.

[3] Sirach iv. 27.

the older Syriac versions actually read 'tell it to the synagogue.' These are the only two places in the four Gospels in which the word 'church' occurs. It is quite possible that Jesus actually said 'synagogue' or 'meeting-house,' though the Greek word 'ecclesia' is used in the LXX for 'congregation.' Our ecclesiastical friends ought to remember that the meeting-house is more primitive even than the church! For xvi. 18—'gates of Hades'—compare the LXX of Isa. xxxviii, 10: 'In the gates of Hades I shall live out the rest of the years'; Wisdom of Solomon xvi. 13, 'Thou leadest down to the gates of Hades.' Evidently this is a Jewish phrase meaning 'death,' and the clause implies that the apostolic succession of confessors like Peter shall never die out. At v. 19 we come to what look like two technical terms of Jewish jurisprudence: 'Whatever thou shalt bind on earth shall be bound in heaven,' &c.; the same power is extended to the other apostles in xviii. 19. In the 'targum'—that is, a Rabbinic comment—upon Cant. viii. 13 we read, 'God says to Israel, "Let Me hear the sound of thy words, when thou sittest to acquit or to condemn, and I will consent to all that thou doest."' The Rabbis said that a ban pronounced upon earth had an enhanced validity before God, while an amazingly bold assertion is to be found in their writings: 'The Holy One, blessed be He, makes His own determination invalid, if it contradict the determination of a pious person'; and, in another place, 'I God rule over men: who rules over Me? The pious, for I enact, and he annuls!' 'Binding' and 'loosing' might, then, be taken as corresponding to the verdict of a Rabbi, who pronounces a thing 'forbidden' or 'permitted' in accordance with 'precedent.' Dalman, however, to whom I owe these quotations, thinks that we should refer to Isa. xxii. 22—cited also in Rev. iii. 7—which records the appointment of Eliakim as comptroller of the King's household; in Rev. iii. 7 the Keeper of the keys is Christ Himself. The story was told that, when the final destruction of the Temple was imminent, its priests threw the keys to heaven, because they had been unworthy keepers; cf. Matt. xxi. 43 and xxiii. 13—the latter peculiar to Matthew as far as the word 'shut' ('Lewis' Syriac version 'hold the keys') is concerned. Peter is to be steward of Christ's house, as Christ Himself of God's. For the contrast between earth and heaven, very frequent in Jewish literature, and often implied, if not always expressed, in the words of Jesus, as they are contained in this Gospel, compare vi. 10 (Matthew only), ix. 6,[1] xviii. 18, 19 (Matthew only). John xx. 23 is much less Jewish in tone; Dalman tells us that he knows of no Jewish parallel to the word translated 'retain' in this verse. I have already referred (p. 149) to the 'whitewashed tombs' of xxiii. 27.

As we should have expected, this Gospel is not only richly Jewish in tone, but is also, on the whole, nationalist in sympathy. 'Israel' is mentioned nine times in Matthew, never in Mark, only twice in Luke, outside the Birth story, in the course of which it occurs four times. Specially noticeable is the phrase 'the land of Israel,'[2] while the words 'the lost sheep of the house of Israel' (cf. ix. 36; xviii. 12, 14) come in at x. 6; xv. 24—in both cases Matthew only; the limitations of the ministry of Jesus and His disciples in the days of His flesh are strongly emphasized. The twelve are not to enter the roads leading to Gentile territory or a Samaritan city,[3] for they shall not have 'gone through the cities of Israel[4] until the Son of Man be come' (Matthew only). This passage seems at first sight to involve a permanent limitation of apostolic ministry, and is difficult to reconcile with xxviii. 19, where the followers of the Lord are bidden to go and 'make disciples of all the Gentiles.'

With such differences of tone in view, it is tempting to infer that two separate sources have been blended in this Gospel, the one universalist, the other nationalist, in tendency. . . . From the former would proceed, according to this theory, such statements as that of xiii. 38, 'The field is the world'; xxiv. 14, 'This gospel of the Kingdom shall first be preached in all the world, for a testimony to all the Gentiles' (here compare Mark xiii. 10); xxvi. 13 (so Mark xiv. 9). In two out of the four cases, it will be seen, Matthew is following Mark, if Mark xiii. 10 is really Mark; xxviii. 19, on the

---

[1] Mark ii. 10 ; Luke v. 24.   [3] Matt. x. 5.
[2] Matt. ii. 20, 21.   [4] Matt. x. 23

other hand, as well as xiii. 38, is peculiar to him, for
Mark xvi. 15 is not part of the authentic Marcan
text. But we have by no means come to the end
of the traces of universalism in Matthew's Gospel, for it
can scarcely be an accident that, out of four women
mentioned before Mary in the genealogy of Jesus, two,
Rahab and Ruth, are Gentiles.[1] Moreover, even in a
context in which our Lord's exclusively national mission
is insistently dwelt upon[2]—'Canaanitish' in v. 22 and
vv. 23–25 are all found in this Gospel only—Jesus does
heal the Gentile woman's daughter, and His wonder at
her faith is brought out more clearly than in Mark, for
'O woman, great is thy faith! Let it be to thee as thou
dost desire!' is also peculiar to Matthew. The Lord is
equally delighted with the Roman centurion,[3] and the
towns of Galilee are unfavourably contrasted with Tyre
and Sidon, Sodom and Gomorrah,[4] 'this generation' of
Jews with the Ninevites and the Queen of Sheba.[5] Luke
xiii. 29 finds its counterpart in Matt. viii. 11, 12; and
xxi. 43 is more, not less, definite than Mark xii. 9; Luke
xx. 16. Mark-Luke have 'to others'; Matthew 'to a
nation producing its fruits.' In this change, it is true,
there may be signs of the influence of the Testimony-
Book, one of the leading topics of which was that of the
two nations, the Church taking the place of Israel (Gen.
xxv. 23; Exod. xxxii. 31, 33; Isa. liv. 1—cf. Gal. iv. 27—
Hos. i. 10, ii. 23—cf. Rom. ix. 25, 26—were passages
quoted).

Upon the whole, the suggestion of two sources of
opposite tendency does not fit the facts; it would rather
seem that the author of this Gospel in its present form did
prefer to think of Jesus as exercising a ministry deliberately
limited to His own people, but at the same time did not desire
to erase the strong universalist elements which he found
in all his sources, not only in Mark, but in Q, for it will
be remembered that the story of the centurion comes
from Q. On the other hand, the mission of the seventy,
thought by some scholars to come from Q also, is left
out by Matthew; and such phrases as 'the Holy City,'[6]

[1] Matt. i. 5. [2] Matt. xv. 22 ff. [3] Matt. viii. 10; Luke vii. 9.
[4] Matt. xi. 21 ff. [5] Matt. xii. 41 ff. [6] Matt. iv. 5, xxvii. 53.

'the [city of the great King,'¦¹ 'in the] Holy Place'ᵃ
(Mark xiii. 14 has 'where it ought not '), 'the saints that
had fallen asleep'ᵃ—all found only in Matthew—bespeak
his devotion to his country's past. All the more luridly
does such a prophecy of doom as that of xxii. 7 stand out,
for 'the Holy City' has now become ¦merely '*their* city,'
while the Roman invaders now form the King's armies.

One or two more passages remain to be noticed in this
connexion. Our author speaks more gently of Bar-
rabbas than do the other evangelists ; he is simply ' a
notorious prisoner ' (cf. Mark xv. 7 ; Luke xxiii. 19).
Matthew, like the others, makes it clear that Jesus Himself was no revolutionist in the accepted sense of the
term ; He was loyal to the temple-tax, not because He
was really a Jewish subject ; He waived His princely
right to avoid offence⁴ ; He also counselled a cheerful
submission to the Government.⁵   In vii. 6 we have a
saying peculiar to this Gospel, which sounds strangely
from the lips of Jesus. A pendant is to be found in
patristic writings (see p. 120) which somewhat modifies
its severity ; but if Luke knew of it, he must have interpreted ' dogs ' and ' swine ' as meaning Gentiles, and
doubted its authenticity. When Jesus calls a Gentile
woman a ' dog,' or rather her daughter a ' puppy,' He
does not use this harsh word⁶ (see p. 46). But the ' dogs '
of Matt. vii. 6, like those of Phil. iii. 2, Rev. xxii. 15, are
the pariah-dogs of Eastern cities ; while the ' swine '
must stand for what is unclean (cf. 2 Pet. ii. 22 and above,
p. 131). We cannot bring ourselves to believe that Jesus
meant Gentiles by these opprobrious terms ; fortunately
another reading of the saying is open to us. One of the
threads running through the teaching of Jesus in
this Gospel is the necessity of avoiding offence.
We are to be careful how we deal with *cynical*
outsiders, with scandalmongers and snarling critics,
who will make the most of any unsavoury episode in the
relations of Christians with one another ; we are not to
' wash our dirty linen in public.'⁷   The context of Phil.
iii. 2 certainly suggests that Paul meant Jews by his use

¹ Matt. v. 35.   ² Matt. xxiv. 15.   ³ Matt. xxvii. 52.
⁴ Matt. xvii. 24 ff.   ⁵ Matt. v. 41.   ⁶ Matt. xv. 26, 27 ; Mark vii. 27, 28.
⁷ cf. Sirach xx., 13 (Hebrew)   consort not with a pig.'

of the word; if so, we may be justified in supposing
that words used by scornful Jewish critics of the Gentiles
had come to be applied to the Jews themselves.[1]   Upon
the lips of Jesus, however, its reference, we should prefer
to think, is more general, and does not apply to
any particular party or nation.   We may notice that
the same wisely exclusive spirit dominates xviii. 17,
'Let him be unto thee as the Gentile and the publican.'
The conjunction of the words 'Gentile' (or 'pagan')
and 'publican' is significant, for no one would infer that
publicans were thought of either by Jesus or our evangelist
as necessarily outside the Kingdom; in xxi. 31 we read,
'The publicans *go before you into* the Kingdom '—'go
before you' is Matthew only.   We must translate 'as
the Gentiles and the publicans are in the synagogue—
outsiders'; for the same association compare v. 46, 47;
—reading with R.V. 'Gentiles' instead of 'publicans'
in v. 47—where the virtues of pagans and publicans are
estimated at their full value.   Luke generalizes in this
last passage—he has no parallel to the other—probably
in order to avoid the use of the word 'Gentile' in a way
which might seem invidious to 'Theophilus,' giving us
'sinners' in both places.[2]   We may say in summary
that, while in Matthew's Gospel the fact of the limitation of the ministry of Jesus and the twelve up to the
Passion is recognized, and indeed emphasized, the ultimate
universality of the Gospel-message is brought out quite
as clearly, nor can any serious student charge our
evangelist with narrowness.

With his nationalist sympathies, this writer combines a
great respect for traditional and legal sanctions.   Where
Luke   has   'injustice,'   Matthew   tends   to   render
'lawlessness'[3];   'lawlessness'   appears   also   in   xiii. 41
(Matthew only), xxiii. 28 (Luke xi. 39, more generally
'evil');   in   v.   17,   19   ff.   we   have   a   passage,
peculiar to this Gospel, which brings out strongly the
eternal   validity   of   the   'law   and   the   prophets,'
so far at least as their main principles are concerned.
I say 'main principles,' for we must not leave out of

[1] For this association of 'dogs' with Jews, cf. the odes of Soloman,
xxviii. 13, 'they came upon me like mad dogs who ignorantly attack
their masters' (Ps. xxii. 17).
[2] Luke vi. 32–34.   [3] Matt. vii. 23; Luke xiii. 27.

sight the fact that elsewhere in the book[1] (much more definite and sweeping than Mark xii. 31), Jesus says that the whole law and the prophets centre round the 'two' great 'commandments,' love to God and to one's neighbour. As to v. 17, it seems quite likely that it was originally to be found in the Third Gospel too ; perhaps Marcion, in his very much revised version of Luke, expurgated to suit the exigencies of his doctrine (see App. IV.) is responsible for its disappearance from our text, for Tertullian, who professes to answer Marcion upon the basis of Marcion's own Gospel (Luke), twice makes use of it. Verse 18 does appear in a modified form in Luke xvi. 17, so that there is some reason for believing that the preceding verse also was originally attested by Luke. Verse 19 is stronger, and was, as we know, turned against Paul like Matt. xiii. 25, 28, where anti-Paulinists saw in him the 'enemy' who sowed tares in the field ; compare ' Am I become your enemy ? '[2] and the Latin gloss attached in some MSS. to Acts xxiv. 18, 19, ' crying out, and saying, " Down with our enemy ! " ' (after ' the Jews from Asia' in v. 18). In the Clementine Homilies (third century A.D.), where Paul appears as Simon Magus, we read in a letter alleged to have been written by Peter : ' Some persons among the Gentiles have rejected my legal preaching, and attach themselves to the lawless and trifling preaching of the man who is *mine enemy*.' Our evangelist may have preserved the saying embodied in v. 19, in view of the laxity which he observed in extreme Pauline circles ; further than this our evidence does not warrant us in going.[3]

Chapter xviii. 17—Matthew only—breathes the same spirit of respect for the recognized courts of justice, if we are right in putting ' synagogue ' for ' church ' here ; but I am a little doubtful about this, for Jesus does not encourage His followers, to say the least of it, to seek for redress in the public courts—the ' synagogue,' of course, was law-court as well as meeting-house. Perhaps we should suggest ' tell it to *your* meeting-house.

---

[1] Matt. xxii. 40 ; cf. xix. 19.   [2] Gal. iv. 16.

[3] The further question—the difficulty of recording v. 19 with the tone of the passage which follows, must be reserved to the end of the chapter.

As might have been expected, Matthew is much more
conservative than Mark in regard to the Sabbath day;
he omits 'the Sabbath was made for man'[1] in xii. 7, 8,
and adds 'or on the Sabbath day' to Mark xiii. 18, in
Matt. xxiv. 20, because pious Jews would not go more
than two thousand steps on the Sabbath, so that escape
to a safe distance would be impossible. Very curious
is the difference between Matt. x. 10 and Luke x. 7;
Matthew has 'the workman is worthy of his maintenance'; Luke, 'the workman is worthy of his pay.'
Methodists follow Matthew, most other Churches
Luke. This is clearly a case of alternative renderings
of the original; but the first evangelist is influenced by
the fact that the Levites were paid in kind, not in cash,
as also perhaps by the custom of the Church in the first
century, for the 'prophets were maintained, *not paid*,
by the members of the churches to which they ministered.'
In the same section of Matthew 'freely ye have received,
freely give,' testifies to the same ideal (Matt. x. 8)
—Matthew only.

But the codifying tendency of this Gospel is everywhere manifest; the Sermon on the Mount is cast into
legislative form, while the teaching of Jesus upon divorce
is twice repeated.[2]   This fact also illustrates our
evangelist's veneration for the married life and home
sanctions, a thoroughly Jewish trait in his character,
in marked contrast to Luke's ascetic and celibate lean-
ings. Matthew's statement of our Lord's position in
the matter of divorce is apparently less sweeping than
that found in Mark x. 11; both in v. 32 and xix. 9 immoral relations with a third party are allowed to be a
sufficient ground for separation.[3]   Into the vexed question
of the choice between the two versions I cannot enter
fully; we shall see that Matthew is specially valuable
for his guarded presentations of his Master's ethical
teaching, so that we need not be surprised to find the

[1] Mark ii. 27.   [2] Matt. v. 31 f., xix. 3 ff.
[3] It has, however, been suggested (*Expositor*, November, 1918) recently
that the words translated 'except for an accusation of fornication' really
means 'notwithstanding the word about uncleanness' (Deut. xxiv. 1).
If so, Matthew agrees with Mark, and we have clearer proof than ever
that Jesus set aside the details of the Mosaic law, and regarded Christian
marriage as indissoluble.

more moderate position represented here. On the whole, I am inclined to think that the First Gospel is right, for I am fairly certain that 'except for (an accusation of) fornication' is not a gloss in either place. If it had been, we should surely have had 'adultery' instead of 'fornication,' since in Jewish law 'fornication' stands for sin before as well as after marriage. The chief emphasis in Matthew's version lies not upon the connubial rights of either party, rather upon the sin against the children involved in immoral relations with another at any time after the first betrothal (cf. i. 18, 19). The strange passage which follows xix. 10 does not contradict what has been said about Matthew's feeling for the sacredness of marriage ; our evangelist is careful to show that it was only in special cases that Jesus spoke of voluntary celibacy as either necessary or desirable.

Behind all this lies the fact that Matthew has a quite extraordinary love for the Old Testament Scriptures and what is called the 'argument from prophecy.' I have suggested already that his Gospel came to be called the Gospel 'according to Matthew' because it was based upon the Book of 'Testimonies,' or quotations from Scripture applied to Jesus, brought together by Matthew the publican. But, apart from definite citations, the author of the Gospel as a whole is steeped in the language and thought characteristic of the sacred literature of his people, with the result that both his phraseology and his narrative are at many points affected. Examples of this tendency can be found on every page of the Gospel ; I need only mention a few of the more striking cases. Chapter v. 48 has 'so then shall ye be perfect,'[1] where Luke vi. 36 gives us 'Be ye pitiful.' We have already mentioned the addition of 'and adulterous' (i.e. 'idolatrous ') in xii. 39 (cf. Mark viii. 12 ; Luke xi. 29) ; the same phrase, with the same addition, recurs at xvi. 4. Chapter xii. 40 is almost certainly no part of the original Gospel (see above, p. 125), for Justin (*Dialogue with Trypho*, 107) does not quote it, though he is dealing with the same saying, and it would exactly suit his purpose. Irenaeus, upon the other hand, does (*adv. haer.* 31, 1). Our inference should be that it became part of the text of the Gospel between the time of Justin (wrote *circ.* A.D. 163) and that of Irenaeus (nearer the end of the second century). As this saying about Jonah's 'sign '

[1] Deut. xviii. 13.

(i.e. his mission, *not* his sojourn in the fish) was associated in (cf Luke xi. 30, 32) with another about Jonah's preaching,[1] it seems probable that this saying has given rise to a preacher's gloss —the gloss may also have found its way into the Book of Testimonies, which was always being supplemented—on the subject of his imprisonment for three days and nights in the fish's belly. Mark viii. 12 perhaps gives us the original form of the pivot-saying about the sign, as it fell from the lips of Jesus. As defenders of the literal historicity of the story of Jonah have made great play with Matt. xii. 40, it ought to be pointed out that its position in the text is extremely precarious.[2] Christian tradition was perpetually growing in this direction ; the last two canonical Gospels to be given to the world in their final form—the First and the Fourth —bear traces of a carefully wrought system of references to prophecy. Sometimes this deference to the letter of the Old Testament may have led to mistakes ; where Mark and Luke stand together against the First Gospel, and we can account for the details of Matthew by the text of the Old Testament, we are justified in suspecting that with the latter the wish that the gospel-history might correspond in all details with its ' types ' has been father to the thought that it did ; or, at least, that our evangelist instinctively gave the preference to the form of narrative which most nearly answered to the old model. Instances of possible error may be found in xxi. 5 ff., where Jesus is apparently made to ride upon two beasts—Mark xi. 7 and Luke xix. 33 confine themselves to one. The foal, of course, might have been led alongside of its mother, but xxi. 7, ' He sat upon them,' looks like a mistake. Our author has probably taken Zech. ix. 9 literally ; if so, he cannot have been an expert Hebraist, for ' riding upon an ass, and upon a colt, the foal of a beast of burden,' simply means ' upon a young ass ' in the language of Hebrew poetry. It is possible, by the way, that we ought to extend the range of this idiom further, and explain 'scribes and Pharisees ' as ' scribes who are Pharisees '—there were Sadducean scribes too—' publicans and sinners.' as ' publicans who are sinners.' In regard to the ' thirty pieces of silver,'[3] this detail has almost certainly come from Zech. xi. 12, 13 via the Testimony Book. In xxvii. 9 the passage from Zechariah is quoted as from Jeremiah. In spite of the fact that ' Jeremiah ' is omitted

[1] Matt. xii. 41.
[2] J. H. Michael (*J.T.S.*, Jan., 1920) argues that the ' sign ' is John the Baptist's preaching, not Jonah's, ' Jonah ' being a mistake for ' John,' as perhaps in Matt. 16. 17 (Barjona).
[3] Matt. xxvi. 15, xxvii. 3, 9.

here by the Old Syriac versions, as well as by the Peshitta (the Syriac ' Vulgate '), Tatian's Gospel-harmony (for these versions see App. III.), and the two earliest Old Latin versions, Dr. Harris thinks that ' Jeremiah ' should still be read, and the mistake attributed to the fact (for another instance, see below) that in the Testimony Book, from which the extract was taken, the section was headed by a quotation from Jeremiah. The ' myrrhed wine ' of Mark xv. 23 has become ' wine mingled with gall ' in xxvii. 34 under the influence of Ps. lxix. 22—also taken from the Testimony Book—and the language of xxvii. 5 has perhaps been affected by the story of Ahithophel's suicide.[1]

In xiii. 35 Ps. lxxviii. 2 is cited as ' the thing spoken through *the Prophet.*' This unusual ascription is best accounted for again by the arrangement of the Book of Testimonies, in which passages from the Old Testament were grouped under a single heading according to topic ; a selection was made for the purposes of this Gospel, without verification in every case. The passages cited in i. 23 ; ii. 6, 15 ; iii. 3, 17 ; iv. 15f. ; viii. 17 ; xi. 10 ; xii. 18ff. ; xiii. 35 ; xvii. 5, 11 ; xxi. 5, 42 ; xxii. 44 ; xxiv. 30, 31 ; xxvi. 15, 31, 64 ; xxvii. 9, 10, 34, 35, almost certainly can be credited to this book. In xi. 10 Matthew has ' Behold *I* send My messenger before Thy face, who shall prepare Thy way,' going on from Mal. iii. 1 to Isa. xl. 3 already quoted in iii. 3. The emphatic *I* comes from Exod. xxiii. 20, as well as the duplicated ' before Thy face . . . before Thee.' Mal. iii. 1 has ' before My face,' but ' prepare Thy wa; ' comes from Malachi—' he shall prepare the way before Thee.' Our conclusion must be that Isa. xl. 3, Mal. iii. 1, and Exod. xxiii. 20 were all associated under one heading in the Testimony Book, Isa. xl. 3 coming first—hence Mark i. 2 quotes Mal. iii. 1 as from Isaiah, while Matthew separates the Isaiah passage from the other two, giving it in iii. 3, and blends Malachi with Exodus ; while Mark, who also uses the Testimony Book, unites Malachi and Isaiah. Eusebius explained the variations from the LXX, so frequent in Matthew, by the theory that the original Gospel according to Matthew was in Hebrew, and made use of the Hebrew Old Testament, while Jerome thought that both Matthew and John made translations of the passages they quoted from the Old Testament which were quite independent of the LXX. It is more likely that the translations were already current in the Testimony Book in Aramaic. In ii. 6 ; iv. 15 ; viii. 17 ; xii. 18–21; xiii. 14, 15 ; xxvi. 31 ; xxvii. 9 these variations are very marked ;

[1] 2 Sam. xvii. 23.

in ii. 15 ; xi. 10 ; xiii. 35, also, Matthew would appear to be dependent upon the same source. His reverence for the details
of the Old Testament Scripture can be seen in xix. 18, where he
alters the ' Do not kill,' &c., of Mark x. 19 to ' Thou shalt not kill,'
&c., as well as in his omission of ' Defraud not ' as not appearing
in the Decalogue, at least in this form. To the enumeration of
five of the ten commandments he adds a statement of the master-
principle underlying them all, as Jesus must have done ' Thou
shalt love thy neighbour as thyself '—Matthew only here—cf. xxii.
40, also peculiar to Matthew. He appears to be dependent upon
the LXX only at i. 23, iii. 3, iv. 4, 6, 7—not in iv. 10.

This Gospel has altogether forty-seven direct quotations of the
Old Testament—more than Mark and Luke taken together. Some
are very striking ; others, to our notions of exegesis, distorted.
As to ii. 15, the idea underlying this strange citation of Hos. xi. 1
—where there appears at first sight to be only a verbal resemblance
—is that Christ is the true Israel ; this is the heading of one of
the sections of the Testimony Book. Upon the whole, we can
say that our evangelist's choice of testimonies is very happy.
Conspicuous amongst them is the passage taken from Isa. xlii.
1–4, in Matt. xii. 18 ff., for it adds a welcome touch to our portrait
of Jesus. He was no loud-voiced agitator, needing with strident
insistence and extravagant gesture to force His hearers to attention.
He did not declaim ; rather He talked in a low compassionate
tone, for He prevailed (v. 20) by His gentleness. We shall come
back to this passage again, but we shall do well to note, in
view of what has been said above (pp. 233–4), the universal colouring
of the whole quotation (especially vv. 18, 21). Another beautiful
suggestion is found in viii. 17, ' Himself took our weaknesses and
carried our diseases.' Jesus had already applied certain features
of the conception of the ' Suffering Servant ' to Himself (cf., e.g.,
Luke xxii. 37), and there can be little doubt that, in the Testimony
Book and elsewhere, the idea of Christ as God's ' Servant ' (cf.
Acts iii. 13, iv. 27, 30, &c., read my ' Servant,' with R.V.,) was
part of the common stock of the Church's Christology in very
early days ; but our evangelist has shown skill and good taste
in his selection of passages. When we compare the testimonies
which occur in the course of the First Gospel with others which
appear, for instance, in Justin, and come from the same source
(the Testimony Book), our favourable impression is deepened.
Needless to say, the citations ascribed to the Lord Himself always
carry conviction. Jesus twice makes use of Hos. vi. 6, ' I desire

brotherly feeling, and not sacrifice '; He also shows a marked predilection for the Books of Jonah, of Deuteronomy, and of Isaiah xl.–lxvi. The Book of Deuteronomy is directly quoted no fewer than seven times by Jesus, the Book of Psalms six times, Jeremiah thrice, ' Second Isaiah ' twice, Hosea twice, Daniel (possibly) four times, Zechariah three times, Micah twice, Malachi and Zephaniah once each; while ' Thou shalt love thy neighbour as thyself,' which comes from Leviticus, is quoted three times in this Gospel —on two of these occasions in Matthew only. The Book of Exodus is used four times—in three of these cases it is parallel to Deuteronomy—and the Book of Genesis referred to three times. These statistics only apply to clear citations or references upon the lips of Jesus Himself. The historical books are not employed by Him very much. A somewhat doubtful reference may be found in xxiii. 35; perhaps the only clear cases are xii. 3, 42, if vi. 29 be not counted. ' Zechariah, son of Barachiah '[1] seems to be a mistake of the evangelist, the ' Zechariah, son of Jehoiada '—the LXX has ' Azariah, son of Jehoiada '—of 2 Chron. xxiv. 20, 21 having been confused either with ' Zechariah, son of Jeberechiah '[2] or with the prophet Zechariah ' son of Berechiah '[3]—Luke xi. 51 has ' Zachariah ' without addition.

We cannot treat the Old Testament quite in Matthew's way, but his use of the Jewish Scripture is important for more reasons than one. We realize how eagerly the early followers of Jesus claimed the Old Testament for their own. In the quotation which Matthew gives us at i. 23—this again comes from the Testimony Book—we have an instance of the help given to the Christian apologist by the LXX. Other Jewish translations, such as that of Aquila (A.D. 129), Theodotion (A.D. 179), and Symmachus, read ' a young woman,' in order to put out of court the Christian use of Isa. vii. 14; but the older LXX text has ' the virgin.' Certainly the Hebrew text might refer either to a young married woman or to a girl, so that the use of the passage as a ' testimony ' to the Virgin Birth is exceedingly precarious. But behind this Christian exploitation—as their antagonists called it—of the Old Testament there lies a sound instinct. ' The coming of Jesus was no caprice, but was part of a well-ordered whole. To the Christian as to the Jew, history means something. To the Greek this was not so; to the Hindu it is not so ' (H. G. Wood). The Church has suffered for her devotion to the Old Testament; there have been continual relapses into Judaism, reactions to the standpoint

[1] Matt. xxiii. 35. [2] Isa. viii. 2. [3] Zech. i. 1.

of the early books. We are witnessing one to-day; the preacher finds texts for 'patriotic' sermons in the early part of the Old Testament, and Bible-readers are turning again to the righteous anger of psalmists and prophets. This may be all to the good, for 'all Scripture was written for our learning'; but Jesus Himself is for Christians the test of the relative worth of different strains of teaching in the earlier revelation; and our investigations have shown that, so far as we can judge from the Gospels, He left upon one side such books as those of Joshua and Judges, the imprecatory Psalms. This does not mean that He did not regard them as Scripture, or that they are without value for us, but it does suggest caution in their use; our conclusions from them must always be checked by comparison with His Spirit (cf. Luke ix. 55, A.V.), and it is quite conceivable that some Old Testament passages prepare the way for Him by contrast, as others by likeness. The gain involved in the appropriation of the Jewish Bible by the Church heavily outweighs any loss there may have been; our conception of the Master Himself is far richer and deeper because we can read the Book in which His own inner life found its normal expression. For the Gospels make it plain that Jesus not only frequently quoted the Old Testament Scripture; He thought in terms of its language. In the story of the Temptation one of the assaults, and all three of His replies, are couched in the actual words of the Old Testament; and this story comes from Q, the earliest and the most authoritative of our witnesses.

A further word should be said about the difficult question referred to in the footnote on page 237. Jesus says, in the most emphatic way, in v. 17 ff. that He has not come to destroy the validity of the older sanctions; in fact, the smallest detail of God's law as revealed in Scripture is not to pass away until every jot and tittle has unfolded its larger meaning. Then He proceeds, apparently, to substitute a new law for the old, a law which seems to contradict the older law at every turn. A closer study of His method reveals the fact that what we are watching Him do is rather this; He takes the great principles underlying the older law in turn, and carries them a stage farther. In v. 21 ff. the law against murder, under which lies the idea of the sacredness of human personality, is not abrogated, but carried on into a prohibition of unreasonable anger, contempt, and abuse; respect for bodily life becomes respect for personality in the larger sense. The same method obviously underlies v. 28 ff.; but in v. 31 ff. Jesus goes behind the Mosaic compromise to the fundamental principle, itself contained in the Pentateuch (cf. also xix. 8 ff.). The law against perjury (v. 33 ff.) becomes an injunction to sincerity and honest downrightness in private conversation; while the law of reprisal, containing the principle of public justice or adequate compensation for injuries received, is shown in v. 39 ff. to involve a prohibition of lawless reprisals. Justice, when properly understood, involves mercy. Finally, patriotism, in v. 43 ff., becomes no longer national, but broadly human. No one is really just to his fellows who is not generous. In any case, it is manifestly unjust to act as judge and jury in your own case.

II

FURTHER CHARACTERISTICS OF THE FIRST GOSPEL

OUR first evangelist's only real prejudice would seem to consist in a definite bias against the Pharisees. Over and over again he puts them in where Mark leaves them out. Instances may be found in Matt. xxi. 45—' the chief priests *and the Pharisees*' recognize that the parable of the keepers of the vineyard has been directed against them (Mark xii. 12 is ambiguous, though xi. 27 seems to implicate at least the Pharisaic leaders, ' the scribes and the elders'). Matt. xxvii. 20 gives us a clearer case, for we read there ' the chief priests and *the elders*' (i.e. probably the Pharisaic members of the Sanhedrin) ' persuaded the crowds' (Mark xv. 11, the chief priests only). In Matt. xii. 14 the Pharisees stand alone in their murderous designs upon Jesus, whereas in Mark iii. 6 the ' Herodians ' are coupled with them. Altogether the Pharisees play a much more prominent part in the conspiracies of Holy Week than is assigned to them either in Mark or Luke. Matt. xxii. 34, 41 are both peculiar to Matthew, and many of the strongest sayings in chapter xxiii. are found in his Gospel only. This does not mean, of course, that they are not authentic; but it does show that the writer of the Gospel in which such emphasis is placed upon their misdeeds was not concerned to allow them to escape their due share of culpability for the shedding of his Lord's ' innocent blood.' In ix. 34, xii. 24 a malicious insinuation, made, according to Mark iii. 22, by ' scribes from Jerusalem,' according to Luke xi. 15 by ' some of their number ' (i.e. of the crowds, v. 14), is ascribed to ' the Pharisees,' while xv. 12, 13 is found only in this Gospel. ' Pharisees,' in association with 'Sadducees,' come to John's baptism, and are addressed as 'generation of vipers,'[1] whereas in Luke iii. 7 the crowd in general is greeted in this fashion. At the other end of the book priests and Pharisees are still working in conjunction.[2] We must remember that the name 'Pharisees' covers a very large party, probably including the majority of what we should call the middle classes. Their 'scribes '—not all the Scribes were Pharisees—had become their leaders in religious matters; the 'elders' were their representatives in political and ecclesiastical life. There were Pharisees as well as Sadducees among the priests, though the 'chief priests' were probably all Sadducees. It follows that the transference, by implication, of blame for some of the most sinister sayings and actions directed against Jesus in the Gospel narrative from a section of their party to the Pharisees as a whole —as in, e.g., ix. 34, xii. 24—would, if pressed, amount to a very serious indictment of Jewish middle-class society in our Lord's time. I prefer to think that for some reason the name 'Pharisee' was specially odious to this writer. If Matthew the publican had anything to do with the kind of tradition which underlies the Gospel, we can well understand how this came about. He does not contradict Mark, for the scribes were Pharisees; but whenever a small group of Pharisees did or said anything more than usually criminal, the 'Pharisees' are the culprits, without differentiation. 'Their scribes' (R.V.)[3] (Mark i. 22, 'the scribes') should also be noticed; Matthew shows us that Jesus had His ideal of the Christian scribe, who has 'new' as well as 'old' things to bring out of his store[4] (Matthew only). It is all the more remarkable, and is a high testimony to the scrupulous honesty of our evangelist, that he alone reports two tributes paid by Jesus to the way of life prescribed by Pharisaic teachers.[5]

But the positive characteristics of this Gospel are very much more important. For one thing, Peter and the rest of the apostles are duly honoured. Three passages concerning Peter are specially noteworthy; none of them appears in Mark. The first, in Matthew's order, is xiv. 28 ff.—the story of Peter's walking on the water 'to

[1] Matt. iii. 7.   [2] Matt. xxvii., 62 ff, xxviii. 12.   [3] Matt. vii. 29.
[4] Matt. xiii. 52.   [5] Matt. v. 20, xxiii. 2, 3.

go to Jesus.' Here we have all Peter's qualities, familiar to us from our studies in his character—his impulsiveness, his tendency to appropriate Jesus, his sudden reactions (cf. Luke v. 8). The whole passage, including the narrative of the miraculous feeding, is curiously prophetic of the Passion. The sixth chapter of John brings out the sacramental meaning of the broken bread, while the Lord's walking upon the water of the lake reminds us of His resurrection, when He came back to the rescue of His friends. On each occasion the disciples are afraid ; though the word used here is a ' ghost,' there a ' spirit,' the idea is the same. When the Risen Lord appears upon the shore of the same lake, Peter again hastens to reach Him before the others—'he girt his fisher's cloak about him . . . and cast himself into the lake, and was swimming, and came ' (' Lewis ' Syriac). But once more, when the first instinctive rush has spent itself, he stops short, and has not a word to say, till the Master challenges him.[1] Still more significant is the fact that, as we read these verses, all the tragedy of Passion-night, as it impressed itself upon the memory of the eleven, passes before us in a revealing flash. ' When evening came, He was alone '[2]; twelve months later, again at the end of a Paschal meal, He is once more alone ; though His chosen three are only a stone's throw away in the garden, they cannot help Him now.[3] And when He had gone altogether from their sight, could their condition be described more adequately than in the words, ' They were already many furlongs from the land, tormented by the waves, for the wind was against them ?'[4] Even during those last hours their Lord was so strange in His power[5] and His humbleness that to them He must have seemed unearthly ; they could only watch His walking on the water, His silent challenging of the tempest of evil passion, in awed amazement. After the first recoil Peter's impulsive loyalty reasserts itself ; he will stand by the side of Jesus, alone if need be, as formerly he would walk on the water to go to Him. When all forsake their Master, Peter follows still ; but now the impulse has carried him as far as it will, his courage ebbs suddenly away, and he feels himself

[1] John xxi. 7 ff., 15 ff.   [2] Matt. xiv. 23.   [3] John xiii. 36, xvi. 32.
[4] Matt. xiv. 23, 24.   [5] John xviii. 6.

sinking.[1] How the Lord saved him in his second and
more dangerous fall, to which the same unsteady impulsiveness had led him, we know[2]; but the words of Jesus[3]
on the water—' O thou of little faith, wherefore wast
thou in two minds '—the same word is used of some of
the other disciples in xxviii. 17—give us the clue to the
denial scene. Peter was caught ' in two minds,' because
in those days he ' walked whither he would '[4];
he was at the mercy of his own changing moods.
Before we leave this passage we should notice that Matt.
xiv. 31 answers exactly to Mark xi. 23, ' is not distracted
in his heart.'

Our second Petrine section[5] is more important still,
' And Jesus answered and said to him, Blessed art thou,
Simon, Jonah's son '—he is called ' son of John ' in John
i. 42, xxi. 15 ff.—' for flesh and blood hath not revealed
it unto thee, but My Father in heaven. And I say unto
thee, that thou art Peter, and upon this rock I will build
My church ' (or ' meeting-house '; see above, p. 232),
' and the gates of Hades shall not prevail against it '
(v. 19 has been discussed above, p. 232). ' Jonah's son '
is perhaps a mistake for ' son of John,' though it has
occurred to me that a play upon the name of Jonah, which
means ' dove,' may underlie it; if so, it might possibly
stand for ' son of the Spirit ' (cf. Luke iii. 22). The other
explanation seems, however, more natural. ' Son of
John ' appears to be a half-playful nickname for Peter,
for no one ever mentions Peter's father's name but Jesus
—at their first[6] and their last meeting in the Gospel[7]
and here, if we read ' son of John.' To everybody else
he was nobody's son, unlike the comparatively aristocratic
' sons of Zebedee.' Jesus will not have him looked down
upon by them or any one else—for the fact that ' the
mother of the sons of Zebedee ' thought her boys superior
to Peter see Matt. xx. 20 ff.—so He gives him a pedigree
too. It can scarcely be accidental that Paul in Gal. i.
16 makes the same claim for himself, and almost in the
same words, 'immediately I conferred not with *flesh and
blood*,' just after the clause ' when it pleased God to *reveal*

---

[1] Mark xiv. 72; Matt. xiv. 30. [2] Luke xxiv. 34; 1 Cor. xv. 5.
[3] Matt. xiv. 31. [4] John xxi. 18. [5] Matt. xvi. 17 ff.
[6] John i. 42. [7] John xxi. 15 ff.

His Son in my case.' Dr. Bacon thinks that the text of Galatians has affected that of the First Gospel here; it is fairly certain, at any rate, that this saying does not come from Q, for Luke is anxious to report all that he can of Peter's doings (see Luke v. 4 ff.; xxii. 31; xxii. 8; xxiv. 34—all Luke only, so far as the mention of Peter is concerned), and is specially desirous to show that Peter and Paul were not really opposed. In the Acts there is a series of parallels between the two leaders who are the writer's heroes (cf. Acts iii. 1-10; xiv. 8-10; viii. 17; xix. 6; viii. 18 ff.; xiii. 9 ff.; ix. 33, 34; xiv. 8, 9; x. 26; xiv. 15; v. 15; xix. 12; ix. 40; xx. 10; xii. 3-12; xvi. 22-40); and at the Council of Jerusalem the writer labours to make it plain that they were in entire agreement.[1] At the same time it is open to us to hold that the First Gospel contains an authentic tradition at this point, and that Paul has a saying something like this in mind; we know that he was harshly criticized by people who compared him unfavourably with the original apostles.[2] Any exclusively Petrine reference is corrected in John xx. 22, 23; but Matthew too makes it clear that part at least of the blessing did not concern Peter only.[3]

With ' on this rock I will build My church ' we may compare a Rabbinic saying : ' When He (God) saw that Abraham, who was going to arise, He said, ' Lo! I have found a rock to build and found the world upon.' The extreme Protestant interpretation, which draws attention to the shade of distinction present in the Greek between ' Peter ' (stone) and ' petra ' (rock), neglects to take account of the fact that the original saying was almost certainly uttered in Aramaic. and that the difference cannot be rendered back into Aramaic. In that language ' rock ' is feminine, as in French; so that Mrs. Lewis is able to render the original ' Tu es Pierre, et sur cette pierre je batirai mon église.' When the text is read in this fashion, its meaning jumps to our eyes ; Jesus will build His Church on the inspired confession of men like Peter. G. K. Chesterton has somewhat suggested that our Lord's supreme discovery was that of the value of the average man—if, indeed, such a being exists—and his

---

[1] Acts xv. 7 ff.   [2] 1 Cor. ix. 1, 5, &c.   [3] Matt. xviii. 18.

interpretation is confirmed by the fact that on the Galilean lakeside the lava-rock is everywhere obtrusive. Cast up from the bowels of the earth, it has been steadily hardening through the centuries. Peter, when Jesus first saw him, is eagerly welcomed as a good specimen of the old Galilean stock, the kind of man for whom He chose to minister by the lake.[1] On the inexpressive but sturdy conviction of such men and women the Church of Christ has been built, and the apostolic succession of people, whose only distinction is their love for their Lord, will never die out.[2]

But there is another allusion in this suggestive saying. Two religions were shortly to contest the world, one represented by a marble temple built on the solid rock near Caesarea Philippi, where the Roman Emperor was worshipped as God ; the other by the motley group of men beneath it. It is as though Jesus said, ' That is what they say about him ; what do you say about Me ? ' When Peter, looking up defiantly at the symbol of the hated imperial power, answers ' Thou art the Messiah, the Son of the real God '—that is what ' living God ' (cf. 1 Thess. i. 9, ' living and real ') means—the Lord turns away from the marble to the man, for He will build His Kingdom in the hearts of men by the way of the Cross ; ' From that time forward Jesus began to show to His disciples,' &c.[3] For even in Peter's confession, warmly as it was welcomed, there was danger ; he had been roused partly by love for his Lord, partly by his mood of reckless contempt for the power of Rome flaunting the insolence of its wealth and security on the very borders of his native Galilee. Jesus hastens to warn His friends against any attempt to rival Caesar. This was the last really happy hour that Peter spent with his Master till He ' appeared to Simon,'[4] for the shadow is beginning to creep over them. The temple has gone ; in its place there is a Mohammedan shrine dedicated to our St. George ; the church remains, for it is built not upon forced labour or wealth won by conquest, but on the enduring rock of God's grace and men's devotion (on the whole scene, see G. A. Smith, *Historical Geography*, &c., p. 473 ff.). Caesarea Philippi was an asylum, or sanctuary, where

[1] John i. 42.   [2] Matt. xvi. 18.   [3] Matt. xvi. 21.   [4] Luke xxiv. 34.

the hand of Herod could not reach the little company ;
only where Peter was safe from the tyrant would Jesus
ask him to commit himself to an allegiance which would,
in the ever-watchful eyes of the jealous government,
have involved high treason. For Himself, Jesus was
not afraid of Herod,[1] but no such pledge of fidelity was
ever again asked for even from His lovers, and in this
case He commands an absolute secrecy.

A third Petrine section[2] has been briefly noticed already ;
but it is interesting to observe that in Galilee, at least,
Peter is recognized by outsiders as the leader of the
twelve. We are not concerned with a real miracle here.
Jesus says, in effect, ' Surely, Peter, you know how to
get a little money when you need it ! Catch a fish, and
pay the tax. Not that it matters much to such as we ;
but it is only a little thing, and we must avoid giving
needless offence.' Ephrem the Syrian father, in his commentary upon Tatian's *Gospel Harmony* (see App. III.),
gives us a curious reading here, a reading also found in
the Peckover MSS. (eleventh century) at Wisbech : Jesus
asks, ' Are the children free? ' Peter says, ' Yes, they are,'
' Then do thou give, as being a stranger unto them,'
answers the Lord. This reading is probably Marcionite
in origin, for one of the watchwords of Marcion (see App.
IV.) was to the effect that Jesus was the Son of the
' Stranger ' God, the God of Love, who had nothing to
do with the God of the Jews, the Creator of the world.
Peter is to pay, because the Lord and His disciples are
foreigners to the Jewish State. It is fairly certain that
the sense of the passage in the authentic text is precisely
the opposite. Jesus and His followers are, like the Levites,
not subject to the tax, because they are not less, but more,
nearly related to the God of the Temple[3] ; all the same,
they will pay to avoid the suggestion, so eagerly adopted
by their enemies later on that they are against the Temple.
For the association of the true Christian priesthood with
the Levites, compare x. 10 and the introduction of the
Sabbath duties of the priests in the Temple service in
xii. 5 (Matthew only) in justification of the priests attendant
upon ' One greater than the Temple '[4] (Matthew only).

---

[1] Luke xiii. 32.   [2] Matt. xvii. 24 ff.   [3] Luke ii. 49.
[4] Matt. xii. 6.

In the treatment of this incident, taken along with v. 20, xviii. 15 ff., xxii. 21, we have a complete programme of politics for the Jewish Christian Church up to the final destruction of the Jewish State; all three 'Petrine' sections have this in common, that they reflect the conditions and meet the needs of the Church in Palestine during the first century, before its entire separation from Judaism.

In Matt. viii. 14, as in Luke iv. 38, Andrew has disappeared behind his brother (cf. Mark i. 29), who is always called in this Gospel 'Simon Peter' or 'Peter'—in xvi. 17 'Simon Barjona' (see above, p. 249)—never familiarly 'Simon,' as in Mark i. 16, 29, 30, 36; iii. 16, *except by Jesus*[1] (cf. Mark xiv. 37 ; Luke xxii. 31). In x. 2 (Matthew only) we have the significant word 'first'; this might appear to recur in John i. 41, if it wêre not that the correct reading there is almost certainly 'early in the morning' (*prôi ton* instead of *prôton*) ; in the Palestinian Church Peter was emphatically the first of the apostles. In xv. 15 Peter asks for an explanation of a 'parable'—here not a story, but a dark saying—cf. xiii. 35 (Matthew only— Mark vii. 17 has 'His disciples asked'). Chapter xviii. 21, 22 is more important ; like the other passages mentioned above, it is peculiar to this Gospel, and it gives us a glimpse of Peter in a thoughtful mood. Evidently he had a way of letting the conversation drift past him to other topics, while he was himself thinking out something the Master had said a little while before. When his thoughts have reached a certain point, he is ready with a question, with which he breaks in upon the monologue of Jesus. 'Then came Peter to Him'—he had been removed, abstracted—'and said, Lord, how often shall my brother sin against me, and I forgive him?' 'Until seven times?' Peter wants a rule of thumb, a fixed limit for his own use ; he brings everything down to the personal question, 'What is Peter to do in a given situation?' I have already suggested (p. 83) that Judas was the offending 'brother' referred to. It is plain that the words in xviii. 15 (Matthew only)—'If thy brother sin,' &c.—have set his mind working; surely there must be a limit. On the Day of Atonement, said the Rabbis,

---

[1] Matt. xvii. 25.

a man must forgive three times. Thought Peter, ' I will make it seven times.' Jesus replies, ' No ; if the sin is merely directed *against you* '—in xviii. 15 He had said, ' If thy brother sin,' according to the best reading— ' there is to be no limit anywhere to your readiness to forgive ' ; for the relation of this passage to Luke xvii. 4, see p. 122. ' Seventy times seven ' should be ' seventy-seven times ' according to Codex Bezae, Tertullian, &c.; in Jewish language this means ' ad infinitum' (cf. Gen. iv. 24 and 666—the trinity of evil—or six recurring, as seven recurring stands for the infinitely good—in Rev. xiii. 18.)[1] There is another case of the same process in Peter's case in xix. 27 ; it is borne out this time by Mark x. 28, Luke xviii. 28. The rich young man has been to Jesus with his question, and has gone sadly away ; a conversation between the Lord and His disciples ensues, in which Peter does not join, for he is thinking out the incident on his own lines. Then at xix. 27 he comes in with his question, direct and personal as usual : ' Lo ! we have left all, and followed Thee '—we have done what this man could not do, ' what shall we have ? ' To be fair to Peter we ought to observe that when he is speaking of rewards, he says ' we ' ; when it is a question of duties, ' I.'[2] In both cases a parable sums up the answer to his question.[3] The Fourth Gospel suggests the same habit of mind in Peter (cf. John xiii. 36, where he refers back, in very much the same way, to xiii. 33.

Turning from Peter to the others, we meet with equal concern that they should receive proper honour. Many of the passages mentioned above (pp. 55, 56) are relevant here ; it will only be necessary to refer to Matt. xiii. 18[4] ; xiv. 33[5] ; xvi. 17 ff., 23[6] ; xvi. 8 ff[7] ; viii. 25[8] ; viii. 27[9] ; xvii. 4, 5[10] ; xviii. 1 ff[11]; xix. 13 ff[12] ; xx. 17[13] ; xx. 20 [14] ; xxvi. 43 [15]. We have already seen that Matthew is a little gentler towards Judas than the others[16]. But the attitude maintained towards the twelve is not merely revealed in these corrections of

[1] Unless the correct reading is 616.
[2] Matt. xviii. 21.
[3] Matt. xviii. 23 ff., xx. 1 ff.
[4] Mark iv. 13.
[5] Mark vi. 51 f.
[6] Mark viii. 27 ff., 33
[7] Mark viii. 17-21.
[8] Mark iv. 38.
[9] Mark iv. 40.
[10] Mark ix. 6.
[11] Mark ix. 33 f.
[12] Mark x. 13, 14.
[13] Mark x. 32.
[14] Mark x. 35.
[15] Mark xiv. 40.
[16] Matt. xxvii. 3 ff.

Mark; it is uniformly appreciative. The 'Sermon on the Mount' is addressed to the disciples (i.e. His most intimate followers, as often in this Gospel), to whom Jesus can speak freely and in confidence; for ' He opened His mouth ' in v. 2 means this, and has no reference to elocution (cf. 2 Cor. vi. 11, ' Our mouth is open to you, O Corinthians '). *They* are ' the salt of the earth,' ' the light of the world '[1] (Matthew only in this form; in Mark ix. 50 they are bidden to ' have salt ' in themselves). *They* are blessed when persecuted, for the Lord turns from generalities to address them in v. 11. ' *They shall* be perfect'[2] (Luke vi. 36 has a command, 'Be ye pitiful'), for God is *their* 'Father' (Luke xi. 2—'Father,' not 'our Father' as Matt. vi. 9). ' The narrow gate ' is open to *them* (Luke xiii. 24 is addressed to an outsider—' Agonize to enter in through the narrow door '), for though ' there be few that shall find the way,' *they* shall have, so to say, the first refusal. That the teaching contained in this discourse was meant for preachers is obvious from vii. 22 (Luke xiii. 26, ' Have we not eaten and drunk in Thy presence? '). On the other hand, vii. 28 seems to imply that the crowd had come up the hill during the Sermon, for they are ' stricken with wonder at His teaching.'

In ix. 9 we notice that this Gospel alone mentions the name ' Matthew ' (Mark ii. 14 has ' Levi the son of Alphaeus '; Luke v. 27, ' Levi ') in connexion with his call; the fact that both Mark iii. 18 and Luke vi. 15, as well as Matt. x. 3, give ' Matthew ' in the list of the twelve suggests that Jesus gave him the name ' Matthew.' The meaning of the name is doubtful. Grimm derives it from ' mat,' i.e. ' man '—in that case it would mean 'My man'—but Bartlet prefers ' Jehovah's gift ' (*Hastings' B.D.*, art. ' Matthew '); in any case, if Matthew the publican had anything to do with this Gospel or with the Testimony Book upon which it was based, it is all the more remarkable that only here is he definitely connected with the ' Levi son of Alphaeus ' of Mark ii. 14, and that Matt. x. 3 calls him 'Matthew the publican,' at the same time putting him modestly behind Thomas —Mark iii. 18, Luke vi. 15, ' Matthew and Thomas '; Matt. x. 3, ' Thomas and Matthew the publican.' This

---

[1] Matt. v. 13, 14 ff.   [2] Matt. v. 48.

is one of several features of the Gospel associated by
tradition with his name which prompt us to wish that
we could ascribe its authorship confidently to him. Matt.
x. 3 puts ' James the son of Alphaeus ' next to ' Matthew
the publican ' ; this association of names, taken with
Mark ii. 14, ' Levi *the son of Alphaeus,*' implies that they
were brothers. Were there three pairs of brothers in
the number of the twelve ? A further puzzling feature
of the list is presented by Luke vi. 16—' Judas, the brother
of James ' takes the place of the ' Thaddaeus ' (V.L.,
' Lebbaeus ') cf. Mark iii. 18. We must content ourselves
with the statement that, according to early tradition,
there were two, if not three, publicans in the apostolic
circle.

'The Spirit of *your* Father'[1] (Luke xii. 12, 'the Holy
Spirit') answers to vi. 9 (' *our* Father '). *They* are the
members of the Lord's household[2] (' Master of the house '
—' members of the household,' Matthew only ; notice
also ' it is sufficient *for the disciple* ' (Luke vi. 40—' every
one when perfected '). The phrase ' *your* Father ' comes
again in x. 29 (Luke xii. 6, ' before God '), while ' *of you* '
is set in the most prominent place at the beginning of the
sentence—in x. 30, 'you' in the next place of honour—the
end of the next sentence (x. 31). We ought to render: ' But
as to you, the very hairs of your head are all numbered.
. . . Of much more value ' (the best reading) ' than sparrows are *you* ' (Luke xii. 6, 7 is much less emphatic in this
particular). Matt. x. 40 has ' he that receiveth you '
(cf. John xiii. 20) ; Luke x. 16, ' he that heareth you.
The disciples of Jesus correspond to the ' prophets and
righteous men ' of the Old Testament who brought blessing upon their hosts[3] (cf. 1 Kings xvii. 9–24; 2 Kings iv.
8–37) ; for the combination of ' prophets and righteous
men ' compare Matt. xiii. 17, xxiii. 29 (Luke x. 24,
' prophets and kings '). Yet though their dignity is so
great they are His little ones[4] ('in the name of a disciple'
—that is, ' because the recipient is a disciple ' ; cf. Mark
ix. 41, ' in the name that ye are Christ's '), but the ' least '
of them is greater than John the Baptist[5], who was equal
to Elijah[6], and the smallest kindness to one of them shall

---

[1] Matt. x. 20.   [2] Matt. x. 25.   [3] Matt. x. 41.
[4] Matt. x. 42.   [5] Matt. xi. 11.   [6] Matt. xi. 14.

not lose its reward (cf. xxv. 40, ' to these very little brothers of Mine '). Some scholars think that Paul is glanced at in v. 19—' he that breaks one of these least commands and teaches men ' (Codex Bezae omits ' so ') ' shall be called least in the kingdom.' This is doubtful in the extreme ; all that we can safely say is that Matthew may have been led to record this saying, in view of anti-nomian laxity in circles calling themselves Pauline. If so, we ought in charity to remember that according to xi. 11, though such men were to be called ' least ' in the Kingdom, they are not excluded thereby, and are indeed reckoned greater than John, who was himself ' more than a prophet.'[1] Our evangelist may be biased in favour of the 'law,' but he is no harsh legalist, breathing out anathemas.

Jesus defends His disciples with special warmth in xii. 7 (Matthew only), and in xii. 49 we have ' and stretching out His hand to His disciples ' (Mark iii. 34, ' looking round about upon those sitting round Him ') He said, ' Behold,' &c. ; ' stretching out His hand ' implies sur-render—compare John xxi. 18, ' Thou shalt stretch forth thy hands,' and the patristic emphasis upon the stretching out of the hands of the Saviour on the cross. The Lord left Himself at the mercy of the men and women whom He called His friends ; not once, but always, He put Himself at the disposal of His friends.[2] *Their* eyes are blessed seeing what they see ; Luke x. 23 omits the emphatic ' your.' In xiii. 18 we notice ' *Do you* then hear the parable ' (Luke viii. 11, ' This is the parable '). The disciples are ' the sons of the Kingdom ' in xiii. 38 —compare Luke xvi. 8, ' sons of the light '—and, like the ' wise ' men of Dan. xii. 3, ' shall shine out as the sun in the kingdom of their Father '[3] (the whole passage Matthew only). Not all the shining is to be left to the future, however ; they are to let their light shine[4] (Matthew only) by their good works, for they are the light of this world too. They are ' the pearl of great price' (see p. 127), which the Divine Merchantman found ; to make them His own He ' sold all that was His '[5] (again peculiar to this Gospel)—cf. 1 Cor. vi. 20, ' Ye were bought at a price '; 2 Cor. viii. 9, ' He made Himself a poor man ' (at one

---

[1] Matt. xi. 9–11.   [2] John xv. 13.   [3] Matt. xiii. 43.
[4] Matt. v. 14, 16.   [5] Matt. xiii. 45.

stroke) ; Phil. ii. 7 ; 1 Pet. i. 18, &c.   The word ' pearl '
comes again in vii. 6, where the fellowship of believers
is the ' holy thing,' the circlet of pearls, which must not
be flung to dogs or swine ; if, to gain the one pearl, the
Lord gave up all, all the more for that reason are we to
value our communion with His Church ' which He bought
with His own blood.'[1]   By a slight change in pointing,
the   Hebrew   for   ' holy   thing '—' holiness '—becomes
' signet-ring,'   which   corresponds   much   more   closely   to
' pearls.'   Here perhaps is another link with the story
of the lost son, in which both ' swine '[2] and ' signet-ring '[3]
occur.   Later on Jesus told a story about a boy who did,
in effect, throw his signet-ring to the ' swine,' and yet
got it back again !   If *they* are greater than the prophets,
they are also, in the best sense of the word, scribes, for a
' scribe who becomes a disciple to the kingdom of heaven'
can ' bring out of his treasure ' (cf. xiii. 44) ' things
new and old,' unlike the orthodox Jewish scribe, who
merely professed to deal in the sayings of the fathers[4]
(Matthew only).   Words spoken to ' all,' according to
Luke ix. 23, are reserved to the disciples in Matt. xvi. 24,
and in his account of the Transfiguration Matthew gives
us an exquisite glimpse of the Lord's tenderness for His
own ; the three disciples have for the first time seen their
Master talking with His peers, and they feel out of it.
They will be quite content to lie out in the snow and watch,
and Peter suggests that three tents should be made for
the three Great Ones, while the three little ones may be
allowed to look on.   But for Jesus, even in the company
of Moses and Elijah, His humbler friends are His first
concern ; the sentence ' And Jesus drew near and touched
them, and said, Arise, and be not afraid,' is found in this
Gospel only.   He has come back to them ; ' He gave the
password of the great,' and came back ' to love plain
ordinary James, to be the friend of Peter till he died,
to give Judas another chance ' (G. S. Lee).
   We never read in this Gospel of the disciples' ' unbelief,'
as, e.g., in Mark iv. 40—' How is it ye have not faith ? '
—only of their ' little faith '[5] (cf. xiv. 31; vi. 30; viii. 26;
xvi. 8—apart from Matthew, only Luke xii. 28).

[1] Acts xx. 28.   [2] Luke xv. 15, 16.   [3] Luke xv. 22.   [4] Matt. xiii. 52.
[5] Matt. xvii. 20 (the best reading 'little faith,' not ' unbelief,' as A.V.).

The saying about the miraculous powers possible to the disciples is twice repeated in Matthew,[1] while the fact that they did not understand what the Master meant when He spoke of His passion[2] is softened into ' and they were very much troubled '[3] (cf. John xvi. 6, ' grief hath filled your heart '). ' Thou hast gained thy brother ' is a splendid phrase, breathing the spirit of xiii. 45, for the Lord's sacrificial devotion to human friendship is to be reflected in the relations of His followers to one another. The best commentary upon these words is to be found in Sirach xix. 12, ' Reprove a friend ; it may be he did it not, and if he did something, he may not do it again. . . . Reprove a friend, for many times there is slander, and trust not *every word* ' (cf. Matt. xviii. 16, ' *every word* '). Compare also the Testament of the Twelve Patriarchs— a Pharisaic book—in which, in the course of the Testament of Gad (vi. 3), these words occur, ' Love ye one another from the heart ; and if a man sin against thee, cast forth the poison of hate and speak peaceably to him ; . . . and if he confess and repent, forgive him ' (cf. Luke xvii. 3). ' And if he be shameless and persist in his wrongdoing, still forgive him from the heart, and leave to God the avenging.' Jesus adds the thought that you may not only *keep* friends, but *make* them, by settling inevitable differences wisely.

In xviii. 18 Peter's new authority is extended to the apostles in a body, and in xviii. 19 unlimited value is assigned to the prayers of two *of them*, if they are in harmony. This passage strikes a note, it should be observed, that is not heard even in the Third Gospel, where such emphasis is placed upon the efficacy of prayer. Individual prayer ' in secret ' is rewarded,[4] but the common prayers of two lovers of their Lord and of each other is invariably successful in its particular object—' about any and every matter concerning which they shall make request.' There is no such explicit statement anywhere else in the first three Gospels, though Mark xi. 24 perhaps approaches it closely, and it deserves our closest attention; there faith, here love, is said to be the condition of effectual prayer ; compare Ignatius to the Ephesians, ' for if the

[1] Matt. xvii. 20, xxi. 21.   [2] Mark ix. 32.   [3] Matt. xvii. 23.
[4] Matt. vi. 6.

prayer of one and a second have such strength.' The
'two' of xviii. 19 become in xviii. 20 'two or three.' Clement
of Alexandria makes the delightful suggestion that the
'two or three' are 'father, mother, and child'; notice
how the third party slips in, as the child becomes part of
the home, almost without the parents knowing it—he has
not to pay his footing; he is just there—and the presence
of this welcome third party is not necessary, for it may be
'two *or* three,' but it helps wonderfully; the 'two' are
the believing husband and wife. The unwritten saying
already discussed provides for the lonely soul (see p. 120),
for 'where one of you is alone, I am with him,' said Jesus—
He must have said it—and that makes two; in John xiv.
23 this pair—Christ and the Christian—becomes a trio,
for where Christ is God is, and that makes three—' we
will come to him,' &c. In the passage in Matthew there is
manifestly a rising note; we pass from power on earth
(xviii. 18) to power with God (v. 19), while in v. 20 heaven
comes down to earth. With v. 20 should also be compared
I Cor. v. 4 and Matt. xxviii. 20 (' I with you ').

'Harmony' is so all-important to Christian prayer ('are
agreed ' is a musical term; cf. Luke xv. 25, 'a symphony,'
a closely-related word) that the Christian must be endlessly
forbearing with his brother[1]; all alike are so deeply in debt
to their Lord that their debts to one another are trifling
by comparison.[2] Matthew's version of the next promise to
the twelve gives us 'in the regeneration'[3]; the word
used here, says Dalman, is distinctly Greek (Luke xxii. 30
has 'in My kingdom '), and cannot be translated back into
Aramaic or Hebrew. The two old Syriac versions, with
the Peshitta, read 'in the new world,' a phrase which
occurs in the Apocalypse of Baruch (xliv. 13), as also
' the world which is to be renewed '; the targum of Onkelos
at Deut. xxxii. 12 gives us 'the world which God will
renew,' while the Books of Enoch (lxxii. 1) and of Jubilees
(i. 29) have the ' new creation ' (cf. Gal. vi. 15 ; 2 Cor. v. 17,
though Paul is speaking of the present spiritual fact, Jesus
in the First Gospel of the future Kingdom). It is more
important for our present purpose to notice the emphasis
placed here upon ' *also yourselves* ' (Matthew only) and
the ' twelve thrones ' (Luke xxii. 30, ' upon thrones,'

---

[1] Matt. xviii. 22.   [2] Matt. xviii. 23 ff.   [3] Matt. xix. 28.

because Judas was to drop out). Luke xxii. 29 ('My Father') may be set alongside of Luke xii. 32 ('your Father') ; and in I Cor. vi. 2 Paul makes it plain that the promise applies not only to the apostles, but to all saints ; not only to the 'twelve tribes of Israel' (Matthew–Luke) but to the 'world.' With xix. 29 may be compared Victorinus on the Apocalypse : 'He shall receive a reward multiplied a hundred times . . . and eternal life, which is a reward doubled a hundred times (in quantity), ten thousand times greater and better (in quality) ' ; and Irenaeus, quoting Papias on the Blessing of Isaac (see App. II.). Jesus adds a caution[1] (Luke xiii. 30 points more directly to Judas 'there are first who shall be last '), and supplements it with a parable, which will come under discussion later. So great is the honour of membership in such a society that each of them should be proud not merely to wait upon the others[2] (Luke xxii. 26), but to be their 'slave '[3] ('slave,' Matthew only). All the nations are to be judged by their treatment of 'one of these very little brothers of the Lord,'[4] and in xxvi. 29 Matthew adds 'with you ' to Mark xiv. 25 (cf. 'with Me '—also peculiar to this Gospel—xxvi. 40). Judas, though a traitor, is still addressed as 'comrade ' (see p. 83), but Judas calls Jesus 'Rabbi,'[5] whereas the others say 'Lord.'[6] Even when they are least satisfactory, Jesus prefers His timorous disciples to 'twelve legions of angels,'[7] and the last words of the book leave us with the familiar note ringing in our ears : 'And behold ! I *with you* all the days to the consummation of the age.' The Old Testament resounds throughout with the note 'Thou shalt ' ; the first book of the New develops a deeper note, 'I with you ' ; the Fourth Gospel, echoed by Paul, carries on the strain till it becomes 'I *in* you.' The transition from 'God with us' (i. 23) to 'I with you' marks the course of Matthew's Gospel.

We are not surprised to find that this writer is exceedingly fond of the words 'disciple,' 'make a disciple of,' and 'brother ' in the Christian sense. In viii. 21 (cf. Luke ix. 59) ; x. 1 (cf. Mark vi. 7 ; Luke ix. 1—here the best MSS. omit 'disciples'); x. 25 (cf. Luke vi. 40) ; xi. 1 ;

---

[1] Matt. xix. 30.   [2] Matt. xx. 26.   [3] Matt. xx. 27.
[4] Matt. xxv. 40.   [5] Matt. xxvi. 25, 49.   [6] Matt. xxvi. 22.
[7] Matt. xxvi. 53.

xii. 2 (cf. Mark ii. 24) ; xii. 49 (cf. Mark iii. 34) ; xiii. 36 ;
xiv. 19 (twice; Mark vi. 41, Luke ix. 16, once each);
xiv. 26 (cf. Mark vi. 49) ; xv. 12, 23, 36 (twice ; Mark viii. 6,
once) ; xvi. 5 (not in Mark viii. 14) ; xvi. 20 (cf. Mark viii.
30) ; xvi. 21 (cf. Mark viii. 31) ; xvii. 6 (cf. Mark ix. 6) ;
xvii. 13 (cf. Mark ix. 10) ; xviii. 1 (cf. Mark ix. 33) ; xxi.
6 (cf. Mark xi. 4) ; xxi. 20 (Mark xi. 21—Peter) ; xxiv. 3
(Mark xiii. 3—Peter and James and John and Andrew) ;
xxvi. 1 (cf. Mark xiv. 1) ; xxvi. 8 (cf. Mark xiv. 4) ; xxvi. 20
—reading ' with the twelve disciples ' (Mark xiv. 17, ' the
twelve ' ; Luke xxii. 14, ' the apostles ') ; xxvi. 26 (cf.
Mark xiv. 22); xxvi. 35 (cf. Mark xiv. 31) ; xxvi. 45 (cf.
Mark xiv. 41) ; xxvi. 56 (cf. Mark xiv. 50) ; xxvii. 64 ;
xxviii. 8 (cf. Mark xvi. 8); xxviii. 16 ('disciples' is found
in Matthew only ; the verb ' to make a disciple (or disciples)
of ' occurs at xiii. 52) ; xxvii. 57 (cf. Mark xv. 43 ; Luke
xxiii. 50 ; John xix. 38, ' a disciple ') ; xxviii. 19, and is
peculiar to this Gospel, as is ' brother '—except for Luke
vi. 41, 42 ; xvii. 3—of the relations of Christians with each
other (v. 22, 23, 24, 47 ; vii. 4, 5; xviii. 15, 21, 35). We are
always to be ready to ' learn '—from Jesus,[1] from the Scriptures,[2] from wild flowers.[3] All these examples come only
from Matthew, for Luke xii. 27 has ' think about the lilies.'

[1] Matt. xi. 29.   [2] Matt. ix. 13.   [3] Matt. vi. 28.

III

JESUS THE SON OF GOD

IF the high regard which all Christians entertained for the
first apostles of the Lord is strongly evident in the First
Gospel, they are never allowed to obscure the figure of their
Master. His Messiahship is described as the subject of the
book in the first verse ; He is ' the Christ '[1] (in i. 18 also
some MSS. omit ' Jesus ' before ' Christ '). His birth
' from (the) Holy Spirit ' is declared twice over with solemn
emphasis[2] ; an ' angel of the Lord ' is sent to set Joseph's
doubts at rest[3] ; Jesus, who ' shall *Himself* save His people
from their sins,' is ' God with us '—compare the final words
of the Gospel, ' *I* with you.'[4] The star ' seen from the
east ' proclaims to the wise men His advent, and they
bring offerings of ' treasures '—' gold '—as to a king ;
' myrrh '—token of coming death and burial; ' frankin-
cense '—they worship Him as God (I follow the order of the
older Syriac versions). The star rests not over Bethlehem,
but over ' the place where the Babe was,'[5] while Herod
is roused by the tidings of the wise men to a massacre of
male children.[6] A curious sidelight upon this tradition is
provided by the pagan satirist Macrobius (A.D. 400), who
tells us that when news arrived in Rome that Herod had
slain children under two years old in Syria, among them a
son of Herod himself, it was said, ' It is better to be Herod's
pig than his son ' (compare what is said on p. 175 of the
reading 'pig' for 'son' at Luke xiv. 5). It would appear
that it had been reported that a ' king of the Jews ' was
involved in the massacre, and that this was taken to mean
a natural son of Herod himself. Justin, in his *Dialogue
with Trypho*, says that the wise men came 'from Arabia '—
he has obviously ' from Arabia ' instead of ' from the east '

---

[1] Matt. i. 17. [2] Matt. i. 18–20. [3] Matt. i. 20.
[4] Matt. i. 23, xxviii. 20. [5] Matt. ii. 9. [6] Matt. ii. 16.

in his text—and quotes from the Testimony Book Num.
xxiv. 17; Isa. xi. 1, 10. The 'Babe'—always in front of
Mary—is mentioned six times in ii. 9–15. The wise men,
like almost everybody else in this Gospel, ' worship Him,'[1]
falling down in deep obeisance. Even Herod professes
his intention to follow their example, for ' all Jerusalem '[2]
is moved at the birth of Jesus, as later at His death.[3] The
word ' Babe,' now sacred, is kept for Jesus, the other
Bethlehem babies being called ' children.'[4] Later on,
however, Matthew will suggest the lowliness of Jesus and
His self-identification with the very little ones by using the
word made so holy by the birth of the Lord of the ' babes '
who were brought to Him, like whom we are to become[5]
(Luke has ' Infant,' ' infants,' alternating with ' babes '
in two places, ' babe ' in the third).[6]
    The language of iii. 13 is dignified : ' Then Jesus *arrives*
from Galilee to the Jordan to be baptized ' (Mark i. 9 has
' came, and was baptized ') ; here, as in iv. 1 (cf. Mark i. 12)
our evangelist is concerned to show that at every stage the
course of Jesus is marked out by Divine Providence. He
must ' fulfil all righteousness '[7] (cf. v. 6, 10, 20 ; vi. 1 ;
xxi. 32—all peculiar to Matthew). The Baptizer's protest
is reported in this Gospel only, while two old Latin MSS.
add to iii. 15 ' and when (Jesus) was being baptized a great
light shone from the water, so that all who had come (together) were afraid.' This would appear to be one of many
secondary deposits of tradition, like Justin's statement
that the birth of Jesus took place in a cave. In iii. 17
Justin, with Codex Bezae, Irenaeus, and several Fathers,
reads ' Thou art My Son, the Beloved ' instead of ' This
is,' &c. ; it is more in the spirit of the evangelist that
Jesus, rather than John, should be addressed. Everywhere
in this stateliest and most carefully wrought of Gospels
the royal dignity of the Christ is proclaimed. People
' draw near ' to Him before they speak, as into the presence
of a king. ' Draw near ' is found—in Matthew only—at
iv. 3 (' the tempter ') ; viii. 2 (' the leper '), 5 (' the
centurion '), 19 (' a scribe ') ; ix. 14 (the disciples of John), 18

---

[1] Matt. ii. 11.   [2] Matt. ii. 3.   [3] Matt. xxvii. 51 ff.
[4] Matt. ii. 16.   [5] Matt. xviii. 2, 3 ; xix. 13, 14.
[6] Luke ii. 12–16, xviii. 15, ix. 46–48 ; cf. xviii. 16, 17, ii. 17.
[7] Matt. iii. 15.

(a member of the local sanhedrin); xiii. 10 (the disciples), 27 (in a parable—it amounts to the same thing), 36 (the disciples); xv. 1 (Pharisees); xvii. 14 (the father of the epileptic boy), 19 (the disciples), 24 (the collectors of the temple-tax—I read with Codex Bezae, 'drew near, and said to Peter'); xviii. 1 (the disciples), 21 (Peter; notice the change in his demeanour—at xvi. 22 he had 'taken' his Lord, now his easy assurance has gone); xix. 16 (the rich young man); xx. 20 (the mother of the sons of Zebedee); xxi. 23 ('the chief priests'); xxiv. 1, 3 (the disciples); xxv. 20, 22, 24 (in a parable); xxvi. 7 (the 'woman' at Bethany), 17 (the disciples), 50 (those who came to arrest Him); xxviii. 9 (the two Marys). In several other places Luke and even Mark use the same word—Mark xiv. 45; cf. Matt. xxvi. 49, of Judas, is a striking instance—but Matthew maintains this atmosphere of reverence systematically; *only the children and the publicans come to Him without the application of this cere-monious word to their approach.* At first the Pharisees merely address Jesus, but they too learn to 'draw near' to Him guardedly (cf. xii. 2, 24 with xvi. 1). Sup-pliants 'worship' Him—viii. 2 (Mark i. 40, 'beseeching and kneeling'); ix. 18 (Mark v. 22, 'falls at His feet,' so Luke viii. 41); xv. 25 (cf. Mark vii. 26); xx. 20 (cf. Mark x. 35); xxviii. 9. The father of the epileptic boy kneels to Him [1]— in Mark he answers a question; in Luke he cries out.[2] Those who know Jesus best wonder at Him, when He stills the storm,[3] saying, 'What *kind of Man* is this?' (Mark iv. 41, Luke viii. 25, in the best MSS. 'Who?'); wonder grows to *worship* when He comes to them walking on the water (xiv. 33—Matthew only). A scribe calls Him 'Teacher'[4] (cf. xxii. 16, 24), Judas 'Rabbi,'[5] His other disciples 'Lord.' This last title might mean no more than 'Sir,'[6]; but in a Gospel so penetrated with the spirit of the Old Testament as this we shall not be inclined to set any limit to the claim implied in its continuous application to Jesus, when we remember that in the LXX 'the Lord' meant 'Jehovah.' In Mark the disciples generally call their Leader 'Rabbi' (ix. 5) or 'Teacher' (e.g. iv. 38); in Luke He is sometimes 'Lord,' rather more often 'Master';

---

[1] Matt. xvii. 14.   [2] Luke ix. 38; Mark ix. 17.   [3] Matt. viii. 27.
[4] Matt. viii. 19.   [5] Matt. xxvi. 25, 49.   [6] cf. John xii. 21.

in Matthew He is 'Lord'—for a typical instance see
Mark iv. 38; Luke viii. 24; Matt. viii. 25. In Mark
vii. 28 we should translate 'Yes, sir'; but
Matthew makes this Gentile woman a witness to the
Messiahship of Jesus,[1] like blind Bartimaeus[2] and the two
blind men.[3]

The beginning of the ministry in Galilee is heralded by
a testimony: He is the 'great light'[4] dawning upon
'Galilee of the Gentiles.' The first act of disobedience
to His command is left on one side[5] (cf. Mark i. 45), and
in the story of the centurion we notice the word 'only'
(' *only* speak with a word '), which is found in Matthew
alone, and ' Jesus *wondered* ' in place of ' Jesus *wondered at
him* '[6]; Matthew does not like the suggestion that Jesus
' wondered ' *at* any man; it was men's part to wonder at
Him. With the word the cure is complete[7] ' in that very
hour,' Matthew only—(cf. ix. 22, xv. 28, xvii. 18—all
Matthew alone; and the instantaneous effect of the cursing
of the fig-tree in xxi. 19—cf. Mark xi. 14, 21). A touch of
His hand is enough to cure Peter's mother-in-law[8] (Mark i.
31, 'taking hold of her hand'; Luke iv. 39. 'He stood
over her, and rebuked the fever '); in viii. 21 the would-be
follower does not wait to be asked, as he does in Luke ix. 59.
Mark iv. 36 says ' the disciples took Him in the boat as
He was'; this will not do for Matthew[9] in whose Gospel
the Lord embarks, *and His disciples follow Him.* He is
the Judge of the dark powers[10] (' before the time ' here
only; cf. Mark v. 7; Luke viii. 28), and ' all the city '
(Gerasa) comes out to meet the terrifying Visitor ('all
the city,' Matthew only[11]—(compare ii. 3, xxi. 10, also
both Matthew only). In ix. 8 the people glorify God,
' who had given such power *to men* '; Jesus lent new
dignity to human nature. Even the Pharisees grow
respectful (' your Teacher,' not in Mark or Luke).[12]

The daughter of the synagogue president is said to be
already dead when His help is asked, but this does not
deter Him from setting off to the house; according to
Mark v. 22 ff., Luke viii. 42 ff., news is brought that she is

---

[1] Matt. xv. 22. [2] Mark x. 47; Luke xviii. 38. [3] Matt. xx. 30.
[4] Matt. iv. 16. [5] Matt. viii. 4. [6] Matt. viii. 8, 12; Luke vii. 9.
[7] Matt. viii. 13. [8] Matt. viii. 15. [9] Matt. viii. 23.
[10] Matt. viii. 29. [11] Matt. viii. 34. [12] Matt. ix. 11.

dead while He is on the way. In the story of the woman with the haemorrhage, the chief interest in Mark and Luke is the courage of the woman; in Matthew the central fact is the power of Jesus, who does not need to look round to see her 'who had done this thing.'[1] 'When He had cast out all '[2] is softened into ' when the crowd was cast out ' in ix. 25 ; Jesus did not find it necessary to take violent action, for His mere entrance was enough (Luke viii. 54 agrees with Mark). Our evangelist avoids Mark's twice-repeated ' child ' (the same word as that translated ' babe ' above, of the Babe Jesus) preferring ' little girl '—notice especially that he alters Mark's ' where the child was ' (Mark v. 40) to ' where the little girl was lying'; 'where the child was ' would be too much like ' where the Child was ' in ii. 9. He also drops out ' and commanded that something should be given her to eat,'[3] but does add a detail about Jesus. In the same spirit he omits the command to secrecy and the reference to the ' ecstasy ' of the parents[4] ; he will leave his readers looking at ' Jesus only.'

Chapter ix. 27 ff. follows, with less vivid detail, upon the lines of Mark i. 41 ff. We notice the same series of words, ' He spoke in stern tones ' (see above, pp. 40, 41), ' see,' ' going out,' ' they spread the story abroad.' At the same time we are reminded of Mark viii. 22 ff. It is no unusual thing to have in Matthew two patients together, where Mark— and Luke where he has a parallel—knows only of one ; for instance, two demoniacs[5] (Mark v. 2 ; Luke viii. 27, one) two blind men[6] (Mark x. 46 ; Luke xviii. 35, one), &c. There is no question here of gradual cure or of the use of saliva, though Jesus does, as in Mark, show a desire to get into conversation with the men. Chapter ix. 32 ff. is exceedingly like xii. 22 ff. In each case the account of the actual healing is somewhat summary, and the effect upon disinterested spectators is set in strong contrast to the futile insinuations of the Pharisees ; both may be compared with Mark vii. 32 ff. In the story of the man with the withered hand both Matthew and Luke omit reference to the anger and grief of Jesus[7] (cf. Matt. xii.

---

[1] Matt. ix. 22 ; cf. Mark v. 30. [2] Mark v. 40.
[3] Mark v. 43 ; Luke viii. 55. [4] Mark v. 43 ; Luke viii. 56.
[5] Matt. viii. 28. [6] Matt. xx. 30. [7] Mark iii. 5.

13; Luke vi. 8); except in Gethsemane, the Lord's anger
and compassion never quite break through the serenity of
His aspect. His attempts at secrecy are not, our evangelist would have us believe, the result of untoward circum-
stance, but of His own self-determination.[1] This feature
of the Gospel obscures the historical development of its
narrative; but what is lost in realism is perhaps made
up for in a deeper understanding of the secret of Jesus.

In xii. 39 the sigh of Mark viii. 12 is omitted, while
xii. 46—'seeking to talk with Him'—is much more
deferential than the 'calling Him' of Mark iii. 31. Chapter
xii. 47 should be left out of the text, in accordance with
the best MSS.; as always in Matthew, Jesus does not
need to be told that His mother wanted Him (Mark iii. 32,
on the other hand, is authentic). In xiii. 55 Matthew,
like Luke (iv. 22), shows his dislike of the word 'carpenter'
in reference to Jesus (Mark vi. 3, 'Is not this the carpenter?'; Matthew, 'the carpenter's son'; Luke,
'the son of Joseph'), and the words of Peter,[2] 'Be it
far from Thee, Lord: this shall not be unto *Thee*' (Matthew
alone), bring out the fact that the friends of Jesus could
not associate the idea of failure and death with Him.
In xvi. 25 Matthew agrees with Luke ix. 24 in the omission
of 'and the gospel'[3]; but in x. 39 he stands alone, for
Luke xvii. 33 drops out 'for My sake.' We are to be
ready, *from sheer love to the Lord*, altogether apart from
the glad tidings that He brings, to sacrifice what is more
precious than all the world.[4] In xvi. 27 he sums up his
statement of the Lord's vast claim in words which are
peculiar to this Gospel—'and then shall He repay to
every man according to his practice' (cf. Ps. lxii. 12; Prov.
xxiv. 12). To find and follow Him is better than life,
for He is our Destiny, the Hidden Treasure of time,[5]
the last Secret of eternity. In the same passage Matt. xvi.
28 has 'the Son of Man coming in *His* kingdom' (cf.
xiii. 41), where Mark ix. 1 has 'the kingdom of God
having (fully) come with power'; Luke ix. 27, 'the
kingdom of God'; not even the Kingdom is ever, in
this Gospel, allowed to take rank with the King.

When we come to the Transfiguration, Matthew gives

---

[1] Matt. xii. 18 ff.   [2] Matt. xvi. 22.   [3] Mark viii. 35.
[4] Matt. xvi. 26.   [5] Matt. xiii. 44.

us our most effective picture of the glory of Jesus. He
tells us that ' His face shone as the sun, His garments
became white like the light,' or, as Codex Bezae has it,
' like snow '; even the morning sun shining upon the
mountain snow was less dazzling than the face and garments
of the Lord (Mark ix. 3, ' His garments became gleaming
very white, so as no launderer on earth could bleach
them '; Luke ix. 29, ' His face became different, and
His vesture gleaming white '—our first evangelist is
evidently the greatest artist of the three). Moses and
Elijah talk *with* Jesus, not to Him, as in Mark—Luke.
Peter is hesitant ; he says ' if Thou wilt,' &c.[1] (Mark—
Luke, ' let us make '). The ' cloud ' appears in Matthew,
as in the other Gospels, but here it is a ' shining' cloud,
tempering the glory of Jesus to their unaccustomed eyes,
without suggestion of the Passion, as in Luke ix. 34.
The fear of the disciples is mentioned in Luke before
the voice; in Matthew after it. In xvii. 7 (Matthew only)
Jesus is active, master of every situation. As in the
case of the blind man (Mark viii. 22 ff.), the healing
of the epileptic boy is completed in Mark ix. 25
ff. in two stages ; in Matthew the convulsion is not
referred to at all[2]; while Luke softens the statement
of its effects, and implies that the ' demon ' caused
no more trouble as soon as the Saviour intervened.[3]
Matthew and Luke both leave out the illuminating Marcan
clause, ' He did not want any one to know '[4]; but it
is more significant that Matthew alone omits Mark ix.
40, Luke ix. 50, though he retains the corresponding
saying (see above, p. 118) found in Matt. xii. 30, Luke xi.
23 ; possibly he sympathized with John's intolerance
of any reluctance to follow his Lord. When the children
are brought to Jesus, Matthew alone has ' that He might
lay His hands upon them, and pray '[5]; the note of serene
royalty is unmistakable. We have already noticed the
strange question, reported in this Gospel, ' Why askest
thou Me concerning the good? ' (see p. 100). Since xix. 17
has, instead of 'Good Master' (Mark—Luke) ' What
good thing shall I do? ' the meaning of the retort of
Jesus must be, ' You ask, " What good thing? " God

---

[1] Matt. xvii. 4.   [2] Matt. xvii. 14 ff.   [3] Luke ix. 37 ff.
[4] Mark ix. 30.   [5] Matt. xix. 13.

is the source of all goodness ; you must go to Him.' The
thought, however, underlying this answer cannot be called
clear, and we must decide against the First Gospel here ;
Matthew is too obviously anxious to avoid any seeming
disparagement of the goodness of Jesus.

In xix. 29 we find ' for My Name's sake ' (Mark x. 29,
' for My sake and the gospel's sake ' ; Luke xviii. 29,
' for the sake of the kingdom of God '). The words ' *being
about* to go up to Jerusalem, *Jesus* '[1] take the place of
Mark x. 32, ' *they* were in the way, going up,' &c.—once
again the Lord steps into the centre of the stage. The
same stately form of words is added to Mark's account
a little lower down (Matt. xx. 22, ' which I *am about to*
drink'; Mark x. 38, 'which I am drinking'), and in xx. 23,
Matthew substitutes ' *My* cup ' for ' the cup which I
am drinking,' omitting, according to the best MSS.,
the Marcan reference to ' the baptism with which I am
being baptized '[2] ; he did not care to think of any one
sharing the baptism of his Lord. The tragic issue of
this scene is to be brought out below in the sequel.
Matthew has ' Lord ' in place of ' Jesus ' in xx. 30 ; according to his account, too, the Master called the blind
men Himself, instead of bidding them be called[3] ; in
xx. 33 he agrees with Luke in the replacement of the
over-familiar title ' Rabboni '[4] (cf. John xx. 16) by ' Lord.'
The reading of Ephrem, ' Lord, that I may see *Thee*,'
seems almost too good to be true. ' *Then Jesus* '[5] (Matthew
only) adds a touch of dignity to the account of the preparations for the Triumphal Entry, and in xxi. 6 we notice
' commanded ' instead of ' said.'[6] The words ' Hosanna
to the Son of David '—that is, ' Save now, Son of David ' ;
. . . ' Hosanna in the Highest '—that is, ' Save now, O
God '—are peculiar to Matthew ; and ' Blessed is the
coming kingdom of our father David ' are dropped from
Mark xi. 10—again the kingdom drops out of sight behind
the figure of the King. The ' whole city ' is ' shaken '
at His Coming, as at His first advent[7] (both Matthew
only). The citizens of Jerusalem ask, ' Who is this ? ' ;
the Galilean pilgrims answer proudly, ' This is Jesus the

---

[1] Matt. xx. 17.   [2] Mark x. 38, 39.   [3] Mark x. 49 ; Luke xviii. 40.
[4] Mark x. 51 (R.V.) ; cf. Luke xviii. 41.   [5] Matt. xxi. 1.
[6] Mark xi. 6 (R.V.).   [7] Matt. ii. 3, viii. 34 ; xxi. 10.

Prophet from Nazareth in Galilee '[1] (again peculiar to this Gospel) ; Matthew has selected from the cries of the crowd such tributes as most redounded to the honour of his Lord. He is fond of associating such words as ' shake' and ' shaking ' (one of the Greek words for ' earthquake ') with signal events in the life of Jesus. At His birth Herod is ' troubled . . . *all Jerusalem* with him '[2]; when He falls asleep on the lake a great ' *shaking* ' takes place on the sea[3] (Mark–Luke more simply, ' a squall ') ; when He falls asleep on the cross ' the earth ' is ' *shaken*,' the ' rocks ' are ' rent,' and the ' tombs ' ' opened '—for another link between the sleep on the lake and the sleep on the cross compare Mark iv. 38 (' on the (?) head-rest '; see p. 29); Luke ix. 58; John xix. 30 (' bowing His head '). His waking on Easter morning is also greeted with a great ' *shaking*,'[4] and ' the watchers ' are ' *shaken* ' with fear.[5] Everywhere in this Gospel natural convulsions accompany the progress of Nature's Lord.

The cursing of the fig-tree takes effect instantaneously[6] (cf. Mark xi. 21) in this Gospel, and ' *began* to drive out '[7] —the word ' began ' denotes, according to the Marcan usage, a new departure (see p. 30)—is altered to ' *drove out* '[8]; with one tremendous blaze of wrath He expels them *all* (' all ' is peculiar to Matthew)—no ' scourge of cords '[9] is needed. But Jesus is never merely destructive ; He does good, as they had done evil, in the Temple, consecrating it afresh by acts of mercy[10] (Matthew only). After His assertion of His lordship over His house, He leaves His critics baffled and helpless ; ' He *left them* ' (xxi. 17) is Matthew alone. In xxi. 22 our author is clearly anxious to avoid the impression, to which the text of Mark xi. 24 might be thought to lend itself, that we receive what we ask for in prayer merely by the exercise of our own faith ; for, instead of ' believe that ye have received, and it shall be yours,' he has ' believing, ye shall receive.' ' *When He came to the Temple* '[11] stands for ' He was walking in the Temple ' (Luke ' teaching the people,' &c.). This is the Lord's last visit, and His entrance and exit are

---

[1] Matt. xxi. 11.   [2] Matt. ii. 3.   [3] Matt. viii. 24 ; cf. xxvii. 51.
[4] Matt. xxviii. 2.   [5] Matt. xxviii. 3, 4.   [6] Matt. xxi. 19.
[7] Mark xi. 15 ; Luke xix. 45.   [8] Matt. xxi. 12.   [9] John. ii. 15.
[10] Matt. xxi. 14.   [11] Matt. xxi. 23 ; cf. Mark xi. 27 ; Luke xx. 1.

marked with a mournful solemnity; compare xxiv. 1, 'departing from the Temple,' with Mark xiii. 1, 'as He was walking out of the Temple.' Notice especially the dramatic effect of these words in Matthew after the last sentence of Matt. xxiii. 38—reading 'your house is left to you.' Jesus proceeds to leave the Temple for the last time. Chapter xxi. 46, 'since they held Him as a prophet,' and xxii. 22, 'and they left Him, and went their way,' are both peculiar to Matthew. The triumph of Jesus is complete; but there was a sombre side to it, for there were those who left Him who said, 'Come unto Me,' though there was 'no need for them to go away'[1] (Matthew only). This is the premonition of His last awful 'Depart from Me,' the undertone of the note so often sounded in this book, echoing the tireless calling and sombre antiphonies of the voice which was like many waters. Also found only here are the words '*His* (angels),' 'with a great trumpet-blast,' '*they* shall gather' (Mark xiii. 27, 'He shall gather'), the 'angels' are His, and they carry out the assembling of the elect, not He.

The phrase 'the sign of the Son of Man in heaven' demands a closer consideration; it appears to mean the 'sign of the Cross.' Tertullian on 'Prayer' should be compared; he says, 'And even the little birds rising from their nests spread abroad the cross of their wings and utter a prayer to God.' The Testimony Book made a great deal of the spreading out of the arms of Moses in the battle with Amalek (Exod. xvii. 8 ff.), and Marcion (see App. IV.) chose this scene as an instance of 'contradiction' between the Old Testament and the New. Perhaps the phrase 'stretching out His hands to His disciples,' which we noticed above to be peculiar to Matthew (in xii. 49) has been coloured by this idea. In the *Expositor* of June, 1918, Mr. Vacher Burch explains Paul's 'conformed to the image of His death,' 'stretching out to what is before,' and 'the upward calling'[2] in this way; and we may add John xxi. 18, 'thou shalt stretch forth thy hands, and another shall gird thee, and carry thee whither thou wouldst not.' The phrase 'stretching out' was first applied to the spreading of God's wings

[1] Matt. xiv. 16.   [2] Phil. iii. 10, 13, 14.

—compare Gen. i. 2 (' the Spirit of God brooded ') ; Deut.
xxxii. 11; Zeph. iii. 17; Luke iii. 22; Matt. xxiii. 37, &c.;
then to man's prayer with outspread arms ; then to the
arms of the God-man extended upon the cross.

The ' Lewis ' Syriac and more than one Old Latin
version omit 'not even the Son '[1] (cf. Mark xiii. 32, p. 100) ;
we should expect Matthew to be chary of this clause.
' At what kind of day your Lord is coming ' (Mark xiii. 33,
' when the time shall be ') is found here only in this form,
though Mark xiii. 34 f. gives us the same idea.   Words
are put into the mouth of Jesus in Matt. xxvi. 1 which
in Mark xiv. 1 take shape in a comment of the evangelist ;
and the foreknowledge of Jesus is made more definite
by the addition of the words ' and the Son of Man is
being betrayed to be crucified ' (Origen and some Old
Latin versions, ' shall be ')—only found in this Gospel.
' For Thee '[2] (Matthew only) sounds the true Matthaean
note.   The same observation applies to ' My time is at
hand' (xxvi. 18), ' to such an one'; both go to show that
the arrangements were not made on the spur of the moment,
for the Lord moved to the cross with ' deliberate speed,
majestic instancy.'   The man ' carrying a pitcher of
water ' (Mark–Luke) disappears in the First Gospel ;
Jesus did not need to use devious methods.   ' As Jesus
commanded them '[3] (Matthew only) reminds us of xxi. 6
(see above) ; and the addition of ' this ' in xxvi. 29—not
found in the true text of Mark xiv. 25; Luke xxii. 18—
glances at the other ' cup ' which the Lord is to drink so
soon.

A beautiful touch of restrained pathos is discoverable in
the words 'Jesus with them '[4] (compare 'with you,' also here
only at xxvi. 29, and also Mark xiv. 32; Luke xxii. 40);
it was the last time, till Easter afternoon, that the Lord
and His disciples were together, for the Marcan ' with
Him ' is dropped at xxvi. 37 (cf. Mark xiv. 33) in the
best MSS.   Though they had been asked to keep awake
with Him   ' with Me '[5] (Matthew only), real fellowship
is, for the time, broken.   By-and-by it is to be renewed,
never to be interrupted again[6] (with ' all the days ' compare
' days shall come when the Bridegroom shall be taken

[1] Matt. xxiv. 36.   [2] Matt. xxvi. 17.   [3] Matt. xxvi. 19.
[4] Matt. xxvi. 36.   [5] Matt. xxvi. 40.   [6] Matt. xxviii. 20.

from them'). 'To be amazed' becomes 'to be sad'
in xxvi. 37; 'kept falling to the ground' is softened into
'fell upon His face.'[1] 'So (could you not)' and 'with
Me' are found only here (in xxvi. 40), and both are full of
delicate suggestion; when they are given the honour
of being for a little while longer the bodyguard of the
King, even so they cannot keep awake. Only in His
first period of prayer, according to Matthew, does Jesus
plead that the cup may pass[2] (Mark xiv. 39 is not so clear);
a less noticeable detail is that Matthew, like Luke (xxii. 47),
rejects Mark's 'Judas arrives,'[3] because he has used the
more dignified word once or twice of Jesus (e.g. iii. 13).
In the same spirit he has already made Judas say, 'Surely
it is not I, Rabbi!' instead of 'Surely it is not I, Lord!'[4]
(cf. xxvi. 22), and Jesus answer indirectly to Judas as to the
high-priest at His trial, 'Is it not?' (xxvi. 64 should
perhaps be translated 'Am I not?' &c.).

Chapter xxvi. 53 is peculiar to this Gospel, as are the
words 'Only I say unto you, "From henceforth"' (v. 64);
Jesus is as masterful with His 'I say unto you,' when on
trial for His life, as He had been in the Sermon on the
Mount. 'Jesus stood before the governor'[5] is found in
Matthew alone, as are 'He answered nothing' (xxvii. 12)
and 'to him not a word' (v. 14). The embarrassed procurator cuts a sorry figure over against the Prisoner; but
the Lord's silence is not that of disdain, but of absorption
in a greater issue; the torrent of accusation rushes past
Him almost unnoticed, for to Him the scene is beyond
protest. The addition of the word 'exceedingly' (xxvii. 14)
just points the contrast between the confusion of the
official and the awful composure of the Lord. Perhaps
there is a mistake in v. 15; Mark xv. 6 seems to imply
that the release of one prisoner was a regular custom,
though the actual words are ambiguous—'at a feast he
used to release' (or 'was for releasing'; this might apply
only to this particular occasion) 'for them one prisoner.'
There is no evidence outside the Gospels for such a practice even if it be limited to the Passover[6]; Matthew has
taken Mark's statement as involving a recognized con-

---

[1] Matt. xxvi. 39; Mark xiv. 33, 35.   [2] Matt. xxvi. 39, 42.
[3] Mark xiv. 43.   [4] Matt. xxvi. 25, cf. v. 49.   [5] Matt xxvii. 11.
[6] John xviii. 39.

cession, but in view of the silence of Luke, who is generally well informed in regard to all that relates to the Roman Government, we must infer that the claim was made by the riotous populace, taking advantage of Pilate's precarious position, and that the governor snatched at the opportunity of getting rid of this inconvenient Prisoner without going further into a dangerous question. ' As he was doing for them '[1] does not settle the matter, for Pilate may well have made the offer immediately upon the arrest of Jesus. The tragic irony of the situation is heightened by the fact, revealed in the ' Lewis ' and Palestinian Syriac versions[2], and confirmed by a passage in Bar Bahlul, the Syriac commentator, who tells us that it was so written in the ' Gospel of the Separated ' —that is, the four Gospels not united into one narrative as they were in Tatian's *Harmony*—that the name of Barrabbas was also ' Jesus.'

Leaving upon one side for the moment the more important of the first evangelist's insertions, we notice ' and destroy Jesus' (xxvii. 20), ' Jesus who is called Christ' (xxvii. 22 ; Mark xv. 12, ' whom ye call King of the Jews'), and the sinister word ' all' (xxvii. 22). The Lord is quite alone ; the same suggestion is offered by ' gathered *against Him* ' (' against Him,' Matthew only) ' the whole cohort' (xxvii. 27). The soldiers proceed to strip Him (Matthew only ; cf. v. 40), and dress Him mockingly in a ' scarlet cloak ' (Mark xv. 17, ' purple '; John xix. 2, ' in a purple upper garment ') ; Roman governors did not generally wear purple (cf. 1 Mac. viii. 14), except in the further East, says Dr. A. Wright ; in Syria they wore a robe of orange-red, much less expensive than Tyrian purple. ' Scarlet ' is the symbol of luxury in the Old Testament (2 Sam. i. 24 ; cf. Luke xxiii. 11), but it is also a sacred colour (Exod. xxv. 4 ; Lev. xiv. 4, 6 ; Heb. ix. 19 ; in Isa. lxiii. 2 we have ' crimson ') ; probably Matthew had a double meaning in his mind, as in xxvii. 25, to be discussed below. ' Going out (of the city) *they found a man* ' is also peculiar to this Gospel (xxvii. 32), marking as it does another stage in the departure of Jesus, who now leaves the doomed city, as He had already left the doomed Temple—both doomed because He left them (cf. xxiii.

[1] Mark xv. 8.   [2] Matt. xxvii. 16, 17.

38, 'is left unto you,' and xxiv. 1). The Lord has to go
outside the city for His one helper, and he is a
conscript ('they conscripted him,' cf. v. 41). A striking
parallel may be found in Jer. v. 1, 'Run ye *to and fro in
the streets of Jerusalem,* and see if ye *can find a man.*'
'If Thou art the Son of God' (xxvii. 40) is found in Matthew
only, as is also ' for He said, I am the Son of God ' (v. 43) ;
while 'waiting upon Him' (xxvii. 55, Matthew only) of the
women who followed Jesus from Galilee reminds us of
viii. 15, where the best MSS. read 'she was waiting upon
Him' for Mark i. 31, 'she was waiting upon *them.*' Mark
simply records the fact that Peter's mother-in-law went
on with her domestic duties, interrupted by a sudden
attack of malarial fever ; Matthew hints that she had no
eyes for any one but Jesus.

But our evangelist's extraordinarily keen feeling for
the sombre irony of the Passion-story shows itself in
greater things than details such as these. All four Gospels
are reminiscent of Jer. xxvi., notably in their threefold
description of the enemies of Jesus (e.g. Luke xxii. 66,
' elders and chief priests and scribes '). Roughly speaking,
the ' people ' in Jer. xxvi. 11 correspond to the ' people '
of Luke, the ' false prophets ' to the Pharisaic members
of the Sanhedrin, the ' priests ' to the Sadducean chief
priests, while the ' princes ' play the part of Pilate. In
the trial of Jeremiah the role of ' all the people ' is not
clear; in xxvi. 16 they join with the ' princes ' in desiring
the acquittal of the accused. The trial of Jesus takes a
more sinister course ; the ' people ' are at first neutral
(Luke xxiii. 5 is uttered by the priests), but then they
turn *against* the Prisoner. But the outstanding difference, apart from their opposite result, between the two
trials consists in the fact that, whereas Jeremiah pro-
tested his own innocence, in the account which Matthew
gives, first Judas[1], then Pilate's wife[2], last of all
Pilate himself[3], declare Jesus guiltless, while the shadow
of blood-guiltiness descends upon them one after another
(vv. 3, 6, 8, 24, 25 ; Jer. xxvi. 15 ; Heb. xii. 24). They
are all—Judas, Pilate and his wife, the people—in the
grip of destiny, nearly all struggling to escape, Judas
by suicide, Pilate by seeking to thrust the responsibility

[1] Matt. xxvii. 4.   [2] Matt. xxvii. 19.   [3] Matt. xxvii. 24.

for his share in the transaction upon the crowd, as their officials had sought to cast the incubus upon Judas, and he upon them (xxvii. 4).

In comparison with these vain attempts to slip out of the entanglements which their weakness or guilt had made for them, there is something almost admirable about the reckless declaration of the people, ' His blood be upon us, and upon our children ! ' When we consider such passages as xxii. 7, xxiii. 35, we might be inclined to assume that our evangelist thought of this sentence merely as a terrible curse, invoked in a mood of savage disappointment upon their own heads by the guilty people, with what result the history of the next fifty years was to show. But we cannot stop there, for it is one of the features of all the Gospels alike that even the enemies of the Lord pay unconscious tribute to the miracle of Love Divine in Him. Though their motives may be mean and cruel, common men are in the region of great revelations when they come into any kind of contact with such a one as He ; they know not what they say or do[1] when they deal with Him, whether they mean well or ill. It was the enemies of Jesus who said, ' Doctor, heal yourself,' ' He saved others : Himself He could not save,' who called Him ' the friend of sinners '[2] ; nor should we forget the meaning of His name, expounded in this very Gospel—' Himself shall save *His people* from their sins,' for the same word is used here, ' all the *people.*'

This haunting sentence is surely the classical instance of a truth upon which early Christian writers and preachers loved to dwell—that the life and death of Jesus had turned all the old curses into blessings. The fatal tree which figures in the story of the Fall corresponds to that life-giving tree, the Cross (cf. 1 Pet. ii. 24) ; the stretching out of Adam's hands to the tree is compared now with the arms of the dying thief extended towards the Cross, now with the outspread arms of the Saviour ; while the spear[3] which gave vent to the cleansing blood, and so admits to Paradise, answers to the flaming sword which drove our first parents out of Eden. Out of the first Adam's

[1] Luke ix. 33, xxiii. 34.
[2] Luke iv. 23 ; Matt. xxvii. 42, &c. ; Matt. xi. 19 ; Luke vii. 34.
[3] John xix. 34.

U

side came Eve, and, with her, death and all our ills : out of the Second Adam's side issues healing and life. As for Eve, who gave birth to the first murderer, Mary, who bore the Saviour, atones for her fault, and the curse of childbearing becomes the blessing of Christian motherhood, as we have it in 1 Tim. ii. 15—' she shall be saved through childbearing '—and perhaps in the reading of Codex Sinaiticus at John xvi. 21, ' she calls to mind no more the anguish for joy that *the* man has been born into the world.' 1 Pet. iii. 20 is specially noteworthy for the curious nuance by which the destructive agent is made to slide off into the channel of salvation. We are reminded of the text quoted above (1 Tim. ii. 15) ; is the Christian matron saved *by* motherhood, or merely kept safe *through* the crisis of motherhood ? The answer is, ' both.' The ' eight souls ' of 1 Pet. iii. 20 were kept *safe through* the water, and also saved *by* the water, from the infection of a corrupt society. In the same way Christian almsgiving atones for the curse of enforced labour (cf. Eph. iv. 28, and especially ' Let thine alms sweat in thy hand '—' the sweat of thy hand ' is a talmudic variant for ' the sweat of thy face ' in the story of the Fall—' till thou knowest to whom to give' (*The Teaching of the Twelve Apostles*, ii. 6). Taking the other reading, ' the sweat of thy face ' suggested comparison with the sweat of the ' Sacred Heart ' in Gethsemane, and gave birth to the mediaeval fancy that crimson flowers sprang from the drops of the Saviour's blood ' falling to the ground,'[1] for is it not written, ' Cursed is the ground for thy sake ; thorns also and thistles shall it grow for thee ? ' So, too, murder atones for murder, the innocent blood of Jesus for that of Abel[2]. Other passages in which this idea of ' salvation by similars,' or, as we might say, homeopathic treatment, can be traced are John iii. 14, 2 Cor. v. 21, and perhaps 1 Cor. xi. 10, ' on account of the angels,' taken along with Gen. vi. 2 ; but the whole subject has been discussed at length in Dr. Rendel Harris's edition of the *Teaching*. Our first evangelist has, it may be, deliberately led up to this strange declaration, and has made ' His blood be upon us, and upon our children ' serve by double suggestion for a promise of hope for his

[1] Luke xxii. 44.   [2] Heb. xii. 24.

own people breaking through the gathering darkness of the trial scene; if it is so, this verse occupies the same position in the scheme of the Gospel as that held by 'Father, forgive them' in the Third, and 'Forthwith there came out both blood and water' in the Fourth Gospel.

To the end of the book the same careful reverence is everywhere displayed. Both Matthew and Luke avoid the use of the word 'corpse'[1] for the body of the Lord; but Matthew alone is responsible for the statement that Joseph laid the body in *his own* tomb, and he adds that epithet 'pure' to 'robe'[2]—the 'Lewis' Syriac has 'new.' The words 'great (stone)'—'great,' Matthew only, xxvii. 60 —prepare the way for the miracle so shortly to follow, and the description of the elaborate precautions taken by the Government (xxvii. 62–66) serves the same purpose. The 'young man clad in a white robe'[3] (Luke xxiv. 4, 'two men in shining clothing') becomes 'an angel of the Lord, coming down from heaven,'[4] who appears to the watchers as well as the women. 'Of Nazareth'[5] is left out because Jesus is no longer to be associated with any particular place, just as the apostles, forbidden before to go to the Gentiles[6], are now to 'make disciples of all the nations.' In xxviii. 9 Jesus Himself appears, and the women worship Him (cf. John xx. 11 ff.); while the story of the bribery of the sentries[7] (Matthew only) is recorded in order to arm young preachers against current Jewish objections—' to the present day,' as in xxvii. 8, is a proof of comparative lateness. The note of 'worship,' so characteristic of the Gospel throughout, recurs in xxviii. 17, and the book ends with a resounding sentence (v. 18 ff., Matthew only) which sums up its message in the familiar threefold rhythm—a claim, a demand, and a promise. The words 'in the name of the Father and the Son and the Holy Spirit' are probably a credal or liturgical addition to the original saying. The triple name was, it is true, used in baptism in very early days, but not in the first century, to judge from the evidence of the Acts and Epistles (Acts ii. 38, viii. 16, x. 48, xix. 5; 1 Cor. i. 13, 15; Gal.

---

[1] Mark xv. 45. [2] Matt. xxvii. 59, 60. [3] Mark xvi. 5.
[4] Matt. xxviii. 2. [5] Mark xvi. 6, cf. Matt. xxviii. 5.
[6] Matt. x. 5, cf. xxviii. 19. [7] Matt. xxviii. 11 ff.

iii. 27 ; Rom. vi. 3). Justin uses the Trinitarian formula, but speaks of Christians as ' enlightened '—that is, ' baptized '—' through the name of Christ.' In regard to Matt. xxviii. 19, moreover, Eusebius sometimes—not always—quotes the passage in the following form : ' Go ye, and make disciples . . . baptizing them in *My* name.' When we bear in mind the centrality of the Person of our Lord in the First Gospel, it seems highly probable that the last-mentioned is the original form of this supreme saying, and that the triple reading, derived from 2 Cor. xiii. 14 or the Church creeds, was beginning in Eusebius's time to replace the other form, so that he possessed MSS. with both readings, and vacillates between the two.

The honours paid to Jesus are balanced by His claims ; these can best be examined in passages where Matthew stands alone, or alone with Luke. We have noticed already ' for My sake,'[1] where Luke vi. 22 has ' for the sake of the Son of Man.' Jesus is Himself the fulfilment of the law[2] (Matthew only ; but see above, p. 237), and has the right to make demands upon His disciples, exceeding those of the scribes[3] (compare by contrast xi. 30, taken along with xxiii. 4). Then He begins to analyse these claims of His ; ' I '—a very emphatic ' I '—comes in like a refrain (v. 22, 28, 32, 34, 39, 44), for He sets Himself by implication above the written word. Reserving the exposition of difficult passages in the ' Sermon ' (chapters xiv., xvi.), we observe that the words ' Verily I say unto you '—the ' I ' is not emphasized here, but solemnity is given by the ' verily '—occur in Matthew only—at v. 18 (in this case some Old Latins omit ' verily '), 26 (Luke xii. 59, ' I say ') ; vi. 2, 5, 16. The ' Sermon ' like other continuous discourses in this Gospel, is followed by a declaration that the great utterance is now over (vii. 28 ; xi. 1, 19 ; xiv. 1 ; xiii. 53 ; xxvi. 1—only vii. 28 has a parallel in Luke vii. 1). In viii. 22 we find the words ' Follow Me ' (Matthew only), and in x. 13 ' worthy,' one of the keywords of the first Gospel. ' Worthy ' occurs at **x.** 11, 13 (twice ; cf. Luke ix. 4 ; x. 5, 6 ; Mark vi. 11), 37, 38 (cf. Luke xiv. 26, 27—in the Third Gospel stress is laid upon the *power* to follow Jesus ; in the First the question is, ' Am I *worthy* of Him ? ') ; xxii. 8 (cf. Luke

---

[1] Matt. v. 11.   [2] Matt. v. 17.   [3] Matt. v. 20.

xiv. 24). The most nearly parallel cases of this use of this idea to be found in the Third Gospel occur at xv. 19, 21, ' I am not *worthy* to be called thy son,' and xx. 35, ' those who are accounted *worthy* to attain that age and the resurrection ' ; but there is a difference between the notion of being worthy of a status and that of being worthy of a Person (cf. Heb. xi. 38). The best explanation of the content of Matthew's phrase is contained in Rev. iii. 4, ' they shall walk with Me in white ; for they are worthy.'

Jesus foretells the persecution of His followers *for His sake* twice over in this Gospel[1] ; in both cases emphasis is laid upon the Person for whose sake suffering is to be endured ; this is also the case in Mark xiii. 9; Luke xxi. 12, but not so clearly in Luke xii. 11. In x. 24 we come upon another great Christian word—' slave ' ; compare Matt. x. 24, 25 with Luke vi. 40, and notice the confirmation of Matthew's version supplied by John xiii. 16 ; xv. 15, 20 ; it should be said that in Luke vi. 40 the ' Lewis ' Syriac has ' there is no disciple that is perfect as his Master in teaching,' which is a little nearer to Matthew's version than is our text (cf. Matt. xxiii. 10). ' The men of His house '[2] reflects the same point of view ; compare the parable of the Tares,[3] that of the two slaves of the king,[4] and xxiv. 45 (Luke xii. 42, ' steward '), 49 (' fellow slaves '—Luke xii. 43 ff. reverts to the word ' slave.'). Corresponding to this recommendation of a proud humbleness in the Christian's relations with his Lord, there is an insistent emphasis upon the absolute supremacy of Jesus. He is ' the Lord,' ' the Householder,' ' the King ' (or ' the King's Son ')—notice ' Is it not lawful to do what I will with *My own* ? '[5] (Matthew only ; cf. John i. 11, with its transition from ' His own property ' to ' His own people '), ' *His own* slaves '[4] (' His own,' Matthew only), '*Mine own* '[7] (Luke xix. 23, ' it '), ' the Lord of those slaves '[8] (cf. Luke xix. 15), and specially the parable of xxii. 2 ff., where the climax of the story comes when one of the guests is turned out for disrespect to the Bridegroom. For the ' robe ' freely given compare Luke xv.

[1] Matt. x. 17 ff., xxiv. 9 ff.   [2] Matt. x. 25.   [3] Matt. xiii. 27, 28.
[4] Matt. xviii. 23 ff.   [5] Matt. xx. 15.   [6] Matt. xxv. 14.
[7] Matt. xxv. 27.   [8] Matt. xxv. 19.

22. The difference in point of view is exceedingly suggestive; what if the returning prodigal had said, in the spirit of the killjoy at the Prince's wedding, 'If my father will not have me as I am, I will not come in at all?' But all these names are 'too mean to speak' the worth of the Lord to His own. His is already the 'name which is above every name'; to His companions in the boat He is 'truly the Son of God'; to Peter, 'the Christ, the Son of the Living God'[1]; and, whereas in Luke xxiv. 49 His last promise to His friends is that they shall be 'clothed with power from on high' (that is, from God, in this Gospel we are left with 'Jesus only' after the Resurrection, as after the Transfiguration which was its prophecy[2] (Mark ix. 8, but not Luke ix. 36, adds 'with themselves' to the 'Jesus only' of Matt. xvii. 8).

Resuming the main thread of the matter common to Matthew and Luke, we observe that Matthew sometimes has 'I' where Luke has 'the Son of Man'[3] (cf. Luke xii. 8, 9; Luke avoids the phrase 'I will deny' by his use of the passive 'shall be denied'—cf. Matt. v. 11; Luke vi. 22). Again, in x. 35, 'I came to separate' is more directly active than Luke xii. 52, 'there shall be . . . divided'; and in x. 37, 'He that loves father or mother more than Me' is at once more intelligible and more definitely based upon the Lord's personal claim than Luke xiv. 26, 'If any one cometh unto Me, and hateth not his own father.' Instead of 'about all these things' (Luke vii. 18) we have in Matt. xi. 2 'the works of the Christ.' Schweitzer argues that John's question was not 'Art Thou the Christ?' but 'Art Thou Elijah?'[4] (cf. xi. 10 and Mal. iii. 1). The Fourth Gospel is our authority for the belief that John did not regard Himself as 'Elijah,' though Jesus repeatedly—Matt. xi. 10, 14, xvii. 12, 13; Mark ix. 13 (Luke omits the Marcan reference to John as 'Elijah,' but not that found in Q; cf. vii. 27)—identifies the two prophets. The difficulty lies in the fact that Mark ix. 12, 13, like Matt. xvii. 11, 12, seems to involve two 'comings' of 'Elijah,' one in the immediate past, the other still in the future. For evidence of Jewish expectation of the coming of Elijah, compare Matt. xxvii.

---

[1] Matt. xiv. 33, xvi. 14.　　[3] Matt. xvii. 8, xxviii. 20.
[2] Matt. x. 32, 33.　　[4] John i. 21.

47, 49, Mark xv. 35, 36 ; he was to be both forerunner
and attendant of the Messiah. Jesus adds to this doctrine
His teaching that ' Elijah ' had already come in the person
of John ; but He does not deny that he will come again.
All that the phrase ' the works of the Christ ' *proves* is
that our evangelist thought of Jesus as the Messiah ;
but the evidence of the Gospels goes to show that John
too meant by the ' One mightier than I '[1] the Coming
Christ.

' His mighty works '[2] comes from Matthew alone, like
the phrase ' I say unto you ' in vv. 22, 24, and the clause
' because if in Sodom had taken place the mighty works
which were wrought in thee,' &c. (v. 23). So we are
carried on to the Lord's appeal to the working people,
which Dr. Granger has beautifully translated, ' Come
unto Me, all you working people with your heavy loads,
and I will refresh you (better, perhaps, " rest you ").
Take My yoke upon you, and learn a lesson from Me,
for I am of easy temper and of homely mind ' ; may I
suggest for the last clause ' and you shall find the secret
of restful living ' ? There is clearly here a reminiscence
of the exquisite image in Hos. xi. 4, and the latter part
of this gracious promise may allude to Jer. vi. 16—' Stand
in the ways and see, and ask for the old paths, where
is the good way, and walk therein, and ye shall find rest
(LXX " purity ") for your souls.' We can only say
that the new prescription for soul-healing is as simple
and definite as the old one is complicated and unsatisfying.
The prophet says, ' Go back ' ; Jesus, ' Come forward.'
But the Wisdom of Jesus the Son of Sirach is much nearer
to the sense of these verses ; cf. Sir. li. 23 ff., ' Come unto
Me ' (' Wisdom '—we have seen reason above for the
belief that Jesus identified Himself with the ' Wisdom '
of the Wisdom Books—see p. 192), ' ye unlearned,
and lodge, in the house of instruction. . . . Put your
neck under her yoke. . . . She is hard at hand to find.
Behold with your eyes how I laboured but a little, and
found for myself much rest ' (cf. also Sir. vi. 27, xxiv. 19).
But comparison with older models only makes the ex-
haustless depth and matchless artistry of the Lord's
' Come unto Me ' the more impressive ; if Matthew had

---

[1] Mark i. 7, &c.   [2] Matt. xi. 20.

done nothing more than preserve this consummate saying, we should have been for ever in his debt. It is tempting to conjecture that Jesus is quoting the sign over the shop in Nazareth in the words 'My yoke is easy,' for Justin tells us that Joseph made 'ploughs and yokes.' What I wish to bring out just now is the enforcement which this saying adds to the claim of Christ. 'I will arise and go to my Father' is an ideal expression of the home-sickness of the soul, but 'Come unto Me' points the way to satisfaction with yet greater clearness; it is better to be told to 'come' than to 'go.' Sometimes this saying has been called an 'erratic bloc,' as though it stood alone in Matthew's Gospel; as a matter of fact, the same note is heard throughout the First Gospel—in ix. 10; xiv. 29; xxii. 4; xxv. 34; xiv. 16—all Matthew alone, in so far as this detail is concerned.[1]

What must have seemed to His hearers a most audacious claim is made in xii. 6 (Matthew only) and in the explanation of the parable of the tares, '*His* angels, *His* Kingdom'[2] (compare in xiii. 43 'the Kingdom of their Father'). The next two parables have been already referred to, but both are important in this connexion. The 'treasure hid in a field' stands for the discovery of Jesus. 'Nor tongue nor pen can show' the joy of it; it is worth a man's while to 'sell all that he has' to buy that field—that is, to give up everything else for the cultivation of the kind of life in which the love of the Lord has been found and can be kept. The sacrament of the love of Jesus is to be 'received' by the man whose path He crosses in a rapture of surprise—'the wonder, Why such love to me?' The second parable puts the other side of the matter, for it is not so much that a man finds his Lord, as that the Lord finds Him. We are the Lord's discovery, as He is the one compensating Fact, dawning upon men and women in the gathering darkness of their disillusioned years (cf. iv. 15, 16—Matthew only). How well, after all, this suits Matthew the publican! It should be observed that our evangelist is specially fond of the word 'find.' On the one side we have 'ye *shall find* rest unto your souls,' 'few there be that find it'[3]; on the other, 'He

---

[1] Compare also Matt. iii. 14, "dost *Thou* come to Me"!   [2] Matt. xiii. 41.
    [3] Matt. xi. 29, vii. 14 (Luke: 'Many shall not be able').

found one pearl of great price,' '*if so be that He find* it ' (Luke xv. 5, 6, 8, 9, 'until He (she) find? and having found' conveys the idea of persistence in search rather than surprise in discovery), 'He *found* others standing '[1] —this last case occurs in one of the most delicately expressed of the parables. The Householder *comes to terms* with the first group of workmen ; He *sees* the second and the third—as Jesus ' saw ' the first apostles,[2] the last-comers He '*found*'—they were *His* men, and He could do as He liked with *His own*[3]; compare I Cor. xv. 8, 'last of all He appeared to me also.' As He found us, so we are to find other unlikely people—' as many soever as *ye shall find*, call to the wedding '[4] (Matthew only).

In xviii. 23 ff. we have another 'subject-parable,' in which, as in xiii. 45, xxii. 2 ff., the Kingdom is compared with a King ; in this instance, like the ' Man ' of xxv. 14 ff, He settles accounts with His ' slaves.' This story has been discussed already, and need not be further enlarged upon here. Our little debts to one another are as nothing when set over against our great debt to our Lord, and the less we say about our rights the better. ' Chosen '[5] (Matthew only) means much the same thing as ' worthy.' In xxiii. 8 ff. the Lord speaks of Himself as the one ' Teacher ' and ' Leader,' as God is the one ' Father ' ; and in xxiii. 32 the Pharisees are bidden to ' fill up the measure of ' their ' fathers ' (Luke xi. 47 is less trenchant, 'and you show your approval of the works of your fathers, because they killed, and you build '— their tombs). The connexion of thought in the Third Gospel is not very clear at this point, for it is not easy to see how the Pharisees showed approval of murders by raising monuments to the murdered men ; unless, indeed, the suggestion is that they buried the prophets under a smothering weight of insincere flattery, really completing the work of their fathers—the fathers killed the prophets ; the sons laid the memory of their teaching respectfully to rest ! But the argument in the First Gospel is overpowering in its directness. According to xxiii. 30, the scribes are made to say ' if we had been (alive) in the days of our fathers, we would not have been partakers in the

---

[1] Matt. xiii. 46, xviii. 13, **xx.** 6.   [2] Matt. iv. 18, 21.
[3] Matt. xx. 15.   [4] Matt. xxii. 9, 11.   [5] Matt. xxii. 14.

blood of the prophets.' 'You are more truly sons of these prophet-murderers than you know,' retorts Jesus ; 'you will commit' (there are several readings here— 'fill up,' 'you shall fill up,' and 'you have filled up') 'the only crime they left undone ! Children of the devil that you are' (that is what 'serpents, vipers' brood' means ; cf. John viii. 44), 'how are you to escape con- demnation to Gehenna ? ' The fact that, while shedding hypocritical tears over the murder of prophets and righteous men, they were themselves plotting the death of Jesus, was the last proof of their desperate insincerity, and consigned them to a place in the infamous succession !

If our author knew that the words which follow— 'Therefore . . . *I* am sending,' &c.—came from a Wisdom Book (cf. Luke xi. 49, and p. 192), it is clear that he identified Jesus with the 'Wisdom of God,' as indeed the Testimony Book did. Dr. Rendel Harris has proved that the source of the Logos doctrine in the Fourth Gospel (John i. 1 ff.) is to be found in the Wisdom literature, for in the language of these books 'Wisdom' and 'Word' mean the same thing. 'Come unto Me '—that is, 'Wisdom' (see above) —suggests that the Logos doctrine comes not from Philo, but from the self-consciousness of Jesus, expressed in Wisdom language—a result very important for apologetic. In any case it is significant that Matthew puts into the first person words which, in Luke's Gospel, are obviously a quotation. The 'Coming' (literally (royal) 'Presence ') 'of the Son of Man '[1] is an instance of technical courtiers' language — Luke xvii. 26, 'in the days of the Son of Man' (cf. Matt. xxiv. 39, 'the Presence'; Luke xvii. 30, 'in the day when the Son of Man is revealed.' The 'oil' in the lamps,[2] like the wedding-garment,[3] symbolizes love for the Lord. In the corresponding parable in Luke xii. 35 f., as in Mark xiii. 35, the emphasis lies upon the duty of keeping awake ; in the parable of the ten virgins, on the other hand, a certain degree of drowsiness is excused,[4] so long as the lamp is kept burning. In the parable of the talents we notice, in place of 'Be thou ruler,' &c.[5] 'Enter thou into the joy of thy Lord ' ; ' It is enough for

[1] Matt. xxiv. 37.   [2] Matt. xxv. 4.   [3] Matt. xxii. 11.
[4] Matt. xxv. 5.   [5] Luke xix. 17, 18.

the slave to be as his lord.'¹ Our evangelist will not put
into the mouth of his Master such words as ' I am a hard
man '² even in irony ; this reminds us of his reluctance
to allow that Jesus said, ' Why callest thou Me good ? '³
The objection made in Luke xix. 25 to the
seeming injustice of taking away the one ' pound,' and
giving it to the man who had ten already, does not appear
in Matt. xxv. 28, for the slave does not argue with his
master.

Chapter xxv. 31 ff. is all peculiar to this Gospel, though
the whole section has many links with such passages
as Rom. ii. 16 (cf. ' the secrets of mankind ' with ' Lord,
when saw we Thee ? ') ;   Jas. ii. 13 ; 2 Thess. i. 7, ii. 1
(Matt. xxv. 31, 32) ; 2 Cor. v. 10 ; Rev. xx. 12.   There
are several typical Matthaean features ; for instance,
the reference to Zech. xiv. 5 in v. 31, where one Greek
Uncial and one Old Latin version have, like the LXX of
that passage, ' all the holy ones with Him ' ; the word
' come ' (v. 34), along with the beautiful suggestion of
' came to Me,' ' came to Thee ' (vv. 36, 39)—to come to
the rescue of the ' very little brothers ' of Jesus is one
way of coming to Him ; you get more than you give.
The idea of the parable may be said to be summed up
in v. 44—' waited upon Thee ' ; they had missed the
opportunity of ' waiting upon ' Jesus (cf. viii. 15, R.V.),
in the person of His ' little ones.'   Other aspects
of this outburst of pure poetry will come under review
presently ; like the ' Lord's prayer ' in Matthew's version,
it is rhythmic in form as well as in substance.   Gentiles,
who had not the happiness of waiting upon the Lord
in the days of His flesh, are the objects of this test.

¹ Matt. xxv. 21, 23 ; x. 25.   ² Luke xix. 22.   ³ Matt. xix. 17.

IV

JESUS THE SON OF MAN

PERHAPS nowhere in the New Testament, except in certain passages of imperishable beauty in the Fourth Gospel, is the perfect union between the overmastering claim of Jesus and the 'meekness and gentleness of Christ'[1] brought out with such subtle force and charm as in this book. At this point we ought to concentrate upon the phrase 'Son of Man.'

It has been suggested that in Palestinian Aramaic 'son of man' would mean simply 'man'; but Dalman denies this. We must remember that the Greek phrase 'Son of Man' means not 'the son of a man,' but 'the Son of the Man'; the Greek words as found in our Gospels are really an attempt to translate an idiom which would be quite natural in Aramaic as the designation of a definite personality—the 'Son of the (ideal) Man'—into a language which does not lend itself to the exact mode of expression desired —in Aramaic 'Bar anasha,' 'Son of Mankind.' The LXX had already coined the phrase 'the sons of (the) men,' which appears also in Mark iii. 28, Eph. ii. 5; and this rendering of a familiar Hebraism may have suggested its equivalent in the singular— 'the Son of (the) Man.' 'Son of Man' in Dan. vii. 13 stands for the personification in a single ideal figure of 'the people of the saints of the Most High'; in the LXX of this classic passage he is said to come ' *upon* the clouds of heaven' (cf. Matt. xxiv. 30, R.V.; xxvi. 64, R.V.; Mark xiii. 26 (Codex Bezae); Rev. xiv. 14-16). The Massoretic Hebrew text, on the other hand, has ' *with* the clouds' (cf. Mark xiv. 62, Rev. i. 7, the accepted reading of Mark xiii. 26, Luke xxi. 27): The difference is important, for the prophecy that He would come ' *upon* the clouds' implies that Jesus directly claimed the perogatives of Godhead; the Messiah would come *with* the clouds—only God could ride *upon* them.[2] It will be seen

<hr>

[1] 2 Cor. x. 1.　　　　　　　　　　[2] Ps. civ. 3.

at once, in confirmation of the view advanced in the last chapter, that Matthew prefers '*upon* the clouds'; Mark and Luke—except in the doubtful case of Mark xiii. 26—follow traditional Messianic language ('*with*' or '*in*' the clouds (cloud)). Certainly the 'One like unto a son of a man' in Dan. vii. 13 comes down from heaven, but He is distinguished from the 'four beasts' as being gentle and inoffensive; 'If ever He is to be Master of the world, God must make Him so' (Charles). The Book of Enoch and the Apocalypse of Esdras agree in regarding the Son of Man as an individual Person, the Messiah. It is by no means certain, says Dalman, that Enoch, chapters xxxvii.–lxxi., is pre-Christian, though these chapters are undoubtedly Jewish; in this section of the famous Apocalypse the 'Son of Man' partakes of the nature of angels (cf. Heb. ii. 16) and of men. According to Joshua Ben Levi (*circ.* A.D. 250), the Messiah would come 'with the clouds of heaven,' if Israel were worthy; if not, 'upon an ass.'[1] Evidently the 'Son of Man' is, to the apocalyptic writers of later Judaism, an ideal figure, supernatural indeed, but not, strictly speaking, divine.

On the other hand, the phrase 'son of man' is employed in several places in the Old Testament for man at his lowliest; for instance, in the Book of Ezekiel the prophet is addressed as 'son of man,' and in Job xxv. 6, Ps. viii. 4, 'son of man' means mere man —man in his naked helplessness. Jesus may well have chosen this title, because it already contained within itself the two ideas of highest dignity and lowliest condescension. We have seen that it was one of many names by which the Coming Messiah was known; but it cannot have expressed the popular conception of His office.[2] If Jesus had called Himself 'Son of David' (Matt. i. 1–20; ix. 27; xv. 22; xx. 30; xxi. 9; xxii. 45) there would never have been any question of His Messianic claim in the minds of Galileans; it is obvious that His preference for the title 'Son of Man' baffled them. Dr. Lukyn Williams thinks that the part of the Book of Enoch referred to was of popular origin, but was not accepted by the Pharisees, coming as it did from Upper Galilee.[3] If so, the Lord's use of the name 'Son of Man' would involve a claim to popular recognition in Galilee; but in the Synoptic Gospels no one except the disciples ever called Him Messiah. Rabbi Abbahu (Caesarea A.D. 280) said, 'If any one say to thee, "I am God," he speaks falsely; if he says, "I am the Son of Man,"

[1] Zech. ix. 9; Matt. xxi. 5.
[2] cf. John xii. 34, ix. 35, 36, reading 'the Son of man.'
[3] John i. 46, vii. 52.

his end is to regret it; if I "ᵀ̤ascend unto Heaven" he will not verify his word.' It seems clearly proved that only in certain circles, as among the school of apocalyptic writers who produced the widely divergent sections of the Book of Enoch, was the ' Son of Man ' commonly recognized as a Messianic title. It was used habitually by Jesus of Himself; almost never by any one else of Him. John iii. 14 perhaps comes from the pen of the evangelist, rather than from the lips of Jesus, but Acts vii. 56 is the only certain exception to this rule, and even here Stephen is quoting the words of Jesus.[1] To the public the Lord is ' Son of David,' to believing friends ' Son of God,'[2] as also to the demons[3] (Mark i. 25, ' the Holy One of God '; cf. John vi. 69 in the best MSS.), and after His Passion to that herald of the world's homage, the centurion[4]; to Himself, though He acquiesces in other titles, He is ' Son of Man ' (cf. Matt. xxvi. 63, 64, where the high-priest asks, ' Art Thou the Son of God ? ' and Jesus answers, ' Am I not? Only I say unto thee : From henceforth ye shall see the *Son of Man* sitting,' &c.; and a similar transition from ' the Son of God,' ' the King of Israel,' to ' the Son of Man ' in John i. 49, 51). Probably the early followers of Jesus did not feel free to call Him the ' Son of Man '; it is a proof of their respect for His actual words that none of the four evangelists attempt to conceal His fondness for the name.

Illustrations of the perfect combination of strength and gentleness in Jesus abound on every page of this Gospel. He will submit to ' come behind ' John ('He that cometh behind me ' is thrust emphatically forward in Matt. iii. 11 ; cf. Mark i. 7, omitted in Luke iii. 16), and be baptized by him, in spite of John's protests, for the lowliness of His temper is part of the perfect rightness of His life, as it was to be lived out here.[5] ' Take courage, child '[6] (cf. ix. 22 ; in both places ' Take courage' is Matthew only) is more tender even than Mark ii. 5, ' Child,' much more so than Luke v. 20 ; was the original ' son of man,' and as Luke got the ' man,' and Matthew–Mark the ' son,' which is not far away from ' child ' ? In ix. 10 we overhear once again the familiar note—'many publicans and sinners *came* and lay down with Jesus ' (' came,'

---

[1] Matt. xxvi. 64, &c.
[2] Matt. xvi. 16, &c.
[3] Matt. viii. 29 ; Mark v. 7.
[4] Matt. xxvii. 54 ; Mark xv. 39.
[5] Matt. iii. 14, 15.
[6] Matt. ix. 2.

Matthew only ; cf. xi. 28 and xix. 14, ' Leave the children alone, and do not prevent them *coming to Me* ' ; Mark x. 14, ' Let the children come unto Me, do not hinder them,' is less emphatic). Friends and enemies alike ' approach ' Jesus ; but the children, like the 'publicans,' 'come,' for His tenderness emboldens them. The Lord warmly defends those who are ' not to blame,'[1] as He has a special interest in the men and women whom nobody wants[2] ; He desires ' mercy '—better translated, perhaps, ' a brotherly spirit '—' not sacrifice,'[3] and it is the *humanity* of His most challenging act of power which appeals to open-minded witnesses[4]—(' had given so great authority to men '—that is, to human beneficence). ' What *man* is there of you ? ' He says, when confronted with the man with the withered hand. . . . 'How much better is a *man* than a sheep!' (Matthew[5] only here). A true *man's* pity overrides his most religious scruples when, in a mere animal, he sees suffering which he can relieve ; how much more should he be moved by the sight of a brother *man's* disability ? Luke xiv. 5 does not bring out so clearly the appeal to the *human* feelings of the critics, for instead of ' What *man* ? ' it has ' Which ? ' The Gospel according to the Hebrews (see App. V.) puts an appeal into the mouth of the man : ' I was a stonemason, and got my living with my hands ; I pray Thee, Jesus, restore my health, that I may not basely beg my bread.' Luke vi. 6, like the ' Lewis ' Syriac version of Matthew, tells us that it was the right hand ; if so, we may be sure that Jesus did not need to be told how pathetic the man's case was. The whole Sabbath question is, in this Gospel, summed up in the words ' It is right to do well on the Sabbath '[6] (Matthew only) ; in other words, the Sabbath was made for *man*,'[7] for such human work as can properly be called humane. No wonder that ' many followed Him ' (' Him,' Matthew only), for ' He looked after them *all* '[8] (' all,' Matthew only). Matthew uses here, as often elsewhere, the more general term ' healed ' (i.e. ' made them feel better ') in preference to the doctor's word ' cured,' which is more common in Luke. I do not need to say much more about

---

[1] Matt. xii. 7. [2] Matt. xii. 7, ix. 13. [5] Matt. xii. 11, 12. [7] Mark ii. 27.
[3] Matt. xx. 7. [4] Matt. ix. 8. [6] Matt. xii. 12. [8] Matt. xii. 15.

the exquisitely appropriate quotation in Matt. xii. 18 ff. ; this picture of quiet and forbearing strength and its assured victory sums up perfectly the meaning of the mission of Jesus to weak and little things and people—' A bruised reed He shall not break, and smouldering flax He shall not quench.' His gospel is the one hope of the world, because it reaches in the sweep of its healing power all possible human conditions. Matthew's order in xiii. 8, 23 is suggestive—' one a hundredfold, one sixty, one thirtyfold,' reminding us of the parable of the talents, where the man who made five and the man who made two receive an equal reward.[1]   Dr. Wright thinks that this order is indicative of disappointment ' ; I should rather say that if it means anything, the impression intended is that of our Lord's toleration of comparatively unsatisfactory results—it is all ' good ground,' and Jesus makes the best of what is forthcoming without comparison with others. (Mark iv. 8 has the opposite order ; while, according to Luke viii. 8, all were equally fruitful).   In xiii. 12, xxv. 29 we read, ' He that hath ' (anything, no matter how little), ' to him shall be given, and he shall have enough and to spare ' ; Mark iv. 25, Luke viii. 18, xix. 26, omit the last clause.   Evidently we are justified in seeing a connexion between the parable of the Sower and that of the talents; the latter points to the same truth from the human side and in terms of men's business.   Matthew also helps us very greatly in the interpretation of the hard saying which follows ; quite half the difficulty of this passage[2] is avoided by his substitution of ' because ' for ' in order that ' (Mark iv. 12 ; Luke viii. 10 ; John xii. 40), for it becomes a statement of fact rather than a declaration of policy.

Our evangelist is everywhere anxious to depict Jesus not only as the Healer, but as the Comforter, of men.   We have already noticed that he prefers a word which might be applied quite as suitably to a nurse as to a doctor to describe the ᶠministry of his Lord to the crowds which thronged Him.   He dwells sympathetically, too, upon the sufferings of those on whose behalf relief was sought: in viii. 6 (cf. Luke vii. 2) we read ' Lord, my servant is at home, in terrible torture ' ; so in xv. 22, ' my daughter is *grievously* demon-possessed ' (cf. Mark vii. 26).

[1] Matt. xxv. 21, 23.   [2] Matt. xiii. 13 ff.

Jesus is touched to the heart by the condition of the two blind men, who met Him as He left Jericho (Matt. xx. 34 alone has 'being moved with compassion'; cf. Mark x. 52, Luke xviii. 42). In this Gospel Jesus is not only the Healer of actual disease, but of sickness; in iv. 23, ix. 35, x. 1 the words 'every disease and every form of weakness' occur (Mark i. 39 mentions only exorcism; and the same observation is true of Mark vi. 5; while in Mark vi. 6b—parallel to Matt. ix. 35—'teaching' is regarded as the central feature of the Galilean ministry; again in Matt. xix. 2, Mark x. 1, we find the same divergence). Luke ix. 1, 2 includes both 'curing' (v. 1) and 'healing' (v. 2) in the commission of the twelve, cf. Luke x. 9, 'heal the sick.' But in Matt. xiv. 14 Jesus does not preach to the crowd of sick and weary people at all, but 'heals their invalids'—the same word is used in Mark vi. 5 of the minor ailments of 'a few sick folk'; Mark vi. 34 only mentions 'much' teaching, and Luke ix. 11 has 'He was talking to them about the kingdom of God, and those who had need of healing He was curing.' It is no mere accident, too, that Matthew alone of the four evangelists tells us of the 'women and children' present at the Lord's picnic-party (xiv. 21, 'not counting women and children'; so xv. 38—cf. Mark vi. 44, viii. 9; Luke ix. 14; John vi. 10). That the same detail occurs (again only here) at the feeding of the four thousand proves that Matthew had an eye and a heart for this sort of thing. Our impression is deepened when we see that Matthew inserts 'all' in xv. 37 (cf. Mark viii. 8). Perhaps the presence of the tired children accounts for the omission of a sermon on these occasions. The same note makes itself heard in viii. 16, 17—' all those who were ill He healed. . . Himself took our sicknesses, and carried our diseases' (Isa. liii. 4, according to the LXX, 'He bears our sins, and suffers pain for us'). This quotation is very striking, for it does not answer to any accepted translation of the Hebrew; it comes, we infer, from the Testimony Book. We may compare Ignatius' Epistle to Polycarp (chapter 1), 'Carry the diseases of all, like a perfect athlete.'

Matthew thinks of men's 'sorrows' and 'griefs' as 'diseases' and 'sicknesses,' arising from a lack of what he would call 'righteousness,' which, from one point of

W

view, means health—without "our" distinction between
physical, mental, and spiritual disease ; from another,
obedience to God's law, for ' man' lives . . . by every
word that issues from the mouth of God.'[1]   This identification of obedience and health, which means happiness,
was the great truth which the best Pharisaic teachers
enforced ; it is enshrined in the one hundred and nineteenth
Psalm, and Jesus declares His adhesion to this Pharisaic
ideal in Matt. v. 20, xxiii. 2, 3 ; the secret of happiness
and efficiency is to obey the law of God, the ' perfect law
of liberty '[2] in things great and small.   He differed from
the Pharisees chiefly upon two counts : they did not
carry out the ' weightier matters of the law,' least of all
the ' royal,' commanding law, ' Thou shalt love thy
neighbour as thyself '[3] ; and, further, they added to the
' light ' burden of the law, rationally expounded, ' the
intolerable deadweight of their own endlessly intrusive
tradition.'[4]   Their wearisome interpolations and their
disregard of essentials alike led to a stultifying unreality ;
even this might have been forgiven, if they had not pre-
tended to themselves and others that they did succeed
in carrying out the law, so becoming not merely mistaken,
but self-blinded ' leaders of the blind '[5]—the corruption
of the best had become the worst.   I must leave discussion
of the meaning of our Lord's campaign against ' hypocrisy '
to a later chapter ; just now we are studying the effect
of this worse than lack of leadership upon the common
people, and our Lord's attitude to them.   Here we ought
to notice a vivid phrase, which the first evangelist adds
to a comment made by Mark, couched in Old Testament
language[6] ; in another context Matthew has,[7] ' And
seeing the crowds, He was smitten with compassion for
them, because they were harassed and dejected ' (Moffatt),
' like sheep without a shepherd.'   There is, indeed, something very pathetic in the aspect of a draggled, tired
crowd ; they wander about with aimless restlessness,
and there is a lost look about them, which went to the
heart of Jesus.   They had no one to look after them,

---

[1] Matt. iv. 4.   [2] Jas. i. 25.   [3] Jas. ii. 8 ; Matt. xix. 19, xxii. 40.
[4] Matt. xi. 30, xv. 6, xxiii 4, 23.
[5] Matt. xv. 14, xxiii. 16, 24 ; Luke vi. 39 ; John ix. 40 ; Rom. ii. 19.
[6] Mark vi. 24 ; cf. Numb. xxvii. 17, LXX.   [7] Matt. ix. 36.

and the Lord's mother-heart led Him to rest and feed them—anything to make them feel better. In the story of the miraculous feeding there is another exquisite touch in Matthew's record : ' There is no need for them to go away '[1] (Matthew only)—the familiar note again; cf. ix. 10; xiv. 28; xi. 28; xix. 14. The obvious forlornness of these people could easily be remedied. But there underlay it a deeper unhappiness in the soul (cf. xi. 30) of these ' lost sheep of the house of Israel.'[2] an unhappiness which could not be removed by the gaiety and comfort of a timely meal, at which these poor folk could enjoy the unusual pleasure of eating food which they had not paid for or cooked themselves, and of being waited upon by the disciples. It was quite as much, as the sequel of the happy picnic-party[3] showed, the fact that the people were being misled, as that they had no real leadership, which roused the pity and anger of Jesus ; the expense of high national spirit in a waste of misdirected passion called forth all His protective instincts.

Perhaps this is the real core of Matthew's delicate but insistent emphasis upon the gentleness of Jesus to the men and women of His own class in His own nation. He had chosen to work beside the lakeside, because the people were capable of so much sacrifice and high endeavour. Whatever the Galileans were not, they were quick-minded and warm-hearted idealists, every one of them ; there was hope for men who could feel so keenly, however mistaken they might be. To them He was always ' of easy temper and a homely mind '[4] ; there is a complete philosophy of reasonably happy living for straitened people in His invitation to them. He did not call them to cross-bearing—at least, not at first—but to a lightening of their burdens. Let them ' learn a lesson ' from Him —learn to share their burdens round, and to be submissive to one another ; for no class understands the meaning of the ' royal law,' ' Thou shalt love thy neighbour as thyself,' better than the very poor have always done ; they know that it is possible to live by taking in each other's washing. The ' three loaves '[5] are generally forthcoming for the exigencies of sickness or hospitality in

[1] Matt. xiv. 16. [2] Matt. x. 6, xv. 24, xviii. 12 ff. [3] John vi. 15.
[4] Matt. xi. 29. [5] Luke xi. 5.

the mean streets. The secret is to take another's yoke upon you, knowing that your own will be lightened by the great Burden-bearer[1]—in other words, to work in a team; for 'I,' says Jesus, 'will look after you, if you see to the needs of one another—I *am with you all the days*.'[2] This last reference leads us to another aspect of the Lord's preaching to plain people; it is brought out in vi. 34 (also peculiar to this Gospel). They must try to temper inevitable worries with a saving trust, and in particular to learn the art of living a day at a time. It is as though He said: ' I know the kind of life you lead, that you have as much as you can do to get through each day as it comes, for every day brings its full measure of perplexities and irritations. Do not let to-morrow overlap into to-day; to-morrow can look after itself. Just about enough for every day is its tiresomeness.' They could not live quite so carelessly as the birds or as gaily as the lilies, but they might learn a lesson from them[3]; if they could not get on so easily, all the more for that reason were they dear to their heavenly Father, who loved the very hairs of their heads, the more because they were too soon grey with the toil of an unnatural way of life. Many poor people, like others of us who are not so poor, are sustained by the belief that somehow they will ' muddle through '; let them translate that fragment of unconscious philosophy into a reasoned trust in their Father, and they shall find the secret of restful living.[4] If the meanest hovel is lit by the kindly light of a generous—this is what ' if thine eye be single ' seems to mean in vi. 22—and patient spirit, the light, like the cottage lamp, which makes even seaside lodgings look cosy and homelike, rounding off the hard outlines of the shabbiest furniture, ' shines out to all in the house.' Adapted to modern conditions, we may render vi. 22 f. thus: ' What the fire is in your room at home, charity and trustfulness will be to you and yours in the circle of your friends and neighbours. It is not so much that life is hard, hard as it is, that is the root-cause of your unhappiness, as a hard and sour-spirited way of looking at life; the source of all the needless trouble which we give ourselves and one another is that we are all in the dark together. We stumble over one

[1] Hos. xi. 4.   [2] Matt. xxviii. 20.   [3] Matt. vi. 26, 28.   [4] Matt. xi. 30.

another, nations and classes and men, we curse and hate and tear at one another, because we are in the dark.' The Fourth Gospel adds here. as so often, the crowning touch to this beautiful teaching. 'Ye are the light of the world,' says Jesus in Matthew[1] (Matthew only) ; 'let your light shine out.' 'I am the Light of the world,' says Jesus in John[2] ; the spirit of generous trustfulness which makes the dreariest life worth living is the Spirit of the Lord Himself, who found His own life here, though the saddest ever lived, so infinitely worth the living.

Coming back for another moment to vi. 34, we notice how clearly it brings out the sympathy of Jesus for the invalid as well as the drudge, thus forming another link with a feature of this Gospel already discussed. The feeling of 'sufficient for the day is its trouble' almost exactly corresponds from one point of view to that of the invalid's hymn,

> Soon finds each fevered day
>   And each chill night its bourn;
> Nor strength need droop, nor hope decay,
>   Till rest or light return;

from another to ' Let him alone, till he shall, as a hireling, get through his day.'[3] In our first evangelist's version of the ' Lord's prayer ' we have ' Give us to-day our bread for the coming day.'[4] The word which, following Debrunner, I have rendered ' for the coming day,' appears to be a coinage of the Gospels, or rather of the source (Q) underlying the First and Third Gospels ; for it is difficult to believe that both Matthew and Luke (xi. 3, ' Give us day-by-day our bread for the coming day ') would have stumbled upon so strange a word independently—a word to which no exact Greek parallel has been found. The presence of this unique word in both versions of the prayer, as well as in that found in the *Teaching of the Twelve Apostles* (viii. 2), is regarded by many scholars as conclusive proof that both Matthew and Luke used a *Greek* translation of Q. The only alternative is to suggest that the book of the sayings of the Lord,

[1] Matt. v. 14.
[2] John viii. 12, xii. 46, cf. i. 4, 5, 9, &c.
[3] Job xiv. 6, vii. 1–4.
[4] Matt. vi. 11.

was still in Aramaic or, less probably, Hebrew, but that in the Liturgy of the Church this Greek word had become, by regular use, the standardized rendering of the original, when our two Gospels came to be compiled. 'For the coming day' appears to be the best English translation; on Monday evening Tuesday might be described either by the words 'for the coming day' or by the more usual expression 'to-morrow', or 'for to-morrow'. If, on the other hand, the prayer was repeated on Tuesday morning, 'for the coming day' would mean 'for Tuesday'; for to-morrow 'for Wednesday.' We notice that Luke's rendering emphasizes regularity of provision, while Matthew's version gives us another illustration of the day-at-a-time philosophy.[1] Before we leave the prayer for daily bread, the reading of the Irish Old Latin MS. lately collated by E. S. Buchanan may be mentioned; it is 'Give us to-day for bread the heavenly word of God.' and would involve in the Greek original 'the bread heavenly' instead of 'the bread for the coming day.' It seems probable that this MS. has been affected by Origen's exposition of the prayer, which goes back to Tertullian, as including really only a petition for spiritual bread; the wish to spiritualize has been the father to the thought of substituting an easy Greek word for a hard one. In xxviii. 20 'I with you *all the days*, to the consummation of the age' rounds off most effectively our Lord's teaching upon the subject of living by the day, of which we have found traces here and there in this Gospel.

In xv. 31 the wonder and relief of the crowds when the Lord had been with them for a little time bubbles out into a kind of breathless music, for 'Christianity', said Borne, a German Jew, 'is the religion of all poor devils.' In this verse the words 'lame men whole' should be omitted, on the strong evidence of Codex Sinaiticus, Old Latin and Old Syriac versions, as well as that of Origen; the omission rather enhances the music of the sentence, making it conform to the threefold rhythm. The same kind of feeling underlies a slight change in xiv. 36—'got perfectly well'—for Mark vi. 56, 'recovered.' In this Gospel the 'evil' always come

---

[1] " Continual bread " is also a possible translation.

in front of the 'good' (cf. v. 45 ; xxii. 10 ; xiii. 47, 'of every kind' ; xx. 8, 'beginning from the last' ; xxi. 31, 'They said, The last,' reversing the order of vv. 29, 30, and reading 'the last' in v. 31). The refrain 'the first shall be last' occurs both in Mark x. 31 and Luke xiii. 30, but is found twice in the First Gospel[1] ; the words ' the publicans and harlots go before you into the Kingdom '[2] draw a much more pointed contrast between so-called bad and good people than does the corresponding passage in Luke vii. 30. This fact is all the more significant, inasmuch as Matthew is, as we shall see, the sternest of moralists. But he has a special concern to bring out the fact that Jesus appealed to men and women who had nothing whatever to recommend them ; He did not so much to make good men a little better, as to make bad men good.

You never can tell how those whom the world labels as hopelessly bad will turn out ; I cannot help feeling that this is one of the ideas underlying the parable of the tares.[3] The slaves of the Householder are forbidden to 'collect' the weeds 'lest by chance they should root up along with them the wheat' (xiii. 29) ; this does not mean that eternally opposed moral distinctions have no meaning, but that we are too clumsy to adjudicate. The history of the Kingdom is, from its very beginning, a series of surprises. Jesus Himself is surprised at the discovery of faith of the right sort in unexpected places[4] ; it was worth coming from heaven to find the 'pearl of great price' on the refuse-heap of this wasteful world.[5] On our side, too, the Christian life begins with a supreme and most surprising discovery[6] ; as we walk with Him through the years He introduces us to His windfalls one by one.[7] But the whole truth will never come out till the end, which will be the greatest surprise of all[8] ; every one, except the King, is rubbing his eyes in astonishment.

This parable brings us to one of those phrases which echo in the memory long after one has laid down the book—'these little ones.' We must set to work to gather

---

[1] Matt. xix. 30, xx. 16. [4] Matt. viii. 10, xv. 28. [7] e.g. Matt. xxi. 30.
[2] Matt. xxi. 31. [5] Matt. xiii. 45. [8] Matt. xxv. 37 ff., 44 f.
[3] Matt. xiii. 24 ff. [6] Matt. xiii. 44.

up the references in the First Gospel to the 'little ones
or 'little brothers' of Jesus. They are as follow : x. 42,
' Whoever shall give one of these little ones a cooling drink,
only because he' (this may mean the giver, or—more
probably—the one to whom the drink is given) 'is a disciple.
. . . He shall by no means lose his reward' (Mark ix. 41
has ' gives you a cup of water . . . because ye are Christ's';
here it is clear that the one to whom the cup is given
is the disciple, but Matthew leaves it open to us to think
that the disciple, because he is *himself* a disciple, asks
no questions, like the Good Samaritan) ; xi. 11 (so, practically, Luke vii. 28) ; xii. 20 (' the bruised reed' and
the 'smouldering flax') ; xviii. 6, 7, ' Whoever is a
hindrance to one of these little ones who believe *in Me*,
(' in Me' not in the best MSS. of Mark, see below),
better for him to have a great millstone hung around his
neck and to be *sunk* in the deep sea!' (compare 'beginning
to sink,' also Matthew only, xiv. 30). ' Woe to the world
because of hindrances ! Hindrances have to come, but
woe to the man through whom the hindrances do come !'
(compare with this passage Luke xvii. 1, 2, ' It is inevitable
that hindrances should come, but woe to the man by whom
they come ! It would be better for him to have a millstone
hung around his neck, and to be flung into the sea,
rather than prove a hindrance to one of these little ones!';
Mark ix. 42, ' And whoever is a hindrance to one of these
little ones who believe, the best thing for him would be
rather if a great millstone were hung around his neck,
and he were thrown into the sea '). Matthew stresses
the personal relationship between some of the little ones
and Jesus—' who believe *in Me*' (' in Me,' Matthew only),
and thrusts the offence to the little ones forward. We
notice, too, a deepening note in the three versions of this
well-attested saying—' thrown,' flung,' ' sunk in the deep
sea' (Matthew). The ' Lewis' Syriac reads in Matthew
(xviii. 7), ' Woe to the world for the hindrances that are
coming ! for the hindrances are ready to come '; while
the First Epistle of Clement—the earliest of our patristic
witnesses—gives us in chapter xlvi. 8, ' Remember the
words of the Lord Jesus : " Woe to that man ! It were
the best thing for him if he had not been born" (cf. Matt.
xxvi. 24 ; Mark xiv. 21) " than to have hindered one of

Mine elect " (cf. Mark xiii. 20, 22) ; "it were a preferable
fate for him that a millstone should be put round (him)
and that he were sunk" (as Matthew) "in the sea, than
that he should pervert one of Mine elect" '—for 'pervert'
cf. Acts xiii. 8, 10. Paul refers to this passage more
than once—e.g. in 1 Cor. xi. 19, 'It is a (moral) necessity
that there should be parties among you ' ; compare also
the whole discussion of 1 Cor. x. 23 ff., Rom. xiv. 1 ff.,
especially vv. 13, 15, 21. The fact that Clement of Rome
(A.D. 75–100) allows this saying to run into another, which
concerns Judas, is extremely interesting, for the one
saying means ' better dead ' (Matt. xviii. 6 f. and parallels) ;
the other, ' better never born ' (Matt. xxvi. 24 ; Mark xiv.
21). How many times we are thrown back upon Judas !
Something more is to be said on this topic when we come
to examine more closely the teaching upon hindrances
in the First Gospel. Dr. Glover, in *The Jesus of History*,
mentions the belief current in antiquity that, when
a man was drowned, his soul perished with his
body, but is not sure whether Jews held this opinion.
At any rate, we know that evil spirits could be disposed
of in that way (Matt. viii. 32 and parallels) ; perhaps
that is the reason why submersion in deep water is prescribed for the mischief-maker.

Proceeding with our list of sayings about the ' little
ones,' we come to Matt. xviii. 10 (Matthew only), ' See
that ye despise not one of these little ones ; for I tell you,
their angels do always look upon the face of My Father
in heaven ' ; then follows the parable of the one ' wandering sheep,' paralleled by the story of the ' lost ' sheep,[1]
but culminating in Matthew in a verse peculiar to him
(v. 14), ' So it is not the will of your Father in heaven
that one of these little ones should be lost.' It is pleasant
to find Jesus lending His authority to the belief in guardian
angels, or representative angels ; compare the ' angels '
of the Churches in Rev. i. 20 ff. and Heb. i. 14, also the
twelve legions of angels attendant upon the Lord Himself. [2]
Are the ' angels ' here ministers of vengeance upon those
who hinder God's purposes for His ' little ones,' or are
they God's hopes for them, His pictures of what He means

[1] Luke xv. 3 ff.   [2] Matt. xxvi. 53, iv. 11 ; Luke xxii. 43 ; Mark i. 13.

the 'little ones' to be—what James[1] calls 'the face of their birth'? According to Rabbinic teaching, there was a good as well as an evil 'yezer,' or 'leaven,' in every man, and the good 'yezer' is sometimes spoken of as though it corresponded to the good angel of mediaeval fancy (see the Sonnets of Shakespeare, 144). The 'angels' of men are spoken of as their spiritual counterparts (Acts xii. 15 and perhaps vi. 15, but cf. 1 Sam. xxix. 9)—compare 'spirit' in Luke xxiv. 37 with 'ghost' in Matt. xiv. 26, Mark vi. 49, an expression which is avoided in the Fourth Gospel.[2] More probably, however, the reference is rather to the angels who pray for the righteous (Enoch ix. 10, xv. 2, xl. 6 (Gabriel), 9 ; Tobit xii. 12, 15 (Raphael) ; Rev. viii. 3) ; in that case the meaning is that the prayers of the little ones always find an easy access to the Person of God (cf. 2 Kings xxv. 19, 'five men of them that were in the King's presence')—they can always 'get through,' as the 'little ones' themselves had ready access to the presence of Jesus (Luke xv. 1 ; Matt. xix. 14 ; see p. 265). We should get a child or a simple believer to pray for us, if we can. On Matt. xix. 12 Schweitzer has an interesting note, suggesting that the 'eunuchs' are the 'little ones' excluded from religious fellowship (Deut. xxiii. 1 ; Isa. lvi. 3–5 ; Wisdom iii. 13, 14). Jesus has a place in His heart for the 'eunuchs that man has made'; He deals first with one class which was out of it in the religious world of His day,[3] then with quite another,[4] for He had a special brief for those who had no place, or had lost their place, in the Church as He found it, the sheep of the house of Israel who had gone astray (Matt. x. 6, xv. 24, xviii. 11–14 ; Luke xiii. 16, xix. 9 ; Matt. ix. 36, xiv. 14 ; Mark vi. 34).

'The last' (xix. 30, xx. 8, 14, 16) is another way of saying 'the little ones.' There is really no 'first' and 'last' in the constitution of the Kingdom; both the man with five talents and the man with two 'enter into the joy of' the 'Lord,'[5] for 'it is enough for the disciple to be as His Lord,'[6] 'slave of all'[7]—He does not say 'last,' though Luke xxii. 26 has 'younger,' in these days a very different thing ! The end of life's working day is to bring equality ;

[1] Jas. i. 23.　　[2] John vi. 19.　　[3] Matt. xix. 12 f.　　[4] Matt. xix. 14.
[5] Matt. xxv. 21–23.　　[6] Matt. x. 25.　　[7] Mark x. 44 ; Matt. xx. 27.

the flat rate of a shilling for the day is not to be despised,[1] inasmuch as it stands for an equal share in the 'joy of the Lord,' for Jesus takes His place with His brethren, and identifies Himself with the 'least' of them.[2] This makes all distinctions absurd[3]; for if He who was 'first-born among many brethren,'[4] 'firstborn of all creation,'[5] was 'in all points made like His brethren,'[6] and came amongst us 'in great humility,' 'taking a slave's rôle,'[7] there can be no first and last. The first should count it an honour to be as the last, for that means to be 'as He was in the world.'[8] We may well regard ourselves as equal now; in any case, when unequally distributed opportunities and faculties are taken into account, we can see that the fairest verdict upon our strange medley of success and failure would be that all alike should just get home at last into the presence of their Lord, where any remembrance of inequalities shall be forgotten in the common joy.

We are to 'humble' ourselves[9] (Matthew only here) as 'this little child,' says Jesus, as He is 'lowly minded'[10] (Matthew only), for our sakes having become Himself 'a little child' (ii. 8, 9, 11, 13, 14, 20, 21—the importance of this repetition has been noticed already; Matthew makes it more striking by calling the other babies in Bethlehem 'children,'[11] not 'little children'). He can be 'hindered,' like the other 'little ones'; like them, too, by His friends[12] ('thou art a hindrance to Me,' Matthew only); such 'hindrance,' if persisted in, involves the offender in such tragic remorse that 'it were better for him that he had not been born'[13]; indeed, any one who causes hindrance to one of these 'little ones,' with whom Jesus all along identifies Himself, is better out of the way of further mischief.[14] Nevertheless, 'hindrances,' in a world like this, are bound to come[15]; only at the 'consummation of the age' will 'the Son of Man gather out of His Kingdom all who are hindrances'[16] (Matthew only; cf. xxv. 31–46 and Zeph. i. 3), for 'every

---

[1] Matt. xx. 9.　　[2] Matt. xxv. 40, 45; x. 40.　　[3] Matt. xviii. 32, 33.
　　[4] Rom. viii. 29.　　[5] Col. i. 15.　　[6] Heb. ii. 17.　　[7] Phil. ii. 7.
[8] 1 Cor. iv. 9; 1 John iv. 17.　　[9] Matt. xviii. 4.　　[10] Matt. xi. 29.
[11] Matt. ii. 16.　　[12] Matt. xvi. 23.　　[13] Matt. xxvi. 24; Mark xiv. 21.
　　　　[14] Matt. xviii. 6; Mark ix. 42; Luke xvii. 2.
　　[15] Matt. xviii. 7; Luke xvii. 1.　　　　　　[16] Matt. xiii. 41.

plant which My Father hath not planted shall be rooted up '¹ (Matthew only). We cause offence sometimes quite unwittingly ; lest we should be driven to despair by His awful words about those who are ' hindrances,' it is made plain in this deep and satisfying Gospel, that in this point too He was made like His brethren. The Pharisees² (Matthew only) and even the disciples took offence³ (Luke omits) at the Lord Himself, careful as He was to give no excuse for misunderstanding⁴; that was part of the inevitable tragedy of His mission. ' The first ' are to become ' last ' ; we need not fear to be last, for He was ' last.'⁵ He became a little child ; so must we seek to be. He was ' hindered ' by those who loved Him ; we must learn to bear with those who hinder us and to believe in them as He still believed in His ' hindrance ' Peter, saving him by His belief and His prayers. Even the offenders may be His ' little ones,' and have their ' angels,' their better selves, which God sees, though we cannot always. They may not know that they are hindering us, as Peter knew not that he was a ' hindrance ' ; and in the complexities of life we may be ' hindering ' them, as Jesus was laid open to hindering Peter, and has suffered from all the irritating frictions incident to co-operation between men of different ways of thinking and feeling. Matt. xviii. 19 gives us the way out : mutual hindrance can be robbed of its power to hurt and thwart by mutual prayer ; where the other will not or cannot pray with you, as Peter could not with his Master, you must pray alone, for the Lord will make the Second ; where He is one of the two, the third will not be long in coming in.⁶ The self-identification of Jesus with all kinds of weak, easily offended people is complete in xxv. 40, 45 ; at the end of every section of our study of this great Gospel we are left looking into His face.

It will be seen with what consummate skill Matthew has woven and interwoven the ¦threads of his Master's teaching. He turns, so to say, one after another of the sayings to the light, until their hidden meanings shine out ; then all the subtle harmonies are united in one massive effect. We have already noticed his mastery

¹ Matt. xv. 13.   ² Matt. xv. 12.   ³ Matt. xxvi. 31 ; Mark xiv. 27.
⁴ Matt. xvii. 27.   ⁵ Matt. xxi. 37.   ⁶ Matt. xviii. 20.

of the arts of tragic suggestion ; here is another case. In xx. 20 we read of ' the mother of the sons of Zebedee ' (' the mother,' &c., is Matthew only) coming with her sons to ask a favour for them. In the course of His reply, Jesus says, ' But to sit on My right hand and on my left is not Mine to give, but (it is) for those for whom it has been prepared by My Father.' This does not read smoothly, and a great improvement is offered us by Codex Bezae —' for others it has been prepared by My Father ' ; while in the ' Lewis ' Syriac of Mark x. 40 we find ' for another ' —surely a direct reference to the ' dying thief ' of Luke xxiii. 42. The reading ' for others ' does not involve any change in the lettering of the Greek, only the dropping of the aspirate. Who were ' the others ' ? The answer is given in Matt. xxvii. 38—' one on the right hand and one on the left.' But the revealing touch comes at xxvii. 56, where our evangelist brings prominently into view the fact that ' the mother of the sons of Zebedee ' was watching the scene. Here we have in one or two swift strokes the tragedy of an ambitious mother's life : instead of a throne, a cross ; instead of her two boys, two criminals —this was what her dreams had come to ! All the smaller tragedies lead us to the foot of the cross, to the universal catastrophe of Calvary. We have already watched Peter, Judas, the Galileans, Pilate ; Matthew adds the mother of the sons of Zebedee, Luke the dying thief, John the mother of the Lord Himself. He is the Son of Man for shattered lives, like that of the man who was crucified with Christ, hopes destroyed, represented by the two mothers standing so forlornly there, the worst forebodings all come true, have ever brought men into the presence of the Passion of the Son of Man, who gathers them up into His heart and prays them through to Easter. Yet is He Son of God, for He gathers them up only by the reach and sweep of His love, most irresistibly triumphant when it stoops the lowest and suffers most, to carry them with Him through their little despairs to the ' Paradise ' of a larger life and a more enduring hope, a perfect love that has now cast out all fear.

V

THE GENTLENESS OF THE CHRISTIAN DISCIPLE

'IT is enough for the disciple to be as his Lord'; as 'meekness' is the characteristic quality of Jesus, the Son of Man,[1] so His follower must be ambitious to become lowly-hearted,[2] a learner all his days, 'led to the mount above through the low vale of humble love.' He must not be a ruthless and self-opinionated revolutionist; the ideal of the Kingdom is not to destroy indiscriminately all old things[3] (perhaps Matthew only), but to ensure the survival of the best in both old and new—the clause 'and both are kept together'[4] is peculiar to Matthew, though the idea is present in Luke v. 39. This Gospel has preserved for us a charming picture of the scholarly Christian disciple, who unites in his own person an inspired originality with a gentle-hearted reverence for things old; he is 'like a householder who produces from his stores things new and old.' He first brings out the new, for he is a disciple of Jesus, and dullness and discipleship should be incompatible terms; then he sets to work to show that, if new, it is not brand-new, for he is a 'scribe,' endowed with the choice learning of an older world, but a 'scribe' who has 'become a disciple,' and is glad to bring his trained mind and store of treasured learning to the feet of his new Master, who alone can illuminate it all[5] (Matthew only). This might be a portrait of our evangelist, with his store of quotations from the Old Testament interpreted anew. No one receives new light so humbly as does the scholar-saint; he not only 'hears' the word, but he 'understands' it[6] ('and understanding' is Matthew only); he has already something to offer his

---

[1] Matt. xi. 29.   [2] Matt. xviii. 4.   [3] Matt. v. 17.
[4] Matt. ix. 17.   [5] Matt. xiii. 52.   [6] Matt. xiii. 23.

Master, and is rewarded at compound interest, so that he has enough and to spare[1] (' and he shall have abundance,' Matthew only). This feature of the First Gospel must, of course, be balanced by the doctrine, expounded in xx. 1 ff., of the final equality of all believers, as also by remembrance of the absolute dependence of the Christian upon his Lord ; he delights to call himself a ' slave,' because he serves for love, not pay, even pay in the form of peace of mind or success ; compare x. 8, ' freely ye have received, freely give ' (Matthew only) with x. 10, ' the workman is worthy of his food ' (not ' pay,' as Luke x. 7).

The story of Peter's walking on the water (Matthew only) exquisitely illustrates the utter dependence of the disciple upon his Lord. The depths of despair possible to man are symbolized by sinking ' in the deep sea.'[2] The service of man is so dangerous a task for men ignorant and clumsy as we in such a world as this that it is like walking on the water ; if we offend one of the ' little ones ' where such offence can be avoided, drowning is too good for us. For men like ourselves, so readily provoked to contempt for people who misunderstand and misrepresent our best, when we read words such as these, despair seems to be within measurable distance, despair not for things that we might conceivably do or say, but for things that we have done and said. Our consolation is that the Lord does not leave us to make our blunders and do more harm than good alone ; when we ' begin to sink,' as men soon come to do when they try to be as He was in the world and walk on the water with Him, we must cry, ' Lord, save me ' ; the Saviour ' stretches out His hand '[3] (cf. xii. 49, ' stretching out His hand,' Matthew only ; see above, p. 257) and takes us back into the boat, giving us again our place in His service, as he restored Peter after his fall.[4] Without Jesus, not simply the individual and more adventurous worker, but the Church itself, would soon be submerged[5] (' buried under the waves,' Matthew only) ; but if *only* (' only ' is peculiar to Matthew in ix. 21, xiv. 36 ; cf. Mark v. 28, vi. 56) the Lord is near, all is well.

Very remarkable is the language of Matt. x. 39, ' He that

[1] Matt. xiii. 12, xxv. 29.   [2] Matt. xviii. 6.   [3] Matt. xiv. 31.
[4] John xxi. 19, 20 ; cf. Luke xxii. 32.   [5] Matt. viii. 24.

finds his soul shall lose it, and he that loses his soul for
My sake shall find it '; compare xvi. 25, 'wishes to save
his soul ' (so Mark viii. 35, 'his own soul'). Luke xvii. 33
reads ' Whoever seeks to make his soul his own shall lose
it ; but whoever shall lose it shall bring it to life again '
(a medical term ; see p. 153 ff.). Perhaps it would be well
to substitute for ' his (own) soul ' the more modern
phrase ' himself.' We noticed above that Matthew's
use of the word ' find ' is worthy of our study. The
Christian ' finds ' his Lord, the Lord ' finds ' him ; now
we see that he only ' finds ' his Lord when he has ' lost '
himself. According to another parallel passage in Luke,[1]
a man must come to ' hate . . . even himself also.' The
Fourth Gospel has ' He that loveth himself is losing himself, and he that hateth himself in this world shall keep
possession of himself to eternal life.'[2] It will be seen that
there is a distinct shade of meaning in the First Gospel.
Matthew is thinking of the ' heart at leisure from itself ' ;
the finder is submerged in the glory of his discovery, so
that it never occurs to him to think of himself at all,
whereas in Luke, and to a certain extent in the Fourth
Gospel too, his remorse has already given rise to an actual
dislike of himself.

The rendering of this great saying offered to us in the
First Gospel has a real message for the modern world,
for we are all—those who seem to be quite indifferent to
spiritual things, and those who are in dead earnest about
them alike—far too much occupied with ourselves, the
many with money-getting, social climbing, or mere animal
comfort ; the few with their own ideas and ' gospels,'
the little corner of the truth which they have made their
own, to them the one thing worth living and dying for,
because it is theirs. The consequence is that we live in
a world full of preachers and almost destitute of listeners,
every one who cares for truth at all snatching at some
fragment which he can appropriate and fit into his scheme
of things, then flinging it into the face of a public which
calls us all cranks together. We need to be set thinking and
dreaming of something outside ourselves, to be smitten into
adoration of an ideal which we cannot appropriate or
manage, but in the glory of which we become so completely

[1] Luke xiv. 26.   [2] John xii. 25.

absorbed as to forget ourselves, our own particular point
of view, altogether. In most modern lives of Christ I am
haunted by the inability of the biographer to lose himself
in his subject. We have been presented with the 'liberal'
view of Jesus, the aesthetic Jesus, the life of Jesus re-
written from the standpoint of modern knowledge and
criticism. The 'eschatological' view of Jesus is almost
the latest, and has been useful in showing us that He has
broken out of all the frames that have been made for Him;
now He is breaking out of this frame too. There is a kind
of patronage, and those who, like the present writer, are
vastly impressed by the picture of the radiantly human
Jesus, must beware of falling into the same snare as the
others. 'Jesus cannot have said this,' we are told ; when
we ask 'Why ? ' various reasons are given, but really they
amount to this—it does not agree with the writer's system.
In the same way we are perpetually warned of the danger
of finding too much in the parables of Jesus ; they must
be expounded in a scientific spirit ; we must remember
that He was a Jew, and lived twenty centuries ago, and
so on. To all these attempts to read the mystery of our
Lord through English or German, liberal or socialist,
narrowly orthodox or 'higher' critical spectacles, our evangelist would say, ' Comrade, how did you get in here without the wedding-garment ? '[1] Disciples and Galileans
alike tried to fit Him into the frames they made for Him in
the days of His flesh ; and He broke away from them,
only coming back to them when His friends were ready to
follow without question, as the word was given to them.
The weakness of church life at its best and keenest in
these days is that there are so many reformers, so
many lovers of some special cause, so few who are content to be merely lovers of their Lord, and to tell the story
without the intrusion of their own comments and explanations. We need to study Jesus, but not for the sake of
finding confirmation of our own ideas or creeds in Him—
we shall do that, for almost all the 'lives' of Jesus are
true, so far as they go—but because we are fascinated
and cannot keep away, whatever we find or fail to find
there. This point is suggested by Matthew's version of
the story of the rich young man, who felt that he only

[1] Matt. xxii. 12 ; cf. xvii. 6.

lacked one thing[1] ('What lack I yet?' is Matthew only). He came to get what he could from Jesus, to complete his philosophy of right living; but the one thing which he lacked was the vital thing. He would fain lend his support to the new movement, if it fell in with his ideas; he was told to 'join up' as a private, to follow for love, without thought of his own personal position. So being caught by the magnetism of the Living Christ, and swept clear away from the morbid self-consciousness which is our bane, we should most gloriously find ourselves; we should 'be found in Him.'[2]

It is our task to trace the steps of this delicately treading worshipper of Jesus, the author of the First Gospel, through his record of his Master's teaching. The disciple must not affect the teacher, or the padre, and there is but one Leader[3] (Matthew only); if the use of the title 'Reverend' is allowed to become anything but a convenient label, it is an insolent usurpation. The call for 'leadership' is a symptom of unbelief and insecurity in the Church; He is the only possible Leader, and we need to think of Him much more, of the sins and incapacities of administrative officials a good deal less. The only pathway to legitimate honour is that, not of the commanding personality, but of general usefulness[4]; 'personalities' are often more of a hindrance than a help in the Church of Christ, which is an anomaly if it is anything more than a democracy under the absolute lordship of Jesus. The supreme trial of the Church in later days He said, would be that the love of 'the many' for their absent Lord would grow cold[5] (Matthew alone). Some will say that He is in the Church ('in the chamber,' Matthew only)[6]; others that He is rather to be found outside the Church than in it ('in the desert'—both these phrases occur in Matthew alone); men are making both these statements in these days, seeking to appropriate Him to their own ecclesiastical or anti-ecclesiastical position. We are not to listen to them. He is everywhere, of all parties and of none; we must wait humbly for His final appearing, and meanwhile recognize Him wherever, by the clear eyes of love, He can be found.

[1] Matt. xix. 21.   [2] Phil. iii. 3, 19.   [3] Matt. xxiii. 8–10.
[4] Matt. xxiii. 11.   [5] Matt. xxiv. 12.   [6] Matt. xxiv. 26.

When, according to our plan, we pass to the record of the sayings of Jesus which underlies the First and Third Gospels, we find the same insistence upon the spirit of self-absorption in Jesus still more clearly in Matthew's peculiarities. ' Blessed are those who feel poor in the spirit '[1] (' in spirit,' Matthew only), ' the mourners '—on account of their own disabilities (Luke vi. 21, ' you who are weeping ')—' the humble ' (heirs of Christ's kingdom on earth, Matthew only), ' those who pine and faint to be perfectly in harmony with the will of God revealed in Him (cf. iii. 15 ; Luke vi. 21, ' you who are hungry now '), ' the pitiful ' (' for they shall receive the pity,' which they know to be their only hope of redemption, so that they are ' pitiful ' in both senses of that most elastic word, pitiful to all because they feel their own pitiful condition ; this ' beatitude ' also is peculiar to Matthew, though Luke vi. 36 has ' become compassionate,' &c.), ' the pure in heart ' (or, as we should say, the single-minded, those who are delivered from the distraction of meaner motives by their passion for the full realization of the blessing to which they know they have no claim, but a glimpse of which has come their way in Jesus ; they shall attain to the beatific vision—this verse also is found in Matthew only), ' the peacemakers ' (who spend their lives in struggling to call men from lesser issues, that they may be free to listen to the one Voice which reconciles them all—they shall be heralded at last as the heralds of the Coming King (cf. v. 45), who will make the ' peace on earth ' of which those other ' sons of God,' the heralds of His first Advent, sang). All those sentences are, so far as the words specially noted above are concerned, found only in the First Gospel, and all of them alike illustrate the evangelist's spirit as truly as they echo his Master's message. The connecting link between all the Beatitudes is the fact, common to them all, that those are pronounced happy in their prospects who are dissatisfied with present conditions and attainments, who have been caught by the fascination of an Ideal which is always beyond their reach. They are on bad terms with popular ideals without being on easy terms with themselves, their only and availing consolation being that their sufferings are ' for righteousness' sake '—that is for Christ's

[1] Matt. v. 3 ff.

sake[1] (Matthew has first 'for righteousness' sake,' then
'for My sake'; Luke vi. 22, 'for the sake of the Son of
Man '). Called tiresome cranks, if not something worse, by
public opinion[2] ('cast out your name as troublesome'),
they are 'the salt of the earth'[3] (Matthew only). Men
are more curious about them than they care to confess, for
their very isolation makes them, willy-nilly, the observed
of all observers[4] (Matthew only). But they are not to
glory in their peculiarities; they must 'let their light
shine,' not to get themselves talked about, but for the glory
of God[5] (Matthew only), and the diffusion of their radiance
in the circle of their influence (v. 15). They are not to
pose as revolutionists, or take pleasure in shocking people[6]
(Matthew only); they are to appreciate all that is best in
accepted ideals, and improve upon them, not so much
by their displacement as by their more perfect practice
(Matthew only; cf. ix. 17, and xiii. 52).

Chapter v. 21, 22 will be most usefully dealt with
under another heading; but v. 23 (Matthew only)
carries the description of the disciple-spirit a stage
farther. So far from glorying in his separation from his
brother Jew, the Christian is to avoid all possible causes
of offence; before engaging in worship he is to make sure
that no one has any possible ground of grievance, legitimate or otherwise, against him; for Christians of other
times and conditions this means that they are not to
come to the Lord's table before they have settled, so far
as they can, all accounts between themselves and their
fellow Christians (cf. 1 Cor. xi. 27, &c.). They are to
use every opportunity of getting on to friendly terms
with persecuting outsiders, if that can be done without
disloyalty to Christian principle, for they are not to allow
difference of theory to drift into personal quarrel. There
is a noticeable contrast in the renderings of the somewhat
obscure saying embodied in Matt. v. 25 offered us by
Matthew and Luke respectively. According to Luke xii.
58 f., the Christian is to 'take pains *to come to terms with* '
his opponent on the way to the law-court, while Matthew
gives us ' *make friends with* thine opponent readily, while
thou art in the way '; Luke defines being ' on the way '

---

[1] Matt. v. 10, 11, 12.   [2] Mark vi. 22.   [3] Matt. v. 13.
[4] Matt. v. 14.   [5] Matt. v. 16.   [6] Matt. v. 19.

as meaning on the way to the magistrate's court, but
Matthew leaves it open to us to translate more vaguely
and broadly ' when you get '—as we say—' in a good
way ' with him. Matthew's version may be compared
with xviii. 15, ' thou hast gained thy brother,' and
v. 41. Notice also that Matthew has nothing corresponding to ' Salute no one by the way ' (Luke x.
4). The Christian's purpose is not so much to
get quit of a troublesome adversary as to get to know
him better. Clement of Alexandria thought that ' the
adversary ' was Satan—' the adversary ' is probably
the meaning of the word ' Satan,' the ' counsel for the
plaintiff ' (cf. Job i. 6, &c.) ; in much the same way as
in v. 39 ' the evil one ' may well mean ' the devil ' (see
above, p. 227). Probably in both passages, as in Luke
xii. 58 ; xviii. 3, behind the human opponent there lies
the idea of the enemy of souls, who delights to entrap
men in quarrels with one another; we are not to ' leave
room for the devil.'[1] Behind the connected organization
of the human law-court, too, lies the shadow of a more
awful tribunal ; in seeking to extract the ' last farthing '
of your rights from your brother man, you are putting
yourself in the power of a yet more rigid system of law,
by which the man who ' keeps his anger for ever '[2] becomes
himself the victim of the relentless justice in which he
seeks to involve his opponent (cf. Matt. v. 22, ' every
one who persists in anger with his brother ' ; Eph. iv.
26 ; and God's questions in Jonah iv. 4, 9). Chapter
v. 38 ff. has been commented upon already, but
we may notice that the ' Sermon ' becomes more
positive as it proceeds. We are first of all to abstain
from resentful bitterness, and avoid offence[3] ; then we
are to be actively friendly in disposition[4] and in deed[5]
with the most uncongenial people. Here the note of
generosity comes in. The disciple is not to be merely
inoffensive ; he is to be lavish in his spending of himself, to
be an expert in the art of making friends with unattractive
people in record time—on the way to the court, for instance, or on a forced march along a stage of a Roman
road in the dust and the heat and the company of a bullying

[1] Eph. iv. 27. [2] Amos i. 11. [3] Matt. v. 23.
[4] Matt. v. 25. [5] Matt. v. 40, 41.

public official.[1] Jesus does not say what we are to give to every one that asks or wants to borrow[2] (cf. Luke vi. 30, 34) ; perhaps if we render, as the grammar of the Greek allows us, ' Give yourself '—the courtesy of your unaffected interest—' to the man who asks,' we shall not get far away from the sense of His command. Even in the inevitable oppositions into which every earnest man finds himself drawn against his will, he will treat those whom he is compelled to resist with a fundamental respect ; he will think of all men as his neighbours,[3] never allowing reviling to provoke him to reviling,[4] never fighting for his own sake, but for the Kingdom, so always fighting effectively, because he fights clean. Jesus does not say that we are to have no enemies, for we can never be literally ' the friends of all, the enemies of none,' if we care very much for principles, but He does bid us never to keep an enemy, if we can in honesty make a friend ; and as for those with whom we cannot come to terms, we must seek, so far as may be, to combat opinions rather than attack men, and meanwhile pray for our enemies all the more earnestly because we find it so hard to understand or help them in any other way. It is worthy of notice that here, as elsewhere, our Lord founds His teaching upon generally accepted principles. ' Keep out of the law-courts,' ' Cut your losses, and settle a dangerous and awkward dispute when you can,' ' There are two sides to every question,' ' Count a man innocent until you have proved him guilty,' ' The judge ought always to be on the prisoner's side,' are maxims accepted in business and the law ; thought out a little further, they lead directly to the ethical teaching of the great Sermon. Men have no idea to what an extent in theory at least, they do accept the elements of the Lord's teaching ; what is called, for instance, the ' sporting spirit ' is not far from the principle of ' Love your enemies.

In chapter vi. this process of illustration is carried a step farther, from outward relationship and demeanour to the realm of inner motive. The Christian is to be self-effacing in his almsgiving,[5] indeed his generosity is not to give him a comfortable sense of his own virtue;

Matt. v. 25, 41.   [2] Matt. v. 42.   [3] Luke x. 36.
[4] 1 Pet. ii. 23 ; Matt. v. 44.   [5] Matt. vi. 1 ff.

his reward is not to be sought in man's acknowledgement of his beneficence or piety, but in the certainty that his heavenly Father rewards both service and prayer. In praying, he will not use words which mean nothing to him (' Use not vain incantations ' ; but Codex Bezae has ' *blattologesete*,' which apparently is closely related to our ' Don't blether ! ') ; he will not indulge in rhetoric, addressing his Maker as though He were a public meeting, for reverence will teach him simplicity ; if he uses a liturgy, it will be that simplest and most profound of all liturgies, the ' Lord's prayer.' When he fasts, he will not ' make a song about' his austerities, but will be, if anything, rather more sociable than usual. He will allow his way of life to speak for itself, his private self-discipline being a matter which concerns God and his own soul only. The whole of this section, with the exception of the ' Lord's prayer,' is peculiar to this Gospel ; but its main feature, the contrast between the Christian and the professional pietist, is to be discussed in a later chapter. The point which concerns us here is that the disciple is not to be a 'superior person,' for it is exceedingly difficult to be different from others without becoming morbidly conscious of the fact. The only way to escape religious snobbishness is that suggested by the whole trend of this Gospel—habitually to dwell upon Christ's love for us, which we share with all men, rather than upon our love for Him, which may well be kept as a dear secret between ourselves and our Lord ; others will know about it soon enough without our telling them. There are some things too sacred and personal to be exposed to the gaze of every onlooker ; the Christian is not to make a display of ring and pearls, which are the love-tokens of his Lord.[1] Nor does it follow, because you have been a successful propagandist, that you will be recognized as one of His own at last ; that depends upon the hidden life of the heart[2] (cf. Luke xiii. 26).

Leaving the Sermon, we come, in the charge to the twelve, to the words ' become as shrewd as serpents, and as guileless as doves '[3] ; here Codex Bezae gives us a most attractive reading—' very generous as doves.' ' Harmless ' must be wrong, for it is out of the question

[1] Matt. vii. 6.   [2] Matt. vii. 22.   [3] Matt. x. 16.

that Jesus would recommend so colourless a quality
as mere inoffensiveness. If 'generation of vipers'
means 'children of the devil,' may not 'intelligent as serpents' stand for 'clever as the devil'?
This is certainly startling, but the teaching of Jesus is
always piquant, and our rendering is more likely to err
through the timidity falsely called reverence, than through
undue boldness. There is precedent in the Gospels for
an unfavourable comparison between 'the sons of the
light' and 'the sons of this age' in point of prudence
('The sons of this age look further ahead . . . than
the sons of the light,' Luke xvi. 8) ; possibly the underlying idea here too may be, 'Do not leave all the cleverness to the devil.' It is a mistake to suppose that because
we are good, we can be as excused from being as clever
as we can ; we need 'all our wits' about us. But it is
possible that the 'serpent' stands for the symbol of
healing ; compare the 'brazen serpent,' and what is
said above of 'salvation by homoeopathy.' If so, the
saying would mean, 'Be wise healers and generous
lovers of men.' The 'dove' suggests affectionateness
and the reading of Codex Bezae might mean 'affec-
tionate.' The missionary is to be as clever at avoiding
offence as he is successful in winning love, not so much
because of his inoffensiveness or his geniality, as from
the fact that his absorption in the love of his Lord, his
beautiful freedom from self-consciousness, shines through
all that he says and does, protecting him from the tactless-
ness of the propagandist, and at the same time winning
respect for his message by the lovableness of the
messenger.[1]

Matt. xi. 12 f. has already (p. 123) been compared with
Luke xvi. 16. If the suggestion made there be accepted,
it will be seen that Matthew's version points a contrast
between the age of ascetic rigidity which found its culmination in John, and that of pacific appeal ushered
in by Jesus, while Luke regards John's preaching as the
beginning of a new and more strenuous period. As the

---

[1] If the 'serpent' stands symbolically for the devil, may not the dove
represent God's Spirit (cf. Luke 3, 22, &c.) ? the rendering "unite the
devil's shrewdness with love like God's' would make this saying more
pungent still.

section lies before us in the First Gospel, its main theme is clearly the difference in method and demeanour between John the hermit-preacher and Jesus ' the friend of publicans.' The case is clearer in Matt. xxvi. 52 f.; Luke xxii. 35 ff., 49; in the First Gospel the disciples carry swords, apparently without the connivance of Jesus, and ' one of those with Jesus ' is sharply rebuked for his attempt to defend him. He does not need human support now; it will only bring disaster. If He chose, He could summon a countless host of heavenly legionaries. According to Luke's account, on the other hand, He tells His followers that they will need swords. Two are immediately forthcoming, and He says—whether ironically or not, it is hard to say—' That will do.' Then, when one of the disciples uses the weapon, which he had been encouraged to bring, Jesus does not rebuke him, but only asks to be allowed to heal the severed ear.[1] This section of the Third Gospel is admittedly obscure, and the words of Jesus[2]—' He was classed among criminals: for my history has come to an end ' (cf. Mark iii. 26)—have been interpreted as meaning that for the moment the Lord had lost hope of a kingdom of peace on the earth. I find it difficult, for reasons stated in a previous chapter (p. 204), to resist the conclusion that there is an undertone of something like despair here. If we translate Mark iii. 26 ' It (Satan's kingdom) cannot stand, but hath come to an end,' we ought to render the same phrase in much the same way in this place too. Perhaps it was of the *speedy* coming of the Kingdom of which Jesus had come to despair; His demeanour at the trial, which follows almost immediately, is sufficient proof that He never really lost hope of its eventual triumph. But the whole subject of the hope and disappointment of Jesus can best be discussed when we come to the eschatological question. There can be little doubt that the passage reflects a very dark moment in the thoughts of the Saviour—for another see the last clause of Luke xviii. 8; the agony of Gethsemane is drawing in upon Him. His immediate concern is the future of His disciples. They are not to fight for Him— so much is clear from Mark xxvi. 52—but they may have to face a struggle for freedom if they did not leave

[1] Luke xxii. 51.   [2] Luke xxii. 37.

Him soon ; He does not intend to resist, and cannot guard
them by the force of His personality any longer. When
they were away on their missionary journeys, they were
His agents, His great name still protected them (Mark ix.
41, ' because ye are Christ's '), and opened all doors.
Now for a time He would not be available ; His name as
' a tainted wether of the flock ' would be under a cloud.
They had best leave Him and arrange for their own
security during the next few hours. Besides, He would
be glad to be alone. He had stayed with them as long
as He could be happy ; now that the ' climbing ' sorrow
is rising too high in His heart for suppression, for their
sake and for His He would have them leave Him. The
struggle must be fought to the end alone, without inter-
ference on the part of His friends. To them His broken
tones sound like an appeal, and they are proud to think
that they have prepared for every contingency beforehand. ' Lord, here are two swords,' they say, and He
answers sadly, ' That will do.' Only three of them are
allowed to go on with Him into the garden, but they are not
to come too near ; if they can only keep awake and pray,
that will be their best security. It is remarkable that
Luke omits the fact of their desertion[1] ; we should gather
that they followed the Lord all the way to the cross if
we had not the evidence of the other Gospels for their
withdrawal (Luke xxiii. 49 implies that the eleven as
well as the other friends of Jesus were watching). After
the futile attempt to defend their Master, however, none
of them, except Peter, take any further part in the action.
Too much stress should not be laid upon their
disappearance in Luke, for the third evangelist has
a way of dropping side-issues when the action tends
to centre more intensely round the pivotal figure
(notice how John the Baptist disappears in the
Gospel, and Peter in the Acts). Our general inference
must be that Jesus did allow the disciples to provide
for their own defence in a special emergency, whereas
Matthew stresses the fact that He would not let them
think of defending Him ; He would spare them, never
Himself. ' He who takes the sword shall perish by the
sword ' states an eternal principle, for war brings

[1] Luke xxii. 53.

destruction in its train, however just the cause. Each evangelist has been led by his own instincts to bring out the aspect of the situation which most appealed to him. It is obvious that Matthew's choice corresponds to the general temper of his Gospel. Force may be a temporary expedient; it can never be a final remedy for anything, and it always reacts upon the man or nation using it.

We are not surprised to find that this book is, *par excellence*, the children's gospel, for everything which the Lord says in its pages about His ' little brothers ' applies to those whom we too call ' little ones.' The ' Child ' Himself is the centre of the Birth story, and the mystery of the Baby-King, the God who was weak and little, is enshrined in the story of the wise men who were wise and humble enough to offer their homage to the Hope of the world in the person of a Child. Matthew alone records the massacre at Bethlehem,[1] and the fact that children were present at the two wonderful supper-parties ; he specially observes that they *all* got their share[2] (' all,' Matthew only). The phrase ' one of these little ones '[3] (Mark ix. 41, ' you ') is peculiar to this Gospel, as also is the record of the fact that ' children ' sang the praises of Jesus so loudly as to attract attention,[4] and the answer of the Master to their critics (xxi. 16). Indeed, the First Gospel contains the Children's Charter.

[1] Matt. ii. 16 ff.   [2] Matt. xiv. 20, 21 ; xv. 37, 38.
[3] Matt. x. 42, xviii. 10, 14, xxv. 40–45.   [4] Matt. xxi. 15.

VI

'HOW SHALL WE ESCAPE IF WE NEGLECT
SO GREAT SALVATION?'

THE emphasis laid by the first evangelist upon the risk of
missing the soul's great opportunity is the reverse aspect
of his insistence upon the greatness of the Lord's Person,
when He offered Himself to undone sinners. He is God's
only Son ('beloved' means 'only' in the language of the
day—iii. 17; xvii. 5), in whom God is pleased to reveal
Himself—'in whom I am well pleased' (only elsewhere
Mark i. 11; Luke iii. 22; but compare Matt. xi. 26; Luke
x. 21). He came as a 'great light' to 'Galilee of the
Gentiles,' where men sat 'under the shadow of death'[1]
(Matthew only), and 'in His name shall the Gentiles hope,'
for 'He shall thrust forth justice to' its final 'victory.'[2]
'Every kind of sin and blasphemy shall be forgiven' men,
blasphemy against the Spirit incarnate in Him never, 'in
this or the coming age'; the words 'in this,' &c., are not
found in the best MSS. of Luke xii. 10.[3] He is Lord and
Judge of all personal spirits[4] ('Hast Thou come to torture
us before the time?' Matthew only); if in the spirit
of God He casts out the demons, then the Kingdom has
already come upon men[5] (Luke xi. 20, 'by the
finger of God'). The gauntlet of mortal conflict has already been cast down before the reigning powers of darkness by the One stronger than they, for the word spoken
by Isaiah *is now* being fulfilled[6] (Mark–Luke, '*that* seeing
they *may* not perceive,' &c.; Matt. xiii. 13, '*because* seeing
they *do* not perceive'), and secrets hidden from the foundation of the world are now coming out[7] (Matthew only). The
issue between good and evil forces has been pressed forward

---

[1] Matt. iv. 15, 16. [2] Matt. xii. 20, 21. [3] Matt. xii. 32. [4] Matt. viii. 29.
[5] Matt. xii. 28.   [6] Matt. xiii. 14.   [7] Matt. xiii. 35.

by the coming of the Lord. ' Weeds ' as well as ' wheat '[1]
have been sown in the world's harvest-field, while men
slept[2]; the ' net ' of the Master's teaching[3] (Matthew only)
has drawn into the scope of the new movement's influence
men ' of every kind ' (compare the symbolism of Luke v. 6,
where the ' nets ' show signs of giving way under the strain
of ingathering, with that of John xxi. 11, where the 'net'
is not broken), and the ' harvest ' is imminent at ' the
consummation of (this) age ' (ix. 37 f.; xiii. 39, 40, 49; xxviii.
20; cf. John iv. 35 ff.; Mark iv. 29) ; compare ' in the
regeneration '—that is, ' in the world to be ' and ' in the
coming age '[4] (both peculiar to Matthew).

It would seem that Jesus thought of the time of His
coming as one of the great creative ages of the world's
history, and it would be comparatively easy to account for
the eschatological atmosphere, so pervasive in the First
Gospel especially, by the suggestion that He looked forward to a succession of such periods, each leading to a crisis
and the birth of a new world. It is clear, at any rate, that
Luke has interpreted sayings which in Matthew seem to
be concerned with the end of the whole world-order
historically of the fall of Jerusalem, which might be called
the consummation of the particular age ushered in by our
Lord. Matthew may have fused with statements which
originally referred to that crisis other sayings which dealt
with an agelong process, of which that catastrophe was an
illustration. We might fairly, I think, argue that the
result of such confusion would be a certain amount of
foreshortening, since none of the evangelists could be
expected to appreciate the range of the Lord's prophetic
vision. But this convenient theory, by which every
prophecy that has not come true may be ascribed to misunderstanding on the part of one or other of the evangelists,
is founded rather upon a wish to counter the suggestion
that Jesus was the prophet of a world-revolution that
has never matured, than upon any very substantial
evidence, except the somewhat precarious argument, ' That
is the way in which things have turned out, and so, whatever the Gospels say or do not say, Jesus must have foreseen
that.'

[1] Matt. xiii. 2 ff., 36 ff. [3] Matt. xiii. 47 ff.
[2] Mark iv. 27 ; Matt. xiii. 25. [4] Matt. xix. 28, xii. 32.

The actual facts of the recorded words of Jesus upon this subject should lead us to suspect all generalizations on one side or the other—to the effect, namely, that He did, or did not, expect a single catastrophic act of God as a result of His life or His death, or both. If, on the one hand, we read that He said, ' There are some of you standing here that shall not taste of death until they see the Kingdom . . . having (fully) come in power'[1] (Matthew, xvi. 28, drops the perfect tense, and substitutes for ' having come in power' ' the Son of Man coming in His kingdom'; Luke ix. 27 stops short at 'the kingdom of God '), and 'you shall not have gone through the cities of Israel till the Son of Man be come '[2] (Matthew only), He also said, according to Mark at least,[3] that He Himself did not know the hour of the end ; according to Matthew[4] (emphasized still more strongly in Luke xix. 11, 12) that He would be away 'a long time.' Mark xiii., with the parallel discourse in Matt. xxiv., presents what looks like a contradiction in the same series of prophecies. It is probable that such discrepancies as exist are due to deficiencies in the media through which the evidence as to what Jesus actually said has come down to us ; sayings which referred to moments in an agelong process have come to be associated with its final issue by men of more contracted vision than was the first Speaker. There can be little doubt, moreover, that the intrusion of the ' fly-sheet ' (see pp. 77, 78) has caused disturbance here. Taken along with the principle, acknowledged by Jewish thinkers and all reasonable men, that the *time of the fulfilment of prophecy* is dependent upon human conditions of faith or unbelief, this consideration may help to reconcile discrepancies in the Gospel tradition, and account for the tendency, already manifest in the Third Gospel and unmistakable in the Fourth, to leave upon one side this dangerous question. It is clear that Christians of the first century did expect a speedy winding-up of the world-process[5] ; Jesus, with His profounder knowledge of the power of evil, was not always so confident as they.[6]   It is much more likely that His

[1] Mark ix. 1.   [2] Matt. x. 23.   [3] Mark xiii. 32.
[4] Matt. xxv. 19, cf. xxv. 5, xxiv. 48.
[5] cf. e.g. 1 Cor. vii. 29 ; 1 John ii. 18 ; Rev. xxii. 20; 2 Pet. iii. 4.
[6] cf. Luke xviii. 8 ; Matt. xxv. 19, xxiv. 6; Mark xiii. 7 ; Luke xvii. 22, xix. 11, xxi. 9.

reporters have interpreted His words in accordance with
their own lively hopes than that the Synoptic Gospels are
later compositions of men anxious to tone down prophecies
which had not, as a matter of fact, come true.

The principal fact which emerges from a careful study
of the material at our disposal is that references to the
imminence of the Kingdom tend to come near the beginning
and so refer to the fall of Jerusalem ; intimations of
possible long delay towards the end of the ministry.
Outside chapter xiii., the last prophecy of a very speedy
coming of the Kingdom occurs in Mark at ix. 1, for xiv. 62
is not decisive ; as to xiii. 30, its position is so dubious
that we cannot be sure that, if it was uttered by Jesus
in the course of the last week of His life, it may not really
belong to vv. 14–23. At the outset of the ' acceptable
year in Galilee, the note of assured expectation rings
out with no uncertain sound. 'The Kingdom of God
is at hand ' must have been the first message of Jesus ;
otherwise we could not account for the misunderstandings
• to which the political interpretation of this war-cry gave
rise in the lakeside towns. Coming towards the end of
His career in Galilee, Matt. x. 23 sounds the same note,
and in Mark ix. 1, when the cross is already full in view,
the Kingdom's final triumph within the lifetime of some
of ' those who stood by ' is still confidently foretold.
But, some time before this, appreciation of inevitable
hindrances to its final coming has become increasingly
evident. For the Lord Himself there is a Cross, for His
followers persecution, for the world war and all kinds of
painful divisions.[1] The parable of the seed growing
secretly combines enforcement of the truth that the
Kingdom moves forward by unseen and gradual processes
with an assurance that, once the harvest is ripe, there
is to be no delay. The seed grows while the Sower ' sleeps
and rises night and day.'[2] This is interesting, because it
hints that Jesus Himself had to preach without visible
result ; ' He knoweth not how' suggests the same thing still
more explicitly. Schweitzer and the extreme eschatologists
hold that to the end Jesus expected the immediate final
coming of the Kingdom, first of all by His preaching and
that of His disciples ; then, when preaching failed, by

[1] Matt. x. 17 ff, 34 ff ; Mark viii. 31 ff.   [2] Mark iv. 26 ff.

the Cross. They explain the agony in the garden and the last despairing cry by the suggestion of an expectation disappointed at the final crisis.

Such a theory, it seems to the present writer, ignores a whole series of facts manifest to any student of the Gospels who does not choose to distort from their natural sense or altogether to cancel passages which do not suit a particular theory. Leaving upon one side Mark xiii. 10, which perhaps should not count if xiii. 30 be excluded upon the other side, there are the repeated references to ' a long time '; there is Luke xix. 11 to be reckoned with, and Mark xiii. 32; for reasons explained in an earlier chapter, there can be little doubt that the last-mentioned verse contains an authentic saying of Jesus. I believe, however, that these interpreters have proved that disappointment had a very great effect upon the thoughts of Jesus. We noticed that the hope of the Kingdom tends to lose its prominence in the teaching of the Master, as His ministry draws towards its close. In Mark ii.–x. 31 ' the Kingdom ' is mentioned ten times by Jesus ; after• x. 32—where, in Mark, the journey to Jerusalem begins in earnest—only twice. For Matthew the figures are (roughly) thirty-four times before xx. 19 ; afterwards six times—thrice in the conventional phrase ' the Kingdom of Heaven is like,' &c. ; once in the phrase ' the Kingdom is taken from you '—in itself a token of disappointment as to the immediate coming of the Kingdom. Statistics in Luke's Gospel follow very much on the same lines.

Our inference will be that, as the ministry went on, Jesus thought less of ' the Kingdom ' considered in itself; more of the part which His own death and resurrection was to play in the coming nearer of God's day. ' The coming of the Son of Man ' takes the place of the coming of the Kingdom. This fact is not merely perceptible in each of the Gospels taken by itself, but it also becomes increasingly evident in the process of Gospel tradition. ' The Kingdom ' is more predominant in Q than in Mark, more central in Mark than in the sections of Matthew and Luke which do not come from Q or Mark, least conspicuous of all in John ; so that the course of early Christian reflexion upon the mission of Jesus corresponds to what may with justice be inferred from the most reliable Gospel sources themselves as to the Master's own development. Indeed, this is what we might have expected. The expectation of the nearness of the Kingdom was the inevitable issue of the Lord's instinctive consciousness of God. For the saintliest amongst us it is hard to imagine God as taking a part in the affairs of men and nations ; we have grown accustomed to the separation of sacred and secular, a distinction which did not exist for Jesus. To come near the realization that God is everywhere is for us a great achievement. For Him the difficulty would be to make real to Himself the fact that we could not take that for granted as He did. That He was 'Son of God' He assumed, but He would not have denied us the same title (see, e.g., Matt. v. 45). We must, of course, be careful in our treatment of His first impressions, for we must remember that He did not begin His ministry without a knowledge of the sin of the world ; much painful experience would come His way at Nazareth, for it was no secluded haunt of innocence. His childhood and working life was passed in face of most of the social ills of an evil time. When He spoke in later days of a boy who left home for the 'far country,' He was reporting what happened continually in the upland villages of Galilee ; Nazareth was close to the great Roman road, the way of the sea, along which lay the kingdoms of the world and the glory of them. Many of His companions went out into the great world to make their fortune, we may be sure, and shocking stories of their experiences would float back to the village. The Temptation scene is enough to show that the romance of adventure had its charm for Jesus, and that the evil of the world, given over to ' the devil,' was part of His stock of experience.

Still, there is no mistaking the quiet confidence of His early preaching. With most of us it is the obvious social evils of our time that first react upon our conscience and rouse our crusading instincts ; only much later do we come to realize that there are worse things than immorality and social injustice, worse because harder to deal with. To some extent people can be made sober by Act of Parliament, more certainly by what Jesus looked for, ' an act of God'; they cannot be made sincere or charitable by any scheme of social betterment. Perhaps

Y

Jesus never believed much in organizing social reform ;
but we can trace in His first preaching, and specially
in the Sermon on the Mount, the conviction that men
only needed to be told about the new way of life, and they
would surely accept it. He knew Himself our Brother ;
how hard it must have been for Him to realize that His
little brothers were so different from Himself ! It is
as though He said, ' Here am I with the good news of the
Kingdom ; one push—all together—and we shall be
there ! ' By-and-by He begins to be surprised at men's
' unbelief,' and in two of His early parables we find, on
the one hand, a very cool analysis of His prospects of
successful propaganda[1] ; on the other, the quiet assurance
that the results were real, though not always immediately
visible.[2] All the time He is aware that there are as yet
only ' few ' who find the narrow way ; but these few are
the ' light of the world,' and for a time He is content
to go on preaching and trust to the power of the message,
of which He was so sure, to do its work. ' Of herself the
earth brings forth fruit ' surely means that one of His
assumptions was that human life, as He found it, was
capable of producing the harvest of the Kingdom by
perfectly natural means. The message which He brought
was already written upon the hearts of His listeners, if
He could only get there !

If He could get there ! That was the problem which
came to weigh upon the mind and heart of the Master
more and more as time went on. The difficulty of making
men feel as He felt led Him to ponder His own spiritual
loneliness. Why was He so different from every one
else ? What did men mean by calling Him ' good ' ?
He is curious to know what they said of Him when His
back was turned.[3] The conclusion to which He was
—we may be sure very reluctantly—forced was that He
was absolutely unique ; this is summed up in the great
saying found in Matt. xi. 27 f. ; Luke x. 21 f. He alone
has the secret of the new way of life which men and nations
must make their own before the Kingdom could come.
In Matthew the claim ' All things have been delivered,'
&c., comes immediately, and most significantly, after
His recognition of the almost total failure of His preaching

---

[1] Mark iv. 1 ff., 11 ff.   [2] Mark iv, 27.   [3] Matt. xvi. 13 ; Mark x. 17.

and works of mercy in the towns of the Galilean lakeside. Somehow men must be induced to come and stay with Him a little while, till they learned to look out of His eyes; they must watch Him live, and see how desirable, how livable, the kind of life He recommended was. What preaching will not do perhaps companionship will achieve: He had already chosen 'twelve, to be with Him'; now He will try to widen the circle of His intimates. I believe that this is the explanation of the feeding of the five thousand; the sacramental interpretation offered in the Fourth Gospel is in principle right. Jesus will, if it be possible, admit all and sundry into His fellowship; He will not speak of 'the many' as 'those who are without'[1] any longer. Notice 'He began'—a new departure—' to teach them many things' (Mark vi. 34). This attempt failed. They would not 'come,' and if they came they would not stay; the more He took them into His confidence, the more flagrantly they misunderstood Him. From this time forward the shadow of the cross begins to darken the thoughts of Jesus.

But before we come to discuss the last phase of the Lord's ministry from this angle of vision, we must say something about two dark problems; they are the fate of the lost, and the meaning of that 'hypocrisy,' so often denounced by Jesus. ' The fire of Gehenna ' (Matt. xviii. 9, cf. v. 29, 30 ; Mark ix. 43, 45, 47 ; Matt. v. 22, xxiii. 15, ' a son of Gehenna,' 33, ' a sentence to Gehenna '; Luke xii. 5 is its only occurrence in the Third Gospel) should not be confused with ' Sheol ' or ' Hades,' the world of the dead.[2] The ' valley of the sons of Hinnom ' is called ' the valley ' in Jer. ii. 23, xxxi. 40 ; ' the accursed valley ' in Enoch xxvii. 2. In the time of Ahaz and Manasseh it had been the scene of human sacrifices,[3] for in this ravine were the ' high places of Tophet ' afterwards defiled by Josiah, but rebuilt under Jehoiakim.[4] Kimchi says that Gehenna was ' a despised place, into which were taken corpses and other refuse, and there was a perpetual fire to burn the refuse and the bones.' This last assertion is challenged by modern scholars, who deny that there is any evidence for other fires than those of Molech (but

---

[1] Mark iv. 11. [2] Matt. xi. 23 ; Luke x. 15 ; Matt. xvi. 18.
[3] 2 Kings xxiii. 10.; 2 Chron. xxviii. 2; xxxiii. 6. [4] Jer. vii. 31.

cf. Heb. xiii. 11). Association with these ill-omened flames led to the symbolic use of the name 'Gehenna' for the 'place of pain,'[1] where apostate Jews were punished in the presence of the righteous 'in quenchless fire.'[2] In the Book of Enoch 'Sheol' has four divisions, two for the righteous and two for the wicked. A special fate is reserved for those who have escaped punishment in this life. After a preliminary course of great pain in 'Sheol,' they are to be raised at the last judgement to receive the punishment of Gehenna, the final place of punishment; while 'Sheol' is intermediate for guilty angels, demons, and kings.[3] In the same book a 'burning furnace' is described as the ultimate abode of fallen angels (cf. Matt. xxv. 41). In the Book of Judith the 'furnace' is the destiny of the heathen generally—contrast the discriminating judgement of the heathen in Matt. xxv. 32 ff. ; and in the Assumption of Moses—quoted in Jude 9 —the Wisdom of Solomon,[4] and the Slavonic Enoch it is the final hell of all the wicked.

In the New Testament Gehenna is a place for spiritual punishment.[5] Its characteristics is 'fire'[6] ('quenchless fire' in Mark ix. 43, 48 ; Matt. iii. 12 ; Luke iii. 17 ; 'agelong fire,' Matt. xxv. 41, xviii. 8 ; cf. xxv. 46) and 'darkness' (cf. Matt. xiii. 42, 50 with viii. 12, xxii. 13, xxv. 30) ; in the Book of Revelation it is called 'the lake of fire' or 'fire and brimstone.'[7] In regard to the 'end-lessness' of this punishment, Dr. Charles thinks that Luke xii. 47, 48 ; Matt. xi. 24 (cf. also Matt. x. 15 ; Luke xx. 47, x. 12, 14) imply a relative mitigation for some sufferers at least ; he is perhaps justified in tracing a suggestion of moral reformation in Luke xvi. 27, and Matt. xii. 32 *seems* to hint that some sins may be for-given in the 'coming age,' while Matt. v. 26 (Luke xii. 59) *can* be taken as holding out a precarious hope of deliverance when the 'last farthing' has been paid. All that we could safely say, apart from the Cross, would be that God rules over Hades,[8] and will always be the merciful Father revealed by Jesus. We have no warrant for the importation into the word which I have translated

---

[1] Isa. l. 11. [2] Isa. lxvi. 24. [3] Matt. viii. 29 ; 1 Pet. iii. 19 f.
[4] Wisdom iv. 19. [5] Luke xii. 5 ; Matt. x. 28. [6] Matt. v. 22, xviii. 9.
[7] Rev. xix. 20, xx. 10, 15. [8] Rev. i. 18, &c.

age-long '—that is, lasting from age to age—the notion of
time limitation, for the very notion of time duration is
outside its scope. In the words of Jesus there is nowhere
any emphasis upon the physical details of punishment,
as in contemporary Jewish literature, the Fathers, and
the sermons of an older day ; Jesus touches the subject
with manifest reluctance, in figures terrible indeed from
their very vagueness, but which would not darken the
imagination of a child, as sermons preached by good
men in our early days could and did. Even if the Passion
of our Lord had no relevance to other worlds than this,
we need not believe that the life of the finally impenitent,
if there are to be any such, is to be one of mere punishment ;
Matt. xxv. 46, xxvi. 24b, xviii. 34, with Luke xvi. 23,
are the most explicit references in the Gospels, and all
may be interpreted of the torment of belated remorse,
like the ' wailing and gnashing of teeth ' of Matt. xiii.
42, viii. 12, xxii. 13, xxiv. 51 xxv. 30—only elsewhere
Luke xiii. 28.

These words, ' destruction '[1] (Matthew only), ' fire,'
and ' darkness,' echo through the pages of this Gospel
very mournfully, and we must steadily refuse to minimize
the threatening character of some of the best attested
words of Jesus. We might conclude that the men and
societies to whom this menacing intolerance is displayed
are those who can best be described by negatives—savour-
less salt, the man without the wedding-garment, the
useless slave, and so on—if it were not that the Lord shows
a special pity for colourless people, unemployed, because
supposed unemployable, within the covers of this same
Gospel.[2] What can be done with the man who has seen
his Lord, or, for the matter of that, has seen his brother,
in need—for these two are one—and turns his back ?
He is to be found in all societies ; but how did he come
to be where he is and what he is ?[3] Is there any cause
in nature for these hard hearts ? Jesus recognized
the fact of the existence of people for whom, as they are,
neither God nor man has any use ; they are ' good for
nothing, but to be cast outside[4] (cf. xxv. 30, xxii. 13)
and trampled under feet *of men* ' (Matthew only ; cf.
Mark ix. 50 ; Luke xiv. 34). Nor is this vein of unrelenting

Matt. vii. 13.   [2] Matt. xx. 7.   [3] Matt. xxii. 12.   [4] Matt. v. 13.

disdain only to be found in one Gospel, though it is most remarkable here ; it hangs like a thundercloud on the borders of the Saviour's most cheering invitations and promises. The men whom the Lord says He will 'cut dead'[1] are the 'whitewashed tombs,' plausible people who compound for the camels which the logic of their practice compels them to swallow by straining out theoretical mosquitoes,[2] sailing away from every encounter with reality in a cloud of traditional claims, of words hallowed by the usage of the pious.[3] To increase their own prestige they will box the theological compass— that is what 'compass sea and land'[4] (Matthew only) seems to mean—for they are regarded by the 'hungry sheep' which 'look up, and are not fed,' as great authorities ; they 'brandish the keys of the Kingdom' in men's faces ; they do not enter themselves, and are a hindrance to easily overawed people, who, but for them, would find their way in[5] (Matthew only).

In order to do justice to this aspect of this stern and tender Gospel, we must discuss a little more fully the meaning of the word 'hypocrite.' It occurs in vi. 2, 5, 16, vii. 5 (Luke vi. 42), as also in the 'Curetonian' Syriac version in vi. 7, vii. 5 (Luke vi. 42) ; in xv. 7 (Mark vii. 6) ; in xxii. 18, xxiii. 13, 15, 23, 25, 27, 29, xxiv. 51 (Luke xii. 46, 'unbelievers' or 'unbelieving'). With the two exceptions noted, all these examples are peculiar to Matthew ; but it should be observed that Luke xii. 1 has 'hypocrisy,' which is absent from Matt. xvi. 6 ; Mark viii. 15, and that Mark alone has the same word at xii. 15 (cf. Matt. xxii. 18 ; Luke xx. 23). In addition to these passages, Matthew only has 'evil things' at ix. 4, 'rapacious wolves in sheep's clothing,'[6] 'false prophets'[7] (xxiv. 24 is paralleled by Mark xiii. 22), and 'brood of vipers'[8] (xxiii. 33, 'snakes, vipers' brood' ; Luke reports the expression as used by John[9] (cf. Matt. iii. 7), but not by Jesus. The Greek word translated 'hypocrite' means 'play-actor,' and this sense is not absent from the Aramaic word used by the Lord Himself. But there was no Jewish drama in the Greek or English sense of the word, and we must

---

[1] Matt. vii. 23.   [4] Matt. xxiii. 15.   [7] Matt. vii. 15.
[2] Matt. xxiii. 24, 27.   [5] Matt. xxiii. 13.   [8] Matt. xii. 34.
[3] Matt. vi. 7, vii. 22.   [6] Matt. vii. 15   [9] Luke iii. 7.

be careful not to read into an essentially Semitic conception associations native only to Greek soil. The terrible strokes of Jesus were not directed merely against the special kind of religious make-believe, commonly recognized as hypocrisy. 'The leaven of the Pharisees, which is hypocrisy'[1] is most dangerous, precisely because it is hidden, masked by good, or partly good, intentions; the original expression covers unconscious as well as deliberate pretence. This consideration gives us the clue to the indignant polemic directed against the Pharisees. At all costs they must be made to see themselves as they really were ; or, if that is impossible, they must be exposed to their dupes. This was the burning centre of the Lord's Passion, that with the great majority of middle-class Jewish people, the very backbone of the nation, He could not get past the mountainous barrier of pride and prejudice which barred His way to their hearts. His complaint at the end would be, 'I never knew *you*.'[2] It was certainly not for lack of trying. If He could not win them by friendliness—Luke[3] tells us how often He went out to dinner at the houses of Pharisees—then He would set Himself to sting them into sincerity, for their own sake and that of the people who followed them so blindly.[4] It was the unseen corroding evil huddled up in the hearts of men and societies, the jealousy called zeal, the narrow-heartedness and cruelty called orthodoxy, the suicidal factiousness called patriotism, that baffled Him. Zeal, orthodoxy, patriotism, are good things, for Jesus was Himself zealous for the best traditions of the past, orthodox, and patriotic[5] ; they become the shelter of the worst evils when they harden into hatred of unaccustomed and uncomfortable light, a pretext for the refusal to think and grow.

So the Lord makes it His business to force out into the light this masked pretence.[6] In the thrust and parry of His Judaean encounters, in words which burn on through the centuries from the pages of the First Gospel, He seeks to carry this barrier by storm—in vain. There is one

---

[1] Luke xii. 1.
[2] Matt. vii. 23.
[3] Luke vii. 36 ff., xi. 37 ff., xiv. 1 ff., &c.
[4] Matt. xv. 14, &c.
[5] John ii. 17 ; Matt. xxiii. 2–3 ; v. 18–19 ; John xi. 52.
[6] Matt. x. 26, &c.

thing yet that He can do : He will draw the arch-enemy's
fire upon Himself, for men must be made to see what this
unrealized evil means ; to see sin at its worst, we must
see the Best at its mercy. At last the devil can hide no longer,
for the sinlessness of Jesus gives him no cover[1] ; Satan
makes his own terms.[2]　We cannot realize the horror
of evil, because we are all tainted ; think of the imagination
of Jesus, who never took a drug ![3]　Evil for evil's sake
must have been unintelligible to Jesus.　In the story of
the woman taken in adultery[4] He seems to be utterly
unable to speak calmly of an actual case of sin so common
that we call it ' the social evil.'　When it was discussed
in general terms He could pronounce upon it clearly[5];
Matt. v. 32 ; Luke xvi. 18, come from Q ; Mark x. 2
(cf. Matt. xix. 3) gives us the context.　When a ' fallen
woman,' that symbol of waste and shame, stood before
Him, He scribbled nervously on the ground, until He
had regained His self-command.　But when He did speak
He was sure-handed as ever.　Before the mystery of
insincerity He is moved rather to scornful protest.　' How
can you talk so well, and be so bad ? ' He exclaimed
once.[6]　This outburst of exasperated incredulity reminds
us of another great soul, incomparably weaker and less
pure, but faintly like Him in his passionate sincerity :
' My tables ! meet it is I set it down ; that one may smile
and smile, and be a villain ! '　This last evil Jesus could
not conquer, yet He could not take it for granted ; He
could only watch men drawing away from Him, their
only Hope, on the very threshold of the hell which He
alone had seen.　He would spring to their side, stand
between them and the edge of perdition, would be their
Brother to the end ; we have already tried to catch a
glimpse of what this meant for Him.　For us it means
that the issue of His self-identification with our sin and
despair is that we can be identified, if we will, with His
perfect righteousness and triumph.[7]

The stages of this tragic victory are all marked out
in this Gospel.　Side by side are set the pity and anger
of Jesus, the ecstasy of those who find Him, the threatened
doom of those who miss Him.　In His denunciations of

[1] John xiv. 30.　　[2] Luke xxii. 31 f.　　[3] Mark xv. 23.
[4] John vii. 53, viii. 11.　[5] Mark x. 2.　[6] Matt. xii. 34.　[7] 2 Cor. v. 21, &c.

sin, in His teaching of righteousness, He is Prophet,
Spokesman of the wrath and gentleness of God; in His death
He is priest; because He was and is both, He is for ever
King. As I read this Gospel, rightly the first, yet once
again, and lay the book down and dream, there is but
One Face that I see, as there is but One that I am meant
to see. It is a Face that looks at first out upon the world
with unclouded eyes. As He says, 'Come unto Me,'
see how they come, as doves to their windows! Men
bring their burdens and lay them down at His feet.[1]
But why do they not all come? The serene Face passes,
and I see Another, yet the Same—a Face in storm with
anger and pity, each kindled by the other, as He turns
to the men who will not come, and would keep others
away.[2] Then again the picture fades, and all that I
can see is a Figure going into the outer darkness after
the men who have shrunk from His appeal, leaving His
lovers behind, out of the upper room, lit by His own
radiant consciousness of God, His joy in the fellowship
of His friends. Then a cry and a great silence; then
the Unclouded Face again, as the Lord brings back with
Him the assurance of a world redeemed. We have passed
from the devil's vaunt, ' I will give Thee all their authority
and their glory because it has been handed over to me,'[3]
to ' All authority hath been given unto Me, in heaven and
on earth.'[4] But I cannot forget those other men, too
proud to ' lay ' their ' reasonings at His feet,'[5] who call
Him ' Lord,' and will not serve His little brothers.[6] I
cannot forget them because they are so much like me.
We do well to pay heed to the warning, so often pressed
in the Lord's teaching that ' many ' will miss the narrow
way of self-forgetting adoration.[7] It is so easy in a hard
and suspicious world to drift into hardness and bitterness
ourselves that there are still but few who keep the child-
heart, humble enough to lose itself in the love of Jesus,
only too happy to look, to listen, and to live. My comfort
is that the Lord's blood was shed, His life was given,
not for the few exceptional people only, but for the
' many.'[8] We may be casual, shallow, prejudiced,

[1] Matt. xiv. 12. [4] Matt. xxviii. 18. [6] Matt. xxv. 24, 44, 45.
[2] Matt. xxiii. 13. [5] Matt. xxv. 24, 30. [7] Matt. vii. 13, xxii. 14.
[3] Luke iv. 6. [8] Matt. xx. 28, xxvi. 28, &c.

too busy or too much worried to listen as thoughtfully as we should to the message of Jesus ; we cannot be too busy to love One who, when He saw the hell of bitterness and shame to which our evil passions were leading us, said, ' I am your Brother ; and if you will not come My way I will go yours ' ; who, even when men like ourselves were tearing Him in their jealous hatred, was willing to forfeit the heaven which He alone knew, and enter the hell which only He had seen, if need were, for their sakes. The sterner side of His teaching remains. We can only trust to the bottomless abyss of the love of God and to the tireless and availing prayers of Jesus, who, when He allowed Himself to be entangled in the net of our sin, yet did not cease to be One with God, and could not be ' holden of death.' Yet with all the hope shed by the Cross and the Open Tomb upon this dark problem, the fact faces us still : to miss Jesus in this life is to doom oneself at least to a very long and very bitter remorse, to a loss which can never quite be made up for. That the very half-realized insincerity which baffled the Master of souls during His ministry proved to be His ground of hope on the cross, we have seen already (p. 203).

VII

THE SECRET LIFE OF THE CHRISTIAN AND ITS FRUITS

WE have already referred to Matthew's use of the word 'righteousness' (iii. 14; v. 6, 10, 20; vi. 1, 33; xxi. 32) and of the adjective 'righteous' (i. 19; x. 41; xiii. 17, 43, 49; xx. 4; xxiii. 35 (Luke xi. 51 omits); xxv. 37, 46). The verb—to 'justify'—occurs once, in a very striking verse, to which reference is to be made directly.[1] 'Righteousness' in this Gospel covers both the Pharisaic ideal of perfect obedience to the will of God in things both great and small, and also the hidden rightness from which alone such obedience can spring. If the roots of the Christian's virtues are more deeply imbedded in his secret life with God than are those of its Pharisaic counterpart[2] (Matthew only), its fruits will be more abundant[3] (cf. iii. 10; xxi. 41). The Christian is distinguished from Pharisee, pagan, and publican alike by the little 'extra' in his achievement, the last straw of virtue which makes all the difference (v. 20, 40, 41, 46, 47; compare xiii. 12; xxv. 29, 'and he shall have abundance'—in both cases, as in v. 20, 47, the words which contain the idea of the 'extra,' the splashing over of the tide of grace, are peculiar to Matthew; but compare Mark iv. 15, last clause). Closely parallel to this association of inward reality with its outward evidences is the use in the First Gospel of the idea of 'reward' in v. 46 (Luke vi. 32, 'grace,' but in v. 35, as in v. 23 (Matt. v. 12), 'reward'); vi. 1, 2, 5, 16 (these references are peculiar to Matthew.) Pharisees have their reward already, cash down—that is what is meant by the phrase 'they have their reward' in the Greek of the period (see p. 36 on Mark xiv. 41). Advertising pietists do win a reputation

---

[1] Matt. xii. 37.   [2] Matt. xv. 13.   [3] Matt. vii. 16, xix. 20.

for sanctity, complacent religionists attain to a kind of peace. That is just the trouble, for when a man has nothing more to pray or hope for he grows old indeed ; he has finished his course in the school of virtue, he thinks, and his transaction with his God is complete. The Christian, on the other hand, is to look for no reward here except to be as his Lord[1] ; his charities, his prayers, his fasting —duties to God, his brother, himself—must all be carried through in secret (vi. 3, 4, 6, 17). In the secret chamber of a man's own soul he shall ever find his God, and his reward shall be that he shall come forth to work out what he has conceived in solitary thought and prayer. Isa. xxvi. 20, as rendered by the LXX, is obviously quoted here : ' Go, my people, enter into the secret chambers, shut the door, be hidden a very little while, until the wrath of the Lord pass ' ; but there is a significant change. In the prophet's word the people is bidden to enter into the chamber and shut the door to escape from God ; here the Christian withdraws to *find* God. At any moment the follower of Jesus can shut his door upon the world, and sit ' calm on tumult's wheel, midst busy multitudes alone ' ; like artist and poet, he retires upon himself, not to find himself, but God, whose presence can most surely be reached not in the round ocean or in living air, but in the mind of man. When he fasts, too, as the Master takes it for granted he will in one way or another, he will take pains not to let his austerities make him austere.

Here again we must allow our understanding of our Lord's teaching its reaction upon our picture of His demeanour as He took His part in the societies of men. If we had seen Him as He bore Himself in the days of His flesh, we should not have been allowed to penetrate His sadness ; He would have appeared to us, in His earlier days at least, the gayest and least self-conscious of all naturally happy souls ; His darker moods and moments He would ever keep to Himself. It has been suggested by Dr. Hogg that the night of the picnic-party by the lakeside was the occasion of a crisis in the life of the Lord, that when He was driven by the well-meant but dangerous attentions of the crowd[2] to break away from them and

[1] Matt. x. 25, xxv. 21, 23.   [2] John vi. 15.

part the twelve from the contagion of their embarrassing enthusiasm,[1] 'He went up into the hills in private, and was there by Himself,'[2] because He saw that this was to be the end of His Galilean ministry. Was the boat which He had at last launched on the troubled sea of the times to suffer shipwreck so soon? In communion with His Father He recovers the peace which was His birthright, and then He turns down to look at the lake. There was the very image of His thoughts! A boat struggling with the wind, His friends already almost at their wits' end! He will carry to their aid His own newly recovered tranquillity, and by the impetus of His love and still in the atmosphere of His victorious prayer He walks upon the water, for their consolation lifted above the limitations of humanity. It is the same at the last supper. Pain breaks through for a moment when He tells His friends that the cup of good fellowship is not for Him just now,[3] for 'the hand of him that betrayeth Me is with Me on the table' (Luke xxii. 21), and an element of discord is still in the company (v. 24); but He turns quickly away to rest in the thought of their faithful love and of the honour which He has in store for them (vv. 28-30); troubles are coming, but He has provided for them already (v. 32). Then, as He feels the 'climbing sorrow' rising to heart and brain, He bids them go (v. 36) in strange, broken words; when they will not leave Him, He lets them come on into the garden, but bids them not come too close, lest they should see more than they can bear (v. 41; Mark xiv. 38, 41). In this respect, too, the disciple is to be like his Lord; he will keep his temporary troubles to himself, and give the world the full reversion of his eternal peace.

That the Christian's demeanour toward his fellows is to convey the impression of light[4] and freedom[5] does not mean that he is not to take pains with the lesser moralities. To himself his inner life will always seem poor,[6] his purity rather one of intention than of achievement.[7] His generous charity for men will be the outward side of his humbleness before God; he will make allowances for others because he knows what allowances have been made for himself.[8] Indifferent to the details of his own merely

[1] Mark vi. 45.   [3] Luke xxii. 18, &c. [5] Matt. xvii. 26. [7] Matt. v. 8.
[2] Matt. xiv. 23. [4] Matt. v. 14, 16. [6] Matt. v. 3.   [8] Matt. xviii. 32, 33.

personal rights and dignities, he will be studiously careful
of the sensibilities of others, ready at any moment to
limit the freedom which is his right, in order to avoid causing
offence.[1] Set free from the tyranny of little things, so
far as they concern himself, he is instinctively scrupulous in
his consideration for those who are still in the toils of the
morbid sensitiveness which is the curse of an unredeemed
culture ; he has a tender heart because he has a tough skin.
We can illustrate this high and lowly courteousness from
almost every page of this Gospel, but a few striking instances must suffice.

In the course of v. 22 there is clearly a rising note in
the urgency of the Lord's warning against certain moods
which are specially perilous to the Christian. Underlying
this passage there runs one of the dominant thoughts of
the teaching of Jesus—that the root of all evil lies in what
He calls the ' heart,' and we should call the will or the
motive (cf. v. 28 ; xii. 34, 35). The old law called to
account the man who kills his fellow.[2] According to the
revised version promulgated in the Sermon, to feel like
killing is equivalent to killing ; there is no particular
merit in stopping short of the act of murder, if your motive
is fear of the consequences or the civilized man's horror
of bloodshed. The ' judgement ' stands for a trial before
the local law-court, where the elders of the synagogue acted
as jury in cases of murder, the ' council ' for the higher
court, or Sanhedrin, specially constituted to hear very
serious accusations ; the ' Great Sanhedrin,' that meeting
in Jerusalem, tried cases of blasphemy, and is probably
referred to here. Moffatt regards v. 22, after 'in danger
of the judgement,' as a Rabbinic comment upon the closing
words of v. 21, and rearranges the material as follows :
' You have heard how the men of old were told, " Murder
not ; whoever murders shall come up for sentence, whoever maligns his brother must come before the Sanhedrin,
whoever curses his brother must go to the fire of Gehenna " ;
but I tell you, whoever is angry with his brother (without
cause) will be sentenced by God.' This suggestion appears
plausible, but I am disinclined to think that Jesus would
have included a comment of a comparatively modern
character in a quotation from what He describes as an

[1] Matt. xvii. 26, 27.   [2] Matt. v. 21.

ancient law. If the last two clauses of v. 22 are Rabbinic, the comment is a very fine and discerning one, and may well have been appropriated by Jesus; moreover, it follows ' whoever is angry with his brother,' &c., in a very telling and effective way, bringing out as it does a feature of the Lord's teaching which seems as clear to me as it is ignored or implicitly denied by most expositors—I mean the delicate sense of subtle shades of difference in social and personal ethics. It is often asserted that the Sermon on the Mount deals with broad general principles, the detailed working out of which is left to the trained Christian intelligence. In a certain sense this is true ; but it ought to be observed that illustrations of the Lord's principle are often given, illustrations which cover a very wide field of application, and that the language used is some-times at least as precise and carefully balanced as that of a legal document. The passage with which we are dealing is a case in point. Even if we have to let the words ' with-out a cause ' go—I am doubtful if the textual evidence now available warrants their omission—no charge of ex-aggeration or of impracticability can fairly be levelled against this saying. The tense of ' whoever is angry ' should be noticed ; it refers either to an angry mood per-sisted in, or to a habitually irritable temper. Anger may be justifiable, as homicide may be justifiable—indeed, it is very often our duty to be angry (cf. Eph. iv. 26, and p. 120 for its ascription to Jesus) ; but it is always dangerous, and if persisted in beyond a time-limit[1] leads, like homicide, to a summons before God's tribunal—the aggrieved man must show cause for his bitterness against his brother. Jesus does not say that persistent anger is always wrong, only that it is exceedingly dangerous ; that the onus of proof lies not upon the man with whom you feel yourself aggrieved, but upon you, if you hug your grievance to your heart ; and that the cause will be tried before a Judge who is always on the defendant's side. But there are more questionable states of mind than anger, and one of them is contempt, generally a meaner and colder thing. ' Raca ' probably corresponds to the Hebrew ' rach,' used in Gen. xli. 19, and meaning ' thin ' ; it had become amongst the Syriac-speaking people of Antioch a term of contempt for

[1] Eph. iv. 26 ; Jonah iv. 1, 4.

the lower classes. Another still more piquant suggestion is that it is equivalent to the French ' conspuer.' We infer that the second member of the saying makes what we should call ' snobbish ' contempt tantamount to blasphemy; it is yet another way of saying the great ' Inasmuch.'[1]

There might conceivably be justifiable contempt, as there is certainly justifiable anger ; but the man who cuts his brother dead is playing with edged tools indeed, and the inquiry which must ensue will be instituted before a higher court upon a more serious charge. The meaning of the third clause is plain : if anger is sometimes justified, and even a measure of contempt might conceivably vindicate itself as the only possible course in extreme cases, abuse gives itself away ; if anger is righteous, it will be restrained ; if contempt is the only course open to the Christian, it will be a silent contempt ; abuse is never, under any circumstances, allowable. It is clear that our expression ' Thou fool ' is far too mild to render the original adequately, for the ' fool ' here is the reckless atheist of the Wisdom Books. The Aramaic term employed was probably ' moreh,' which, though borrowed from the Greek of the day, had taken a darker hue ; it is used in the simple Greek sense in xxv. 2 f. ; the ' foolish virgins ' were certainly not reckless atheists. The element of anathematization contained in this word gives it a more sinister flavour. ' Rach ' damns a man in this world ; ' moreh ' in the next. In modern speech we should perhaps render, ' Whoever says " Damn you "—and means it—shall be damned himself.' Perhaps Jesus had overheard His disciples abusing each other in the full-blooded Galilean way (cf. Mark xiv. 71) and was warning them of the ominous meaning of bad words so lightly used.

Our consideration of this passage brings us to a very interesting feature of this Gospel ; it gives us a summary of our Lord's teaching upon the use and abuse of language. The relevant passages are v. 22, 33 ff. (cf. James v. xii, and above p. 123) ; vi. 7 ; vii. 21; xii. 32 ff. ; xxiii. 16 ff.—most of this material being peculiar to Matthew. The cardinal passage is perhaps xii. 36, 37, and we will begin there. Great importance is clearly attached to talking, for

[1] Matt. xxv. 40.

the distinction, so obvious to us, but in many ways so mis-
leading, between actions and words, has almost disappeared:
' From thy *words* thou shalt be justified, and from thy
words thou shalt be condemned ' (cf. Luke xix. 22, ' Out
of thine own mouth I judge thee ' ; it is curious that this
clause is absent from the First Gospel).   Sooner or later a
man's talk betrays him, be he ever so much upon his guard ;
for even if words are used to conceal thoughts they will
prove him a liar and a hypocrite ; diplomacy avails not at
all with God, and not for long with man.   ' God knows the
heart,' and what God knows men will soon begin to find
out ; you cannot keep a secret.   But words may be ' idle '
—that is, meaningless, empty ; hence it follows that ' a
word "spoken even against" the Son of Man' will be forgiven.   The word may only evidence misunderstanding,
or it may be uttered in a sudden heat, soon repented of ;
on the other hand, when it represents a real rebellion of
the sin against ' the Holy Spirit,' a deliberate partisanship
with evil in antagonism· to what is known to be good, when
it betrays ' the lie in the soul,' it is unforgivable.   Grieved
astonishment (see above on xii. 34) pervades our Lord's
attacks upon men who never seemed to mean what they
said, and could not be induced to say what they meant.
A note of warning is perceptible in His indignant question ;
they could not for ever go on saying the right thing with
evil in their hearts—they could impose upon all the people
some of the time, and some of the people all the time, but
not all the people all the time[1] ; and, as for God, their
meaningless words told Him more about them than the
most explicit expression of their malice could have done,
for they manifested their falseness as well as their wickedness.   Though you do not mean anything much by many
of the things you say, you are warned that everything
you say will be used in evidence against you.[2]

This does not imply that we are always to be serious, for
social life would be intolerable if we weighed every word,
and no room was left for humorous exaggeration and mere
pleasantry.   There are really no such things as meaningless words.   What we call frivolous talk or banter either
has a good effect or a bad one ; in either case it ceases to
be, in the strict sense of the word, ' idle.'   Real humour

---

[1] Matt. x. 26.   [2] Matt. xii. 36.

is not a morally neutral thing ; it is a beneficial exercise
of a God-given faculty.   In the passage quoted more than
once already from Ephesians[1] Paul speaks of a ' good word '
or *bon mot*—compare ' on account of this word[2] '—a
saying which produces upon the hearers a pleasant impression (compare also Col. iv. 6).   But our strongest
vindication of the place of humour in the life and conversation of the Christian is the example of the Lord Himself,
whose stories and sayings are set to the measure very
often of a quiet spirit of laughter.   The tide of truth
sweeps up into the channels that human life and language
have made for it, and splashes over, sparkling and bubbling
in the sun.   But laughter with the flavour of malice in it
has no place in the Lord's armoury.   Irony is not uncom-
mon in His words, but I cannot detect any laughter in
His irony ;   it is indignant and pitiful, but there is no
trace of that subtle sense of enjoyment in the use of the
weapon which suggests a secret laughter.   In His table-
talk at the Pharisee's house we hear Him for once dis-
coursing in a sarcastic vein, when He advises the mannerly
but ill-mannered guests how to manœuvre for precedence[3] ;
here, as elsewhere, His humour does not lie far away from
tears.   ' Every idle word that a man shall speak ' perhaps
means that the speaker must prove that his word was really
' idle ' ;   that, in effect as well as in intention, it was innocent
of mischief, for we are as truly responsible for the impression which our unguarded talk produces as we are for
the effect it was meant to produce.   The plea ' I did not
mean any harm ' is put out of court, for we have no business not to mean any harm ;   we should mean good by every
word we say ;   even flippancy has its place, and may
mean good.   ' There is many a true word spoken in jest.'
' Idle ' words are not really ' idle ' ;   indeed, it is possible
that more lasting harm has been done by things said ' half
in jest, half in earnest,' than by statements quite obviously
meant to be taken seriously.   We feel that at least we
know the worst when a man tells us what he thinks of
us in plain prose ;   but the light word which may mean
anything or nothing poisons the imagination, setting the
hearer morbidly searching for the hidden innuendo.   Everything depends upon our knowledge of the man or woman

[1] Eph. iv. 29.   [2] Mark vii. 29.   [3] Luke xiv. 7 ff.

addressed. Jesus was never sarcastic with stupid people. If the other man knows you well enough, and has sufficient humour not to take you over seriously, you may be as free-spoken as you please ; the Christian will always regulate the exercise of his faculty of humour according to his knowledge or ignorance of the person with whom he is dealing ; he will deny himself the pleasure of being facetious at the expense of any but his intimate friends. In any case, judgement by our ' idle ' talk is the fairest test to which we can be subjected ; we reveal ourselves not when we are measuring our words, but when we are off our guard—in our carpet-slippers at home, for instance.

So we are led along to the consideration of the two sections of our Lord's teaching which deal with the use of oaths, both of them peculiar to this Gospel[1]; the corresponding passage in the Epistle of James[2] has been referred to already (see p. 123). The commandment ' Thou shalt not take the name of Jehovah thy God in vain ' has quite as much to do with veracity as with reverence ; this aspect of the case is brought out clearly in the Lord's quotation of the more positive form of the same ordinance : ' Thou shalt not commit perjury, but shalt render unto the Lord thine oaths.'[3] The Oriental always swears when he wishes to be believed. The third commandment meant ' If you must swear, at least tell the truth when you swear ' ; Jesus says, ' You should never need to swear at all.' In xxiii. 16 ff. He tears to shreds the elaborate system of casuistry by which the consciences of man not habitually truthful in proportion to the vehemence of their speech are cased. The reference here is plainly to the habit of playing with truth by emphasis upon subtle distinctions which are forthcoming when you want them, but were not present to the mind when the strong word was uttered, to a clever escape from an uncomfortable position created by a man's own boastful or exaggerated talk.

In v. 33 ff. the analysis of the idea of truthfulness probes yet more deeply into the roots of conduct. Let your language be proportioned, as exactly as you can make it, to the strength of your feeling ; as you do not quite know yourself, or how long your present mood is likely to last,

[1] Matt. v. 23 ff., xxiii. 16 ff.
[2] Jas. v. 12.   [3] Matt. v. 23 ; Lev. xix. 12 ; Ex. xx. 7.

it is well rather to understate than exaggerate. Truthfulness for the Christian is sincerity, a margin being left to allow for his lack of self-knowledge, as Justice is concerned with his treatment of others, always inclining to mercy, because he is yet more ignorant of their true meanings and deserts than he is of his own. To use great words for small thin feelings is a form of profane swearing not generally recognized. We often say ' I am frightfully tired ' or ' I am dying for my tea,' when we mean we are a little weary or hungry. This abuse involves a degradation of language which has come down to us, and for the maintenance of which in its purity and effectiveness we are responsible ; but it also undermines our own power of expression, and it is vitally necessary that we should be taken seriously when the time comes when words shall be the only means available if we are to make ourselves understood. The man who is for ever playing with words finds them fail him when he wants them badly. We must keep this weapon sharp and ready. Slang is perhaps indispensable for all societies with an exclusive life of their own ; but it should involve the creation of new words, not the corruption of the old. ' By heaven ' was, as it still is, only a cautious evasion of the name of God. Teaching upon this subject was not new to Jewish Christians. ' Accustom not thy mouth to an oath,' wrote the author of the Wisdom of Jesus the son of Sirach (xxiii. 9–11), ' and be not prone to the naming of the Holy One. For as the servant that is continually scourged shall not lack a bruise, so he that sweareth and nameth God continually shall not be cleansed from sin.' This precept could be carried out if the name of God were avoided, and Philo (*Special Laws*, § 2) says, ' However, if a man must swear, and is so inclined, let him add, if he pleases, not indeed the highest name of all, . . . but the earth, the sun, the stars, the heaven, the universe, for these things are most worthy of being named.' In the Talmud there is a discussion as to whether certain words, such as ' heaven,' ' earth,' &c., necessarily contain a reference to God or not ; evidently Jesus takes the stricter view upon this matter. ' Earth ' is as sacred as ' heaven ' ; the very hairs of a man's head [1] as truly under the care and control of God as ' the city of

[1] Luke xii. 7, xxi. 18.

the great King.'[1]   The Rabbis said that oaths were not
binding if circumlocutions were used for the Sacred Name ;
the oath ' By Jerusalem ' not binding if the swearer did
not turn that way as he spoke ; other evasions of the same
nature are pilloried in xxiii. 16 ff.   Chapter v. 33 f. means
' Let your speech be confined to a double yea or nay '—
compare the ' Amen, Amen' so frequent upon the lips
of Jesus in the Fourth Gospel and the ' Yea, Amen ' of
Rev. i. 7 (cf. Rev. xxii. 20) ; in other words, if you desire
to make a specially solemn affirmation, repeat ' yes ' or
' no ' twice without an ugly oath.   Whatever goes beyond
a simple assertion of this kind is superfluous, anyhow, and
betrays a nervous attempt to assure the listener that the
speaker is for once not lying ; such over-anxiety makes the
wise man suspicious.   We are always inclined to suspect
a man who is for ever proclaiming his integrity ; if he
were really honest, he would not need to say so much about
it.   Indeed, experience has taught us that such over-
emphatic assertions do come, as Jesus says, from the devil.
Our hectic journalism and flaming advertisements breed
an unwholesome suspicion of all statements which we
cannot verify for ourselves—witness the general impression
that no newspaper is to be trusted nowadays ; Peter only
used an oath when he denied his Lord.[2]   The saying reported by James,[3] and perhaps alluded to by Paul,[4]
bears   a   different   meaning;   Paul   is   answering   the
charge of what we should call 'shilly-shally'; like other
subtle thinkers and statesmen, he was accused of clothing his
utterances in such ambiguous language that,when challenged,
he could make them mean either one thing or the other,
to suit the occasion.   Commenting upon Lev. xix. 36,
the Talmud has ' that the yea may be a true yea, and
the nay a true nay ' ; we are to learn the art of free and
hearty assent to the truth, to say ' Yes ' without reserve and
grudging to all legitimate demands.   If you mean to give
to a good cause, give right out and have done with it,
without   waiting   to   be   asked.   It   is   equally
necessary to learn to say ' No ' frankly and bluntly to the
suggestions of evil.   We might sum up the First Gospel
as being the Gospel of the double ' Yes ' and ' No '—' Yes '

[1] Matt. v. 35.   [3] Jas. v. 12.
[2] Matt. xxvi. 72.   [4] 2 Cor. i. 17–20.

emphatically to the call of the Lord ; ' No ' to all evasions of His claim.

In vi. 7 we have ' do not use vain repetitions ' (A.V.). The ' Lewis ' Syriac version has ' do not say vain things,' a phrase which reminds us of the ' idle word ' of xii. 36 ; ' Words without thoughts cannot to heaven go.' Reference to the ' heathen ' suggests ' incantations,' which in derivation is suspiciously near ' intoning.' In the Moulton-Milligan dictionary two alternatives are propounded. One is based upon the reading of Codex Bezae (' Do not blether ') ; the other upon ' Battos,' a nickname of Demosthenes, corresponding to our ' windbag.' In prayer we are only to say what we mean, and mean intensely ; we are not, like the Pharisee in the parable [1] (see p. 156), to repeat one set of words aloud, and be thinking ' within ourselves ' of something quite different. We are not to do lip-service to Jesus.[2] It should be observed in this connexion that Matthew brings out the shrinking of our Lord from the kiss of Judas[3]; He still calls Him ' comrade,' but this is no time for a display of affection. The true devotion is that of humble obedience, and this is, to say the least of it, conspicuous by its absence in the case of Judas : ' Why call ye Me Lord, Lord, and do not the things that I say ? '[4] The same kind of recoil is evident in Luke xxii. 48, ' Betrayest thou the Son of Man with a kiss ? ' Before we leave the subject of truthfulness in speech Matt. xviii. 16 should be noticed, for there we catch the same note: ' in order that at the mouth of two or three witnesses ' (for ' two or three ' compare xviii. 20) ' every word '— or perhaps ' sentence '—' may be established '; compare Sirach xix. 15, ' trust not every word.'

Throughout this Gospel we can trace this emphasis upon moral realism, this recurring protest against pretence of any kind. Matthew's heart is in the Sermon on the Mount ; he will take his Lord's words seriously, for to him it is law. He would have had little sympathy with those of his modern interpreters, who, after their explanations, leave us with a few general rules for carefully restricted application in some departments of life. But he leaves us with the teaching of his Master made easy[5] by His presence in the

[1] Luke xviii. 9 ff.   [3] Matt. xxvi. 50.   [4] Luke vi. 46.
[2] Matt. vii. 21.   [5] Matt. xi. 30.

daily perplexities in which the attempt to carry His words into practice involves us—' Teaching them to keep all the many things I have commanded you, and lo ! I am with you all the days.'[1]   There are no moral accidents, John the Baptist and Jesus agree in insisting.[2]   Words are deeds, for with God there is no great and small, trivial and serious.[3] Sacred things are not to be played with,[4] and all life is sacred[5] ; the Lord's coming does not make the world more comfortable, but rather at first sharpens men's hostility to one another, for both sides to every moral conflict will care more and fight more desperately because He has so forced the pace[6] (Luke xii. 51, ' division '). But the final result is to be that ' Wisdom shall be vindicated of all that she has done '[7] (Luke vii. 35, ' children '), for the issue shall justify the long agony of the centuries.   It may be that Christendom is fated to blunder on for much more than twenty centuries of painful disillusionment before she discovers that force is, after all, no real remedy for anything ; even so, it will have been worth while, for one of the pillar-truths of the teaching of Jesus will have been vindicated.   Meanwhile Christians must be thorough-going in their obedience ; they must give the ' leaven ' a fair chance to spread in the ' three measures of flour,'[8] private life, business life, and citizen life[9] (cf. Matt. v. 38–41). They must give an object-lesson of the Lord's teaching in practice, proving in their own persons to a sceptical world that self-discipline is not incompatible with sociability,[10] that non-resistance to personal injury does not involve backbonelessness or insipidity ; they must be ' careful without care,' puritan without being puritanical, for they have imposed upon them the task of making goodness for its own sake desirable to a world that does not want to be good, and that has never really learned to like good people.   For our own training in this Christian discipline we have the teaching of the Lord, at once so clear in its outlines and so refined in its shading ; and where words fail, as even His words must, if they are only words, His Spirit will inspire as it is reflected back[11] upon and into

[1] Matt. xxviii. 20.
[2] Matt. iii. 10, vii. 19, xv. 13.
[3] Matt. xii. 36.
[4] Matt. vii. 6.
[5] Matt. v. 34 f.
[6] Matt. x. 34.
[7] Matt. xi. 19.
[8] Matt. xiii. 33.
[9] Matt. v. 39ff.
[10] Matt. v. 16, vi. 17.
[11] 2 Cor. iii. 18.

those who are willing to spend much time in looking at Him, thinking about Him, listening to Him, until the difficult art of saintly living becomes second nature, and the yoke has proved itself easy to wear after all, for in Him we have found ' rest to our souls '—we have got there !

One or two parables remain to give us a last illustration of the evangelist's purpose. That of xviii. 23 ff. ends upon the same realistic note, ' unless you forgive each one his brother *from your hearts.*'[1] In the parable of the two sons[2] there is a curious cluster of various readings in regard to the reply given by the Pharisees to Jesus.[3] In different MSS. we have ' the first,' ' the second,' ' the last,' and so on. In a privately circulated account of his last fateful journey Dr. Rendal Harris gives us, incidentally, the secret of these confusions ; I reproduce with his permission. He quotes Dr. Mackie, a Scotch missionary in Eygpt, who told the story to a class of women in Syria, ending with the question, ' Which of the two,' &c. The unanimous answer was ' the first,' the one who said he would go, and did not, the reason given being that a day's work in the vineyard was a little thing, but to say ' No ' to your father's beard was a very serious matter indeed. The various readings are the outcome of a real difficulty. An interesting parallel to this view of the case is to be found in one text of Sirach xix. 21, 'A servant that saith to his master, "I will not do according to thy will," though he do so afterwards, angereth him that feedeth him.' All the more necessary to Eastern hearers must have been our Lord's insistence upon the superiority of practical obedience even to good manners. In xxi. 41 we detect the same emphasis ; ' who shall render to Him their fruits in their seasons ' is peculiar to this Gospel. Both the ' call to work ' parables are found in Matthew only, and the quotation from Hosea demanding ' brotherly feeling, and not sacrifice,' is twice repeated.[4]

We have now traced the picture of the Lord and His teaching built up in this most subtle of the Synoptic Gospels ; it is clear that it is based upon a series of paradoxes. Jesus nowhere makes higher claims than He does

---

[1] Matt. xviii. 35.   [2] Matt. xxi. 28 ff.   [3] Matt. xxi. 31.
[4] Matt. ix. 13, xii. 7.

here ; yet nowhere is His lowly and even-tempered gentleness more boldly and delicately expressed—for instance,
in the sequence of xi. 27, 28 ff. ' The Friend of publicans,'[1]
He is also the sternest of moralists[2] ; though His ' yoke
is easy,' it is only easy to a great devotion. He demands
an exact obedience[3] in small things as in great,[4] but
correctness of conduct is nothing without a personal
loyalty to Himself[4] ; the ' house ' of the generation of
comparatively respectable Jewish people to whom He
came, though ' swept clean ' and garnished with all the
proprieties of a great tradition, became again the home of
purposes viler than all the uncleanness of Gentiles and
publicans, because it was ' empty ' (' empty,' Matt. xii. 44
only), untenanted by love. So pitiful to the ' bruised
reed,'[5] so ready to make men's ' ailments ' and ' diseases '
His own[7] that they came to Him from every side and
found relief in telling Him their troubles,[8] He is the eternal
Judge of men and angels.[9] Yet He does not advertise Himself, or ' cause His voice to be heard in the streets '[10] ;
always in the presentation of Jesus there is the sense of
power ungrasped at.[11] That He was the Son of God He
took for granted ; He needed not to call Himself by that
name, for when men looked into His face, in their hearts
they knew Him for what He was ; in xxvi. 64, ' Thou hast
said ' may be translated ' You know I am '—compare
xxvi. 25, where Moffatt renders the Lord's reply to Judas's
question, ' Surely it is not I, Rabbi ? ' ' Is it not ? '
It is all the more significant that Matthew does not shrink,
as Luke does, from the cry of desolation upon the cross[12] ;
indeed, the fact that, earlier in his Gospel (xix. 17, see p.
100), he has shown himself unwilling to believe that Jesus
was ever baffled, makes this, the last utterance reported in
the first two Gospels before the Lord's passing, all the more
pregnant with tragic meaning. The clue to this great
paradox is to be found in the title our Lord chose for
Himself : He is Saviour, Lord, and Judge, because He is
' Son of Man.'· In Ezekiel's vision, described in chapter 1
of the book of his prophecies, ideal manhood is discovered in

[1] Matt. xi. 19.   [2] Matt. v. 20.   [3] Matt. xix. 17.
[4] Matt. v. 19.   [5] Matt. xix. 21.   [6] Matt. xii. 20.
[7] Matt. viii. 17.   [8] Matt. xiv. 12.   [9] Matt. xvi. 17, viii. 29.
[10] Matt. xii. 19.   [11] Matt. xxvi. 53 ; Ph. ii. 6.
[12] Matt. xxvii. 46 ; cf. Mark xv. 34.

the seraphs and in God Himself, and immediately afterwards[1] the prophet is addressed as 'son of man.' Jesus
is one with man, because He knows what we might have
been, and may become ; this conception of His Person
lies behind both His lowly demeanour and His exalted
claim.   One with us by nature, He set Himself to become
one with us in experience, to learn for Himself and realize
for us what obedience means and costs for men, fallen as we
are in such a world as this.[2]   The incarnation of the Son
of God assures us that it is He who meets men in conscience,[3] in nature,[4] in the daring dreams of youth[5].   But
there is more than this, for, if this were all, we have no
gospel for a world that has outlived and outsuffered its
dreams, or for us, whose conscience has been tampered
with and seared, who are visited by the great moment
more rarely as life goes on, but know ourselves to be
helpless, undone sinners all the time.

When Jesus came, He came prepared to take all the risks
of coming as He did ; that is why we meet Him not only
in our dreams, but in our despairs.   When the whole
history of our times cries out against our easy idealism,
and we are faced by a horror of great darkness into which
we dare not look far, and then, turning to the Church
and to ourselves, we find ourselves utterly helpless, helpless not because the world will not listen to us, but because
we know that we are guilty too, for the sins which spilt
His precious blood are our sins ; when we come to the point
at which we say to ourselves, ' These deeds must not be
thought after these ways—so it will drive us mad,' and
we try in vain to pray ; when, after life has hammered
home upon us our own entire failure, and the worst failure
of all is that we cannot be as sorry as we know we ought to
be—then we find the Lord struggling for us, praying for
us, facing out for us the logic of our sin, and somehow,
we know not yet how, winning through to hope
and victory, not for Himself alone, but for us.   He
let us carry Him down with us ; we have to let Him carry
us up with Him.   When we lose ourselves in love for Him,
we begin to live the risen life of victory over sin.   Almost
without our knowing it, we are lifted above the vicious

[1] Ezek. ii. 1.   [2] Heb. v. 8.   [3] Luke v. 8, &c.
          [4] Matt. xvii. 2.   [5] Matt. xiv. 28.

circle of self-indulgence and self-despising in which our thoughts have come to move, for now we do not think about ourselves at all, but of Him ; our ' bitter-thoughted heart ' is 'sweetened' by His Cross, and our work in life is narrowed and deepened to the task of making others look, not at our own ideas, but at Him, as we have learned to look.

Carried over into social life, this self-forgetting becomes our master-key to all the problems of saintly living. Every point in the great Sermon may be illustrated from the Lord's own behaviour ; at every turn, the tradition of His teaching is balanced by the story of His life. Preaching ourselves, our own ideas of Christian truth, mere sup-porters of a ' cause,' we soon become partisans, and shall be betrayed into all the faults and failures, all the bitterness in disappointment, of the partisan spirit ; preaching Him we shall be delivered from touchiness about ourselves. Realizing our oneness with Him, the Elder Brother who keeps the home together, we shall come instinctively to feel our oneness with one another, and we shall love men and women, not simply because they appeal to us or think our way, but as His ' little brothers ' ; we shall learn to love God and man, because He who was both ' first loved us.' In a word, the Kingdom of God will come when a sufficient number of men and women behave to everybody as, in self-respecting families, brothers and sisters behave to each other at home. And He has taught us the way. We are not to think so much of their chance relations with us as of their eternal relationship to Him.

APPENDICES

I

The Story of Ahikar (pp. 81, 131).

THIS Eastern fable is extant in Syriac, Arabic, Armenian, Ethiopic, Greek, and Slavonic versions, and concerns the history of one Nadan (or Nadab) and his relations with his uncle, called variously Ahikar, Khikar, Haiqar, and Akyrios, who adopted him, and introduced him to the Court of Sennacherib, King of Assyria, whose vizier he was, as his own destined successor. He proceeded at once to take more than a son's place at home, and more than a successor's right at Court—I follow Dr. Harris's language. Finally, after a threat of removal emanating from his injured patron, his disloyalty comes to a head in the forging in his uncle's name of treasonable letters of office, under Ahikar's seal, addressed to neighbouring sovereigns, letters which Nadan promptly betrays to the king. Ahikar is sent off to execution; but a slave, whom he had formerly saved from the monarch's wrath, and who is now ordered to perform the act of beheading, finds a substitute, and conceals Ahikar in an underground cell beneath the vizier's house, where he can hear the sound of Nadan's revelries and the shrieks of his beaten men and maidservants (cf. Matt. xxiv. 48 ff.; Luke xii. 45 f.). By-and-by, however, the tables are turned. Complications with the King of Egypt arise, and Ahikar is sadly missed in the crisis which ensues. Then the slave plays the friend's part by confiding to the King of Assyria that the sage is still living. The wasted and withered old man appears, with nails grown like eagle's talons and hair like a beast's (cf. Dan. iv. 30). When Ahikar has proved himself the saviour of his country, and has been re-instated, he proceeds to take vengeance upon his wretched nephew. Nadan is flung into a black hole, after a severe flogging (cf. Luke xii. 47), and is fed on bread and water, while his uncle points the moral to him at great length and with extraordinary fertility of illustration. Thereupon the nephew swells up and, bursting asunder, goes down into darkness.

We have already noticed parallels to this story in the parable of the Unfaithful Slave, where the strange expression ' shall cut him asunder'—i.e. with reproaches; as we say, a 'cutting' speech —has come straight from this old story; and on page 81 we have traced the origin of Peter's account of the end of Judas (Acts i. 18, 19) to the same description of a traitor's doom. Here is another fairly clear case, occurring in the course of Ahikar's address to his nephew : ' And Haiqar said to him, " O my boy ! thou art like the tree which was fruitless beside the water, and its master was fain to cut it down, and *it* said to him, ' Remove me to another place, and if I do not bear fruit, cut me down'"' (cf. Luke xiii. 9). The difference between the two parables consists in the fact that in the older story the tree seeks to defend itself; in that uttered by Jesus the ' Vinedresser ' wishes to spare it. 2 Pet. ii. 22 also comes from the same 'sermon' (see p. 131), and another interesting point is that Nadan appeals to his uncle to put him to feeding the pigs (cf. Luke xv. 15). Obviously the fable of Ahikar's treatment of his adopted nephew was in the Lord's mind when He told the story of the father's so different dealing with his prodigal *son*.

II

FOR the convenience of readers, I give here the text of the saying quoted here, translated from Irenaeus and the Coptic Encomium (p. 130):

Irenaeus (quoting Papias on the Blessing of Isaac) : ' The Lord said, " Days shall come wherein vineyards shall grow, each having ten thousand main shoots, and each main shoot ten thousand branches, and in each branch ten thousand sprigs, and upon every sprig ten thousand clusters, and in every cluster ten thousand grapes, and every grape pressed shall yield twenty-five measures of wine ; . . . and when any one of the saints shall lay hold of a cluster, another cluster shall say, ' I am a better cluster; take me, by me bless the Lord.' " ' Judas the traitor questions this, the fragment proceeds to tell us, and Jesus answers, ' Those who see it will come to this state of affairs.' Something like this is found in the Book of Enoch (150 B.C.) and the Apocalypse of Baruch (first century A.D.). In the Coptic Encomium we read : ' The Saviour said, " I will hide nothing from you concerning the things about which you have questioned Me. As regarded the vine of Paradise . . . there are ten thousand grapes upon it, and each bushel will produce six measures of wine. As regardeth the palm-trees in Paradise, each cluster yieldeth ten thousand dates, and each cluster is as long as a man is high. So likewise it is in the matter of the fig-trees ; each shoot produceth ten thousand figs, and if three men were to partake of one fig, each of them would be satisfied," ' and so on about wheat, apples, and the thourakim-tree. ' These,' the Encomium continues, ' are the good things which I have prepared for every one who shall celebrate the Commemoration of My Beloved One and My kinsman John upon the earth. Blessed is every one who shall be worthy to inherit these good things.' If the tradition underlying these fragments gives us a real re-miniscence of a saying of Jesus, we must take it that they set the seal of our Lord's approval upon part, at any rate, of the Book of Enoch. But their tone sounds altogether unlike the general tenor of His teaching, and we must ascribe the attribution of them to Jesus to the millenarian tendencies of Papias.'

It may be well at this point to give a selection from the ' Un-written Sayings' (see pp. 120, 121, &c.) not mentioned already in the text of this book.

1. From the Oxyrhynchus papyri (Grenfell and Hunt) :

' Jesus saith, " Let not him who seeks . . . cease until he finds, and when he finds he shall be astonished ; astonished he shall reach the Kingdom, and having reached the Kingdom he shall rest." ' Part of this saying is quoted by Clement of Alexandria as found in the Gospel of the Hebrews, and it comes in his *Stromateis* again in a form more nearly corresponding to the papyrus.

' Jesus saith, " (Ye ask) who are those who draw us to the Kingdom if the Kingdom is in heaven ? . . . The fowls of the air and all beasts that are under the earth or upon the earth, and the fishes of the sea, these are they that draw you, and the kingdom of heaven is within you (Luke xvii. 21) ; and whoever shall know himself shall find it. (Strive therefore) to know yourselves, (and) ye shall be aware that ye are the sons of the (Almighty) Father ; and ye shall know that ye are in (the city of God !), and ye are (the city) "—I follow the Grenfell–Hunt reconstruction of this difficult saying.

' Jesus saith, " Except ye fast to the world, ye shall in no wise find the kingdom of God ; and except ye make the Sabbath a real Sabbath, ye shall not see the Father." '

' Jesus saith, " I stood in the midst of the world, and in the flesh I was seen of them, and I found all men drunken, and none found I athirst among them, and My soul grieveth over the sons of men, because they are blind in heart and see not." '

' Jesus saith, " A prophet is not acceptable in his own country, neither does a doctor work cures upon them that know him." '

' Jesus saith, " Thou hearest with one ear, but the other thou hast closed." '

2. A fragment of a lost gospel found at Oxyrhynchus contains the words, ' Ye are far better than the lilies which grow and spin not. Having one garment, what do ye lack (cf. Mark vi. 9) ? . . . He Himself will give you your garment.' ' His disciples say unto Him, " When wilt Thou be manifest to us, and when shall we see Thee ? " He saith, " When ye shall be stripped, and shall not be ashamed . . . " ' (cf. Gen. iii. 7, 10, 11). Compare with this a strongly ascetic passage from the Gospel according to the Egyptians (see below, App. V.) quoted several times by Clement of Alexandria : ' When ye trample upon the garment of shame ; when the two become one, and the male with the female neither male nor female ' (also in the letter known as the Second Epistle of Clement).

III

MSS., &c., mentioned in the text.

The Sinaitic Codex (p. 278).—A Greek MS. of the New Testament now in the library of Petrograd, discovered by Tischendorf in 1844 at the monastery of St. Catharine on Mount Sinai. Dates from the fourth century, and, like the Vatican Codex, written probably at Caesarea.

The Vatican Codex (p. 177).—At Rome. Also fourth century, and very closely connected with the last-mentioned MS. On these two MSS. were based in a very large measure Westcott and Hort's recension of the Greek text of the New Testament, and, through that, our Revised Version of 1881.

Codex Bezae.—At Cambridge. A Graeco-Latin MS. of the sixth century, containing the Gospels and Acts. Theodore Beza acquired it from Lyons, and presented it to the University of Cambridge. Probably comes from the Rhone Valley, and specially interesting because of its many various readings, very frequent in Luke and Acts. Many of its most striking readings, the importance of which Westcott and Hort tended to discount, except where serious omissions in the last few chapters of Luke were concerned, have been forced into notice by evidence which has come into prominence since 1881. Old Syriac and Latin Versions seem to belong to the same school, and this group, representing what is often, though not very happily, called the 'Western text,' is more and more becoming the storm-centre of Textual Criticism.

The Old Syriac versions are the 'Lewis'—sometimes called the 'Sinaitic'—and the 'Curetonian' Syriac. In 1892 Mrs. Lewis and Mrs. Gibson, of Cambridge, found some palimpsest leaves of a Syriac MS. of the Gospels, dating from the fifth century, in the monastery of St. Catharine on Mount Sinai, containing in a legible form about three-fourths of the Gospels. By 'palimpsest' is meant a writing covered with wax above the original letters, and in the scarcity of writing materials used again for another book. In this case fragments of the lives of women saints were at the top, the older Gospel-text below. This extraordinarily interesting text was transcribed by the late Canon Bensly, Dr. Rendel Harris, and Professor Burkitt, and published in 1894. For a clear account of its peculiarities written for English readers, see Mrs. Lewis's *Light on the Four Gospels from the Sinai Palimpsest* (Williams & Norgate).

The Curetonian Syriac was discovered by the late Dr. Cureton in 1847, and published in 1858. It contains some fragments of a fifth-century MS. of the Gospels, brought by Archdeacon Tattam in 1842 from the monastery of St. Maria Deipara in the Nitrian desert. It is now in the British Museum. At the beginning of Matthew's Gospel it has the title 'Gospel of the Separated '— that is, the Gospels are not harmonized into one story running straight on as they are in Tatian's *Harmony*. The fact that the Appendix to Mark (Mark xvi. 9-20; see pp. 37, 38) is present in the Curetonian but not in the 'Lewis' Syriac Version, is accounted for by Mrs. Lewis by the fact that Tatian (160 A.D.) came in between. This makes the 'Lewis' Syriac Version, which itself is a translation from a yet older Greek MS., *our most primitive witness* to the Gospel-text. Tatian was born, according to Zahn, about A.D. 110, and was a pupil of Justin Martyr at Rome. About 160 he composed a *Harmony of the Four Gospels*. In 1836 the Armenians of the Mecharitist monastery of St. Lazaro in Venice published a copy of a commentary on Tatian's *Harmony* by Ephrem, a Syriac Father of the Fourth Century, which they possessed in an Armenian version. Moesinger translated this, and Zahn and other scholars have reconstructed the text of the *Harmony* by the aid of the commentary. The Rev. J. Hamblyn Hill has also translated the *Harmony* itself from the Arabic version, and there is a Latin version in the Codex Fuldensis of the Vulgate. However, Ephrem is still our most reliable authority, for both Arabic and Latin versions have been tampered with to make them agree with the usual text in their respective languages. The reason why this *Harmony* has disappeared so completely is that in 172 Tatian came under the ban of the Church as a heretic, and his *Harmony* was carefully replaced by the ' Separated ' text throughout the Syrian Church.

The Peshitto, or Peshitta, is the Syriac Vulgate, the Authorized Version of the Syrian Church, made by Rabbula, who was appointed Bishop of Edessa in 411.

The Palestinian Syriac Version (p. 120) is a Lectionary, made, according to a subscription of a monk named Elias of Abud, in the monastery of the Amba Musa at Antioch in the year 1029. Of the Old Latin versions, the most important are the Codex Bobiensis and the Codex Palatinus. The latter belongs to the fourth or fifth century ; the former to the sixth century.

IV

Marcion. (pp. 174 (note), 187, 237.

A famous heretic of the second century, who carried the Pauline opposition to Judaism to such an extreme that he tried to cut the Old Testament out of the gospel, in the process reducing the gospel itself to tatters. His theory was to the effect that there were two Gods, the Just God, who made the world, and was the God worshipped by the Jews, the God of the Old Testament ; and the Good God, the Father of Jesus, who only intervened when the Just God, in His vengeful punishment of man's disloyalty, was condemning His creatures wholesale to Gehenna. Marcion published a Bible of his own, in which ten Pauline Epistles, with the Third Gospel, mutilated to suit the exigencies of his theory, took the place of the New Testament, and a list of ' Contradictions ' between the Old and New Testaments was substituted for the Old Testament. The present writer has referred in the text to an article upon Marcion published under the title ' A Protestant of the Second Century ' in the *London Quarterly Review* of October, 1913.

V

The Gospel according to the Hebrews (pp. 173, 291).

KNOWN to have been in existence in Aramaic as early as A.D. 150, Harnack has proved that it was in use in the Jewish Christian community in Alexandria, ' The Gospel according to the Egyptians ' being in vogue in the native Church. Its most interesting peculiarities seem to have been its inclusion of the story of the woman taken in adultery ; the answer of Jesus to His mother and brethren, when they asked Him to go with them to be baptized by John, ' In what have I sinned, that I should go and be baptized by him ? Unless perhaps this which I have said be ignorance '; the account of the descent of the Spirit at the Lord's baptism—' the whole fountain of the Spirit came down and rested upon Him, and said unto Him, My Son, in all the prophets I awaited Thy coming, that I might rest upon Thee. For Thou art My rest ; Thou art My firstborn Son, who reignest for ever '—the fact that the Holy Spirit is called Christ's Mother ; ' bread for to-morrow ' in the Lord's Prayer; the insertion mentioned on page 279 ; and additions to the story of the Rich Young Ruler. When, according to this Gospel, the young man heard the terms laid down by Jesus, ' he began to scratch his head, and it did not please him.' Whereupon the Lord rebuked him for claiming to have fulfilled the law, when he had neglected the offices of mercy. ' How sayest thou,' Jesus is reported as saying, ' l have done the law and the prophets ? since it is written in the law, Thou shalt love thy neighbour as thyself, and, behold, many of thy brethren, the sons of Abraham, are covered with filth and dying with hunger, while thy house is full of many good things, and nothing at all goes out to them.' After the Resurrection, Jesus is represented as appearing first to James, the Lord's brother, to release him from a vow which he had taken at the Last Supper. ' James had sworn that he would not eat bread from that hour, after he had drunk the Lord's cup, until He should see him risen from those that are asleep.' ' He that wonders shall reach the Kingdom, and having reached the Kingdom shall rest,' is an abbreviated version of the saying found also among the Oxyrhynchus papyri and in Clement of Alexandria (see above, App. II.). ' Never be glad, except when ye look upon your brother in love ' is a welcome addition to our collection of the sayings of the Lord, for it strikes the true note, and the Gospel also records a saying to the effect that it is one of the greatest offences that one should sadden the spirit of one's brother. It is probable, on the whole, that this Gospel contains some genuine sayings of Jesus. A. F. Findlay, in the *Dictionary of Christ and the Gospels*, expresses the opinion that the author used both Matthew and Luke. There are evident traces of a desire to elevate James, the Lord's brother, the head of the Jewish Christian Church, above the original apostles.

The ' Gospel of Peter ' (p 143) is only extant in a fairly long fragment discovered at Akhmin in Upper Egypt, in the winter of 1886–7, by the French Archaeological Mission, and published in 1892. This fragment deals with the Lord's Passion and Resurrection. Herod is regarded as the real judge of Jesus ; he refused to wash his hands with Pilate. On the cross Jesus ' held His peace, as in no wise having pain.' One of the malefactors reproached the Jews standing round the cross, not his fellow sufferer, as in Luke. The cry of the Lord is given as ' My power, My power, why hast thou forsaken Me ? ' It has been mentioned on page 186 that ' the Power ' was used as a name for God. It is probable that this title was used because it suggested that the man Jesus was really forsaken by the Spirit which descended upon Him at His baptism. The belief of the Docetists—who had a very large following in the first and second centuries—was that God could not suffer. If the Lord cried out in agony upon the cross, He cannot have been God any longer. Either the Holy Spirit had forsaken the man Jesus, or a mere phantom suffered on the cross, or Simon of Cyrene was crucified by mistake, while the Son of God passed through the midst of His enemies and went away, as He had done before (Luke iv. 30). A strong reason for believing that Luke xxii. 44 is part of the original Gospel—in spite of Westcott and Hort—is that these heretics would certainly remove his realistic description of the ' bloody sweat ' of the Saviour if they could. Dr. Rendel Harris thinks that it has been removed by their influence from the early MSS., in which it is conspicuous by its absence—or rather from the document which they copied.

AN INDEX

TO THE CHIEF PASSAGES EXPLAINED IN
THE FIRST THREE GOSPELS

Index